Economic Development and Social Change

T0373636

Some of the greatest thinkers in the history of economic thought have been instrumental in advancing the study of development economics. In this volume, leading scholars are brought together to illuminate this tradition, with particular emphasis on the question of growth and development.

Economic Development and Social Change examines the influence that has been exerted by both pre-classical and classical thought on modern-day development economics. It provides a synthetic analysis of the classical vision of growth and development from the Mercantilist era to Physiocracy, before examining Adam Smith's contribution to growth theory. The book then goes on to explore Marxian thinking and ideas, and the political developments that gave rise to state functions in post-war theory.

George Stathakis is at the Department of Economics, University of Crete, Rethymno, Greece and **Gianni Vaggi** is at the Faculty of Economics, University of Pavia, Italy.

Routledge studies in the history of economics

Economic Development and Social Change

Historical roots and modern perspectives

Edited by George Stathakis and Gianni Vaggi

LONDON AND NEW YORK

First published 2006
by Routledge
2 Park Square, Milton Park, Abingdon, Oxon OX14 4RN

Simultaneously published in the USA and Canada
by Routledge
711 Third Ave, New York, NY 10017
First issued in paperback 2012

Routledge is an imprint of the Taylor & Francis Group, an informa business

© 2006 Selection and editorial matter, George Stathakis and Gianni Vaggi; individual chapters, the contributors

Typeset in Baskerville by Wearset Ltd, Boldon, Tyne and Wear

All rights reserved. No part of this book may be reprinted or reproduced or utilized in any form or by any electronic, mechanical, or other means, now known or hereafter invented, including photocopying and recording, or in any information storage or retrieval system, without permission in writing from the publishers.

British Library Cataloguing in Publication Data
A catalogue record for this book is available from the British Library

Library of Congress Cataloging in Publication Data
A catalog record for this book has been requested

ISBN13: 9-780-415-64733-5 (pbk)
ISBN13: 9-780-415-33468-6 (hbk)
ISBN13: 9-780-203-41722-5 (ebk)

Contents

Figures

Tables

Contributors

Amit Bhaduri is professor emeritus at Jawaharlal Nehru University in Delhi and professor of political economy at the University of Pavia. He has taught at various academic institutions in Mexico, the US, Italy, Germany and Austria. His research work deals with the economic structure of backward agriculture, growth and capital theory, and policy issues related to globalization. He has published many papers and a number of scholarly volumes, among them *On the Border of Economic Theory and History* (Delhi: Oxford University Press, 1999), *The Intelligent Person's Guide to Liberalization* (Delhi: Penguin Books, 1996) (co-authored), and *Unconventional Economic Essays* (Delhi: Oxford University Press, 1993).

Robert Boyer is an economist at CEPREMAP, Paris, senior researcher (Directeur de Recherche) at National Center for Scientific Research (CNRS), head of the Research Unit (URA 922: Régulation, Human Ressources et Public Choice), professor (Directeur d'Etudes) at l'EHESS, member of the Council of Economic Analysis (1997–2001) and president of the Association Research and Régulation (Recherche et Régulation). He is the author of several books and articles on regulation theory, history of economic ideas, development and international economics and institutional economics.

Jorge Braga de Macedo is professor of economics at the Nova University in Lisbon. He has held many positions in Portugal and in international organizations. He was a Minister of Finance of Portugal, chairman of Ecofin, president of the Development Centre of OECD, and advisor to OECD and the European Commision. He has been in various occasions a consultant to the European Bank for Reconstruction and Development, the United Nations, the World Bank and the IMF. He has taught in many universities in Europe and the US, among them Princeton and the Institut d'Études Politiques in Paris. He has published extensively on exchange rate regimes, globalization, ethics, the European integration, and development policy.

Alain Clement is a senior lecturer in economics at François Rabelais University in Tours, France. He is a specialist in the history of economic thought applied to food and social affairs. In 1999 he published a book, *Nourrir le peuple: entre Etat et marché, XVI–XVXe siècles.* He is also the author of innumerable articles published in major international journals.

Shelagh Eltis is a historian and graduate of Somerville College Oxford and expert on French enlightenment.

Walter Eltis is emeritus fellow of Exeter College and was a lecturer in economics at the University of Oxford from 1963 until 1986. He is currently visiting professor at the University of Reading. In 1986 he became economic director and in 1988 director-general of the National Economic Development Office. He has been Chief Economic Adviser in the Department of Trade and Industry from 1992 until 1995. He has written numerous books and articles in the field of history of economic thought and also in contemporary policy debate.

Hagen M. Krämer is professor of economics at the Karlsruhe University for Applied Sciences, Germany. He studied at the University of Bremen, where he received his PhD in 1995, and at the New School for Social Research, New York. He then went on to work for Daimler-Chrysler as a business economist for six years before taking up his current position in Karlsruhe. His main fields of research are structural change and the service economy, income distribution and technological progress, and the history of economic thought.

Heinz D. Kurz is professor of economics at the University of Graz and director of the Graz Schumpeter Centre. He is the author of several books and articles in scholarly journals, several of which were co-authored by Neri Salvadori, including *Theory of Production* (CUP 1995; paperback 1997). He is a managing editor of *The European Journal of the History of Economic Thought* and *Metroeconomica* and in the period 2006–2008 serves as president of the European Society for the History of Economic Thought.

Sandrine Leloup is teaching at the University of Paris I, Phare and is a researcher at the Pole d'Histoire et d'Analyse des Représentations Economiques. Her research work focuses on the re-interpretation of the ideas of Smith and Bentham.

Andrea Maneschi has taught at Vanderbilt University since 1970 and is the director of the postgraduate program in economic development. He has taught in many universities in Brazil, the US, Italy and Australia. His research interests span the theory of international trade, the history of economic thought, and economic development. His articles have appeared in *Journal of International Economics, Review of International*

Economics, Oxford Economic Papers, Cambridge Journal of Economics, and in
journals that specialize in the history of economic thought. In 1998 he
published *Comparative Advantage in International Trade: A Historical
Perspective.*

Antoin E. Murphy is a professor of economics and fellow of Trinity
College, University of Dublin. He is one of the joint managing editors
of the *European Journal of the History of Economic Thought.* His books
include *Richard Cantillon: Entrepreneur and Economist* (Oxford University
Press, 1986); *John Law: Economic Theorist and Policymaker* (Oxford University Press, 1997); *Du Tot – Histoire du Système de John Law (1716–1720)*,
edited by Antoin E. Murphy (Paris: I.N.E.D., 2000).

Tatsuya Sakamoto is currently professor of the history of social and economic thought at the Faculty of Economics, Keio University, Tokyo. He
specializes in the social sciences in the Scottish Enlightenment. His
publications include *David Hume's Civilized Society* (in Japanese) (Tokyo:
Sobunsha, 1995), *The Rise of Political Economy in the Scottish Enlightenment*,
edited with Hideo Tanaka, (London: Routledge, 2003), and he recently
edited *Economic Science in the Dawn* (in Japanese) (Tokyo: Nihon Keizai
Hyoronsha, 2005).

Neri Salvadori is professor of economics at the University of Pisa. He has
been visiting professor at many universities in France, Spain, Austria,
and Mexico. His research interests focus on theories of production,
growth and distribution, classical economics and the economics of
Sraffa. Among his many books published are *Classical, Neoclassical and
Keynesian Views on Growth and Distribution*, edited with C. Panico (Chel-
tenham: Edward Elgar, 2006), *Innovation, Unemployment and Policy in the
Theories of Growth and Distribution*, edited with R. Balducci (Cheltenham:
Edward Elgar, 2005), *Classical Economics and Modern Theory: Studies in
Long-period Analysis*, with H. Kurz (London: Routledge, 2003).

George Stathakis is professor of political economy at the University of
Crete. His research interests include Greek economic history, Marxian
political economy and development economics. His most recent books
are *The Marshall Plan in Greece* (in Greek) (Athens: Vivliorama, 2004)
and *The reform of CAP and rural development in Southern Europe*, with C.
Kasimis edited, (Aldershot: Ashgate, 2003).

Philippe Steiner is professor of sociology at the Université Charles de
Gaulle, Lille, France. His current research topics are contemporary economic sociology and the history of French political economy and social
sciences. He has recently published *L'école durkheimienne et l'économie.
Sociologie, religion et connaissance* (Geneva: Droz, 2005).

Gianni Vaggi is professor of development economics at the University of
Pavia. He holds a PhD in economics from the University of Cambridge.

He is the director of the Centre for the Co-operation with Developing Countries of the University of Pavia and of the European School of Advanced Studies in Co-operation and Development of Pavia. He has written several books and articles on history of economic thought, particularly on classical political economy, and in development economics. He has been visiting professor at St. John's College Cambridge and Vanderbilt University and has held seminars and lectures in more than forty universities around the world.

Richard Werner is professor in international banking at the Management School of the University of Southampton. He has over a decade of experience in the financial sector, including many posts in Japan and is currently the chief investment advisor to the Profit Funds. His more recent books are *New Paradigm in Macroeconomics: Solving the Riddle of Japanese Macroeconomic Performance.* (Basingstoke: Palgrave Macmillan, 2005), *Central Banking and Structural Changes in Japan and Europe* (Tokyo: Soshisha, 2003), *Dismantling the Japanese Model* with Kikkaawa (Tokyo: Kodansha, 2003) and *Princes of the Yen, Japan's Central Bankers and the Transformation of the Economy* (New York: M.E. Sharpe, 2003).

Preface

This book originated from the sixth annual conference of the European Society for the History of Economic Thought that took place at the University of Crete in April 2002. The title of the conference was Economic Development and Social Change in the History of Economic Thought.

The aim of the book is to bring at the forefront the long tradition in the history of economic thought concerning the question of growth and economic development. The search for the causes of the wealth of nations has been a key issue in pre-classical and classical economics and has inspired modern growth theories. Nowadays, development economics has largely evolved from pure growth models to a wider analysis of social change. History of economic thought has been largely instrumental in producing some of these changes.

Neither the conference nor the book would have been possible without the help of many people. Ioanna Yiotopoulou was the coordinator of the conference and many students worked long hours during it. Ioanna also worked hard to produce the edited version of the book. Lois Woestman did all the editorial work and provided helpful advice on the successive revisions of the manuscripts.

We would like to thank Bertram Scheffold and Erich Streissler, the two ex-Presidents of ESHET, for advice, continuing assistance and the benefit of their experience. Financial support came from the University of Crete, the Bank of Greece, the Ministry of Foreign Affairs of Greece and Ernst & Young.

We also thank the editors at Routledge, Robert Langham, Terry Clague and Taiba Batool, for their great assistance in the preparation of this book.

George Stathakis and Gianni Vaggi

Introduction

Economic development and social change: the classical view and the moderns

George Stathakis and Gianni Vaggi

Presentation of the book

The aim

During the last thirty years of the twentieth century, an increasing number of authors have gone back to Smith and to the other founding fathers of economics in their analysis of development and change; to mention only two among the most famous ones: Albert Hirschman (1977) and Amartya Sen (1987). The importance of the classical inheritance is taken for granted in many development analyses; from increasing returns to endogenous growth, from Smith's sympathy to human and social capital.

The analysis of the causes of the wealth of nations is the founding origin of the history of economic ideas, as the title of Smith's *An Inquiry into the Nature and Causes of the Wealth of Nations* indicates. The search for the causes of the rise, and sometimes fall, of nations was a key issue of eighteenth-century economics and has inspired modern growth theories, from Harrod's work in 1939 to the so-called "new growth theories" of the 1980s. Capital accumulation and investment, and more recently R&D, and externalities and increasing returns are some of the recurring issues in modern development theory. This collection offers a blend of essays of history of economic thought and development economics and tries to suggest a particular point of view.

One could think that the increasing references to the old economists and in particular to the eighteenth-century views is due to the fact that these theories and visions are nothing else but a nice and useful "tool box", where anyone can dig out what he or she requires to show that certain views have a long tradition of authoritative predecessors. This may be the case but we believe that in classical political economy, by which we mean the strand of thought that goes from Physiocracy to Smith and to Ricardo and Marx, there is also a precise vision and a precise model of long-term development. This introduction is dedicated to this model. In our opinion there is nothing wrong in the predecessors' tool-box approach, but the tools in the box are a part of well-defined development theories. Two corollaries descend from this point of view.

First, the chapters of this book highlight some particular aspects of classical development analysis. These elements are part of a more general vision, which aims at an explanation of the essential features of the process of development.

Second, inside the classical view of development, we can find a mixture of different approaches to science that range from economics to other social sciences. During the last part of the twentieth century, development economics has largely evolved from pure growth models to a wider analysis of social change. The evolution of the different sectors of economic system, the classical structural change, is only one aspect of social change. Nowadays, it is a widely shared view that development is a complex phenomenon and analysis of the evolution of societies requires the examination of a multiplicity of aspects: institutions, human motivations, population, democracy and spatial location. This way of looking at economic evolution was also typical of the classical economists of the eighteenth century.

The first section of the introduction presents the essays that make up the book and highlights some of the major themes that link modern development theories to past views. The second section provides a synthetic analysis of the classical vision of growth and development from the Mercantilist era to Physiocracy. In the third section we discuss Smith's contribution to the growth theory and present a synthesis of the classical model of development and growth. In the fourth section we explore Marx's ideas. Finally, we refer to the political developments that gave rise to state functions and to development theories in the post-war period. All sections include references to the relationships between the visions and the concepts proposed by the founding fathers of economics and some features of the most recent evolution in modern development thinking and debates.

Division of the material

The book is divided into two parts. Part I begins with a presentation of some modern assessments of the evolution of development thinking by Boyer and de Macedo and continues with articles that examine some of the founding elements of classical development theories. The reader is immediately asked to compare the "state of the art" in development theories with the model of growth and development which emerges in classical political economy. Boyer makes an extensive survey of post-war development theory from an institutionalist point of view, while Braga de Macedo emphasizes modern debates on development policies. Bhaduri deals with increasing returns both in the view of Smith and in modern theories bridging history of ideas and more recent growth theories. Similarly, Kurz and Salvadori discuss the new endogenous growth theories in a classical perspective. Werner introduces the theme of institutions and of "credit guidance" policies in the process of development, while Kramer discusses the notion of the constant wage share in income-distribution theories.

The chapters in Part II highlight some of the many possible relationships between the economic growth model and social institutions. Two main themes flow through the various essays. First, the story becomes more complicated with respect to the simple economic development view because many "variations on the theme" are possible. In a certain way the classical model is open-ended. Second, the classical authors suggest policies designed to foster development and well-being, but the positive outcomes are highly influenced by social customs, human motivations and the institutional setting. Murphy takes us to the debates on money and credit in the early eighteenth century. Sakamoto highlights the role of social customs and habits, a system of manners, in Hume. Clement examines the problem of the attitude towards renewable resources and labour in Mercantilism and in classical economics, while Steiner discusses the role of agents and elite in French economics in the aftermath of the Revolution. Walter and Shelagh Eltis' chapter discusses the analytical features of the Physiocratic growth model with emphasis on the issue of luxury. With the essay of Leloup we go back to Adam Smith and we see that investment decisions and the attitude towards risk can revert the natural economic growth, thus leading to different development paths. Finally, Maneschi presents Ricardo's view on the relation between machinery and comparative advantage in international trade.

Growth views from Mercantilism to Physiocracy

The traditional foe: Mercantilism and its policies

Without Mercantilism, history of economic ideas would have been completely different and certainly so would have been the classical vision of economic development. In the eighteenth century Enlightenment, Mercantilist views and policies represented a traditional example of what *should not have been done* to increase the well-being of a nation and of its citizens. The defeat of Mercantilism in England and France took place during twenty years, between 1756 when Quesnay published his first article and 1776 when Adam Smith's *Wealth of Nations* appeared. The analysis of the causes of national wealth was an object of investigation common to Thomas Mun, who is perhaps the most famous among the Mercantilist writers, and also common to Quesnay and Smith. However, Smith's and Quesnay's answers to the problem of economic growth were drastically different from those of the Mercantilists.

It is commonly believed that the Mercantilists defined national wealth as precious metals, but this is a limited view of their theory of wealth; the so-called "bullionist" phase of Mercantilism characterized the sixteenth century (see Appleby 1978, p. 202). As early as the 1620s, the most outstanding Mercantilists did not regard precious metal as wealth in itself. Mun clearly defines wealth as commodities, or necessities, which he calls natural wealth, or "manufactures and industrious trading with forraign commodities", which he calls artificial wealth (Mun 1623, p. 7; see also pp. 71–3). Nevertheless, the country's treasure, in today's terminology the stock of reserves of international currency, provides a good measure of national wealth, because it provides a synthetic indication of the command of a nation on goods and services and thus of her power.

In mature Mercantilism the causes of increase in the stock of national wealth have not to be searched into credit policies but rather into the trade balance of a country. This view leads to some fundamental changes in the policies which are aimed at increasing national wealth. Flows of precious metals depend upon the balance of trade. In modern terminology the capital side of the balance of payment simply reflects the current-account balance. Thus, the level of interest rates and the strength of the domestic currency have no direct influence on international capital flows and hence on the wealth of a nation. Much more important is the direct control of both imports and exports – the former have to be limited, the latter fostered. Strict trade control and export promotion increase national wealth, which is the ideal political economy in the age of merchants.

In England during the late sixteenth and early seventeenth centuries, some merchants became producers and entrepreneurs, particularly in the textile sector (see Appleby 1978, pp. 190–219; Rubin 1929, p. 31). The emergence of industrial activities brings forth the idea that there is a relationship between the cost of production and the price of commodities and between these prices and competitiveness in international markets by domestic producers. Competitiveness is the key factor in achieving a surplus in the balance of trade. Costs are made up of raw materials, sometimes imported, and, above all, of wages, which must be as low as possible (the essay by Clement discusses this point in more detail). The merchant-producers ask the government to protect domestic industry from foreign competitors, and this leads to the emergence of the protectionist variation of Mercantilist thought.

Commercial policies must favour the achievement of trade surplus, and the state must support national manufactures and national trading companies with a set of other policies too. Interest rates may influence the cost of the circulating capital and hence the competitiveness of domestic products on international markets, both of which should be kept low. Low money wages will also contribute to cheapen the prices of domestic products and this will foster exports (see Mun 1623, pp. 8, 12; Appleby 1978, pp. 160ff.). Mun uses some brilliant arguments to support the idea that the national wealth derives from foreign trade; he justifies the export of money by the fact that it will enable the country "to bring in more forraign wares, which being sent out again will in due time much increase our Treasure"(p. 15; see also Mun 1621, pp. 21–2).

The single Merchant aims to achieve a "profit upon alienation", since his gain derives from buying cheap and selling dear (see Mun 1623, p. 26). But only a favourable balance of trade can increase national wealth; it follows that a country can only enrich itself at the expense of her trading partners. In the end, *international trade is a zero-sum game*. The Mercantilists maintain that once national wealth has been increased thanks to the supportive policies of the government, then all sections of population will benefit. The inflows of precious metals due to a surplus in the balance of trade will be beneficial to the entire society.

During the seventeenth century, this analytical framework successfully interprets and guides the growth of the English economy, thus proving to be an adequate paradigm. The economic struggle among the nation-states of Europe is an accepted feature of this vision. In 1601 the British East India Company is founded and a year later it is the turn of the Dutch one. In 1651 Cromwell proclaims the first Navigation Act, according to which all trades with Great Britain and with her colonies should take place with English vessels. This is an obvious way of profiting from freights and shipping services; the Mercantilists discover the difference between the current- and the trade-account balance. In the second half of the seventeenth century in France, Colbert, the Minister of Finances for Louis XIV, implements policies designed to protect the then rising domestic manufactures from foreign competitors. The term '*colbertisme*', which refers to the protection policy of infant industries, comes from the name Colbert.

Hutchison notices that the balance of trade theory of wealth is not unanimously accepted throughout the seventeenth century. In 1623 Misselden writes in favour of natural liberty in trade, and towards the end of the century Barbon, North and Martyn believe that commodities are designed to satisfy men's needs and to make their life more enjoyable rather than just to enrich the coffers either of the merchant companies or of the State (see Hutchison 1988, p. 22). These considerations open the way to a view of free trade which is beneficial to all countries, thus opposing the balance of trade theory of wealth. However, by the end of the century the critics of Mercantilism fails to produce a new theory of economic growth and development, but some ideas are already available.

Towards a new principle of wealth: Petty

Sir William Petty is the first author to stress the role of the techniques of production in a theory of economic growth.

First, Petty underlines the peculiar role of the agricultural sector which, by producing necessaries, provides the basis for the development of population and of manufacturing. He also highlights the concept of surplus, and of agricultural surplus in particular.

In his *Treatise of Taxes and Contributions* Petty writes:

> if there be 1000. men in a Territory, and if 100. of these can raise necessary food and raiment for the whole 1000. if 200. more make as much commodities, as other Nations will give either their commodities or money for, and if 400. More be employed in the ornaments, pleasure, and magnificence of the whole; if there be 200. Governors, Divines, Lawyers, Physicians, Merchants and Retailers, making in all 900 . . . there is food enough for this supernumerary 100.
>
> (Petty 1662, p. 30)

Like a human body, society is a complex organism in which different groups of people have different roles, all of them necessary to the functioning of society. This is possible thanks to agriculture. This sector maintains all other economic activities, because its output is larger than the input required in its production. The existence of a surplus implies that some men produce food and other necessaries in excess of their own needs, and therefore there is subsistence for other people, and this provides the necessary ground for manufacture, trade and other activities to arise. The very existence of activities different from the agricultural ones is a proof that there is a surplus in agriculture. It is thanks to the surplus of necessaries that societies can diversify their activities and the structure of employment.

Second, Petty's other important notion is that of social division of labour, which is quite obviously a twin concept to that of surplus. If the surplus of the economy springs out of the primary sector, it is the manufacturing sector which can take advantage of the technical division of labour; this is another important piece in the process of modification of the Mercantilist theory of wealth.[1] Petty believes that the division of labour reduces the cost of production of commodities (see Petty, 1676, p. 260) and hence anticipates the Smithian theory of wealth. Lower production costs lead to lower prices, as it is described in the famous example of watches in the 1682 work *Another Essay on Political Arithmetick* (see Roncaglia 1977, pp. 93–4).

Petty does not deny the importance of foreign trade as a source of national wealth, but at least exchange is no longer the only economic activity capable of increasing the wealth of nations. Notwithstanding these important analytical innovations, Petty does not abandon the balance of trade theory of growth.

The modernization of French agriculture: Quesnay

With a long jump we arrive in the middle of the eighteenth century with François Quesnay and the Physiocratic school.[2] The twenty years from Quesnay's first economic article, *Fermiers*, in 1756 to Smith's *Wealth of*

Nations changed the notion of wealth and laid the foundations of economics as an independent science. Quesnay is the first author to state explicitly that no gain can derive from trading activities: "trade is only an exchange of value for equal value" (*Sur les travaux des artisans*, p. 897; see also *Réponse au Mémoire de M.H.*, pp. 757–8; both in INED 1958). Thus in the trading process commodities are exchanged for commodities of equal value. Therefore, trade cannot lead to an increase of private as well as national wealth unless the state protects the merchants by granting them exclusive privileges in trade, but this would be against the natural order of things. This is so not only in domestic trade; it is impossible to increase wealth in the sphere of circulation of commodities, including foreign trade. Therefore, trade cannot be a source of wealth.

Following Petty, Quesnay considers agriculture as the core of society. More than that, he regards the primary sector as the only one capable of earning a surplus over the means of production which have been invested, hence agriculture is the only productive activity or sector, while industry, along with trade, is a sterile occupation. According to Petty, only agricultural surplus is the true source of wealth of the country. This is a very peculiar position which of course will receive the criticism of Smith, otherwise a great admirer of Physiocracy. But certainly it is a clear step towards an alternative principle of economic growth with respect to the Mercantilist notion of "balance of trade".

Quesnay's next step in the analysis of the causes of wealth is even more interesting. Being part of the primary sector is a necessary but not sufficient condition for bestowing the quality of productive on an activity; something else is needed. This further feature of a productive activity is disclosed in the article *Farmers*, with the fable of the oxen and the horses (see *Fermiers* in INED, pp. 438–41). Oxen are used in most regions of France, where they use a plough with a wooden spade, which Quesnay considers to be small-scale cultivation that yields little or no surplus. Horses are used in most of England in large-scale cultivation and they can use the iron spade in the plough. The latter is a superior technique of production capable of yielding a large net product over the inputs of cultivation.

For Quesnay, only those agricultural activities whose output is considerably higher than their inputs are a source of surplus and hence of economic growth. In a large-scale cultivation, agricultural production takes place under the supervision of rich farmers, who can rent large amounts of land and make large annual and original advances, what we now call circulating and fixed capital. The latter includes horses too. In a small-scale cultivation and *métayage* (crop sharing), farmers are poor; they cannot afford the advances necessary to make agriculture really productive and they hardly have a surplus on top of the expenses of cultivation.

It is the existence of a large stock of capital which allows cultivation to be productive; surplus is not a gift of nature, but the result of modern and efficient techniques of production. It is thanks to the fixed capital that the productivity of cultivation can increase, and it is possible to adopt the best technology and to have a modern and prosperous agriculture.[3]

For Quesnay, industry is sterile largely because it lacks fixed capital; industrial activities are carried on by poor artisans, who can only recover their production expenses, that is to say their wages and the cost of raw materials (see *Sur les Travaux des Artisans* in INED 1958, p. 896). According to Quesnay economic development depends on the amount of capital employed in cultivation, because this will transform the poor French agriculture into a productive sector. Technological improvements depend on capital accumulation.

We are getting close to the principle of economic growth in terms of accumulation with endogenous technical progress, but two further points must be mentioned.

First, Quesnay's analysis of the causes of economic growth is strictly linked to his view of the general working of the economic system. The economy is analysed as an entity which has to reproduce itself; thus reproduction and surplus are the fundamental notions on which Quesnay builds his economic analysis. Of course the concept of capital is the key element in moving from the notion of gross product to that of *produit net* or surplus. Quesnay's view of a reproduction economy is highlighted in several works, the best known being the *Tableau économique* that first appeared in 1758 at Versailles. The *Tableau* is a two-sector model with agriculture, the productive sector, and industry, the unproductive one, plus one expenditure class, the landlords. Thus we have some concepts which will become crucial both in economic theory and in development thought. For Quesnay, the circulation of commodities strictly depends on the structure of the inputs of production, but can also be influenced by government policies and by the consumption decisions of the landlords out of their rent, (this mechanism is explained in Eltis' essay).

Second, Quesnay provides a new view of development related to technology and capital accumulation; by itself this is a remarkable step forward in the direction of *Wealth of Nations*. However, Quesnay's analysis is not limited to the purely material and technological aspects of production. He understands that some social transformations are needed in order to carry on that "accumulation with best technology" process, which alone can lead to growth and prosperity. Without some radical changes in the way in which corn prices are determined, French agricultural entrepreneurs would have no incentive for continuing the cultivation of land and re-investing their savings in it (see Vaggi, 1987, pp. 80–6). Capital accumulation and technical progress in agriculture are the causes of growth and both depend upon the re-investment of farmer's profits,[4] this process must be triggered and sustained by the enlightened rulers with an appropriate set of policies. They go from the single tax on landlords' rents to the liberalization of the corn market in order to foster the exports of French corn.

As a matter of fact, this was the only Physiocratic policy to be partially implemented. Between the end of 1763 and the first months of 1764 the Controlleur Général Bertin declared some edicts in favour of the exportation of some agricultural products; on 18 July his successor de L'Averdy proclaimed the free export of all kinds of corn by sea and land (see Weulersse 1910, vol. II, pp. 222–4). Trade liberalization should have led to an increase in the wholesale prices of corn for the French producers and hence in profits and in investments. In the second half of the 1760s, several bad harvests resulted in a sharp rise of corn prices at the wholesale level, but also in the retail markets in the cities. French public opinion regarded free exportation as the main cause of the rising price of bread in the cities and there was growing hostility towards Physiocratic policies, which were regarded as a threat to the people's subsistence. After popular uprisings and hostile pronunciations by local parliaments in 1770, the new Controleur Général Terray abolished the free exportation of corn.

For the Physiocrats, the final aim of all policies must be the modernization of French agriculture. This process requires a transition from a backward to an advanced agriculture; capital accumulation by the agricultural entrepreneurs is the decisive element of the process itself. However, this would require a redistribution of surplus towards the farmers, the social group which is in charge of investments, and this could be achieved through major reforms in the French kingdom: fiscal and commercial reforms, a change in the expenditure decisions of the rich classes and an increase in the length of land-lease contracts. Quesnay is no revolutionary, but the extent of reforms required to lead France to development is impressive.

The Physiocratic attempt to reform the economic policy of the *ancien régime* failed for social and political reasons (see Fox-Genovese 1976, pp. 11, 238–42) as well as for some analytical flaws in Quesnay's economics, such as his view on the sterility of manufacture, but his deep and wide analysis of the causes of development and growth opens the way to Smith.

Adam Smith and the classical growth model

The division of labour

Building on Quesnay's contributions, Smith provides an alternative definition of national wealth to that of Mercantilism. The "Introduction and Plan of the Work" in *Wealth of Nations* defines "the real wealth, the annual produce of the land and labour of the society"(Smith 1776, Introduction, 9). Wealth is now a flow concept, very much like the modern GDP notion and Smith also distinguishes between the gross and net revenues of a country (Smith 1776, II.ii.5).[5] The first three chapters of Book I of the *Wealth of Nations* answer the other major question: which are the causes of growth and decline of nations? Smith's answer is straightforward and it is already clearly included in the title of Book I: the main cause of economic growth is the improvement in the productive powers of labour (Smith 1776, Introduction, 3–5). This is the new principle of wealth and it is still today the main principle behind all the explanations of economic prosperity.

It must be noticed that in the title of Book I Smith says that he will also investigate the distribution of the produce of labour among the different ranks of people. Contrary to productivity, the distribution of income between wages, profits and rents is a rather forgotten aspect in development theories but it occupies the final four chapters of Book I.

But what gives occasion to the improvement in the productivity of labour? "The greatest improvement in the productive powers of labour, and the greater part of the skill, dexterity, and judgement with which it is anywhere directed, or applied, seem to have been the effects of the division of labour"(Smith 1776, I.i.1). Thus, division of labour and productivity increases are the major causes of economic development and of the bettering of human conditions.

But what is the division of labour? There are two types of division of labour, the technical one and the social one, both of which play a fundamental role in the process of economic growth. The rest of Chapter I is dedicated to an elucidation of the advantages of technical division of labour. By splitting the production process into simple operational units, the division of labour brings about an increase in the skills and dexterity of labourers, and this leads to the improvement in labour productivity (Smith 1776, I.i.3–4). Smith refers mainly to specialization of activities within each sector of the economy; in a famous example Smith examines "the trade of the pin-maker". Here it is possible to separate production into eighteen different operations, each one being performed by a different worker. The product per worker per day greatly increases with respect to the case of a single labourer performing all eighteen operations. This idea fits well in a "human capital" view of growth, where knowledge is at the heart of technical progress and productivity increases and fits well into some of the recent "endogenous growth theories". Knowledge, education and human capital are typical positive externalities to individual firms and help to explain the existence of non-decreasing returns to scale.

The increases in the productivity of labour lead to the separation of trades inside each branch of society; it is a separation of arts, of branches, of employments, of trades (Smith 1776, I.i.4). The rest of Chapter I provides several explanations of how the separation of trade into simpler operations leads to an increase in labour productivity. First, by concentrating on one operation only the worker specializes, increases his rapidity and produces more units of a commodity than if he had to look after other activities (Smith 1776, I.i.6). Second, the worker saves the time which is commonly lost in passing from one work to the other (Smith 1776, I.i.7). Third, and most interestingly, process innovations are much easier when a labourer can concentrate on only a few operations, a fact which is also true in the production of machines (Smith 1776, I.i. 8 and 9).

Chapter II of *Wealth* focuses on the social division of labour. Chapter II includes some of the best known sentences in the whole of *Wealth of Nations* and perhaps of the entire economic thought. We find the famous example of the "triple B": the butcher, the brewer, the baker (Smith 1776, I.ii.2). Here Smith is talking of the separation of arts and branches, of trades and activities, of occupations in different activities and sectors. The technical or process division of labour gives room to the social division of labour, the separation of activities in the sense that individuals dedicate themselves entirely to a single employment and they specialize in the supply of a single produce. The "tribe of hunters and shepherds" becomes a civilized society made up of a variety of separate trades: armourers, carpenters, smiths, braziers, tanners, dressers (Smith 1776, I.ii.3). A social division of labour based on the specialization of activities becomes the normal feature of a civilized society.

The simple and unique principle of the division of labour presents two aspects, which are of course linked to each other and go hand in hand in the explanation of the growth in the well-being of some human societies. However, Smith seems to believe that the increases in the productivity of labour due to technological division of labour explain and justify the separation of trades and employments. This is a precondition for the social division of labour. "The separation of different trades and employments from one another seems to have taken place in consequence of this advantage ... In a tribe of hunters or shepherds a particular person makes bows and arrows ... with more readiness and dexterity". He finds that by exchanging these products for cattle or for venison he can get more of both, "than if he himself went to the field to catch them"(Smith 1776, I.i.4). It is then in the interest of each man in society to specialize in the production of one commodity and then use exchange to fulfil his other needs.[6] The social division of labour depends on the advantages of the technological one, but then the specialization in different branches of production reinforces the technical division of labour in each production process.

Capital accumulation

In order to carry on the technological division of labour we need capital, at least in the form of anticipated wages, an idea originating from Quesnay. This is the topic of Book II of the *Wealth*. Smith points out the existence of two major sectors in economy, a productive sector and an unproductive one, respectively the sectors producing material goods and those that produce services (Smith 1776, II.iii.1). The key to the increases of labour productivity is the accumulation of capital in the productive sectors. This is a very important legacy to many modern theories – from Lewis' model to export-led growth theories, to state versus market views – which either explicitly or implicitly adopt the idea that there are more and less productive sectors, even if sectors are no longer described in Smith's terms.

Apart from the improvements in labour productivity, growth can also derive from moving labour from unproductive to productive activities (Smith 1776, II.iii.3), and this depends "upon the proportion between the part of the annual produce, which ... is destined for replacing a capital, and that which is destined for constituting a revenue, either as rent, or as profit" (Smith 1776, II.iii.8). If the annual surplus is reinvested in production by bringing more workers into the productive sector we have an "extensive" growth. Growth is of the "intensive" type if it is due to productivity increases of productive labourers. The investment and accumulation process is the key to economic growth. The capitalist-entrepreneurs who control the process of capital accumulation are motivated by profit (Smith 1776, II.iii.6)[7] and they can introduce innovations which lead to technical progress.

Three more points must be underlined. The first point is that, as for Petty and for Quesnay, the social division of labour requires a surplus of food, of agricultural products, hence the improvement of agriculture is a necessary prerequisite to secure a surplus produce to the country and to achieve economic growth (Smith 1776, I.ix.c.7, and III.i.2). This explains why Smith ascribes priority to agriculture in what he considers to be a sort of natural order of investments, according to which capital accumulation follows a precise sequence in society (Smith 1776, II.v.1.12, 19–20). In Chapter V of Book II "Of the different Employment of Capitals", Smith clarifies the sequencing of investments in the different sectors of economy, when the surplus produce begins to be employed in activities outside the primary sector (Smith 1776, II, v, 3–7).

First, there are investments in agriculture making it productive and rendering the country self-sufficient in food. Second, capital accumulation moves to manufacturing, where division of labour can play a larger role than in agriculture. Third, investments concentrate in some internal commercial activities, for example transport that favours and facilitates exchange, then capital accumulation moves to foreign trade. By following this order, a nation can enrich herself and progress over time. (Leloup's essay has more on this problem and on the "retrograde order of investments".) It is worth noticing that the only passage of *Wealth* where we find the invisible hand is in Book IV, where Smith maintains that each individual is led by an invisible hand to prefer domestic to foreign trade and in this way he "labours to render the annual revenue of the society as great as he can", without explicitly intending it (Smith 1776, IV.ii.9).

The second point is that Smith's theory of economic growth provides the foundations for his views on international trade. The title of Chapter

III of Book I is "That the Division of Labour is limited by the Extent of the Market". For Smith, the purchasing power of the domestic market might be a possible limitation to capital accumulation and hence to both the social and the technical division of labour. By allowing to sell the output in excess of domestic consumption, foreign trade favours the improvements in the productivity of labour. It is the so-called "vent for surplus" problem (Smith 1776, II.v.34, IV.i.31). Then Smith's economics is open to the influence of foreign trade on growth (see Myint 1977, pp. 231–2, 242). Smith praises Physiocracy for advocating liberty as "the only effectual expedient" to increase annual produce (Smith 1776, IV.ix.38); foreign trade is carried on for the mutual advantage of all the exchanging countries. However, these benefits are fundamentally of a dynamic nature and concern the possibility of achieving increasing returns to scale. Of course there may be negative effects also for a rich country, in particular when there is no competition. Most of Book IV is a vigorous attack on Mercantilism and its policies, but it is important to underline that Smith is in favour of free trade because he is against big monopolies and the alliance between the big merchant companies and the state.

Third, Smith is very cautious in his description of the relationships between rich and poor nations. He does not think that the latter ones will benefit from free trade anyway (see Myint 1977, pp. 246–8). In the so-called *Early Draft of Part of the Wealth of Nations* he writes, "it is easier for a nation, in the same manner as for an individual, to raise itself from a moderate degree of wealth to the highest opulence, than to acquire this moderate degree of wealth (see Smith 1763?, p. 579). There is no automatic mechanism which guarantees the catching up, or convergence, of the poorer countries towards the level of income of the rich ones. On the contrary, wealthy nations have an interest in trading among themselves because of their rich markets, rather than with poor countries (Smith 1763?, p. 578). Smith lists at least six major impediments facing the poor countries in their first steps of a development process. Quite often poor countries do not have the resources to adopt the same techniques of production of the rich ones; productivity increases and technical progress depend on the accumulation of capital – of all the impediments this is the really binding one.

We can now sketch a growth model which largely reflects Quesnay's and Smith's indications:[8]

Surplus ⇒ profits ⇒ savings ⇒ investments [⇐ expected rate of profit] ⇒ capital stock increases ⇒ (structural change *and* division of labour) [⇐ extent of the market] ⇒ increases in labour productivity ⇒ increases in surplus and profits.

Most of the above links sound familiar,[9] but it should now be clear that the arrows do not have a character of strict determinacy, as many things can "go wrong" in moving from one step to the next. The classical growth models highlight some clear relationships of cause and effects, which reflect "natural laws" but modifications are possible, from bad governance to excess of market power by monopolistic firms, to quote only the best-known variations. With an appropriate simplification of the sequence, it is possible to reproduce most of the modern views of growth and development. We can have an "endogenous growth" model or a dualistic model of the Lewis' type (see Lewis 1954). The sequence *per se* fits well a Kaldorian view of growth with industrialization, and of course if we are prepared to leave aside non-decreasing returns, one can end up with Solow's growth model. Here we only intend to highlight two points.

First, structural change can hardly been taken out of the picture when analysing development processes. This is particularly clear in Physiocracy, but it is equally relevant in Smith's natural order of investments and in the process of extensive growth.

Second, in Smith's view the lack of free competition, that is monopoly, is not the only cause which can prevent growth and development. Also other elements can modify the "stylized facts": customs and habits or the system of manners, the quality of labour, social institutions, for instance in agriculture, the initial conditions of the country. Of course, most of the political economists of the age of enlightenment believed in natural laws. However, in classical political economy a variety of elements are required in order to trigger the path towards prosperity. By the same token, many things may go wrong and lead to unexpected outcomes; in many ways development and growth are an open-ended story. As a result of this, institutional and social changes go hand in hand with economic development.

Some of the complications of the long-run development model are discussed by Malthus and Ricardo; the former examines the demographic problem and the possibility of crisis, the latter analyses income distribution, natural resources and foreign trade.[10] However, most economists in the early nineteenth century abandon Smith's rather optimistic view about development and progress and have, among them Marx, a more critical view of the evolution of history.[11]

Karl Marx's vision of boundless growth

The Communist Manifesto

The most dynamic perception of capitalism lies with Marx. From his early work onwards – such as the *Communist Manifesto* – capitalism is presented through a Promethean lens, as a system with immense capabilities to generate growth. It is shown to be a process of transformation and revolution of what Marx defined as productive forces and relations of production. Capitalism's geographical expansion was equally impressive. Capital was reaching "every corner of the globe" and pre-existing societies had all to adjust to the requirements of capital. In a word, capital was re-making the world in its own image.

In reality, in the middle of the nineteenth century, world domination of capital and the transformation of western and non-western societies alike was less impressive (Dobb 1963; Hobsbawm 1998). However, Marx is making a point which has theoretical aims and is not intended for empirical verification. Capital is perceived as self-expanding value undermining any form of stability, economic, social, ethical or cultural, that was conceived as being sustainable. Marx is already "thinking in terms of totality", in recognizing that nothing existed outside the limits of human history, and the limits of history are set by this powerful expansion of capitalism. Capital is meant to be both the empirical fact of this new historical era and the conceptual perspective on this totality.

Marx introduces a whole range of new terms: mode of production, productive forces and relations of production, class struggle, base and superstructure. Most of these concepts are probably lacking in clarity and precision. Yet in the simplifying vision expressed in the *Manifesto* there is enormous power as it brings into comprehensible order an otherwise bewildering multiplicity of historical facts. Theory in this respect is not an actual description of historical development but a model for understanding it.

The rise of capitalism is identified with industry, whose development relies on the scientific discoveries. These technological advancements free productive forces from any physical constraint, and keep up the pace of growth (Polanyi 1957). Nevertheless it is the relations of production, that is the capital–labour relation, which accounts for such a transition. As with Smith and Ricardo, labour is the source of wealth. Yet Marx's perception of labour as a commodity implies that the capital–labour relation is a social one. This approach allows him to move beyond the "trinity formula", the economic approach that identified capital, labour and land as factors of production engaged in a technical process, that is production. Thus, the production of wealth, this very space of political economy, encompasses the social contradictions that produce political conflict in the industrial society.

In the *Manifesto* capitalist accumulation takes place in relation to the world market. Globalization is viewed as a slow process that began in the sixteenth and seventeenth centuries. Global expansion of capital is not the result of a saturation of capital accumulation within the national boundaries. This point opposes what the theories on imperialism implied later on. For Marx, the rise of capitalism is from the outset a global phenomenon and the destinies of industrial and rural economies are viewed as a common process within the global framework. In the *Manifesto* there is a strong impression of a methodology that presaged the ideas of the dependency school (Frank 1969; Amin 1974) and the world-system approach (Wallerstein 1974). Moreover, the formation of nation-states is considered as being compatible with the globalization process. The strong nation state and liberal politics are part of this process.

In his later writings, such as *Capital*, Marx shifts his emphasis to primitive accumulation and the search for the roots of capitalism in agriculture, as Quesnay and Smith had done before him. But still his global perspective remains strong. The debate among Marxists as to the national or global roots of the transition from feudalism to capitalism produced one of the most lively debates in the Marxist tradition (Hilton 1976; Aston and Philpin 1985).

The dynamics of capitalism and crisis

Marx's later works present a more detailed analytical investigation of the growth process. Marx starts his theoretical discourse exactly from the same point as Smith and Ricardo had done, namely from the market, where the exchange process takes place under competitive terms. As the Physiocrats had done before him he soon moves from exchange to production in order to identify the process generating surplus. Yet the exchange process remains predominant in terms of the analysis of the dynamic element of capital accumulation. The competition among individual capitals within the same market leads to the homogenization of the conditions of production and provides incentives for innovations of the Schumpeterian type. Continuous technological change is a sine qua non for individual capital aiming to increase its profitability or prevent its devaluation.

Marx from the outset removes all constraints from capital accumulation. Neither population, as Malthus had indicated, nor the level of wages, as many others had indicated, among them Senior, could prevent the slowing down of the accumulation process. If they did it could not last for long. The only remaining obstacle was land. Here Marx seems to follow Ricardo, with his main thesis that the scarcity of land and rent could prevent the accumulation of industrial capital as it would keep wage levels up and squeeze the profits. Yet Marx is more optimistic concerning the capabilities of technical progress to prevent diminishing returns in agriculture and felt that through various means (imports, land reform, capitalist investment) rent could be checked.

Having removed all other obstacles, capital was faced with only one obstacle; itself. This is probably the best part of the Marxian perspective on growth and capitalist dynamics. His reproduction schemes, inspired most likely by Quesnay (Gehrke and Kurz 1998), indicate that a specific balance among the various sectors of the economy is necessary in order to have a positive growth rate. The pace of growth is given by the sector-producing means of production (Rosdolsky 1977). On the other hand, his law on the falling tendency of the profit rate indicates that extra profits that compensated the innovative activity of individual capitals produced a constant replacement of labour by capital. This may increase labour productivity but threatens average profitability across the economy (Foley 1986). However, there are counter-tendencies which can sustain the profit rate, so again the balance is open-ended. Yet the optimism generated by increased profitability could easily lead to over-accumulation of capital, which after a certain point was unable to find profitable investments.

An additional element is wages. Private motivation on the side of capital is to keep wages close to the subsistence level and the relative share of wages has a declining tendency. Improved productivity of labour and the cheapening of commodities (even if not of all commodities according to Ricardo) asks for such increases in wages that would keep consumption at an equal footing to increased productive capacity, in order to avoid under-consumption (Bleaney 1976). Luxury consumption could provide a solution but this in its turn is influenced by the pace of a business cycle.

These are among the various partial perspectives through which Marx attempts to come to terms with the periodic instability of the growth process. This element may have been privileged in the Marxist tradition as it produced many debates on capitalist crisis (Shaikh 1978). None of the above partial perspectives on cyclical crisis generated any concern for the long-term dynamics of the system. And there is little doubt that such perspectives, no matter how partial they may have been, provided the background to most of the research on modern growth theory and business cycles, starting with Domar as the obvious example (Kühne 1979).

In the unfinished third volume of *Capital*, Marx attempts to elaborate more on the socialization process. He views the centralization and concentration of capital as manifestations of this process, as well as the changes in the organization structure of the firm: the rise of the joint-stock company and a managerial class distinct from the owners of the firms. The analysis of finance capital and the fictitious forms of money, in effect the emergence of the money and capital markets, opened up new space for a different theorizing of the accumulation process and crisis (Harvey 1982).

The politics of socialization and the state

The management of the welfare, the prevailing conditions at the production place and after a certain point the regulation of wages become the political agenda of what Marx had defined as class struggle. From the French Revolution onwards the basic principles of *freedom*, *equality* and *brotherhood* come to dominate political developments within the emerging liberal regimes. From the middle of the nineteenth century, right- and left-wing parties are formed with more or less clear-cut agendas concerning the economy.

The Right predominantly interprets the equality and freedom principles in economic terms, that is as private ownership and free trade. The Left uses the third principle, that of brotherhood redefined as social solidarity, as indispensable to the former two. A new concept – the social economy – emerges under different names in the European countries (Procacci 1991). The welfare state becomes the result of a compromise between the Right and the Left. The economy is to function among the market principles as long as a significant part of the economy organizes itself on social principles arising from solidarity.

Under the circumstances the welfare sector is to be organized only by the state and the emergence of such a sector is identified with a new "science of policies". Public administration was already organized in hierarchical form and had incorporated techniques of management that provided a certain degree of bureaucratic rationale. The welfare state becomes the new area of extension of such rationale.

Economic crisis, and in many cases war, produces new arrangements that came out of this political compromise during the twentieth century with the capitalist economy moving to more articulate forms of regulation. After the 1929 crisis and by the end of the Second World War the state moves beyond public administration and the organization of the welfare. The new area of compromise includes economic policies and the regulation of income distribution.

The adjustment of the system of government, of the ideas on policy and of the techniques of management is what allows the state to survive, to redefine what is within its competence and what is not, that is internal and external at the same time. Governments had by then established general tactics of governing through a combination of laws with administrative practices. The political economy in the nineteenth century provides not only a new object, the economy, and a new mechanism, the market, but also a combined perception, of population, administration and territory (Foucault 1991). The state emerges not only as an institution dedicated to certain functions but it comes to be captured as the object of rational action, capable of protecting the general interest.

The formation and development of the market economy is combined with a parallel process which may be called state formation. The state becomes not only the cartographer of the social and economic conditions prevailing among a population within a territory but these factual outcomes become the source of government practices according to principles different from those emerging from the market.

Development theory

Development and underdevelopment

Development economics are founded on the aftermath of World War II. In effect the drastic political changes brought the development agenda at the forefront. De-colonization, the Cold War and the increased competition among superpowers provides the political background for ideological assumptions of both theory and practice in development. Practice teaching and research in economic development interlinked through key paradigms draw on a diversified stock of knowledge. Yet substantive theory is very much the same, as they all lead to the basic idea that intervention and planning are possible.

In economic theory Keynes had already formed this political agenda (Napoleoni 1972). He provides the theoretical possibility of a normative science that made comprehensible the decision-making process of the politicians and the public administrators. Fiscal and monetary policies, industrial and agricultural policies, social policies, regional and urban planning, and policies on a whole variety of other areas become the subjects of a new "policy science". Social science is supposed to provide answers to the rational ordering of decisions in complex modern societies. Institutions are enabled to control their social environment and through deliberate actions achieve a preferred state of affairs.

Social sciences were until then preoccupied with the industrial society. The "discovery" of the Third World brings a paradigm shift as it has to respond to the realities of societies that had remained primarily rural. The use of the same conceptual framework is highly problematic. The dual-society thesis emerges as a way to recapture the dichotomy between "modern" and "traditional" sectors in these societies. The modernization paradigm brings a whole range of ideas of how the transition from the one stage to the other may be implemented, of how the "backward" sector is to be integrated in this very process of modernity.

For the emerging dependency school, any theorizing that would be more reflexive to the actual conditions of the Third World could not but search for new epistemological paths. This theoretical perspective soon turns into a critic of economism and neoclassical thinking and for the same reason it soon turned against classical Marxism. It questions this very validity of mainstream theorizing for the developed world as well (Seers 1979). Development is in this respect emerging as an ethical-political issue, identified with social reform and distinct from any technical growth-oriented scheme.

Economic theory has already legitimized the various forms of intervention. The first growth models undermine the wisdom surrounding the pure economics of the market. Harrod's 1939 famous paper extends the short-run static analysis to long-run macro-dynamics and indicates that savings have not only an employment effect but also turn into a growth-promoting, capacity-increasing aspect. Harrod's analysis also highlights the intrinsic instability of the system. Solow's 1956 model is an attempt to bring into neoclassical thinking an area of economic knowledge which could threaten the weakness of marginal economics for both economic analysis and policies. The American version of growth theory is pushing towards the neoclassical–Keynesian synthesis, the integration of Keynesianism within a strict neoclassical paradigm.

Dependency theory on the other hand attempts to provide predominantly economic and sociological explanations as to the roots of underdevelopment (Furtado 1964; Dos Santos 1970; Cardoso and Faleto 1979). Underdevelopment implies a stagnant economy unable to enter the typical growth pattern of the developed economies. Even if growth is present it concerns a small part of the economy with weak linkages to the rest of the economy. In the underdeveloped countries the missing elements are capital and technology. Land, no matter whether it produced corps for the internal or the external market, is incapable of rising productivity due to the abundance of labour. Industrialization is crucial for any break with underdevelopment.

Two theories at the time came up with a solution. Lewis (1954, 1955), with his two-sector model, recommends that the rise of savings could provide the break. Balanced growth (Rosentein–Rodan 1943; Nurske 1953) emphasizes that the parallel establishment of a group of industries could break the cycle of underdevelopment and initiate a viable industrialization process.

Rostow (1960) goes even further. He brings back the stages theory and feels that peripheral industrialization is both possible and feasible. He argues that it is a matter of time and institutional reforms that could be implemented within a liberal economic framework.

Myrdal (1957), who had already focused on institutional reform, is less optimistic on this issue. His theory of cumulative growth indicates that the liberal framework in international economic relations increases rather than decreases regional inequalities. The reversal of this process requires that international trade, investment and economic aid should be regulated by international institutions so as to benefit the less developed regions. Furthermore, the state in the underdeveloped world, which was lacking the qualities of the state in advanced societies, must be subject to institutional reform before becoming a reliable agent of development. As with Hirschman (1958) the emphasis is on the "diffusion of development" and the "linkages" that generate external economies to the productive system.

Mainstream economics remains sceptical towards such ideas. All issues concerning income distribution had been expelled from the "value-free" economic theorizing. If income redistribution is not considered as an important issue in the developed world, the same goes for redistribution of wealth on the international scale. Even the extreme income inequalities in the Third World are viewed as normal for economies being in the initial stage of development. The maturity of these economies would smoothen such income inequalities.

Capital, technology and labour become the issues of debate between two clear strategies: the export-led strategies giving emphasis, to foreign investment, liberal economic policies, free trade and monetary stability; and the import-substitution strategies giving emphasis to industrialization through tariff protection, credit orientation and state-induced forms of industrialization (Chang 2002). The former approach is the predominant

American view initiated by the Marshall Plan and extended in the early 1950s to the underdeveloped world as well. In reality the path followed by most countries was a combination of the two. Even in countries dedicated to export-led growth, import-substitution policies are extensively practised.

The economic crisis of the 1970s brought huge restructuring and readjustment in the world market. Neo-liberalism appeared as a system of ideas that would give new dynamism to the stagnant economies. By the early 1990s, the collapse of communism and other political developments left little space for rethinking. Globalization theories proclaimed that with very few variants there was one economic strategy for developed and underdeveloped countries alike.

Diversified theorizing

Mainstream doctrine seems unchallenged. The collapse of communism and the retreat of dependency theories left an open space which a reformed neoclassical approach was quick to fill. It incorporates both the traditional liberal dogma and many of the elements of the critic. The issue of economic development is one of economic growth. This is the typical old kind of argument. Growth is generated by the freedom of the market and the distribution of economic factors among sectors and activities in the most efficient way. Thus the liberalization of the world trade and the international movement of capital and commodities provide much of the foundations of the basic argument. Yet markets are not perfect. Asymmetrical information, economies of scale, human capital, monopolies and a whole area of other economic structures, social constraints and institutional failures indicate the need for reforms. Good governance and institutions seem to matter. The IMF and the World Bank seem to have incorporated recently most of these reformist ideas into what is called a Post-Washington consensus.

Although a unified dogma seems to dominate the scene from West to East and from North to South, many critical voices are raised to question the established orthodoxy. Thus, the crisis of the orthodox thinking appears at the very moment of its success. Among the new ideas are: a growing awareness of the limits of abundant natural resources in sustaining civilized life; a new ecological ethic; a greater concern with questions of equity and income distribution, particularly in countries that had successful periods of economic growth; a deeper understanding of the contradictions of globalization; a reassertion of the principles of self-governance and decentralized decision making; a more comprehensive understanding of the relation between markets and institutions; a reassertion of the superiority for democratic processes in tackling poverty and social space; a growing suspicion as to the merits of liberalization of the international financial markets; a deep concern about the restrictive trade practices of the developed economies. If it accomplishes nothing else, this reconstruction of the meaning of socio-economic development is forcing a serious re-examination of economic growth doctrines as well (Ruttan 1998; Meier and Stiglitz 2001).

The continuous transformation of economic theory has established a spectrum which allows for all kinds of outcome and diversified theorizing. As we have seen, the neoclassical paradigm itself has started moving into non-economic areas, facing the question of institutions, of human and social capital and all kinds of situations at variance with the perfect competitive market assumption. As soon as the perfect competition assumption is relaxed a whole variety of outcomes are possible inside the neoclassical paradigm. At the same time there is a growing variety of theoretical paradigms facing questions such as the relation between institutions and the market, and the association of democratic politics to economic development. It is rather early to tell whether a paradigm shift is in process. Yet it seems certain that the agenda of the classical thinkers is becoming an indispensable part of modern debates.

Notes

1 For a discussion of Petty's notion of division of labour, see Aspromourgos 1986, pp. 29–32.
2 For a more detailed analysis of the changes in the theory of wealth from Mercantilism to Quesnay, see Vaggi 1992.
3 Quesnay's ideal economy has been appropriately defined as a sort of agrarian capitalism (see Hoselitz 1968, pp. 661–2).
4 Unfortunately in Physiocracy the profits of the cultivators represent a magnitude of uncertain existence and unstable size, which can hardly explain and justify the process of long-run transformation of the economy envisaged by the Physiocrats (see Vaggi 1987).
5 Smith criticizes the idea that money should be considered as wealth (Smith 1776, II.iii.23–5).
6 Smith underlines the fact that the different specializations are not due to differences in natural talents of men; see the example of the street porter and the philosopher (Smith 1776, I.i.4).
7 On the notion of rate of profit in Smith, see Vaggi 1990.
8 A much wider analysis of the growth models by the classical authors is in Eltis 1984.
9 We assume that structural change takes place together with division of labour in the more productive sectors. Structural change alone could result in "extensive growth" due to labour movements from the less to the more productive sectors, without necessarily having an increase of labour productive in these sectors.
10 Rostow 1990 provides an extensive description of the evolution of growth theories during the nineteenth and twentieth centuries.
11 For an analysis of the so-called "four stages theory" in the age of the enlightenment and in Smith, see Meek 1976 and Groenewegen 1999.

References

Amin, S. (1974) *Accumulation on a World Scale*, New York: Monthly Review Press.

Appleby, J. (1978) *Economic Thought and Ideology in Seventeenth-Century England*, Princeton: Princeton University Press.

Aspromourgos, T. (1986) "Political Economy and the Social Division of Labour: The Economics of Sir William Petty", *Scottish Journal of Political Economy*, 33 (1), February.

Aston, T. and C. Philpin (eds) (1985) *The Brenner Debate: Agrarian Class Structure and Economic Development in Pre-industrial Europe*, Cambridge: Cambridge University Press.

Bleaney, M. (1976) *Underconsumption Theories: A History and Critical Analysis*, London: Lawrence and Wishart.

Cardoso, F. H. and E. Faletto (1979) *Dependency and Development in Latin America*, Berkeley and Los Angeles: University of California Press.

Chang, H. J. (2002) *Kicking Away the Ladder: Development Strategy in Historical Perspective*. London: Anthem Press.

Dobb, M. (1963) *Studies in the Development of Capitalism*, London: Routledge & Kegan Paul.

Dos Santos, T. (1970) "The Structure of Dependence", *American Economic Review*, 60: 231–6.

Eltis, W. (1984) *The Classical Theory of Economic Growth*, London and Basingstoke: Macmillan.

Foley, D. (1986) *Understanding Capital: Marx's Economic Theory*, Cambridge, Mass.: Harvard University Press.

Foucault, M. (1991) "Governmentality", in G. Burchell, C. Gordon and P. Miller (eds), *The Foucault Effect: Studies in Governmentality*, Chicago: The University of Chicago Press, pp. 87–104.

Fox-Genovese, E. (1976) *The Origins of Physiocracy*, Ithaca and London: Cornell University Press.

Frank, A. G. (1969) *Capitalism and Underdevelopment in Latin America* (revised edition; first edition 1967), New York and London: Modern Reader Paperbacks.

Furtado, C. (1964) *Development and Underdevelopment*, Berkeley and Los Angeles: University of California Press.

Gehrke, C. and H. Kurz (1998) "Karl Marx on Physiocracy" in H. Kurz and N. Salvadori (eds), *Understanding "Classical" Economics. Studies in Long-period Theory*, London: Routledge.

Groenewegen, P. D. (1999) "Productivity of Labour, Thrift and Economic Progress: Adam Smith's Optimistic View of Economic Development", in G. Forges Davanzati and V. Gioia (eds), *Reflections on Economic Development*, Lecce: Edizioni Milella.

Harrod, R. (1939) "An Essay in Dynamic Theory", *Economic Journal*, 49: 14–33.

Harvey, D. (1982) *The Limits to Capital*, Chicago: The University of Chicago Press.

Hilton, R. (ed.) (1976) *The Transition from Feudalism to Capitalism*, London: Verso.

Hirschman, A. O. (1958) *The Strategy of Economic Development*, New Haven Conn.: Yale University Press.

—— (1977) *The Passions and the Interest*, Princeton: Princeton University Press.

Hobsbawn, E. (1998) Introduction to *The Communist Manifesto: A Modern Edition*, London: Verso.

Hoselitz, B. F. (1968) "Agrarian Capitalism and the Natural Order of Things: Francois Quesnay", *Kyklos*, 4.

Hutchison, T. (1988) *Before Adam Smith*, Oxford: Blackwell.

INED (1958) *Francois Quesnay et la Physiocratie*, Institut Nationale d'Etudes Démographiques, vol. II, Paris: Presses Universitaires de France.

Kühne, K. (1979) *Economics and Marxism*, London: Macmillan.

Lewis, W. A. (1954) "Economic Development with Unlimited Supplies of Labour", *Manchester School*, 22, May: 139–91.

—— (1955) *The Theory of Economic Growth*, London: Allen & Unwin.

Meek, R. L. (1976) *Social Science and the Ignoble Savage*, Cambridge: Cambridge University Press.

Meier, G. and J. Stiglitz (2001) *Frontiers of Development Economics: The Future in Perspective*, Oxford: Oxford University Press.

Mun, T. (1621) *A Discourse of Trade*, London: Nicholas Okes; reprinted New York: Augustus M. Kelley, 1971.

—— (1623) *England's Treasure by Forraign Trade*, London: Thomas Clark, 1664; reprinted New York: Augustus M. Kelley, 1968.

Myint, H. (1977) "Adam Smith's Theory of International Trade in the Perspective of Economic Development", *Economica*, 44.

Myrdal, G. (1957) *Economic Theory and Underdeveloped Regions*, London: Duckworth.

Napoleoni, C. (1972) *Economic Thought of the Twentieth Century*, London: Martin Robertson.

Nurske, R. (1953) *Problems of Capital Formation in Underdeveloped Countries*, Oxford: Basil Blackwell.

Petty, W. (1662) "A Treatise of Taxes and Contributions", London: Brooke; in C. H. Hull (ed.), *The Economic Writings of Sir William Petty*, vol. 1, Cambridge: Cambridge University Press, 1899.

—— (1676) *Political Arithmetick*, London: Clavel and Mortlock, 1690, in ibid.

Polanyi, K. (1957) *The Great Transformation*, Boston: Beacon Press.

Procacci, G. (1991) "Social Economy and the Government of Poverty", in G. Burchell, C. Gordon and P. Miller (eds), *The Foucault Effect: Studies in Governmentality*, Chicago: The University of Chicago Press, pp. 151–68.

Roncaglia, A. (1977) *Petty – la nascita dell'economia politica*, Milano: Etas Libri.

Rosdolsky, R. (1977) *The Making of Marx's Capital*, London: Pluto Press.

Rosenstein-Rodan, P. N. (1943) "Problems of Industrialization in Eastern and South-Eastern Europe", *Economic Journal*, 53: 201–11.

Rostow, W. W. (1960) *The Stages of Economic Growth*, Cambridge: Cambridge University Press.

—— (1990) *Theorists of Economic Growth from David Hume to the Present*, Oxford: Oxford University Press.

Rubin, I. I. ([1929] 1979) *A History of Economic Thought*, London: Ink Links, 1979.

Ruttan, V. (1998) "New Growth Theory and Development Economics", *Journal of Development Studies*, 35: 1–26.

Seers, D. (1979) "The Congruence of Marxism and Other Neoclassical Doctrines", in A Rothko Chapel Colloquium, *Towards a New Strategy or Development*, New York: Pergamon Press, pp. 1–17.

Sen, A. (1987) *On Ethics and Economics*, Oxford: Blackwell.

Shaikh, A. (1978) "An Introduction to the History of Crisis Theories", in *U.S Capitalism in Crisis*, New York: Union of Radical Political Economics, pp. 219–40.

Smith, A. (1763?) "Early Draft of Part of the Wealth of Nations", in R. L. Meek, D. D. Raphael and P. G. Stein (eds), *Lectures on Jurisprudence*, Oxford: Clarendon Press, 1978.

Smith, A. (1776) *An Inquiry into the Nature and Causes of the Wealth of Nations, WN*, R. H. Campbell, A. S. Skinner and W. B. Todd (eds), Oxford: Oxford University Press, 1976.

Solow, R. (1956) "A Contribution to the Theory of Economic Growth", *Quarterly Journal of Economics*, 70: 65–94.

Vaggi, G. (1987) *The Economics of Francois Quesnay*, London: Macmillan.

—— (1990) "The Classical Concept of Profit Revisited", in D. E. Moggridge (ed.), *Perspectives on the History of Economics Thought*, vol. 3, Aldershot: Edward Elgar.

—— (1992) "The Theory of Wealth, the Ancien Régime and the Physiocratic Experiment", *International Journal of New Ideas*, 2.

Wallerstein, I. (1974) *The Modern World System*, New York: Academic Press.

Weulersse, G. (1910) *Le mouvement physiocratique en France (de 1756 . . . 1770)*, 2 vols, Alcan Editeur; reprinted Paris: Mouton, 1968.

Part I

Development theory

Classical and modern perspectives

1 Half a century of development theories

An institutionalist survey

Robert Boyer

Introduction: the need to take a new look at a half-century of theories and strategies of development

Development economics offered a double specificity when it first emerged as a separate discipline at the end of the Second World War. For some analysts, it constituted an exception to the theories that were assumed to be operative in the developed economies. Others felt that the developing world could become a new zone of application for such theories – as long as they were adapted to its main characteristics. However, in both cases, development economics was only of secondary importance. As Axel Leijonhufvud humorously wrote in 1973:

> The priestly caste (the Math-Econ), for example, is a higher "field" than either Micro or Macro, while the Develops just as definitely rank lower.... The low rank of the Develops is due to the fact that this caste, in recent times, has not strictly enforced the taboos against association with the Polscis, Sociogs and other tribes. Other Econ look upon this with considerable apprehension as endangering the moral fiber of the tribe and suspect the Develops even of relinquishing model-making.
>
> (Cited in Bardhan 2000: 1)

This sort of tongue-in-cheek attitude fell out of fashion in the late 1990s, when development issues found themselves at the heart of some bitter controversies. Even more importantly, development studies have made a great deal of progress at the conceptual level, with many of its advances working their way into the very core of general economic theory. There are a number of examples. Theories of imperfect information and of "principal-agent" contracts (Stiglitz 1987) have nurtured thinking about the basic characteristics of a rural economy (Bardhan 1989b). Externalities relating to co-ordination problems have led to formalisations that deal as much with endogenous growth (Lucas 1993) as with the existence of multiple equilibria whenever preferences and strategies are interdependent (Hoff and Stiglitz 2001). As such, both the developed and the traditional economies' characteristic problems can be dealt with as part of a unified framework.

However, in the end, a number of these strategies for development turned out to be failures, causing the world's top theoreticians to raise questions as to why so many theories, based as they were on mechanisms that were simple and unique, had such limited capacities for explaining development. In the words of Irma Adelman:

> Like chemists' futile quest for the philosopher's stone, over the past half-century the search for a single explanatory factor guided both theoretical and empirical research into development. As a discipline, economics seems incapable of recognising that this sort of factor does not exist, and that a policy of development requires an otherwise more complex understanding of systems, one that combines economic, social, cultural and political institutions, whose interactions themselves change over time. That as a result, interventions must be multiform. That what is good for one phase of development can turn out to be unfavourable at a later stage. That certain irreversibilities create path-dependency. In sum, that the prescriptions a given country receives at a certain moment in time should be rooted in an understanding of its situation, and of the trajectory that has led it to the present through a long period of history.
>
> (2001b: 104–5)

A number of similar statements can be found in recent stances taken by top experts in development, as well as by other pacesetters in the field of economics (Emmerij 1997a; Sen 1997; Stiglitz 1998; Meier 2001; *Revue d'économie du developpment* 2001). This convergence raises two issues.

How and why did development theories converge, in the late 1990s, towards a systemic and institutionalist conception diametrically opposed to a "purely economic approach" that usually focuses on technologies, demography and markets? It would be illuminating to carry out an analysis, however brief this may be, of the stages that development economics passed through from the end of the Second World War until modern times. Development is a concept with a long history. The same can be said of those factors that are considered to be crucial in terms of the perpetuation of under-development – they too have changed greatly over the course of the past half-century.

At the same time, it would also be useful to revisit the period's main governmental strategies, sometimes characterised by trust in a 100 per cent state system, and sometimes by the temptation to leave resource allocation – and even certain strategic choices – up to the market.

As regards the theories that are involved, the most notable studies into the potentiality of (and conditions underlying) a market economy have revealed a whole array of structural limitations that can undermine the efficiency of the market's allocations (Ingrao and Israel 1990) or of its very functioning (White 1981) – not to mention the problem of its institutionalisation (Fligstein 1999). In short, a market is a social construction. In return, and quite symmetrically, public-choice theoreticians have concluded that it is not necessarily possible for the state to compensate for market failures, given that it suffers from the opportunistic behaviour of politicians (and of the senior civil servants in charge of implementing their decisions).

Therefore, if we are to answer the issue that lies at the heart of the present essay with any confidence, we will have to show that there are a multiplicity of reasons today why we should kick this habit of alternating between a belief in the state as an agent of development, and the belief that all we have to do is respond to the market's signals. In other words, we do not in fact have to be slaves to the cyclical Kondratief-like thinking that seems to have marked the history of ideas, doctrines and economic theories on development-related matters. There may be another way of formulating this paradigm.

A half-century of trials and errors

The development concept's long history

From the outset, economic policy-making was dealing with problems that today come under the heading of theories of development. The founding fathers often wondered (and argued) about the respective roles that the state and the market should be playing in this complex process. William Petty, François Quesnay and Adam Smith raised some significant questions. Does the market need the state; or to the contrary, will the market's success deprive the state of its attributes? To encourage development, do we need more or less of a state? (Sen 1988: 10).

Development theory per se was only seen as a distinct discipline after the Second World War. Since then, the development concept has gone through an endless series of redefinitions and reinterpretations. To carry out a forward-looking analysis of development, it would be useful to take a quick look at the different definitions that have been attributed successively to the processes at work in those economies that were once described as "peripheral" (see Figure 1.1).

The first and most elementary definition stresses the self-perpetuating nature of growth, as opposed to simple phases of acceleration in a transient economic situation. This criterion relates to an important aspect in development, that is a country's entering a phase of permanent growth as opposed to its tendency to stagnate, or to experience the sort of slow increases in output that were rife during the sixteenth century (Braudel 1979; Bairoch 1995).

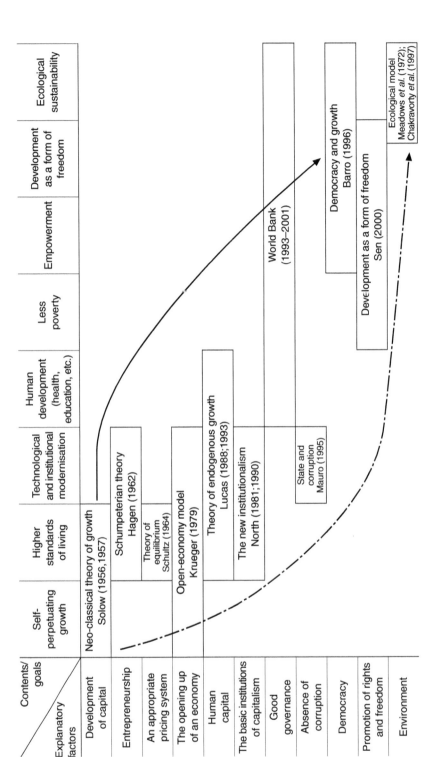

Figure 1.1 A historical look at the substance and at the purpose of development.

Of course, growth could be a product of demographic changes rather than of rising standards of living. Hence a second definition stressing a quasi-continuous rise in per capita consumption as a criterion of development, considered here in the strictly economic sense of the term. It is this definition that theories of growth usually use, in line with a tradition that goes all the way back to Harrod or Domar models – although the canonical form is found in a neo-classical type of emblematic formalisation (Solow 1956, 1957).

Still, neither of these meanings accounts for a third essential component: the transformations of technologies, organisations and institutions that accompany the economic growth process per se. The development concept itself introduces the idea of a qualitative transformation and finds a significant reference in the Schumpeterian theory of development, as long as this application is not limited to entrepreneurs alone or to an entrepreneurial frame of mind.

This notion can be extended further by incorporating one of the main findings of historical demography, to wit, the spectacular human development that has taken place over the past two centuries. This has occurred at different levels: physical (growth in people's average size); health-related (longer-life expectancies at birth); and intellectual (rise in collective and individual knowledge through training in reading and mathematics, and more generally by learning to think analytically and abstractly).

It is important to note that these variables define the objectives and contents of development, and not just one of its pre-conditions as has been assumed in recent studies of endogenous growth (Lucas 1988, 1993; Romer 1990). This received wisdom is the basis of the human-development indicators the World Bank uses. Published at regular intervals, these indicators lend themselves to a ranking that is somewhat different from classifications based on per-capita income (e.g. World Bank 1998). This demonstrates the multidimensional nature of development.

An analogous divergence crops up when national performances are measured by growth rates or by reductions in levels of poverty. Of course, economic dynamism provides the necessary resources for reducing distribution-related conflicts (Collier *et al.* 2001), but nothing guarantees that the least well off will receive their fair share of the fruits of growth. Much depends on the distribution of property – and on the institutions that shape the pricing and rewards systems (Adelman 2001a: 84). Hence a sixth definition of development as a reducer of poverty – the latter term being defined here as when people are deprived of a decent life.

Development analysis and theories of justice can be linked in an attempt to come up with a more general definition. According to Rawls (1971), development can be defined as the recognition that all individuals have basic rights, notably the right to operate in a framework that enables everyone to fulfil his/her potential as far as possible. This conception finds its extreme version in a definition that is radically opposed to a purely economic vision, and which assimilates development with freedom in the social, political and economic order (Sen 2000).

Lastly, increasing environmental problems have caused certain analysts to stress the ecological sustainability of a given mode of development. This is the criterion that is ultimately transplanted into the idea of the primacy of the economic regime's social acceptability and political sustainability. This final definition has a distant origin in the Malthusian interpretation of development as a conflict between an economic dynamic and the exhaustion of nature resources. It has, however, taken on new forms, first when oil and raw materials prices skyrocketed during the 1970s (Meadows *et al.* 1972), and later during the 1990s, due to the fear of global warming (Godard *et al.* 2000).

All in all, over the past half-century, the development concept has been considerably transformed, to the point that it now encompasses a whole series of objectives relating to: the quality of the economic policy being followed; the investments being made in health and education as part of the reproduction of a society's overall structure; political acceptance of a given economic order; without forgetting the economic activity's place in the ecosystem. From its original ad hoc and limited relevancy in a domain that was purely economic (and even economistic) in nature, the concept's definition has been extended to cover most of the orders that comprise a society, as well as the interrelationships between them. This has been achieved through the use of a systemic approach – even if this term has been rarely used (Adelman 2001a). An analogous trend has been observed with the different schemes for interpreting development, as well as systematic non-development.

From technology to modes of government: the progress made in the explanatory factors of development

Figure 1.1 highlights a remarkable parallelism between the changes in development-related ideas and the changes in the explanatory factors that theoreticians and analysts use.

At first, development economists drew their inspiration from the advances that had been achieved in the various theories of growth. Whether inspired by Keynes or by the reaffirmation of a balanced growth model, they saw the investment rate as the key factor over the long and medium term. In fact, cross-national econometric studies asserted that this was one of the most robust explanations for differences in growth rates over a period of one or several decades (Bradford de Long and Summers 1991).

The optimal growth theory shows that this type of relationship is not linear. Moreover, the experience of the Soviet economy confirms that it is important for social and economic institutions to define incentives to encourage the productive utilisation of the resources that have been allocated to investment and to innovation. Society's ability to absorb technologies and innovations also cropped up as a key variable explaining differential rates of growth (Abramowitz 1986). Industrialising countries' ambitious but unsuccessful development plans were sometimes attributed to a lack of talent in economic management, not to mention a shortage of entrepreneurs.

This raises a major issue, to wit, the main institutions of an economy that is being run according to market logic. On the one hand, economists tend to stress mechanisms such as price-based allocations, where non-development can only stem from the blocking of market mechanisms (Schultz 1964). On the other hand, the new institutionalism implies the need to transcend a logic that is based on property rights alone (North 1981) so as to focus on the constitutional and legal support system in those societies where the level of economic activity reflects all of these incentives and constraints (North 1990).

One interpretation decries the hindering of a market logic; the other highlights the importance of policy and law. Ultimately, both incorporate the mode of government, or "governance" using current jargon. This refers not only to the way in which the state is being governed and managed. It applies more generally to the distribution of power throughout the entire social order, including in the economic sphere (Théret 1992). Roughly speaking, the idea here is that development stems from good governance, which can mean, for example, the application of an appropriate pricing system for those goods whose production and allocation can be structured to match the markets' organisation.

It remains that good governance can be analysed in a number of different ways. The World Bank believes, for example, that this should entail an efficient management of public goods and of externalities (World Bank 1997, 2001). For other analysts, the key to the inhibition or blocking of development lies in the corruption that can be caused by state intervention (World Bank 1995; Rose-Ackerman 2000). Other economists focus on the complementarity between democracy and development, once a threshold of per-capita income has been surpassed (Barro 1996). As for those economists who draw their inspiration from the advances that have been made in political philosophy – but also those who chart the basic characteristics of under-development – individual rights are the key to overcoming the poverty and shortage that is generated by an unequal access to basic goods (Sen 2000).

Finally, given the persistence of famine in certain countries, people become periodically aware that deteriorations in the natural environment can undermine the economic activities of a traditional society. Together with rapidly rising raw materials prices, this reminds them that in the long run ecological constraints will determine the future of the planet and therefore of economic activity.

It is clear that, a half-century on, the term "development" no longer refers to the same definitions nor to the same explanatory factors. We should thus try to verify whether the same changes apply for all of the vectors and strategies of development.

Theories of development: historical controversies, recent convergences

At first, development economists were highly sceptical about the market's aptitude for promoting a steady accumulation of capital in developed economies, and especially about other countries' ability to catch up with them (Meier 1987). For Marxists (e.g. Preobrazhenski 1924), and later for structuralists (e.g. Prebisch 1971), market extension should be a limited phenomenon involving neither capital goods nor credit. Quite the contrary: it is up to planning and/or state intervention to promote a type of growth that respects national autonomy as well as a modicum of social justice.

Neo-classical economists were quick to rebel against this vision, putting forward the idea that the impoverished state of farmers in the Third World in no way constitutes an impediment to the development of a *homo oeconomicus* type of rationality – meaning the ability to respond to the price signals that are conveyed by a market (Schultz 1964, 1980). Here the problem is framed the other way around: the developing countries are said to be suffering from not enough of a market orientation rather than from an excess thereof.

Between these two extremes, the early (e.g. Domar 1957) and later Keynesians (e.g. Stiglitz 1988) stressed that the market creates an unbalanced allocation of credit and labour. In so doing, it affects investment whilst providing a satisfactory outcome for most standard goods, that is merchandise whose quality has been clearly defined independently of its price (see Figure 1.2). Market extension should neither be too great nor too small. This contradicts both the neo-classical and the structuralist points of view.

Similarly, the state's relationship to the market is the subject of a wide variety of conceptions. For the founders of development economics, whether Marxists or structuralists, it is up to the state to replace the market inasmuch as the latter is usually unable to pilot accumulation with any degree of success. This view also holds the market responsible for a whole series of crises that can be damaging to almost all members of society: capitalist entrepreneurs, wage earners and bankers. It is therefore imperative to resort to planning, be this of the authoritarian or the indicative variety, so that governments can promote an orderly type of development.

It is just as necessary that a collective authority intervenes in areas such as land and raw materials management, that is in environmental matters. This is an idea that goes back a long way (Malthus specifically refers to it)

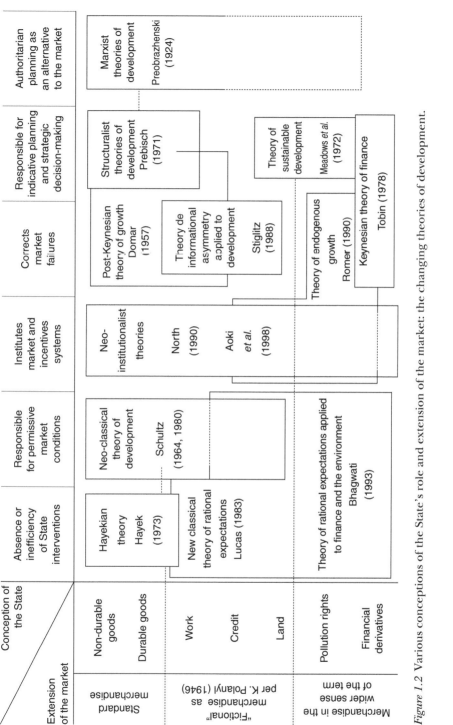

Figure 1.2 Various conceptions of the State's role and extension of the market: the changing theories of development.

and was rejuvenated after the first oil shock. The first ecological models tended to demonstrate that pure-market adjustments would be unable to keep humankind from running out of natural resources, thus leading to a no-growth situation (Meadows *et al.* 1972).

There is an even stronger argument concerning threats to the environment, specifically the deterioration of the ozone layer, as demonstrated in the 1990s by the Rio and Kyoto international conferences. Still, it is difficult to convert this concern into instruments of intervention that can be used for environmentally related economic decision-making: should there be norms and rules, or instead should market mechanisms (i.e. pollution rights) prevail? This again raises the question of the relationship between collective choices and the market, all the more poignantly so inasmuch there is no world government to tax polluters or to determine norms that can be applied to everybody.

Observing the functioning of Soviet-type regimes (or of economies featuring strong state interventionism), neo-liberal theoreticians have concluded that statist *constructivism* is condemned to fail since it is unable to manage the complex information flows that are characteristic of modern economies, and which only a myriad decentralised markets are capable of handling (Hayek 1973). This theory was primarily applied to the older industrialised economies, but it also has major implications for the developing countries. In lieu of "planning", this school of thought recommends "allowing market pricing to do the work". In this view, a frugal and modest *state* is the best way of supporting development. It remains that the neo-liberals' argument does not refer to a Soviet-type of authoritarian planning alone, inasmuch as it tends to question the efficiency of almost any type of state intervention.

In this view, as long as agents are entirely rational and can extrapolate the consequences of government decisions, the state loses all ability to disturb market equilibrium, which is deemed to operate independently of any one individual's wishes. The rational expectations hypothesis can therefore be said to have given a second wind to the classical school's pro laissez-faire arguments, despite the existence of temporal interdependencies (the phenomena for which planners have traditionally been responsible (see, e.g., Lucas 1983)).

This reasoning is also applied to environmental problems: as long as all actors are familiar with the model governing the interdependency between the economic system and environmental processes, the pricing system will be responsible for revealing and then resolving whatever imbalances may emerge. This is all the more valid since rising standards of living will supposedly raise general awareness of environmental matters (Bhagwati 1993).

Research carried out since the mid-1980s has enabled us to transcend this relatively Manichean dichotomy. On one hand, having witnessed for example the transformation of the Soviet economy (World Bank 1996), theoreticians – even neo-liberals – and international organisations now recognise that the state has a significant responsibility in building the institutions that the market needs if it is to fulfil its potential. It also is responsible for providing a supportive framework for entrepreneurship: a stable currency, an efficient system of payment, codified accounting practices, business law, a stable legal system, state monopolisation of legitimate coercion, and a minimum of transport and communications infrastructures to reinforce the unity of the national entity. All of these factors are necessary pre-conditions for setting up a market (Hollingsworth and Boyer 1997: 55–93). The considerable economic problems that have arisen in Russia, and to a lesser degree in the rest of Eastern and Central Europe, are merely an expression of a lack of understanding of these institutional conditions (Boyer 2001).

On the other hand, theories that focus on the asymmetrical nature of information generally conclude that market equilibrium has been suboptimal, for example when price is both a mechanism of resource allocation as well as an indicator of quality. This leads to rationing in the labour and credit markets, the end result being that corrective state interventions can improve the lot of all economic agents (Stiglitz 1994). This argument is entirely applicable to the developing economies, characterised as they are by relatively shallow financial markets and by atypical employment contracts (Stiglitz 1988; Bardhan 1989a).

Can finance be totally controlled via market-based adjustments? Does speculation always enable convergence towards a security's or a financial asset's true value? Keynesian theories of finance provide convincing arguments for a negative response to this conjecture (Tobin 1978; Shiller 2000). Central Bank interventions, prudential regulations and the existence of a lender of the last resort are all factors that sustain the viability of a developed financial economy. The state's function in this case becomes to correct market failures.

There is, however, another corpus of literature that is more directly related to development itself: the theory of endogenous technological progress, which stresses the role played by those positive externalities that are associated with innovation and with the human capital which is being trained within an educational system or a firm. Given that the social returns are greater than the private returns in this case, growth optimisation is predicated on state intervention – for example, on the subsidising of R&D expenditures or on the guarantee that basic education remains free of charge (Romer 1990).

This issue is a particularly poignant one for the developing countries, inasmuch as the knowledge or technologies that they use are usually imported at such times as they make a purchase of capital goods and patents. Thus the general framework that is applicable to endogenous growth has to be adapted to the developing countries' circumstances. Even the Asian Tigers, during the halcyon days of their era of growth, seemed to be unable to increase their total factor productivity (Lau 1996). As a result, developing countries' economic and technological policies should probably be distinct from the developed world's, instead of being a mere carbon copy of it (World Bank 1998).

In modern theories, the state retrieves a role, one that the market is incapable of fulfilling. Not only does it correct the markets' failures but it also institutes a number of market systems, thanks to its promulgation of highly specific rules that ensure their viability (one model being today's financial markets). Neo-institutionalist theories also highlight the key role that is played by the constitutional and legal order, which shapes the incentives system, hence the forms of organisation and innovation, and therefore the economic dynamic itself (North 1990).

This makes it difficult to imagine that only one form of market economy exists, possibly gravitating around a Walrasian equilibrium. A wide range of forms already seems possible. As long as economic institutions are congruent, their changes cannot be explained by the efficiency principle alone. Moreover, these institutional architectures will be all the more successful if they encourage market adjustments for standard goods, whilst recognising that credit and employment contracts will for the most part be unaffected by such adjustments – this being another source of diversity for modes of development (Aoki and Okuno-Fujiwara 1998; Aoki 2001).

All in all, modern research has revealed a significant convergence, resolving the somewhat Manichean debates that had presided over the emergence of development economics.

Most theoreticians agree that the market can allocate and produce standard goods efficiently, but that labour and credit cannot be completely run by a market logic, meaning that state interventions or collective agreements are needed for their management. This is even more important for the financial markets (Orléan 2000; Shiller 2000) and for any process that implements significant indivisibilities or complementarities. This configuration crops up frequently in traditional rural economies (Bardhan 1989b), but also in the industrialising economies (Hoff and Stiglitz 2001). It is paramount to have a form of co-ordination that operates outside of market strictures to govern the choices that are being made in terms of public infrastructure, the environment or education and research policies.

The theory of endogenous technological progress recycles some of the main intuitions that can be found in the structuralist theories of development (Rosenstein-Rodan 1943) when it shows, for example, that a country with an initial handicap can be permanently stuck in a poverty trap in the absence of any forms of co-ordination that have been organised by its state or collective entities (Murphy *et al.* 2000; Hoff and Stiglitz 2001). Inversely, by synchronising investment or innovation, this obstacle can be overcome. This generates stronger growth and benefits all of society. As such, the state can spur a creation of additional wealth, and is no longer a simple predator in a zero-sum game.

In theoretical terms, the modern era has witnessed the abatement of the radical conceptions that had long dominated discussions about development economics. Neither authoritarian planning nor a full-scale generalisation of the market system is being looked for. All that is at stake is a very moderate balance between state intervention and decentralised adjustments. A range of World Bank annual reports illustrates this growing awareness (World Bank 1993, 1996, 1997, 1998, 2001) and seems to herald a turnaround – even a bifurcation – in the development conceptions found in the international organisations themselves.

This conception can be broken down into two diverging conceptions of the state's role. For neo-Keynesian theoreticians, the authorities' function is to correct the market's imperfections (Stiglitz 1988). For some of the new institutionalists, the political order is a catalyst for economic incentives. Here the economy's overall performance is deemed to be derived from its incentives system. There is no absolute criterion of efficiency guiding the development and selection of economic systems (North 1990).

For this reason, most governments across the world have adopted a stance that had been expressed for the American economy by the Council of Economic Advisers (CEA):

> The role of government ... is not to stimulate economic activity through public expenditures but, in a more subtle fashion, to provide individuals and companies with the tools they need to prosper thanks to their own efforts ... Government should be used to supplement and not to replace the market and the private sector. This is the basic principle guiding the economic strategy of this administration.
>
> (Council of Economic Advisors 1998: 87)

"100 per cent state" and "100 per cent market": two failed development strategies

Leaving theory aside to concentrate on the strategies that states have been pursuing, it is reassuring to note that a number of convergent lessons can be drawn from the history of the twentieth century. Development plans that bet everything either on a complete organisation of economic life by the state or on a total delegation of collective responsibilities to the market have all failed more or less miserably (Théret 1999). In the absence of any exhaustive analysis, this can be illustrated by a number of national trajectories (see Figure 1.3).

There is no better example of the failure of the "100 per cent state" approach than the changes in the Soviet economy. Centralised economic power was supposed to engender rapid growth and allow the USSR to

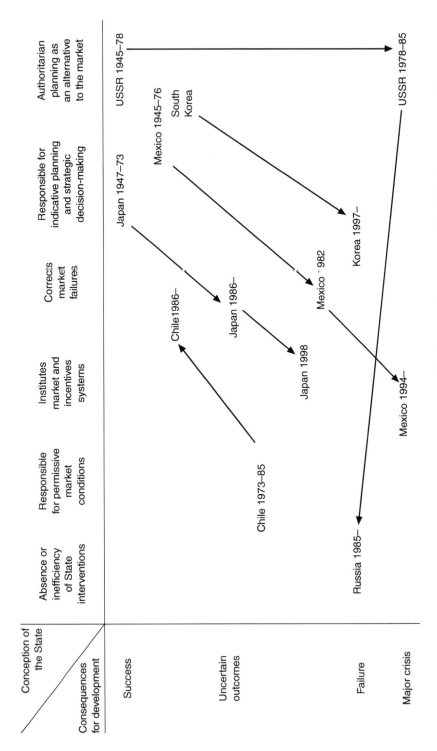

Figure 1.3 Various conceptions of the relationship between State and Market – and impact on national development strategies.

catch up with the living standards found in the rival capitalist economies. However, one should not underestimate its initial successes in building up a heavy industry and in diffusing the most essential collective services. The Soviet regime's maturity process was eventually stunted by a complete evaporation of productivity gains and its inability to make a successful transition to mass consumption – not to mention the political tensions that arise in an authoritarian system (Sapir 1989). It is no surprise that reforms initiated in the mid-1980s to overcome these obstacles triggered a major structural crisis, accompanied by a deep recession that lasted for nearly a decade (Sapir 1996).

Still, the subsequent trajectory of the Russian economy does offer a second lesson, one that is almost symmetrical to the first. It is not enough to simply banish the monopolisation of political power by the Communist Party, or the role of the Gosplan in economic management, for a market economy to prosper. The country's recurring difficulties provide proof that a market does not possess the property of being self-implementing (Fligstein 1999). Without a legitimate state endowed with the power to establish the rules of the game, what ends up prevailing is a trend towards autarky and the fragmentation of the economic and social space.

In contrast, the dynamism of the Chinese market shows how very important the state can be in the emergence of a market economy. Far from being the enemy of the market, the state can be a catalyst. On the one hand, it sets up the necessary institutional foundations: property, contracts, currency and market supervision. On the other hand, it supports agents during their internalisation of a market-based logic.

This somewhat extreme example can be reinforced by an analysis of other national trajectories (Pieper and Taylor 1998, Aoki and Okuno-Fujiwara 1998, Emmerij 1997b, Ranis 1997). In the 1980s and 1990s, state-driven growth strategies experienced difficulties that were aggravated by the conflict between national regimes that were undergoing strong governmental supervision and accelerated financial deregulation. Recent developments in Japan and later in Korea are good examples of this. The suddenness of the 1997 crisis that broke out in South East Asia raises an important theoretical question. Many analysts had believed that this area's earlier success had been the result of an economic policy that had encouraged the advent of a market system (World Bank 1993; Aoki *et al.* 1998). Yet when they opened up to financial innovation, what became apparent was the deferred impact of this extension of the market. It had been efficient for standard goods, but its impact was much more problematic in terms of credit and financial products (especially derivatives; see, e.g., Boyer 1999a) and labour (Boyer 1994). Following another path, modern theoreticians have thus recycled those intuitions that once served as a foundation to Karl Polanyi's analyses (1946).

It remains that there is probably no better example of the limitations of a "100 per cent market" approach than the Chilean trajectory (Pieper and

Taylor 1998: 46–7). After 1973, Chile adopted a strategy that was highly
geared towards a market-based logic, broken down into every sphere of
economic activity. This strategy led to the destruction of most of the state's
previous interventions, yet this is not what drove the "Chilean miracle". In
actual fact, from the 1980s onwards the state was forced to correct the
imbalances that were the product of the previously extremely neo-liberal
strategies, so as to develop state structures that could encourage exports,
regulate short-term capital inflows and above all maintain control over the
proceeds from copper exports. This led to the reintroduction of a complementarity between state intervention and the market (Odaka and Teranishi 1998). Much more systematic comparative studies have confirmed
that many Latin American countries' past successes did not stem from
their adoption of "100 per cent market" friendly strategies, but, on the
contrary, from an earlier correction phase that had reintroduced a
modicum of state control (Inter-American Development Bank 1995).

Thus, the analysis of development strategies confirms the lessons
derived from changes in theories. There is convergence towards a balanced conception of the relationship between state and market, moving
away from the succession of radical positions that had previously dominated this field.

Interventionists and neo-liberals: an ongoing battle?

If we put the development strategies that were being pursued during the
interwar period into perspective, what shows up is a series of contrasting
positions: vigorous state interventions designed to be a response to the
failures of deregulation, and, inversely, the limitations of a state-driven
type of development triggering a reorientation in favour of market-based
adjustments. Looking to the future, it is worthwhile remembering the
reasons for this swing, which is somewhat reminiscent of the long waves
Kondratief thought he had identified in his study of the history of capitalism (see Figure 1.4).

The interwar period was marked by the unfavourable repercussions of
the crisis in the industrialised economies on other countries' development
potential. This is exemplified by the Latin American countries, which at
the time were very open in trading and financial terms to the international economy. The consensus back then was that neo-liberal strategies
had failed, causing Cambridge economists (including John Maynard
Keynes) to look for a new theoretical framework. For countries on the
periphery, external dependency was considered an impediment to
national development, and financial capital as a destabilisation of their
earlier specialisation. Governments who supported open-door policies and
deregulation lost legitimacy – and often power.

This was the breeding ground that nurtured, from the 1950s onwards,
a developmentist state conception that was supported by structuralist

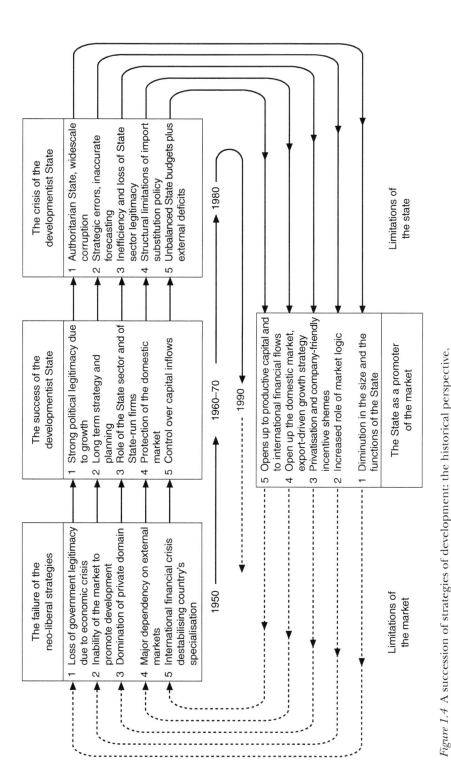

The failure of the neo-liberal strategies

1 Loss of government legitimacy due to economic crisis
2 Inability of the market to promote development
3 Domination of private domain
4 Major dependency on external markets
5 International financial crisis destabilising country's specialisation

The success of the developmentist State

1 Strong political legitimacy due to growth
2 Long term strategy and planning
3 Role of the State sector and of State-run firms
4 Protection of the domestic market
5 Control over capital inflows

The crisis of the developmentist State

1 Authoritarian State, widescale corruption
2 Strategic errors, inaccurate forecasting
3 Inefficiency and loss of State sector legitimacy
4 Structural limitations of import substitution policy
5 Unbalanced State budgets plus external deficits

5 Opens up to productive capital and to international financial flows
4 Open up the domestic market, export-driven growth strategy
3 Privatisation and company-friendly incentive shemes
2 Increased role of market logic
1 Diminution in the size and the functions of the State

The State as a promoter of the market

Limitations of the market

Limitations of the state

1950   1960–70   1980   1990

Figure 1.4 A succession of strategies of development: the historical perspective.

theories (Prebisch 1950, 1971). Here the state and the public sector are meant to take the initiative for those strategic decisions that will have an impact over the long run, for example via planning procedures or by controlling access to credit or to imported capital goods. To avoid having to suffer from the uncertain nature of the international economy, the domestic market is highly protected by a policy of high tariffs, with exceptions possibly being made for capital goods destined for priority sectors. Capital flows are subject to state controls and certain financial transactions are prohibited or severely restricted.

In the 1960s and 1970s, governments following this orientation enjoyed a great deal of legitimacy, if only because strong growth generally allowed for a resolution of those tensions that inevitably accompany the changes in industrial structures and social equilibria which lead to development. This success was generally forgotten during the 1990s but it was a reality and it transformed a number of societies, including in Latin America.

Paradoxically, it is the very success of the developmentist state that led to criticisms thereof, starting in the 1980s. The multiplicity of state interventions causing corruption and authoritarianism meant that democracy movements began to rise up. In addition, given the growing uncertainty that the international system was transmitting via raw materials prices, interest rates and market growth rates, governments committed strategic errors and planners were guilty of an ever-greater variance between forecasts and actual performances. The state sector seemed to be more and more inefficient, often because it was impossible to implement the import substitution policies any further than they had been. Lastly, slower growth and the ensuing economic instability exacerbated distribution-related conflicts, provoking major imbalances in state budgets – and often in external accounts as well. The need for an alternative strategy became clear to governments, regardless of their ideological orientations or initial policies.

Development projects therefore adopted a strategy that involved supporting the market in most areas of economic activity. People felt that it was necessary to open up to productive capital and to international financing. This meant that the domestic market was supposed to open up and deregulate, with exports becoming increasingly viewed as the main driver of growth. Then came a plethora of privatisations and company-friendly incentive schemes, both domestically and abroad. Price mechanisms tended to replace state interventions, resulting in a considerable transformation of the state and of the economy.

Not only were these convergent efforts meant to diminish the amount of money that the public sector was taking out of the rest of the economy, but the state also turned itself into a promoter of the market system and of entrepreneurship. It was during this period that an opposition arose between the trajectories of those Latin American countries that had belatedly taken to this path and the changes in those South East Asia countries (see, e.g., Boyer 1994; Marques-Pereira and Théret 2001) that had supposedly been pursuing company-friendly policies since the 1950s (Aoki and Okuno-Fujiwara 1998). In the end, and up until the mid-1990s, the newly industrialised countries' successes were attributed to their having adhered to a market principle, and to their successful insertion into the international division of labour.

And yet, once again, the euphoria brought by past successes is an early warning for the next crisis. Countries pursuing this sort of strategy experienced a whole series of crises. Mexico was severely hit in 1994 by the divorce between the slow transformation of its productive apparatus and the speed with which foreign capital was withdrawn. Most of the countries in South East Asia suffered a complete reversal of fortunes in 1997, again because the international financial community changed its opinion regarding the stability of these economies and markets, which were said to be "emerging".

Governments were subjected to major social and political tensions. Their adherence to a market orientation was a problem, including in those countries that were most in favour of free trade and laissez-faire attitudes. The influence of the international financial markets increasingly came under fire, given that it was wreaking havoc on countries' social and industrial organisation. Their firm footing in the international division of labour, previously considered to be a boon, seemed to undermine their ability to control their national economic situation and, more generally, their own style of development. There were open discussions about the limitations of a strategy that was entirely run according to a market orientation, a debate that took place both in those countries that were suffering from the crisis as well as in international organisations such as the International Monetary Fund and the World Bank (Stiglitz 1998).

The late 1990s were somewhat reminiscent of the interwar period: were governments again going to shift towards strategies that gave primacy to the state as an alternative to the market?

From the market's failures to the state's limitations: the contributions of "big theories"

In all likelihood, such a conclusion would be precipitous. First, the two periods featured productive structures, social and political conditions and international economic configurations that were quite different, so it was highly improbable that there could have been an identical repetition of the catastrophic chain of events that took place between 1929 and 1932. In addition, we should not underestimate the clarifications that have been provided by theoreticians' research into the respective merits of the market and the state (Stiglitz 1987, 1994; Wolf 1990) and of organisations (Arrow 1974).

Symmetrically, note should also be taken of the advances that were being made in multidisciplinary approaches (Hollingsworth and Boyer

1997) that put the role and the power of the market into perspective, taking other forms of co-ordination as a benchmark. Indeed, above and beyond the passion of these political debates and the ideological oppositions involved, economic theory and political science concluded that there can be a durable co-existence of state and market failure, and that neither of the two co-ordination procedures should pretend to be the only one capable of organising and managing modern economies (see Figure 1.5). It is important that we present the essential characteristics of this approach – developed to a greater extent in other studies; see, for example, Boyer 1997 – inasmuch as it has had a definite impact on development issues.

General equilibrium theoreticians have, in this respect, done a great deal of work. They have demonstrated under which conditions Adam Smith's assertions can be verified, particularly his notion that the search for individual interests can ensure a favourable collective outcome as long as the market is mediating these interactions, without any other interference (Ingrao and Israel 1990). The net result is that the existence, stability and optimality of a market economy's equilibrium is much harder to guarantee than we have been led to believe by the founders of political economy since Adam Smith.

Among other things, money has to be exogenous, competition must be perfect, quality assessments have to be seamless, no public equipment can exist, production techniques must feature constant returns, innovation cannot manifest any positive externality, no more than pollution can produce any negative externalities. It is also important that the disruptive effects of expectations be nullified thanks to the creation of futures markets for all goods, covering all time periods and operating in every country of the world – even though, in the real economies, a small number of financial markets actually ensure all by themselves the co-ordination of people's views of the future. Last but not least, considerations of social justice cannot exert any influence on the allocation of resources and on the conditions of a Pareto-type of efficiency.

If one or the other of these seven conditions is not satisfied, other co-ordination mechanisms become necessary. Each will create its own pathology, something that should be compared with the reassuring image of an invisible hand: absence of equilibrium, multiple equilibriums, variance versus Pareto optimum.

In this view, collective interventions to organise the markets or ensure an alternative form of adjustment derive their legitimacy from all these advances in economic theory. They therefore have an effect on the analysis of development. First of all, money is a collective institution that is the basis of all markets but which does not itself stem from a market mechanism (something that Karl Polanyi already discusses in his 1946 work). Similarly, the preservation of competition depends on actions taken by state authorities – it does not stem from some unadulterated and automatic

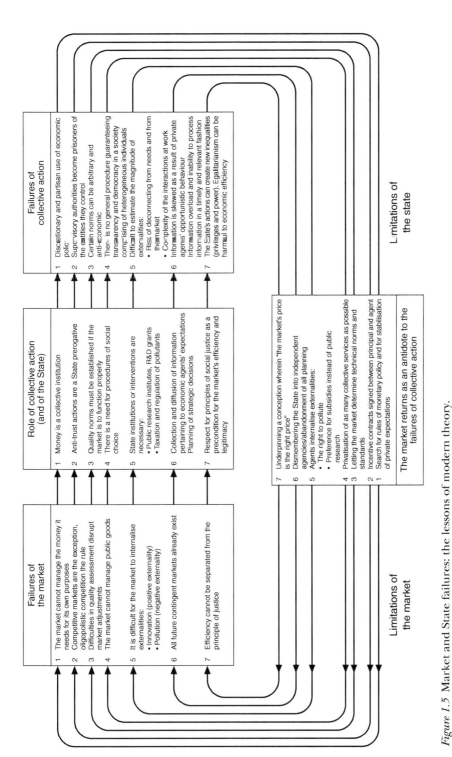

Figure 1.5 Market and State failures: the lessons of modern theory.

Failures of the market

1 The market cannot manage the money it needs for its own purposes
2 Competitive markets are the exception, oligopolistic competition the rule
3 Difficulties in quality assessment disrupt market adjustments
4 The market cannot manage public goods
5 It is difficult for the market to internalise externalities:
 • Innovation (positive externality)
 • Pollution (negative externality)
6 All future contingent markets already exist
7 Efficiency cannot be separated from the principle of justice

Limitations of the market

Role of collective action (and of the State)

1 Money is a collective institution
2 Anti-trust actions are a State prerogative
3 Quality norms must be established if the market is to function properly
4 There is a need for procedures of social choice
5 State institutions or interventions are necessary:
 • Public research institutes, R&D grants
 • Taxation and regulation of pollutants
6 Collection and diffusion of information pertaining to economic agents' expectations Planning of strategic decisions
7 Respect for principles of social justice as a precondition for the market's efficiency and legitimacy

7 Underpinning a conception wherein "the market's price is the right price"
6 Dismembering the State into independent agencies/abandonment of all planning
5 Agents internalise externalities:
 • The right to pollute
 • Preference for subsidies instead of public research
4 Privatisation of as many collective services as possible
3 Letting the market determine technical norms and standards
2 Incentive contracts signed between principal and agent
1 Search for rules of monetary policy and for stabilisation of private expectations

The market returns as an antidote to the failures of collective action

Failures of collective action

1 Discretionary and partisan use of economic policy
2 Supervisory authorities become prisoners of the entities they control
3 Certain norms can be arbitrary and anti-economic
4 There is no general procedure guaranteeing transparency and democracy in a society comprising of heterogeneous individuals
5 Difficult to estimate the magnitude of externalities:
 • Risks of deconnecting from needs and from the market
 • Complexity of the interactions at work
6 Information is skewed as a result of private agents' opportunistic behaviour Information overload and inability to process information in a timely and relevant fashion
7 The State's actions can create new inequalities (privileges and power). Egalitarianism can be harmful to economic efficiency

Limitations of the state

adjustment that may or may not be taking place in a decentralised economy. Furthermore, markets for goods, even the most traditional ones, can only function if there is already some agreement about quality and technical norms, generally reached by organisations that operate outside of the market (certification authorities, trade associations, etc.). As for the supply of public goods, something that is so important in today's economies, this implies the existence of procedures of collective choice that cannot be based on market procedures.

Externalities, whether positive or negative, presuppose either regulation or else incentive mechanisms that are intended to create a convergence between private and collective interests, and between social and private returns. Since only a very small number of contingent markets actually exist, and given that financial markets are capable of disturbing macroeconomic equilibrium, there is a need for collective procedures that can ensure a modicum of co-ordination between decisions whose effects can manifest over several time periods. This was one of the specific objectives of the indicative planning that has taken place in both the industrialised economies (Shonfield 1965) and the developing countries.

Lastly, if economic efficiency is predicated on a minimum of respect for social justice, economic decisions and political options can no longer be separated, something that justifies, for example, transfers relating to taxation or social protection. All in all, from a modern economic point of view, state interventions, if they are adjusted correctly, make it easier to obtain an equilibrium that is more satisfying in both economic and social terms.

As for public-choice theoreticians, they contest economists' suggestion that the state should be analysed as a functionalist entity, emphasising instead that state interventions have also encountered a number of limitations (Buchanan 1979). These limitations would seem to be different from the ones that the market has had to face, but potentially they are just as formidable (Wolf 1990). Governments can in fact use monetary policy (and, by extension, budgetary policy) towards purely political ends that have nothing to do with the quality of the macroeconomic equilibrium or with the stimulation and regularity of growth. The entities responsible for the supervision of competition can be "captured" by the private interest groups they are responsible for; the magnitude of the state's economic interventions would then be offset by a rise in corruption. The quality norms that the state authorities have set up could turn out to be barely functional and quite harmful, for example, to the dynamism of innovation.

It will not necessarily be possible to come up with a satisfactory solution for determining the volume of public services via mechanisms of political arbitrage. This is because the theory of social choice shows that no convergence towards stable and unambiguous outcomes can be achieved when a society comprises autonomous individuals with highly heterogeneous preferences.

Nor is it easy to correct externalities, since to do so people need to have at their disposal detailed information that state entities are not necessarily able to gather – especially in light of the fact that economic agents often behave opportunistically and hide whatever private information they may possess. Furthermore, it may well be that the compilation and processing costs, and the time that is needed to carry out such operations, would be so significant that the state's actions would always be lagging behind events. Finally, political action intended to correct market-generated inequalities might in turn create other sources of inequality through its distribution of privileges and of the conditions for accessing power. An extreme form of egalitarianism could also be harmful to economic efficiency.

All of these lines of thinking countermand what the general equilibrium economists have been suggesting about the market's limitations. All in all, public-choice theoreticians and new economic policies reveal the failures of collective action, distinct from market failures but just as numerous and no less daunting.

Research programmes in the 1990s often studied the effects of an introduction of more competition and of a great number of market mechanisms in an effort to overcome the shortcomings of collective action. This strategy could be broken down into the various areas of state intervention. For example, macroeconomic theories proposed the abandonment of discretionary monetary policies and the search for rules to stabilise private expectations and ensure the credibility of the central bank. This conception was widely diffused throughout the developing countries, often leading to the redefinition of a regime of growth.

"Principal/agent" theories renewed both conceptions about the organisation of public services, attempting to reconcile collective objectives with incentives for greater efficiency, such as the ones that are traditionally conveyed by the market. Models that formalised technological choice (in the presence of increasing returns) suggested that, under certain conditions, the determination of technical norms and/or quality assessment could be the products of an unfettered competition between firms vying for one and the same market, such that direct public intervention would not always be necessary.

Externalities can be partially internalised thanks to subsidies or taxes that compensate for the gap between private and social outcomes (two examples of this being innovation and pollution). In certain situations, the creation of a market (of technological expertise, of environmental pollution rights, etc.) changed the conditions surrounding public action. Similarly, given the specificity that is the wont of each area of intervention, modern theories suggested the creation of independent agencies that raised doubts as to whether an all-encompassing type of planning could be efficient. Lastly, certain theories of justice broke with the Rawlsian tradition (which emphasised improving living conditions for the worst-off) and tried to build upon the hypothesis that in the end the market-price system is a fair one, with regards to products and to factors of production, inasmuch as it records and evaluates individuals' competencies.

Three lessons can be derived from this extremely rapid review of the literature. First of all, the renewed interest in market mechanisms (meant to overcome some of the shortcomings of state intervention) does not mean that we should forget the basic findings harvested from theories of general equilibrium: the market must be supervised by state interventions and will only deliver outcomes that are favourable for society if the products involved are standard ones; and under certain well-defined conditions.

Second, a spotlight should be cast on the similarity between two chronologies: the first relates to the various strategies of development (see Figure 1.4); the second to the different ways in which general economic theory has changed (see Figure 1.5). It is tempting to hypothesise the co-development of theories and of modes of development, via mediations that in reality are very complex. Do theoreticians exert a critical influence on the policies that are being pursued or, conversely, does economic theory, however abstract it may be, seek to elucidate the consequences of strategies that have been selected totally independently of governmental input?

Last but not least, this analysis tends to deny the hypothesis that the same sort of debate is destined to take place time and again, inasmuch as economic theories have clearly been making progress at a conceptual level (even if their forecasting capabilities remain as problematic as ever). The development strategies of the 1990s are in no way, shape or form the same as the ones that prevailed a half-century ago.

Development theories have become systemic and institutionalist

The 1990s as a crossroads

In actual fact, many different lines of reasoning, relating as much to theoretical precepts as to the correction of erroneous development strategies, argue in favour of the emergence of a more balanced conception of development. We cannot help but acknowledge the role that institutions play – and the need for a more systemic approach (see Figure 1.6).

At a theoretical level, researchers are no longer handcuffed and forced to talk solely about the limitations of the market. This is because they have explained the role played by extra-market co-ordination mechanisms in the appearance of growth paths or in the emergence of types of equilibrium that are more favourable than the ones which would result from a mere interaction of market-based strategies functioning in the marketplace alone. This allows us to interpret the emphasis that has been placed

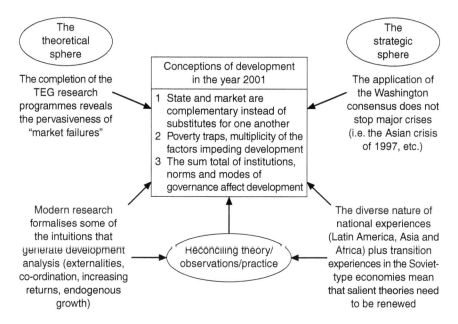

The theoretical sphere

The completion of the TEG research programmes reveals the pervasiveness of "market failures"

Modern research formalises some of the intuitions that generate development analysis (externalities, co-ordination, increasing returns, endogenous growth)

Conceptions of development in the year 2001

1 State and market are complementary instead of substitutes for one another
2 Poverty traps, multiplicity of the factors impeding development
3 The sum total of institutions, norms and modes of governance affect development

Reconciling theory/ observations/practice

The strategic sphere

The application of the Washington consensus does not stop major crises (i.e. the Asian crisis of 1997, etc.)

The diverse nature of national experiences (Latin America, Asia and Africa) plus transition experiences in the Soviet-type economies mean that salient theories need to be renewed

Figure 1.6 Towards a systemic and institutionalist approach to development: changes during the 1990s.

on imperfect information; the interdependent nature of actors' strategies; and of course those externalities that are associated with education, research, or even with some of the public infrastructures that can be found in traditional rural economies (as well as in many developed ones).

By so doing, today's researchers are returning to intuitions first held by the founders of development studies – with the novelty that they are now in a position of producing formalisations that can enable a clear explanation of the logic driving interactions which can lead, for example, to societies' becoming stuck in a poverty trap, or to equilibria being based on low levels of education and on high fertility rates (and therefore on low income levels). As Hoff and Stiglitz have stated:

> In many respects the theory of development has gone the full circle. 30 or 40 years ago, there was an emphasis on the different links between the social and economic spheres ... Nowadays formalised theory has been extended to a number of areas relating to imperfect information and incomplete contracts. These studies have shown that, in a variety of configurations, extra-market interactions lead to complementarities that can be associated with multiple equilibria. ... These no longer only involve endogenous types of institutions, choices and prices – but also preferences and technologies.
>
> (2001: 427)

This type of approach also incorporates one of the main self-styled facts to have appeared over the past fifty years, to wit, the great diversity of the national experiences of development – something that cannot be accurately reduced to a simple opposition between a pure canonical model and various degrees of imperfection. In addition, the allegedly impossible economic development of those countries that are "lagging beyond" took place in a certain number of national configurations.

Nevertheless, even within those countries that were able to initiate a process of development, it took on forms that varied from one country to the next, given that, in the words of Adelman,

> The process of economic development is simultaneously multidimensional and essentially non-linear. It leads to dynamic transformations not only in the modes of production and technology but also at the level of its social, political and economic institutions, as is the case with human development models.
>
> (2001a: 67)

Examples of this abound. It suffices to compare the different countries of Latin America to notice major differences (Quemia 2000), even greater than the variations that can be accounted for by the traditional opposition between a typical Latin American industrialisation strategy (based on import substitution) and the South East Asian preference for an export-driven type of growth.

Similarly, the Asian countries' 1997 financial crisis did not fit into the same model as the Latin American countries' crises, since each involved differing styles of development, political choices and types of finance-driven disruption (Marques-Pereira and Théret 2001). Lastly, the Eastern European countries' development clearly reveals contrasting trajectories in terms of privatisation, the reconstruction of the state and economic restructuring, with the political environment playing an essential role in the economic and social system's capacity for transformation.

Third, we should not neglect the way in which the Asian crisis led to questions being asked about the Washington consensus, which had been trumpeting the general principles that it considered to be valid everywhere: budgetary discipline, fiscal reform focusing on economic incentives, financial deregulation, elimination of barriers to international trade and to competition, privatisation and liberalisation. As stated by John Williamson, considered the father of this conception of development, such principles are not necessarily erroneous – but they have to be applied flexibly, and rounded out by at least two more ingredients.

First of all, there is a need "(to build) key institutions such as an independent Central Bank, a strong budgetary administration, an independent and incorruptible judiciary and agencies to develop such productivity missions". Second, it is important to "increase spending on education and to redirect this towards the primary and secondary sectors" (Williamson 1997: 58). By so doing, it should be possible, in this view, to fill the gap that has steadily arisen between advances in economic research and the prescriptions of international organisations such as the World Bank and the IMF – even if this current inevitably created a degree of tension within these very same organisations (see, e.g., Joseph Stiglitz's resignation from his post as head of the World Bank).

All of these factors have made it increasingly likely that there will be no return to previous conceptions of development. First of all, the main issue is no longer one of choosing between alternative and unilateral principles of co-ordination: the market or the state? An ever-increasing number of analysts recognise that "an appropriate mix between the state and the market is necessary to the promotion of development. This mix has to be adapted dynamically so that it can stay in tune with advances in development" (Adelman 2001b: 103).

Furthermore, no single factor can explain the blocking of development, since a whole range of factors are generally at work in any trajectory we observe. The diagnostic therefore needs to reflect the context. Finally, the development process is characterised by its strong sense of history, inasmuch as "the choices that are being made give birth in turn to the initial conditions of later development" (Adelman 2001: 72). This is an economic historian's point of view, one of whom concluded by calling for "a little more history and a little less of a regression-based interpretation of growth" (Crafts 2001: 326).

A final quote summarises the road that has been travelled by a half-century of development:

> Development processes and policies are interdependent and present a multiform, dynamic and non-linear nature. Development thus continues to imply a modification of the mechanisms, modalities, agents and institutions that are necessary for its promotion. The only constant in development is systematic dynamic change.
>
> (Adelman 2001a: 108)

The title of the present essay can be explained by these sorts of considerations. However, there are also a number of other reasons relating to changes in economic theory itself.

Multiplicity of co-ordination mechanisms and the rise of institutionalist theories

The aforementioned developments are largely part of the state–market axis, assuming that these are the two only forms of co-ordination currently operating in the world's economies. Quite symmetrically, both of these pure and unadulterated forms are limited. The concept of a mixed economy has therefore become a meaningful one, even if its usage has dropped dramatically since the 1970s (Shonfield 1965). This is the view that one way to reconcile the two approaches is to look for an optimal combination of market mechanisms and state-driven co-ordination. It is the first approach to try to reconstruct a theory of development capable of accounting for all of the lessons that we have learnt from economic history – as well as the diversity of national configurations.

It remains that modern research offers at least two other forms of co-ordination that are capable of playing a significant role in these economic changes: the organisation (or the firm) on one hand; and civil society on the other (see Figure 1.7).

The fact that firms fulfil a resource allocation role to complement, or else to accompany, the market may already have been recognised in Adam Smith's *Wealth of Nations* – but it is also a topic that Karl Marx dealt with in

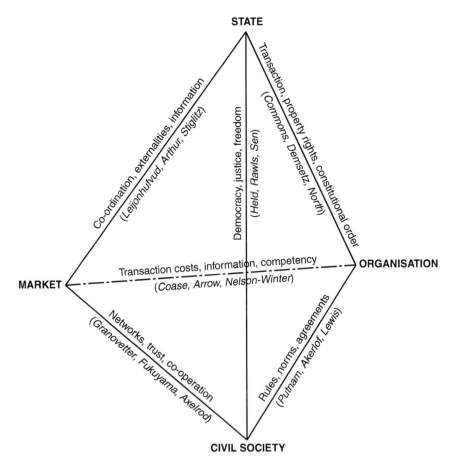

Figure 1.7 Beyond the opposition between State and market: the "diamond" of institutional economics.

Das Kapital. It was not until the interwar period that economists began to wonder why firms actually exist (Coase 1937). Nearly forty years elapsed before this original form of resource allocation drew their attention – first at an organisational level (Arrow 1974), and then at a more general level of the institutions of capitalism (Williamson 1985).

The contribution that this school of thought made was to show that in the presence of significant transaction costs resulting from an (over-)reliance on the market, or where it has been difficult to compile and to process information (Simon 1982), organisations can develop internal resource allocation and information circulation routines that are potentially superior to those that the market can deliver. This is especially true in those instances (i.e. if there are quality problems and/or increasing returns) where there is no possibility of organising a viable market (White 1981). Lastly, insofar as individuals develop specific competencies within their organisation, this can become an arena for the accumulation of idio-syncratic knowledge and know-how whose production or allocation cannot be governed by market logic. This is nothing other than a straightforward neo-Schumpeterian vision of the reasons why firms exist, one that has propped up many of the trials and errors that have been committed in the field of innovation and technological change (Nelson and Winter 1982).

Over the past twenty years, research into explanations for differences between regional, national or even firm performances has revealed the importance of a fourth entity – civil society. The main idea is that this is the matrix within which agents will act to forge a whole series of agreements, rules and habits that then enable and facilitate purely economic transactions by shaping networks (Granovetter 1978); by creating and preserving the trust that is needed for successful market trading (Fukuyama 1996); or by helping co-operation to emerge (Axelrod 1984).

However, civil society also maintains relations with organisations, inasmuch as the rules it imposes on them are not necessarily recognised by the state or conveyed via the market, that is in employment-related matters (Akerlof 1984). The democratic process (Held 1987) is not unrelated to the maturation of sociality at a local level (Putnam 1993), whilst concern for social justice has had an obvious impact on the demands being made of the state (Rawls 1971). This fabric of social relationships maintains multiform relations through transactions that are purely economic in nature, meaning that in certain cases this factor is key to explaining the real economic dynamism of a given region or country.

Figure 1.7 shows both the extremely simplistic nature of the canonical opposition between state and market as well as the way in which the enrichment of these categories of analysis can help us to understand the various styles of development's diversity. The main issue no longer relates to the exact location of a cursor such as a mixed economy. Instead it is the compatibility of a whole set of behaviours that unfold simultaneously in different spheres and according to varying logics.

Moreover, the state has a rejuvenated role to play in this process: it is at the heart of the distribution of power, and it is key to the way in which the constraints and incentives that other actors are having to face will be shaped. In a sense, this is the convergent conclusion of historians' studies (North 1990) and political scientists' research projects demonstrating the importance of the constitutional order, derived from the political world, as a means for creating a coherency between (and transforming) a whole set of forms of logics and organisation (Sabel 1997) – not to mention studies from the field of economic sociology that have revealed the importance of such societal constraints for firm's strategies and innovation drives and, by extension, for their forms of competitiveness (Streeck 1997).

The diversity of institutional arrangements and the need for a multidisciplinary type of research

Accounting for these different forms of co-ordination implies the need to progress beyond strictly mono-disciplinary approaches that usually revolve around political factors, the role of law, the nature of the social contract and the general logic underlying a given action – and no longer principles of economic rationality alone. A first effort in this direction has already been made. It is possible to put together a taxonomy of forms of co-ordination, which can be put to good use by the various disciplines of social science (Hollingsworth and Boyer 1997). Roughly speaking, most of the forms that have been observed can be described using a double characterisation (see Figure 1.8).

First of all, it is important to contrast purely horizontal relations between agents who are basically endowed with the same powers, and relations that to the contrary are vertical and based on unequal status, information and wealth. Typically, a market, which is a form of horizontal co-ordination, exists in opposition to a private hierarchy, whose flagship form is the firm.

The logic underlying the action itself can be part of two clearly distinct registers. Either purely individual interests guide actions, as indicated in both economic theory and in rational-choice analysis, or else it is the strength of the social, moral and cultural contract – in short, the obligation that determines the actions of a *homo sociologicus*, traditionally contrasted, on a trait-for-trait basis, with *homo oeconomicus*.

These two criteria make it possible to come up with at least six major types of institutional arrangements. The market combines a form of horizontal co-ordination with an action logic that is governed by individual interest, usually apprehended in its utilitarian form. Private hierarchies such as the firm apply this same conception to unequal relationships, inasmuch as their drivers (in this case, their owners) possess a power that enables them to dispose of their employees' time at work.

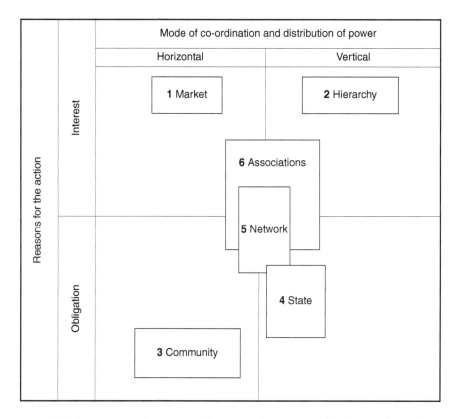

Figure 1.8 State and market are nothing more than two specific forms of co-ordination and institutional arrangements.

Inversely, the community operates within the register of an obligation that is attached to the strength of the social contract – in theory at least, it is based on relationships that are supposed to be egalitarian. It is within this space that a subtle process of trust is born. Networks occupy a central role within this typology since they combine obligations and interests (in variable proportions) and can be broken down according to a variety of modalities that are predicated on the more or less egalitarian nature of the relationships that exist between the various members of the network.

This form of co-ordination is central in modern innovation processes. Partnerships have very often been involved in the development of those rapidly changing new technologies that have come out over the past few years, advances that imply large-scale investments that, from a rational point of view, it would be best to share. Along these lines, associations, whether trade groups or labour unions, generally combine a defence and promotion of interests that can be economic, political and social in nature. As opposed to networks, which operate according to a market-based production logic, an association's function often involves the management of collective goods: codes of conduct, technical norms, vocational training for a given sector of activity, the representation of the constituency's interests to the state. Last but not least, the state has a unique position, combining an obligation principle (citizens are not free to rid themselves of its authority and have to pay taxes) with a clearly asymmetrical type of power (laws apply to each citizen, whereas not everyone is involved in the making of laws).

All in all, modern economies can no longer be defined only on the basis of the extent to which they mix market and a state-oriented logic. Instead, the focus should be on the variety and complementarity of these six institutional arrangements. Indeed, it is possible to show that no form of co-ordination, in and of itself, is capable of replacing all other forms, without taking into account the sector, era, and social, political and technological environment (see Table 1.1).

First of all, each form necessitates highly specific conditions of implementation. For example, building a market in good and due form is in no way an automatic undertaking, nor is it feasible at all times and in all places. It implies a stable monetary regime, an acceptance by all of society of a market-based logic and an agreement on trading rules (i.e. the quality of goods).

Second, all forms can complement any other form that satisfies its prerequisites. Using the same example, institutionalising a market implies the involvement of associations (i.e. agents authorised to trade on securities markets such as Wall Street), networks (such as those that define quality or technical norms) or state entities (led by those that control the banking and payment system, without forgetting the crucial role played by business law).

Furthermore no institutional arrangement has shown itself to be superior to all other arrangements or to be dominant in the long run. Depending on the circumstances, assessment will be made according to criteria such as the efficiency with which resources are allocated, the aptitude for supplying collective goods and for "internalising externalities" or the ability to satisfy the desire for justice that will be more or less implicit or explicit, depending on the society in question. A similar demonstration as the one carried out with respect to the markets can be reiterated for almost all of the other types of institutional arrangements, and is briefly summarised in Table 1.1.

As such, the issue no longer involves choosing between the state and the market or selecting those institutional arrangements that are going to be the most efficient in absolute terms. Each arrangement satisfies a different objective, and overall macroeconomic performance is the product of the combination thereof. In this case, it is the quality of the institutional architecture that is the main determinant of the viability of a strategy of growth.

This type of approach is particularly relevant to development, inasmuch as the interaction between political determinants, economic change and cultural factors is frequently evoked as a explanation for both success and failure (*Revue d'économie du développement* 2000, 2001). Approaches to development have been given a second wind by this realisation, and there is no reason not to believe that this (re)discovery of the importance of institutions and organisations is a great deal more significant than a simple shift in economists' research orientations.

Politics at the heart of development

This vision is not without consequences for the relationships that tie the economic sphere to the political arena. Traditionally, economists will analyse conditions of development without any explicit mention being made of political processes. Political scientists on the other hand focus on the general shaping of policies, without referring to economic factors. Both assume that the two spheres are independent of one another. Recent interest of international organisations in corruption attests to an increased awareness of certain interdependencies – with a large proportion of whatever surplus may exist being lost because of corruption (and spent in a non-productive manner), chances for an endogenous type of development are lessened.

The theoretical approach confirms the existence of a close interdependency that can be played out at several levels.

Historical studies of the way in which markets are formed (Braudel 1979) and political-science research into competition policy in the United States (Fligstein 1999) have clearly highlighted the crucial role played by governmental authorities and by the state itself in the emergence of markets in good and due form, i.e., which possess a modicum of viability. An acknowledgement and precise definition of the property rights that are associated with each good and with each asset; shared quality assessments, currency units and means of payment; a commercial jurisdiction that enables the resolution of legal disputes – all of these are pre-conditions for the existence of a market and can only be satisfied by an authority operating externally to supplier and buyer interest.

In terms of development studies, in some of the countries that are deemed to be lagging behind, the state has been the driving force for the institution of markets. On the one hand, this is because it is the guarantor thereof, while on the other, it is because it organises the teaching of those types of behaviour that are necessary if such markets are to function efficiently. In a certain sense, this is an analysis of a configuration in which state and market are complementary, as recognised in the classification adopted in Figures 1.2 and 1.3.

However, a much more general approach to economic systems does exist, one which makes the role of the state central to its analysis. Although economic theories derived from Walrasian analysis focus on the

Table 1.1 Each institutional arrangement has its own strengths and weaknesses

Co-ordination mechanisms	Property				
	Conditions of implementation	Aptitude for supplying collective goods and incorporating externalities	Efficient allocation of resources	Suitability for objectives of social	Possible contribution to development
Market	Stable monetary regime Acknowledgement of a commercial logic Agreement re: rules of trade Agreement re: quality of goods	Extremely difficult in general, except where suitable schemes have been implemented by State authorities (taxation or subsidies)	Significant with regards to the allocation of standard goods that are fungible and whose quality is recognised	Difficult in a pure market since it carries with it an implied principle of justice (people are assessed as per their market value)	Stimulates supply of essential goods (food, etc.) not featuring any externalities
Community	Feelings of trust and loyalty, based on feeling of belonging	Internalisation of those collective goods that manifest externalities in the community space	Moderate since limited by the size of the group and dominated by the stability of the social relationship	Ensured by integration of the economic sphere into the fabric of social relationships	Ambiguous. Supply of local collective goods, causes solidarity, but limited in terms of the search for efficiency and innovation
Network	Strategic complementarity between the different members' contributions	Good as long as externalities can be internalised within the network	Good as long as the network manifests a modicum of stability	Possible as long as the network supersedes the economic sphere	Positive role in innovation matters, once a certain threshold of development has been breached

Association	Recognition that interests and objectives are shared	Good with respect to the establishment of norms and rules or for the supply of specific collective services (i.e. vocational training)	Good for the supply of collective services; moderate for standard goods	Problematic if there is a Balkanisation of associations, with each having its own explicit aims	Relatively positive but ambiguous; implementation of collective services but potential appropriation of rents
Hierarchy	Recognition of the asymmetrical nature of power; Beneficial effect of internalising the division of labour	By definition, inexistent or weak, except in the case of State intervention	Generally large in production matters, but the organisational costs limit the degree of advantage	Complete deconnection except in exceptional circumstances (cooperation and performance)	Acts in association with the market, positive role as regards the division of labour and innovation
State	Recognition of the legitimacy of the political order; Balance of power (executive, legislative, judiciary, administrative)	Significant if information is perfect or sufficient, more problematic for highly differentiated services	Conditioned by relationships between citizens/the people in power, or between the political sphere/the administration	Possible if clearly identified by the political process, and if a coalition makes it possible to achieve this	Socialisation and diffusion of relevant information; Supply of basic collective services (education, health, transport); Actor in catching up process, blocking agent if strategy is not adapted to overall trends

interaction between preferences and technological potentialities (mediated only by a complete set of markets), current research recognises the role played by different institutional arrangements in price formation, income distribution and even innovation dynamics (Amable *et al.* 1997). Carrying on from the preceding analysis, a constitutional order will define the framework of the constraints and incentives that serve as a basis for the various institutional arrangements that can be deployed.

In turn, organisations (both public and private, i.e., firms) are only viable insofar as they fit in with the constraints and incentives that are conveyed by these institutional arrangements. Agreements, born out of spontaneous and recurring interactions between agents, have also come to play an ever-increasing role, one that is often important for agents' socialisation and for organisations' viability. As a result, scarcity constraints no longer appear in a direct form, insofar as they are partially mediated by myriad institutional arrangements that codify the relationships that exist between organisations and individuals (see Figure 1.9).

The usefulness of the new institutionalist theories (Aoki 2001) is that they have shown how, in these sorts of circumstances, neither institutional arrangements nor organisations are being chosen any longer on the basis of changes in pure economic efficiency. On the one hand, the basic role of institutional arrangements is to define actors' positions, reduce the uncertainty that is inherent to strategic behaviour and orient general behaviour. This is a major contribution to the viability of an economic system (North 1990).

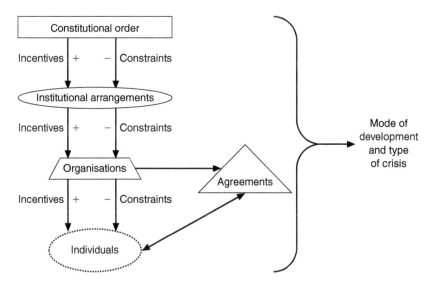

Figure 1.9 Politics help to shape economic dynamics (source: Loosely taken from North (1990) and Sabel (1997)).

On the other hand, these arrangements are characterised by significant path-dependency and by the primacy of the past, something that, in certain aspects, is governed by mechanisms that are functionally equivalent to the ones which drive changes in norms and techniques, typified by their increasing returns (Boyer and Orléan 1992; Arthur 1994). These mechanisms are combined in a way that brings about a lasting and significant diversity of economic institutions, even in the developed countries, in an era of financial globalisation (Boyer and Souyri 2001). There is no better example of the persistence of differing institutional architectures than Japan's trajectory throughout the 1990s (Boyer and Yamada 2000).

This allows us to interpret development successes as well as failures.

For some countries and at certain moments in time (often after wars or major political upheavals), the institutional architecture (which is a product of past and present political compromises) engenders dynamics for organisations and for economic actors that result in a continuous process of wealth creation and social transformation. Remember the fallout of the Second World War in several European countries and in Japan – they were able to largely catch up with the lead that the USA had taken in technology (Boyer 1999c). The same has happened in certain South East Asian countries: the differences between the economic trajectories of countries such as Taiwan and Korea versus the Philippines suggest a preponderance of political (and not just cultural and religious) factors in development dynamics.

Inversely, for other countries (i.e. those that are the victim of an inherited specialisation and dependency to the world economy, one which is based on raw materials exports and/or on major inequalities left over from the colonial period), the political order actually encourages the sharing of rents rather than the creation of wealth. This is why some theoreticians have spoken of the "development of under-development", an image that is in no way excessive when we consider the highly unfavourable development of most African countries over the past few decades (Bourguignon and Atkinson 2000).

More generally, the political consequences of the financial crisis in South East Asia (Contamin and Lacu 1998) has cast renewed attention on the relationship between the political and the economic spheres (Boyer 1999b). On the one hand, an ever-greater number of observers agree that the state, which is the guardian of the general interest and which possesses sufficient resources, is a necessary prerequisite for the implementation of a development strategy. The example of Russia is a timely reminder of how the disintegration of a former Soviet-type state can compromise the transition to a market economy. Note the absence of monetary stability and of a satisfactory definition (and effective guarantee) of property rights; the lack of a payment system covering the entire national territory; the inability to collect the tax revenues that are needed to sustain the expenditures that should be made in the collective interest; and so on.

China and Poland exemplify the paramount nature of state and government in market transition situations, and for carrying out economic, technological and social modernisation. Yet private organisations and institutions are necessary since by their decisions they channel resource allocation and so they galvanise a dynamic of wealth creation. It is difficult for the state to play its role when it does not have the power to collect the resources it needs to operate (Théret 1992). In other words, the political and the economic spheres must develop hand-in-hand. The very success of a growth strategy depends on this synchronisation. It may be imperfect – but in the long run it is indispensable.

Conclusion: development economics at the heart of institutionalist research

This panorama of the theories and strategies of development lends itself to certain fundamental conclusions that will allow us to answer the questions that were raised in the introduction to this chapter.

Yes, development economics has become systemic and institutionalist, given that this field has benefited from the lessons learnt from history and from theoretical advances; and also because it is now imbued with its own conceptual foundations.

Comparative development analysis and modern economic theory constitute useful antidotes against those dogmatic visions and ideologies that attempt to pit interventionist conceptions against the neo-liberal vision. The end result is that no pure and unadulterated strategy, that is one that is based either on "100 per cent state" or on "100 per cent market", has been successful – and theory has confirmed the innate limitations of any economic regime that is based on only one of these two mechanisms of co-ordination. A first step towards a solution thus consists of offsetting market failures by the appropriate state interventions and, vice versa, transcending the state's limitations thanks to processes that mimic market competition wherever possible.

The crises that were observed throughout the 1990s reinforce this diagnosis. Whereas in the 1980s certain instances of under-development could be attributed to excessive interventionism, the financial crisis of 1997–8 showed that the extension of the market to the financial sphere (and to derivative financial products) could also lead to a destabilisation of even the most dynamic modes of development (e.g. South East Asia). Too much market can be harmful to development. The 1998 disintegration of the "Washington consensus", which had previously dominated international organisations' conceptions of development, attests to this awareness. Political leaders and experts have been looking for a new doctrine (in the noblest sense of the term). Most have recognised the need for a new institutional architecture, or at least for new rules for running the international financial system.

This is the second path that is opened up by the attempt to solve the state–market dilemma (see Figure 1.10). On the one hand, we now know that successful development depends on the complementarity between these two logics, and not on the affirmation of one or the other. Remember that the market is a social construction whose emergence and viability are predicated on a rich set of legal rules, codes and supervisory bodies. In addition, modern institutionalist research has stressed that the many institutional arrangements, other than the state and the market (i.e., associations, communities, partnerships, etc.) can play a crucial role in reconciling the imperatives of dynamic efficiency (such as higher productivity or living standards) and social justice, construed here as aiming at a more egalitarian distribution of the fruits of growth.

It is therefore illusory to blame one single factor for the hindrance of development. An approach that is based on interdependency, externality and complementarity is far superior. The systemic and changing nature of development has to be acknowledged.

All in all, development economics has become a favourite field for research into different economies' institutional foundations; for exploring the conditions that give birth to path-dependency; and therefore for analyses of the reasons underlying the persistence of a wide variety of different institutional configurations (hence of modes of regulation). This research programme also applies to analyses of the older industrialised

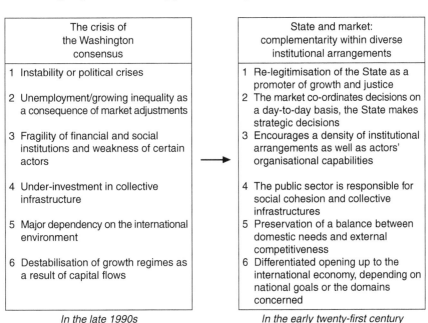

The crisis of the Washington consensus	State and market: complementarity within diverse institutional arrangements
1 Instability or political crises	1 Re-legitimisation of the State as a promoter of growth and justice
2 Unemployment/growing inequality as a consequence of market adjustments	2 The market co-ordinates decisions on a day-to-day basis, the State makes strategic decisions
3 Fragility of financial and social institutions and weakness of certain actors	3 Encourages a density of institutional arrangements as well as actors' organisational capabilities
4 Under-investment in collective infrastructure	4 The public sector is responsible for social cohesion and collective infrastructures
5 Major dependency on the international environment	5 Preservation of a balance between domestic needs and external competitiveness
6 Destabilisation of growth regimes as a result of capital flows	6 Differentiated opening up to the international economy, depending on national goals or the domains concerned
In the late 1990s	*In the early twenty-first century*

Figure 1.10 A conception of development that revolves around institutional innovation.

economies. How long will people who agree that the developing economies have been experiencing a variety of different trajectories refuse to grant this same diversity to other economies, under the pretext, for example, that ICT has created some sort of "one best way" capable of explaining all social and financial organisation?

Would it not be preferable to look for an institutional architecture that is suitable for a particular country in light of the specialisation which that country has inherited from the past; of its general conception of the social contract; and of the political choices it wants to make as regards its international insertion strategies? Surely the road to success involves synchronising institutional and organisational sophistication with a deepening of the division of labour. This lesson would also appear to be universal in nature, since it applies both to the developed and to the developing countries.

Development strategies can either opt for an endless repetition of the canonical opposition between state and market – or innovate through the advent of theories that are more respectful of the diversity of local circumstances and cognizant of the lessons derived from long-run history.

Acknowledgements

This is the translation and adaptation of an article entitled "L'après consensus de Washington: institutionnaliste et systémique?", initially published in French in 2001 in *l'Année de la régulation 2001*, 5: 13–56, Paris: Presses de Sciences-Po. We thank the publishers concerned for permission to reprint the translation here.

References

Abramowitz, M. (1979) "Rapid Growth Potential and its Realization: the Experience of Capitalist Economies in the Postwar Period", in E. Malinvaud (ed.), *Economic Growth and Resources: The Major Issues*, London: Macmillan.
—— (1986) "Catching-up, Forging Ahead, and Falling Behind", *Journal of Economic History*, 46 (2): 385–406.
Adelman, I (2001a) "Cinquante ans de développement économique: les principales leçons", *Revue d'économie du développement*, 9 (1–2): 65–113.
—— (2001b) "Fallacies in Development Theory and their Implications for Policy", in G. M. Meier and J. E. Stiglitz (eds), *Frontiers of Development Economics*, Oxford: Oxford University Press.
Akerlof, G. (1984) *Economic Theorist's Book of Tales*, Cambridge, MA: Cambridge University Press.
Amable, B., R. Barré and R. Boyer (1997) *Les systèmes d'innovation à l'ère de la globalisation*, Paris: Ost/Economica.
Aoki, M. (2001) *Towards a Comparative Institutional Analysis*, Cambridge and London: MIT Press.

Aoki, M. and M. Okuno-Fujiwara (1998) "Beyond the East Asian Miracle: Introduc- ing the Market-Enhancing View", in M. Aoki, H. K. Kim and M. Okuno-Fujiwara (eds), *The Role of Government in East Asian Economic Development*, Oxford: Claren- don Paperbacks Press.

Arrow, K. (1974) *The Limits of Organization*, New York: Allen and Unwin.

Arthur, B. (1994) *Increasing Returns and Path Dependence in the Economy*, Ann Arbor: The University of Michigan Press.

Axelrod, R. (1984) *The Evolution of Cooperation*, New York: Basic Books.

Bairoch, P. (1995) "The Main Trends in National Economic Disparities since the Industrial Revolution", in B. Van-Ark (ed.), *Economic Growth in the Long Run*, Cheltenham: Elgar.

Bardhan, P. (1989a) "Alternative Approaches to the Theory of Institutions in Eco- nomic Development", in P. Bardhan (ed.), *The Economic Theory of Agrarian Insti- tutions*, New York: Oxford University Press.

—— (1989b) "A Note on Interlinked Rural Economic Arrangements", in P. Bardhan (ed.), *The Economic Theory of Agrarian Institutions*, New York: Oxford University Press

—— (2000) "Economics of Development and the Development of Economics", in P. Bardhan and C. Udry (eds), *Readings in Development Economics*, Cambridge, MA: MIT Press.

Barro, R. J. (1996) "Democracy and Economic Growth", *Journal of Economic Growth*, 1 (1): 1–27.

Bhagwati, J. (1985) *Essays on Development Economics*, vol. 1, Cambridge, MA: The MIT Press.

—— (1993) "The Case for Free-Trade", *Scientific American*, November.

Bourguignon, F. and T. Atkinson (2000) "Pauvreté et inclusion in une perspective mondiale", *Revue d'économie du développement*, 8: 13–32.

Boyer, R. (1994) "Do Labour Institutions Matter for Economic Development? A 'Régulation' Approach for the OECD and Latin America with an Extension to Asia", in G. Rodgers (ed.), *Workers, Institutions and Economic Growth in Asia*, Geneva: ILO.

—— (1997) "The Variety of Unequal Performance of Really Existing Markets: Farewell to Doctor Pangloss?", in J. R. Hollingsworth and R. Boyer (eds), *Contemporary Capitalism: The Embeddedness of Institutions*, Cambridge: Cambridge University Press.

—— (1999a) "Deux enjeux pour le XXIe siècle: discipliner la finance et organiser l'internationalisation", *Techniques financières et développement*, 53–4, décembre 1998–mars 1999.

—— (1999b) "Le politique à l'ère de la mondialisation et de la finance: le point sur quelques recherches régulationnistes", *L'Année de la régulation*, 3: 13–75.

—— (1999c) "Une lecture régulationniste de la croissance et des crises", in P. Combemale and J. P. Piriou (eds), *Nouveau manuel sciences économiques et sociales*, Paris: La Découverte.

—— (2001) "Les économistes face aux innovations qui font époque", *Revue économique*, 52 (5), September: 1065–115.

Boyer, R. and A. Orléan (1992) "How do Conventions Evolve?", *Journal of Evolu- tionary Economics*, 2: 165–77.

Boyer, R. and P. F. Souyri (eds) (2001) *Mondialisation et régulations*, Paris: La Découverte.

Boyer, R. and T. Yamada (eds) (2000) *Japanese Capitalism in Crisis*, London: Routledge.

Bradford De Long, J. and L. H. Summers (1991) "Equipment, Investment and Economic Growth", *Quarterly Journal of Economics*, May: 445–502.

Braudel, F. (1979) *Civilisation matérielle, économie et capitalisme XV–XVIIIe siècles*, 3 volumes, Paris: Armand Colin.

Buchanan, J.-M. (1979) *What Should Economics Do?*, Indianapolis: Liberty Press.

Chakravorty, U., J. Roumasset and T. Tse (1997) "Endogenous Substitution among Energy Resources and Global Warming", *Journal of Political Economy*, 105: 1201–34.

Coase, R. H. (1937) "The Nature of the Firm" *Economica*, 4: 386–405; trans. (1987) "La nature de la firme", *Revue française d'economie*, 2 (1): 133–63.

Collier, P., D. Dollar and N. Stern (2001) "Cinquante ans de développement économique: bilan et expériences", *Revue d'économie du développement*, 9 (1–2): 23–64.

Commons, J. R. (1934) *Institutional Economics*, New York: Macmillan.

Contamin, R. and C. Lacu (1998) "Origines et dynamiques de la crise asiatique", *L'Année de la régulation*, 2: 11–63.

Council of Economic Advisors (1998) *Economic Report of the President*, Washington DC: U.S. Government Printing Office.

Crafts, N. (2001) "Historical Perspectives on Development", in G. M. Meier and J. E. Stiglitz (eds), *Frontiers of Development Economics*, Oxford: Oxford University Press.

Demsetz, H. (1967) "Toward a Theory of Property Rights", *American Economic Review, Papers and Proceedings*, 57: 347–59.

—— (1982) *Economic, Legal, and Political Dimensions of Competition*, Amsterdam: North Holland.

Domar, E. (1957) *Essays in the Theory of Economic Growth*, New York: Oxford University Press.

Emmerij, L. (1997a) "Development Thinking and Practice", in L. Emmerij (ed.), *Economic and Social Development into the XXIst Century*, Washington, DC: Inter American Development Bank/Johns Hopkins University Press.

—— (ed.) (1997b) *Economic and Social Development into the XXIst Century*, Washington, DC: Inter American Development Bank/Johns Hopkins University Press.

Fligstein, N. (1999) "Ruling Markets: A Political-Cultural Approach to Market Institutions", mimeo, Department of Sociology, Berkeley, University of California, June.

Fukuyama, F. (1996) *Trust: The Social Virtues and the Creation of Prosperity*, New York: Simon and Schuster.

Godard, O., P. Gouyon, C. Henry and P. Lagadec (2000) "Le principe de précaution: différents cas de figures et différents points de vue", *Revue d'économie du développement*, 8 (1–2): 175–86.

Granovetter, M. (1978) "Threshold Models of Collective Behavior", *American Journal of Sociology*, 83 (6): 1420–43.

Hagen, E. E. (1982) *On the Theory of Social Change*, Homewood: Dorsey Press.

Hayek, F. von (1973) *Law, Legislation and Liberty*, vol. I, London: Routledge and Kegan Paul (vol. II 1976, vol. III 1979).

Held, D. (1987) *Models of Democracy*, Stanford: Stanford University Press.

Hoff, K. and J. Stiglitz (2001) "Modern Economic Theory and Development", in G. M. Meier and J. E. Stiglitz (eds), *Frontiers of Development Economics*, Oxford: Oxford University Press.

Hollingsworth, R. and R. Boyer (eds) (1997) *Contemporary Capitalism: The Embeddedness of Institutions*, Cambridge, MA: Cambridge University Press.

Ingrao, B. and G. Israel (1990) *The Invisible Hand: Economic Equilibrium in the History of Science*, Cambridge, MA: MIT Press.

Inter-American Development Bank (1995) *Overcoming Volatility: Economic and Social Progress in Latin America*, Baltimore, MA: Johns Hopkins University Press.

—— (1996) *Making Social Services Work. Economic and Social Progress in Latin America*, Baltimore, MA: Johns Hopkins University Press.

Krueger, A. O. (1974) "The Political Economy of the Rent-Seeking Society", *American Economic Review*, 64 (3): 291–303.

—— (1979) *The Developmental Role of the Foreign Sector and Aid*, Cambridge, MA: Harvard University Press.

Lau, L. J. (1996) "The Sources of Long-Term Economic Growth: Observations from the Experience of Developed and Developing Countries", in R. Landau, T. Taylor and G. Wright (eds), *The Mosaic of Economic Growth*, Stanford: Stanford University Press.

Leijonhufvud, A. (1973) "Life Among the Econ", *Western Economic Journal*, 11 (3): 327–37.

—— (1981) *Information and Coordination: Essays in Macroeconomic Theory*, New York: Oxford University Press.

Lewis, D. K. (1969) *Convention: A Philosophical Study*, Cambridge, MA: Harvard University Press.

Lucas, R. (1983) *Studies in Business Cycle Theory*, Cambridge, MA: The MIT Press.

—— (1988) "On the Mechanisms of Economic Development", *Journal of Monetary Economics*, 72: 3–42.

—— (1993) "Making a Miracle", *Econometrica*, 61 (2): 251–72.

Marques-Pereira, J. and B. Théret (2001) "Régimes politiques, médiations sociales de la régulation et dynamiques macroéconomiques", *L'Année de la régulation*, 5: 105–43.

Mauro, P. (1995) "Corruption and Growth", *Quarterly Journal of Economics*, 110 (3): 681–712.

Meadows, D. H., D. L. Meadows, J. Randers and W. W. Behrens III (1972) *Limits to Growth*, New York: Universe Books.

Meier, G. M. (ed.) (1987) *Pioneers in Development*, Oxford: Oxford University Press/World Bank.

—— (2001) "The Old Generation of Development Economists and the New", in G. M. Meier and J. E. Stiglitz (eds), *Frontiers of Development Economics*, Oxford: Oxford University Press.

Murphy, K. M., A. Shleifer and R. W. Vishny (2000) "Industrialization and the Big Push", in P. Bardhan and C. Udry (eds), *Readings in Development Economics*, vol. 1, Cambridge, MA: MIT Press.

Nelson, R. and S. Winter (1982) *An Evolutionary Theory of Economic Change*, Harvard: The Belknap Press of Harvard University Press.

North, D. C. (1981) *Structure and Change in Economic History*, New York: Norton.

—— (1990) *Institutions, Institutional Change and Economic Performance*, Cambridge and New York: Cambridge University Press.

Odaka, K. and J. Teranishi (eds) (1998) *Markets and Government: In Search of Better Coordination*, Tokyo: Maruzen.

Orléan, A. (2000) *Le pouvoir de la finance*, Paris: Odile Jacob.

Pieper U. and L. Taylor (1998) "The Revival of the Liberal Creed: the IMF, the World Bank, and Inequality in a Globalized Economy", in D. Baker, G. Epstein and R. Pollin (eds), *Globalization and Progressive Economic Policy*, Cambridge: Cambridge University Press.

Polanyi, K. (1946) The Great Transformation, New York: Rinehart.

Prebisch, R. (1950), *The Economic Development of Latin America and its Principal Problems*, New York: United Nations, Economic Commission for Latin America.

—— (1971) *Change and Development: Latin America's Great Task, Report to the Inter-American Development Bank*, New York: Praeger.

Preobrazhenski, E. ([1924] 1965) *The New Economics*, Oxford: Clarendon Press (1965).

Putnam, R. D. (1993) *Making Democracy Work: Civic Traditions in Modern Italy*, Princeton: Princeton University Press.

Quemia, M. (2001) "Théorie de la régulation et développement: trajectoires latino-américaines", *L'Année de la régulation*, 5: 57–104.

Ranis, G. (1997) "Successes and Failures of Development Experience since the 1980s", in L. Emmerij (ed.), *Economic and Social Development into the XXIst Century*, Washington, DC: Inter American Development Bank/Johns Hopkins University Press.

Rawls, J. (1971) *A Theory of Social Justice*, Cambridge, MA: Harvard University Press.

Revue d'économie du développement (2000) *Gouvernance, équité et marchés mondiaux, sélection des Actes*, Conférence ABCDE-Europe, Paris, 21–23 June, 1998 (1–2), numéro spécial, Paris: Pesses Universitaires de France.

—— (2001) *Penser le développement au tournant du millénaire*, Conférence ABCDE-Europe, Paris, 26 au 28 juin 2000, 9 (1–2), numéro spécial, Paris, PUF.

Romer, P. (1990) "Endogenous technological change", *Journal of Political Economy*, 98 (5): 71–102.

Rose-Ackerman, S. (2000) "Corruption bureaucratique et responsabilité politique", *Revue d'économie du développement*, 8 (1–2): 145–50.

Rosenstein-Rodan, P. N. (1943) "Problems of Industrialization of Eastern and South-Eastern Europe", *Economic Journal*, 53: 202–11.

Sabel, C. (1997) "Constitutional Orders: Trust Building and Response to Change", in J. R. Hollingsworth and R. Boyer (eds), *Contemporary Capitalism*, Cambridge, MA: Cambridge University Press.

Sapir, J. (1989) *Les fluctuations économiques en URSS, 1941–1985*, Paris: Éditions de l'École des Hautes Études en Sciences Sociales.

—— (1996) *Le chaos russe*, collection "Cahiers Libres", séries "Essais", Paris: La Découverte.

Schultz, T. (1964) *Transforming Traditional Agriculture*, New Haven: Yale University Press.

—— (1980) "Nobel Lecture: The Economics of Being Poor", *Journal of Political Economy*, 88 (4): 639–51.

Sen, A. (1988) "The Concept of Development", in H. Chenery and T. N. Srinivasan (eds), *Handbook of Development Economics*, vol. I, Geneva: Elsevier Science Publishers B.V.

—— (1997) "Development Thinking at the Beginning of the XXIst Century", in L.

Emmerij (ed.), *Economic and Social Development into the XXIst Century*, Washington, DC: Inter American Development Bank/Johns Hopkins University Press.
—— (2000) *Development as Freedom*, New York: Anchor Books.
Shiller, R. J. (2000) *Irrational Exuberance*, Princeton: Princeton University Press.
Shonfield, A. (1965) *Modern Capitalism, the Changing Balance of Public and Private Power*, Oxford: Oxford University Press.
Simon, H. (1982; 2nd edn 1983) *Models of Bounded Rationality, Behavioral Economics and Business Organization*, Cambridge, MA: The MIT Press.
Solow, R. M. (1956) "A Contribution to the Theory of Economic Growth", *Quarterly Journal of Economics*, 70: 65–94; and also in A. Sen (ed.) (1970) *Growth Economics*, Harmondsworth: Penguin.
—— (1957) "Technical Change and the Aggregate Production Function", *Review of Economics and Statistics*, 39: 312–20.
Stiglitz, J. (1987) "Dependence of Quality on Price", *Journal of Economic Literature*, 25: 1–48.
—— (1988) "Economic Organization, Information, and Development", in H. Chenery and T. N. Srinivasan (eds), *Handbook of Development Economics*, vol. I, Geneva: Elsevier Science Publishers B.V.
—— (1994) "Whither Socialism?", *Wicksell: Lectures*, Cambridge and London: The MIT Press.
—— (1998) "More Instruments and Broader Goals: Moving Towards the Post-Washington Consensus", mimeo, Washington, DC: World Bank.
Streeck, W. (1997) "Beneficial Constraints: On the Economic Limits of Rational Voluntarism", in R. Hollingsworth R. and R. Boyer (eds), *Contemporary Capitalism: The Embeddedness of Institutions*, New York: Cambridge University Press.
Théret, B. (1992) *Régimes économiques de l'ordre politique*, Paris: puf.
—— (1999) "Vers un socialisme civil? L'épreuve de la contrainte démocratique de différenciation de la société", in B. Chavance, E. Magnin, R. Motamed-Nejad and J. Sapir (eds), *Capitalisme et socialisme en perspective*, Paris: La Découverte.
Tobin, J. (1978) "A Proposal for International Monetary Reform", *Eastern Economic Journal*, 4: 153–9.
White, H. C. (1981) "Where Do Market Come from?", *American Journal of Sociology*, 87 (3): 517–47.
Williamson, J. (1997) "The Washington Consensus Revisited", in L. Emmerij (ed.), *Economic and Social Development into the XXIst Century*, Washington, DC: Inter American Development Bank/Johns Hopkins University Press.
Williamson, O. (1985) *The Economic Institutions of Capitalism*, New York: The Free Press.
Wolf, C. J.-R. (1990) *Markets or Governments, Choosing between Imperfect and Alternatives*, Cambridge, MA: The MIT Press.
World Bank (1993) *The East Asian Miracle: Economic Growth and Public Policy*, Washington, DC: World Bank.
—— (1996) *From Plan to Market*, Washington, DC: World Bank.
—— (1997) *State and Development*, Washington, DC: World Bank.
—— (1998) *Knowledge for Development*, World Development reports, Oxford: Oxford University Press.
—— (1999) *Governance, Equity and World Markets*, World Bank European Conference on Development Economics, Paris, 21 June.
—— (2001) *World Development Report*, New York: Oxford University Press.

2 Comparative development and institutional change

Jorge Braga de Macedo

Little else is requisite to carry a state to the highest degree of opulence from the lowest barbarism, but peace, easy taxes, and tolerable administration of justice.

(Adam Smith, 1776)

[C]apitalism was supposed to accomplish exactly what was soon to be denounced as its worst feature.

(Albert Hirschman, 1976)

Introduction

Invoking the philosophy of Adam Smith – those who do not compare cannot adapt, just like those who do not remember the past are condemned to repeat it – this essay draws attention to three tenets of economic thought on development. First, comparing development experiences reinforces "peer pressure" for institutional change. Second, expectations play a role in the success of institutional reforms. Third, governance closer to the citizen is required if globalisation is to be "inclusive".

The process beginning with the Marshall Plan and leading to the creation of the Organisation for Economic Co-operation and Development (OECD) illustrates all three aspects. At the OECD, the Development Assistance Committee (DAC) and Development Centre (DEV) co-ordinated foreign aid among members, monitored its effectiveness and promoted policy convergence between developed and developing countries. DEV's programme of work for 2001/2002 included a retrospective 40th anniversary publication entitled *Development is Back* (Braga de Macedo *et al.* 2002) (cited by chapter number (e.g. *DiB*1), in this chapter and its appendix). The overarching theme of this programme of work was the interaction between globalisation and governance (also *DiB*12).

While the interaction between globalisation and governance may be positive or negative, the three aspects of economic thought on development covered here imply "development as hope" (Braga de Macedo 2001; *DiB*3; Cohen and Soto 2002). In his celebrated attack on the Marxian and

Weberian interpretations of capitalist development, Hirschman warned that similar circumstances at different points in time may give rise to "*identically flawed* thought-responses if the earlier intellectual episode has been forgotten (1976: 133, emphasis in original; Santiso 2000). Losing hope in development seems to have been a case of interruption of the learning process for sustained institutional change at the domestic and international levels. Moreover, the September 11 attacks generated a sense of insecurity which brought a renewed awareness about the importance of passions along with that of interests. It became clear that, without security, globalisation cannot be inclusive.

The chapter is organised into three sections, plus introduction, conclusion and appendix. The implications of the Marshall Plan for international development policy are traced in the first section. The restriction to the OECD area of concepts such as complex interdependence (Keohane and Nye 1977) and yardstick competition (Schleifer 1985) may have lessened the awareness of positive globalisation and governance interaction, thereby interrupting the learning process evoked by Hirschman. The second section suggests that rising awareness of the need for good governance at national, regional and global levels does not imply that reforms are actually implemented. In turn, the combination of a history of poor governance and limited adaptive capacity dampens the role of expectations and institutional change. The third section emphasises the principle of proximity as an additional argument for better governance and inclusive globalisation, even though the European experience in applying it remains below expectations. The overall conclusion of the chapter is that, without finer attention to culture in development thinking, peer pressure will remain absent from development practice.

International development policy

Having inspired similar efforts in favour of countries in Eastern Europe, central Asia and Africa, the Marshall Plan remains the benchmark of international assistance for reconstruction and development. The reason may be that recipients agreed on how to allocate the payments through multilateral surveillance procedures which pioneered those of the Exchange Rate Mechanism (ERM) of the European Monetary System (Eichengreen and Braga de Macedo 2001).

Monitoring development goals

Passionate debates about globalisation have involved protests on the occasion of meetings of international organisations dedicated to trade, finance and development. These same international organisations influence the field of development economics, which:

> ...was born from the marriage between the new insights about the sui generis economic problems of the underdeveloped countries and the overwhelming desire to achieve rapid progress in solving these problems with ... large-scale foreign aid. A factor in "arranging" this marriage, in spite of the incompatibilities involved, was the success of the Marshall Plan in Western Europe.
>
> (Hirschman 1981: 13)

The influence of international organisations notwithstanding, there is recurrent evidence of institutional inertia and reform reversals, which has led those who emphasise expectations to be sceptical about "large-scale foreign aid" inducing reforms. At the same time, anxiety about the implications of the institutional change required for national economic and social development is often due to the inability or unwillingness of policy-makers to specify the prerequisites of enduring reform.

The combination of challenges and responses is specific to each national experience. This general lesson from comparative development is consistent with the emphasis on designing and implementing a global partnership for development, which is the eight of the goals adopted by all 189 Member States of the Union Nations at the Millennium Summit in September 2000. It is also the crucial element of the Monterrey declaration on Financing for Development, named after a conference in early 2002 involving the UN, IMF, World Bank and WTO, together with business and civil society.

The global partnership for development and the other seven goals contained in the Millennium and Monterrey declarations presume rising per capita income, but go beyond it. Hirschman concludes his essay by claiming that the western economists who looked at developing countries at the end of World War II were convinced that their major problems would be solved:

> ...if only their national income per capita could be raised adequately.... In sum, like the "innocent" and doux trader of the eighteenth century, these countries were perceived to have only interests and no passions. Once again, we have learned otherwise.
>
> (1981: 24)

The design and implementation of the global partnership for development should not obscure the fact that the first seven goals cover dimensions that were largely unconsidered in post-war Europe. These are: eradicating extreme poverty and hunger; achieving universal primary education; promoting gender equality and empowering women; reducing child mortality; improving maternal health; combating HIV/AIDS, malaria and other diseases; and ensuring environmental sustainability. These goals have been guiding the development agenda since the DAC approved "ambitious but realisable" goals for 2015 in terms of economic well-being, social development and environmental sustainability and regeneration (OECD 1996: 2). The importance of the eighth goal is precisely to raise awareness among developed countries about the need for a durable partnership with developing countries. It would seem that adapting procedures from the Marshall Plan could contribute to achieving this goal.

In effect, the evolution of economic thought on development and the calls for an interdisciplinary approach thereto have led to greater consensus on the goals of development. Drawing on Charles Oman and Ganeshan Wignaraja (1991), the appendix to this chapter looks at the evolution of development thinking until the time when Deepak Lal concluded that "the demise of development economics is likely to be conducive to the health of both the economics and the economies of developing countries" (1983: 109). This was also a time when Amartya Sen (1983: 745) and Pranab Bardhan (1988: 66) called Hirschman's piece cited above "an obituary of development economics". Dudley Seers went even further:

> In the retrospective perception of the twenty-first century, development economics may perhaps be seen as a transitional stage in the metamorphosis – and the Manchester conference of 1964 (on the "Teaching of Development Economics: Its Position in the Present State of Knowledge") will appear as signalling the start of its death throes and the conception of its successor.
>
> (1979: 717)

Yet, according to Sen, the fact that "neo-classical economics did not apply terribly well in underdeveloped countries ... need not have caused great astonishment, since neo-classical economics did not apply terribly well anywhere else" (1983: 746). This more cheerful view of the future of development economics was echoed by concern with showing how information-theoretic considerations "can provide insights into markets and market failures in less developed economies, to show how it can provide explanations for institutions which in neo-classical theory appear anomalous and/or inefficient" (Stiglitz 1989: 156).

After the Monterrey declaration, in effect, it would seem that the difficulties in development reside in the implementation rather than in matters of principle. The declaration itself reflects the greater consensus about appropriate policies that has been emerging over the last fifteen years in matters of principle, such as the relevance of governance at national, regional and global levels. This emerging consensus has not been matched by agreement over the relative importance of these three levels of governance in different issue-areas and therefore over the proper sequencing of reforms. An appropriate analytical framework to evaluate these reforms may also be lacking. Nevertheless, the management practice of benchmarking has encouraged institutional change by allowing for more systematic monitoring in corporate and political governance. While this monitoring has not prevented a succession of scandals in corporate governance, let alone perceptions of widespread corruption at all levels of government, it has become less likely that such practices would evade scrutiny and therefore punishment. When pay-offs are well defined, benchmarking increases the accountability of managers or policy-makers as shown in applications of the literature on yardstick competition (e.g. Besley and Case 1995). While benchmarking is not a panacea, the identification of best practices does help to improve performance reviews by peers in intergovernmental organisations and indeed by financial markets.

Given the emergence of complex interdependence among major OECD members, the question is how portable its benchmarking methods might be outside the membership. The success of the euro can be rooted in the multilateral surveillance procedures that originated in the Marshall Plan, and peer pressure brought to bear on the members of the ERM well beyond the monetary and exchange rate areas. The case can be made for their portability to regional arrangements in other continents, such as MERCOSUR's Macroeconomic Monitoring Group or the Chang Mei Initiative among ASEAN members, China, Korea and Japan (*DiB*9).

Even if portability of the benchmarking methods to emerging markets is granted, the design should fit particular circumstances (*DiB*12; Braga de Macedo 2002a). The New Partnership for African Development (NEPAD 2001), for example, is a step in the right direction if the process of peer reviews (not made explicit in the original document) actually works. Peer monitoring, together with regional peace and security initiatives, are issue areas that make particularly strong use of the democratic basis of NEPAD (Kanbur 2001: 8). When there is no local capacity for benchmarking, however, results may not come quickly enough to sustain the attention of the donor community, let alone of the countries themselves when reward and punishment have not been defined. With respect to the desired "mutual accountability" between DAC donors and least developed countries, it is even less clear how it may be implemented outside of the existing procedures for peer reviews.

Whilst born with the Marshall Plan, yardstick competition remained largely confined to broad economic guidelines in the OECD membership until the fall of the Berlin Wall and the demise of the Soviet Union. The advent of true global economic progress seemed then to follow the triumph of the market over the state. The recommendations of the Bretton-Woods institutions combined with American preferences to form what came to be known as the "Washington Consensus" (Williamson 1994). It was widely believed that globalisation promoted and rewarded appropriate policies at national, regional and global levels. As shocking policy failures emerged at all three levels, the role of governance at corporate, public and political levels began to be part of development thinking (World Bank 2002; *DiB*7 and 8).

Global policy convergence?

One of the crucial debates in economic and social development is about how to ensure that the poorer countries grow more rapidly than the richer countries, so that there may be convergence in living standards and increasing cohesion in the world economy. Angus Maddison (2001) documents in his millennial perspective on international development how uneven the increase in productive capacity and per capita incomes have been. Since 1820, world per capita income rose more than eightfold, and life expectancy almost threefold. But the 2:1 gap in terms of per capita income between Western Europe, its offshoots in Australasia and North America and Japan ("the West") and "the Rest" became 7:1 in 2001. If Asia's catching up continues, the gap will decline to 6:1 in 2015 (*DiB*2).

If the rich get richer and the poor get poorer, the gap between rich and poor nations will widen over time. Cohesion – be it global, regional or even national – will be threatened. Reforms will stall.

For interpretations of development relying on deterministic models, perhaps only countries with an adequate initial level of human capital endowments can take advantage of modern technology to enjoy the possibility of convergent growth. Alternatively, "reasonably efficient economic institutions" might be the major requirement for economic growth and convergence of incomes per capita worldwide.

The emphasis on open markets (for the international trade of goods, services and assets) and on institutions to protect property rights (including hidden taxes, regulatory reform, etc.) underscores the importance of micro-behavioural responses to incentives, be they domestic or external in origin. Poor economic management stems from the absence of secure property rights, or from autarkic trade policies and inconvertible currencies. The failure to grow is rooted in wrong policies as much as in inadequate technology or insufficient human capital. The convergence club is better defined according to policy choices rather than initial levels of human capital; poor policy choices are not irrevocably linked to low levels of income (*DiB*4).

Sachs and Warner (1995a) use a sample of 117 countries – covering approximately 90 per cent of the world population – for which data on policy convergence are available as of 1985. They establish that countries with "appropriate policies" and initially low per capita income grow more rapidly than richer ones. Countries whose policies related to property rights and to integration of the economy into international trade do not qualify as appropriate do not converge. The published version of these findings (Sachs and Warner 1995b) takes the argument too far both conceptually and empirically insofar as it bases the convergence criterion on trade openness alone. On the contrary, subsequent work (Hall and Jones 1997; Cohen and Soto 2002) makes the property rights argument more precise by adding a link between social institutions and the yield on human capital. The result is that the preconditions for convergence become more exacting (*DiB3*).

Income convergence is therefore predicated on a process of economic reform that requires appropriate policy responses to the emergence of a global economy, building on the failure of import-substituting industrialisation and the demise of central planning. The institutional change prerequisites revealed by such reform processes confirm the importance of good corporate, public and political governance. In other words, globalisation and governance are two complementary sets of requirements for sustained development.

The capacity to cope with a volatile international environment is the main difference between emerging markets and mature democracies that are clustered in "the West". The response to crises is often more drastic at "the periphery" than at "the centre" because policy is supposed to have higher credibility in mature democracies with a higher credit rating and more transparent public and private partnerships. Lower ratings go with less transparency, signalling a weaker financial reputation and higher perceived risk to international investors.

Including recent members of the OECD in "the Rest" rather than in "the West", the former's population share in the world total rises by 9 percentage points between 1950 and 2001, but at current trends is expected to increase by one percentage point only from 2001 until 2015. On the contrary, the per capita income share of "the Rest" in the world average rose by 4 percentage points between 1950 and 2001, and at current trends is expected to increase by 8 percentage points from 2001 until 2015. All told, the ratio of Rest to West per capita income fell by 5 percentage points between 1950 and 2001, and is expected to increase by 3 percentage points from 2001 until 2015 (*DiB2*).

A particularly troubling implication of the emerging markets crises of the late 1990s was that the difference between the reputation of the West and the Rest shrunk. The G-7 summits enlarged to include Russia, and some of the other "systemically important countries" gathered in groups such as the G-20. In Asia, where the trouble originated, the difficulties of Japan continued. The combination of the 2001 recession and the September 11 attacks called for a rethinking of the consequences of globalisation along globalisation and governance lines (World Bank 2002). On the other hand, the resilience of the US economy made co-ordinated policy responses less necessary.

Experience with the reform process has shown that privatisation and liberalisation are not simply complementary but, in many areas, are necessary preconditions for each other and cannot go forward unless they do so together (*DiB7* and 8). In practical terms, this is reflected in the basic regulatory function or abilities of the state – abilities which may be either inadequate without further investment in public administrative capacity, or threatened by liberalisation itself, especially with respect to financial markets. As a consequence, the sequencing of domestic liberalisation policies must be done carefully: the appropriate response to the competitive pressure of globalisation may be a restriction of trade in assets until banks are effectively supervised (*DiB*9 and 10).

Policy reform must also be accompanied by attention to its impact on poverty, inequality and social cohesion (*DiB*6). Policies of poverty alleviation take on a salience in poor and rich countries that middle-income countries may find surprising and often confusing. On the one hand, the dynamics of the process of development are so intense in an emerging economy and society that widespread poverty alleviation may seem impossible or undesirable or both, and have been often ignored, especially in recent years with the focus on creating appropriate incentives. On the other hand, especially after mass consumption is achieved, poverty alleviation becomes a moral imperative of civil society, so much so that economic incentives in recipient countries are often forgotten in the rush to provide humanitarian aid (*DiB*11).

The success of these reformist pressures has deepened and broadened the scope of development studies. During the Cold War, centrally planned economies were seen as developed in terms of their command over resources, education and health and the comparison with market economies emphasised the difference in economic system in ways that were conceptually very different from the comparison of developed economies with underdeveloped ones. Because the latter were seen as poorer versions of the former, economic growth was enough to bring about the transformation into the desired system. As the failure of central planning began to be acknowledged, the idea of an equivalence between economic systems was progressively abandoned. Market-oriented transition strategies were believed to advance economic, social and political development and this was in large part why they were embarked upon. It is now recognised that, whilst necessary, economic growth is not sufficient to sustain development. In this respect, the concept of sustainable development applies to countries along the entire development path and not just when they reach certain levels of income per capita (*DiB*5).

As shown in the next section, the specific timing and sequencing of reforms continues to depend on initial conditions and national adaptive capacity. Indeed, policy convergence guards against a single path that might attain the terminal condition faster but could not be sustained thereafter. This is perhaps the most relevant lesson of the apparent demise of the principle whereby economic efficiency is deemed independent of social cohesion and majority voting.

Expectations and institutions

The importance of network externalities in a country's institutional framework means that organisations that are well adapted to and evolve in that framework will often capture increasing returns from it. Incremental change in a country's institutional framework comes from the perceptions and expectations of political, economic and social entrepreneurs and organisations that they could do better by altering the existing framework. Those perceptions and expectations depend crucially both on the information they can acquire, and its cost, and on how they process it.

As information and transaction costs are not negligible either in economic or in political activity, the choices made and actions undertaken by entrepreneurs and organisations do not necessarily produce a set of institutions and transactions that deliver the common good. The costs of specifying, monitoring and enforcing contracts and property rights, including the judiciary and other dimensions of the political system, may determine whether or not a particular society will find a positive globalisation and governance interaction.

In order to establish the relevance of peer pressure as a governance response consistent with expectations and policy convergence, it helps to go back to the balancing act between market and government failures under imperfect information, which is to be performed on a case-by-case basis (Stiglitz 1989). It is widely acknowledged that this balancing act cannot neglect history, but is also determined by expectations – because it involves institutional change. Even when there is a decisive element of self-fulfilling prophecy, the role of expectations differs from central planning to the extent that it is consistent with information available in world financial markets and cannot therefore be manipulated by national authorities. In other words, the fulfilment of the prophecy is credible. Thus hope, translated into economic analysis, implies what Paul Krugman (1991) called an overlap between history and expectations as determinants of the development path.

Expectations and interdependence

In a world of increasing returns, it is possible to establish both the "big push" theory of economic development (Rosenstein-Rodan 1943) and Krugman's (1981) own model of "uneven development" in which the division of the world into rich and poor nations takes place endogenously. The central implication of external economies (e.g. the rate of learning in a sector is larger the larger the sector, as in Krugman 1987) is that there will be multiple equilibria, and therefore that a policy choice arises about how to reach the most desirable equilibrium.

In this regard, there are those who think that the choice is essentially resolved by history (past events set the preconditions that drive the economy to one or another steady state). Indeed, there is a strong tradition arguing that history matters precisely because of increasing returns. But there is an alternative view, according to which the key determinant of choice of equilibrium is expectations.

The role of expectations is recognised in the responses of two Nobel laureates to the letter dated 15 February 2000, whereby the managing editors of the *European Journal of the History of Economic Thought* asked them to list the five most significant developments in economics in the twentieth century (Editorial 2001: 285). Listing rational expectations as the fifth such contribution, James Buchanan *et al.* (2001: 289) mention the work of Robert Lucas, whose 1985 Marshall lecture (1988) revived interest in growth theory and launched a large literature on "endogenous growth" (Krugman 1991; Matsuyana 1991; Bardhan 1995). Kenneth Arrow listed economic growth and development as the fifth "most significant development". His assessment of endogenous growth theory reads as follows:

> The most interesting questions are the explanation of international and intertemporal differences in productivity, especially those in terms of economic incentives. But, while the field is very active, there has not emerged much of a consensus. Perhaps the most advanced part of the work has been the study of the effects of research and development expenditures on the growth of productivity. But it is also clear that variables such as the quality of government and culture, not usually thought of as economic, are also of great significance.
>
> (2001: 303)

Many development economists might start evoking the doctrinal core of their field with history rather than with expectations, as indeed was done here. According to Krugman, history alone will determine the equilibrium if three conditions are met. First, "if the future is heavily discounted, individuals will not care much about future actions of other individuals, and this will eliminate the possibility of self-fulfilling prophecies". Second, "if external economies are small there will not be enough interdependence among decisions". Third, if "the economy adjusts slowly, then history is always decisive. The logic here is that if adjustment is slow, factor rewards will be near current levels for a long time whatever the expectations, so that factor reallocation always follows current returns" (1991: 664).

In an application to urban development in the United States, Timothy Harris and Yannis Ionnides (2000) find that history "dominates the process by which one city becomes a metropolis and another languishes in the periphery". The empirical verification that farmland values and housing values did not anticipate urban development reinforces the importance of institutional change and of yardstick competition with respect to appropriate policies.

As expectations include the tendency towards convergence, they impose tighter and tighter constraints on inadequate policies. Also, even though future generations are not represented in majority voting, greater awareness of the need to implement sustainable policies brings pressure on elected governments to clarify the intergenerational effects of current policies (*DiB*5). This applies to the physical and cultural environment as well as to the provision of public goods and transfers through taxation. The awareness is also rising that excessive taxation, whether overt or hidden in the form of inflation, discourages saving and stifles growth. This may appear not to be a developing country problem, but the difference arises mainly in the mix between overt and hidden taxes, as the latter dominate in developing countries.

As growth prospects fall due to the absence of incentives to save and invest, so does employment, reducing future consumption and increasing social deprivation. In due course these policies will be corrected. Yet, without adequate institutions, there may be reversions into inadequate policies. For Jose Tavares and Romain Wacziarg (2001), one of the paradoxes of democracy may be pressure for current consumption, even to the extent of mortgaging future savings. In that sense, faster economic adjustment helps prevent policy reversals for any given level of interdependence in time (low discount rate) and in space (large externalities). Conversely, high interdependence induces institutional change and adaptation.

Institutions and credibility

Calls for an interdisciplinary approach to development, and the emphasis on its internationally agreed goals, should not obscure the essential prerequisite of higher economic growth. In spite of agreement that market-based economic growth is key for the prevention of poverty and hunger, discussion continues about which kind of economic growth strategy to follow in developing countries (*DiB*6). Sometimes this discussion tends to focus on macro-economic conditions and the functioning of markets in a narrow sense, neglecting the legal, political, social and cultural institutions of a well-functioning market economy.

A successful strategy for higher economic growth would therefore be based on developing those institutions in ways that are appropriate both to the local culture and to global financial markets. For example, Hernando de Soto (2000) has shown the empirical importance of unclear property rights in developing countries. Besley and Andrea Prat (2001) show that freedom of the press improves governance. Federico Bonaglia *et al.* (2001) show that more open economies, enjoying more foreign competition and investing abundantly in institution building, register lower corruption levels.

According to Tavares and Wacziarg (2001), countries with democratic political systems tend to generate higher economic growth with wealth shared by a wider population than countries with non-democratic regimes. Jacques Drèze and Sen (1989) stress that democratic countries have managed to prevent famines, even though they have more trouble avoiding malnutrition and Sen (1990) points out that the persistence of severe famines in many of the sub-Saharan African countries – both with "left-wing" and "right-wing" governments – relates closely to the lack of democratic political systems and practice.

The responses to a questionnaire sent to thirteen economists representing the best professional opinion world-wide about social and ethical aspects of economics provide a variety of views on the role of markets in economic growth and development, but reveal a consensus: markets operate in particular environments and their performances depend on that of other institutions – economic, social and political (Musu and Zamagni 1992). These responses were used in the preparation of the Encyclical Letter *Centesimus Annus*, whose emphasis on the rejection of central planning as a viable alternative to the market was accompanied by a strong defence of the natural and human environment and by the promotion of the global common good. Ten years later, the views of Nobel laureates about the most significant contributions to economics in the twentieth century confirm the relevance of the global common good (Editorial 2001; Malinvaud and Sabourin 2001: 27–9).

There are many specific examples that governance and institutions matter for development (Lin and Nogent 1995), but exactly how the independence of the central bank and appropriate budgetary procedures interact with political accountability in particular institutional settings is not known. Since "change is the rule" in this environment, economists can contribute to understanding institutional change. Jurgen von Hagen and Ian Harden (1994 and 1996) look at the budget laws of various countries and discuss in what ways one can compare the budget approval procedures in their various phases from cabinet to parliament. Similar work had been done by Alex Cukierman (1992) and others on the central bank and other monetary institutions; William Branson *et al.* (2001) apply similar analyses to transition countries.

Torsten Persson, Gerard Roland and Guido Tabellini (1997) find a general trade-off between independence and accountability that provides support to the separation of powers argument from eighteenth-century political philosophy. In particular, the separation between executive and legislative powers is applied to the budget process as an illustration of the benefits of democratic governance. Building on their notion of complex interdependence, Keohane and Nye (2001) show that, with the spread of free information, the credibility of policy becomes essential – a direct consequence of the role of expectations.

Nevertheless, there are few applications of these insights to developing countries, so that the burden of the initial conditions makes institutional change less credible. In establishing credibility, three additional difficulties must be overcome pertaining to data, analysis, culture. Inadequate data is a very serious problem everywhere, but the phenomenon is even more pronounced in developing countries. Following fads, set modes of thinking and, as the opening quotes imply, recurrent instances of *déjà vu* lead to faulty analysis, and possibly to reinventing past theories, rather than to analytical advances. And third, focusing on the attitudes of a culture toward change may help to understand whether reforms will be accepted or rejected by public opinion.

For example, to ensure the long-term success of reforms, budget-relevant data must be universally accepted. In the European Union, fiscal policy is the domain of the individual EU countries, but authority over the data on budgets, debt and related metrics lies with the European Commission. This creates a situation in which securing the data is the responsibility of a third party.

Governance is an issue not only for states or corporations, but also for NGOs and for international organisations. The idea that the "soft power" of persuasion is now more important than military might may be questioned in an era of global insecurity but it nevertheless suggests that an organisation's credibility relates directly to its transparency. Improving transparency can help to prevent some of the problems that have occurred in the past, thus enhancing the credibility of information. Whether the perceived increase in transparency is vindicated by subsequent outcomes, and becomes "real", is a separate question.

Business associations (as distinct from major businesses, which can be quite different in nature) are often essential intermediaries in the fight against corruption. There are many instances in which a government working alone or in partnership with NGOs has degenerated into something from which no solution can emerge. By adding non-profit business associations to the mix, we add a component that understands the extent to which business is the victim of corruption. Coalitions that include civil society organisations and business associations should expect difficulties. But when business associations feel as though they are participating, they are more at ease.

It is relatively easy to apply norms to macroeconomic variables, such as deficits and debts, because these variables are easy to measure. The same is not true of structural policies. Even the European mechanisms of surveillance of structural issues have not overcome the danger of procrastination and the interaction of surveillance with the election cycle can significantly delay reforms (on such "Euro hold-up" see Braga de Macedo 2001).

Governance, national and international

Among international organisations, a broad reformist approach originated in the report by Lester Pearson (1968) and became part of the "basic needs" approach, but it was largely forgotten until the Comprehensive

Development Framework (CDF) was launched (World Bank 1999, 2001). Possibly influenced by this reformist approach, and encouraged by favourable public opinion, aid donors tended to give increasing prominence to poverty reduction until they agreed on the development goals listed above.

The ways in which the complementarity between national governance of economic actors and global competition works itself out vary across countries and over time, enhancing growth in some cases and stifling it in others. This is why creating new institutions capable of delivering the desired role of the state in economic life remains a matter for national choice. Preferences vary widely, and initial conditions, economic, social and political, are equally diverse. A reformist government being replaced by a nationalist or populist one will change the policy response to globalisation, for example.

But, as Krugman (1994) has vividly illustrated, reforms are often rhetoric rather than a revelation of a plan or a genuine commitment on the part of policy-makers. The reason for this anti-reform bias pertains to a possibly perverse interaction between voters and the media, whereby new initiatives are broadly rewarded by public opinion but their implementation is blocked because existing entitlements are fiercely defended by those who benefit from them. In addition, since the losses are often clearer than the gains, even though the latter may potentially be much larger, uncertainty about the political redistribution mechanism may also impart a "status quo bias", as illustrated in the context of protection by Raquel Fernandez and Dani Rodrik (1991).

The ability to redistribute power and real resources to the population at large suggests that some social groups are able to distribute external resources among themselves in a more or less co-ordinated fashion. For some purposes, groups can be identified with parts of the government, in particular spending ministries (e.g. public works, education, health), possibly in alliance with industry or union lobbies (construction, teachers, pharmaceuticals). In other cases, groups can be identified with traditional institutions, like the church, the military and the judiciary (Tommasi 2002). This group influence on the tax/transfer mechanism implies some form of "common access" to the aggregate capital stock, when taxable sector coincides with exports whereas the "informal" sector involves import or import substituting production. Each powerful group ignores the effect of the transfer it extracts on the taxes levied to balance the government budget (Tornell and Lane 1996, 1998, 1999).

As a consequence of each group's voracity, aggregate transfers rise more than proportionately. The associated "fiscal euphoria" has dissipated terms of trade improvements in many countries, especially those with weaker institutions. When an increase in the rate of return to capital in the taxable sector leads to a more than proportional increase in discretionary redistribution, then the power of vested interests is perverse for society as a whole. On the other hand, better co-ordination among powerful groups, perhaps due to a unitary rather than a divided government, decreases the "voracity effect".

Given the widespread awareness of reform rhetoric and of the resilience of vested interests, currents departing from mainstream development thinking have become more difficult to classify neatly in terms of method and ideology. The Comprehensive Development Framework (CDF) is seen as a response to the perception that globalisation leads to increased poverty. Successful development assistance reflects four principles: (1) long-term, holistic strategy; (2) country ownership; (3) partnership (with business interests and civil society); and (4) results orientation (as opposed to stress on inputs like the percentage of aid in GDP). None of the principles is new, and they all raise difficult choices.

The joint articulation of the four CDF principles as a framework to promote coherent aid programmes linked with poverty-reduction strategies has been influential in building the "Monterrey consensus" – even though the positive globalisation and governance interaction they presuppose needs to be made specific in order to be useful for policy-makers. Therefore judicious adaptation of these principles to diverse country circumstances is critical to success.

With respect to "partnership and results orientation", for example, partnerships often make policy-making more difficult due to various forms of transactions costs. There are instances in which the granting of more power to communities and to lower levels of government has actually decreased the quality and efficiency of aid. The European experience suggests that supra-national and international mechanisms can provide defences against the danger of regulatory capture but cannot eliminate it. Similarly, results orientation by itself cannot overcome voracity effects (Braga de Macedo 2003).

Proximity and inclusive globalisation

The crucial policy issue is how states and markets should interact when the latter become global. The desired interaction, it is surmised, will result from changes in corporate and political governance, thereby raising normative issues that bring back the interplay between the passions and the interests mentioned at the outset. While such philosophical underpinnings are often neglected by national and international development organisations, they have been at the heart of economic thought on development, as the examples from European eighteenth-century intellectual history illustrate.

The existence of a "global common good" has become more widely acknowledged, but there is no way the existing global institutions can provide for the common good without relying on national and local entities. Sometimes, perhaps because of contradictory positions of the member states, the UN, WTO, IMF and World Bank are unable to co-operate effectively with each other in areas where their combined mandates and areas of expertise would have produced better results.

In addition to the Monterrey process, there have been occasions when the global economic and financial institutions have co-operated with the UN system. Some pertain to conflict resolution on the ground (e.g. El Salvador, East Timor), others to joint ventures such as the joint publication of *A Better World for All* by the IMF, OECD, UN and World Bank.

Nevertheless, the democratic accountability of global institutions, let alone of regional ones, remains remote. National legitimacy remains the source of their democratic accountability. If we postulate both national legitimacy and democratic accountability, the preferred domain of political governance will remain the nation-state. However, this in itself is no reason for concern. The appropriate level of governance response should only be changed when the level of the nation-state is found to be sufficiently inadequate due to changes in technology or in preferences, or both.

As global markets remain only part of policy environments, institutional changes at global level are not prerequisites for most policy reforms. Indeed, the principle of proximity suggests the opposite – governance responses at the local level, through the combined action of elected officials and civil society. Moreover, the European example demonstrates that regional institutions may provide for the common good.

The quality of governance can be improved by solving the problem closer to the citizen than the often cumbersome national administration would allow. This is why the principle of proximity is explicitly recognised in the 1992 *Treaty on European Union* (article 1, second paragraph, and article 2, second paragraph, mention the principle of subsidiarity, referring to article 5 of the 1957 Treaty establishing the European Community; see also no. 58 of the Encyclical Letter *Centesimus Annus.*).

For many issues, improving governance calls for international policy co-operation. There are even calls for new international institutions. Barry Herman (1999), for example, discusses some of the concerns leading to the Monterrey process (also *DiB*9). The quest for appropriate regional institutions echoes both concerns, as there are sub-national and supra-national regions. Among the latter, the institutional frameworks of the EU and of the OECD deserve notice because both are built on the belief that peer pressure among them can bring about better policies.

In addition, the EU´s combination of unity with diversity may be an appropriate response for a "globalisation of solidarity". In order to ensure this, a greater awareness of the common European good is called for. This presumes that the EU will play its part in the globalisation of solidarity, from its own enlargement to the reinforcement of its development policies. At the moment, the amounts reported to the DAC cannot be meaningfully consolidated and therefore remain scattered and with diminished impact.

Given the incoherence among aid policies, looking at the overall volume of public development assistance is not going to establish a European identity in development. This is especially true in an environment of economic and financial globalisation, where democratic governance has become the undisputed norm and poverty reduction has become the ultimate development objective. Moreover, governments, businesses and other parts of civil society process information about development which goes far beyond the levels of public development assistance as a percentage of gross domestic product.

The achievement of social cohesion within the EU, together with the success of the convergence towards financial stability which led to the creation of the euro, are recognised world-wide. These internal achievements have a bearing on development insofar as they provide lessons for policy reform in developing countries. All too often, the "common European good" invoked for internal purposes is not perceived as such in the global arena because Europe's achievements are not brought to bear on the issue. In addition, there are the implementation difficulties stemming from the uneasy co-existence of sixteen systems of aid governance.

The ability to present the collective advantage of policy reform in each particular case is the essence of political leadership. Yet, too often policymakers do not care to explain the changes and their consequences for public administration, let alone for firms, trade unions and civil society at large. As a consequence, social groups fear losses of income or entitlements, resist change as a matter of principle, and become less sensitive to national interest than to their perceived group gains or losses.

Comparative development calls for a dialogue about policies, as development has become a two-way street rather than an "institutional technology transfer". Comparative analysis and policy dialogue naturally involve mutual feedback: globalisation has blurred the analytical distinction between the West and the Rest (*DiB*2), and it has underscored the perception that the problems of income distribution and skills are global (*DiB*6). The sense that globalisation, not poor governance, has reinforced inequality is behind much of the recent confrontations around the international trade and investment agenda.

Analysis is not enough to completely prevent this perception. Moreover, a communications campaign would also run out of steam unless it were based on a credible demonstration of the benefits of tariff liberalisation in and of greater market access for developing countries. The theme of inclusive globalisation (prominently featured in the work on globalisation and governance) has acquired new salience after the September 11 attacks, as it – drawing on several UN resolutions – is in line with the broad coalition built by the United States and its traditional allies to fight terrorism. Other international organisations have also recognised that the debates on globalisation can no longer neglect the security dimension of national, regional and international governance.

The responsibility in promoting – or hindering – development of global as opposed to national institutions should not be decided on philosophical grounds, as the practical implications of global markets escape no one concerned about development. Nevertheless, "forgetting" the philosophical roots requires that the development community periodically rediscover them, as with the Monterrey consensus.

If the main responsibility for change is global, in effect, citizens and policy-makers in developing countries can only wait for a better international order. Gordon Smith and Moises Naim (2000) mention prevention of deadly conflict, providing opportunities for the young, and managing climate change as specific areas of competence of the UN system. Yet, its Secretary-General cannot carry out minimal global governance tasks, let alone provide correspondent "global public goods" (Kaul *et al.* 1999). If the main responsibility rests with the citizens and policy-makers, then the focus shifts from global to national, local or regional governance. Greater proximity to decision-making brings hope, but it also calls for deeper and more immediate institutional changes towards the global common good. While this includes the provision of global public goods (Kaul *et al.* 2002), it does not imply a world government. Indeed, in many cases it may be achievable through peer pressure among national governments along the lines of what is observed at the OECD or the EU.

Conclusion

National development is based on economic growth, social cohesion and political stability within a democratic framework. It implies a sustained improvement in people's welfare. As the economic history of mature democracies reveals, the path of long-term development depends crucially on policies pursued along the way with respect to opening to foreign trade and to preserving property and civil rights. Institutions promoting the rule of law and the role of civil society make these policies compatible with social cohesion and good government.

Given the economic, social and political conditions prevailing before the take-off into sustained growth, features of the system of international relations may foster or hinder improvements in governance. This is particularly true for the path from an aid-dependent to an emerging market situation: coherence among donors should help reward policy reforms and could discourage poor performance.

From its creation in the wake of the Marshall Plan, the OECD serves as a yardstick for development. This is not only because its members include virtually all the donors, but also because its members – in spite of their heterogeneity – are seen as successful reformers. The OECD is therefore well placed to contribute to the debates surrounding globalisation and poverty reduction – what may be called the quest for "inclusive globalisation".

Cultures are not deterministic, backward-looking realities that prevent some countries from developing and help other countries to develop. Methods of "soft co-operation", enforced by peer pressure, are appropriate not only for the countries that are part of the OECD club, but also for other countries that may feel like-minded in some specific area. The idea that dialogue between cultures is possible and desirable is an important part of the quest for inclusive globalisation. There is a development path, maybe diverse, but in line with some values and notions of change that may at least be compared in a meaningful way over the medium term.

Better data, sounder analysis and finer attention to culture motivate the need to agree on national and regional comparative procedures capable of improving the quality of domestic institutions. While, in the short run, domestic policies may be more valuable than pursuing globalisation at all costs, the role of external pressure is appropriate to macroeconomic stabilisation whereas peer pressure might be required to embark on sustained institutional change. The difficulties pertaining to data and analysis as well as of culture may be immense. However, progress on the first two has immediate effects on the third – what are the attitudes of a culture towards transparency, which is a key to the credibility of free information – itself a crucial element of soft power.

Belonging to regional arrangements that combine external and peer pressure is only one example of ways in which national governance may be improved. Clearly, there are many institutional improvements called for by each national development strategy, and the portability of the European experience to a development context cannot be presumed. But as the NEPAD may soon illustrate, the investigation of the scope for more peer pressure is especially important for poorer countries that face serious trade-offs between complying with international agreements and investing in basic development infrastructures such as education, health and social security. The overall message is: the positive effect of globalisation on governance cannot be sustained through the developing process without the required improvements in local and national governance.

Appendix: DEV@40(25)

As mentioned in the introduction to the chapter, development is a field of economics where nearly all others are relevant. For example, the last volumes of the monumental *Handbook* edited by T. N. Srinivasan, the late Hollis Chenery (1988 and 1989) and Jere Behrman (1995a and b) include the following selected list of topics: savings, credit and insurance; technological change and technology strategy; institutions and economic development; poverty, institutions and the environmental-resource base; poverty and policy; power, distortions, revolt and reform in agricultural land relations; human and physical infrastructure: investment and pricing policies; structural adjustment, stabilisation and policy reform: domestic and international finance; trade and industrial policy reform. Whilst welcome, this diversity makes it impossible to survey the evolution of development thinking without a particular vantage point, which the admittedly cryptic short-hand title evokes, as the time horizons implied by the institutional memory of the OECD Development Centre, established in 1962.

The series of essays quoted in *DiB* were prepared by current associates who wrote the following chapters: (2) Angus Maddison, (3) Daniel Cohen, (4) Jean-Claude Berthelemy, (5) David O'Connor, (6) Maurizio Bussolo and Christian Morrison, (7) Andrea Goldstein, (8) Oman, (9) Reisen, (10) Ki Fukasaku, (11) Henri-Bernard Solignac-Lecomte and Ida McDonnell.

These essays should be read against the background of the evolution of development thinking carried out around the time of the DEV 25th Anniversary Symposium, as reflected in the DEV book by Oman and Wignaraja (1991; see also Gustav Ranis and Paul Schultz 1988, celebrating the 25th anniversary of Yale's Economic Growth Center).

Given the greater convergence in development thinking of the last fifteen years, some of the categories used then – such as reformist or heterodox – appear less relevant today when confronted with the mainstream, then called orthodox or neoclassical school of thought. The most relevant parts of the text for this discussion can be found under four headings: Cold War roots (pp. 2–4), foreign economic policy (pp. 67–9, 81–2), reformist pressures (pp. 121–4), development planning (pp. 223–6).

References

Arrow, K. (2001) "The Five Most Significant Developments in Economics during the Twentieth Century", *European Journal of the History of Economic Thought*, 8 (3): 298–304.

Bardhan, P. (1988) "Alternative Approaches to Development Economics", in H. Chenery and T. N. Srinivasan (eds), *Handbook of Development Economics*, vol. 1, Amsterdam: North Holland.

Bardhan, P. (1995) "The Contributions of Endogenous Growth Theory to the Analysis of Development Problems: an Assessment", in J. Behrman and T .N. Srinivasan (eds), *Handbook of Development Economics*, vol. 3B, Amsterdam: North Holland.

Behrman, J. and T. N. Srinivasan (1995a) *Handbook of Development Economics*, vol. 3A, Amsterdam: North Holland.

—— (1995b) *Handbook of Development Economics*, vol. 3B, Amsterdam North Holland.

Besley, T. and A. Case (1995) "Incumbent Behavior: Vote-seeking, Tax-setting and Yardstick Competition", *American Economic Review*, 85 (1): 25–45.

Besley, T. and A. Prat (2001) *Handcuffs for the Grabbing Hand? Media Capture and Government Accountability*, London: London School of Economics.

Bonaglia, F., J. Braga de Macedo and M. Bussolo (2001) "How Globalisation Improves Governance", London: CEPR Discussion Paper no. 2992.

Braga de Macedo, J. (2001) "Globalisation and Institutional Change: A Development Perspective", in E. Malinvaud and L. Sabourin (eds), *Globalization: Ethical and Institutional Concerns*, Vatican City: Pontifical Academy of Social Sciences.

—— (2002) "Towards an African Multilateral Framework", mimeo, Paris: OECD Development Centre.

—— (2003) "Partnerships: the Crucial Role of the State", in A. Liebenthal, O. Feinstein and G. K. Ingram (eds), *Evaluation and Development: the Partnership Dimension*, London and New Brunswick, NJ: Transaction.

Braga de Macedo, J., D. Cohen and H. Reisen (2001) *Don't Fix, Don't Float*, Paris: OECD Development Centre.

Braga de Macedo, J., C. Foy and C. Oman (eds) (2002) *Development is Back*, Paris: OECD Development Centre.

Branson W., J. Braga de Macedo and J. von Hagen (2001) "Macroeconomic Policy and Institutions in the Transition towards EU Membership", in R. MacDonald and R. Cross (eds), *Central Europe towards Monetary Union: Macroeconomic Underpinnings and Financial Reputation*, Boston: Kluwer Academic Publishers.

Buchanan, J., G. Debreu, L. Klein, M. Friedman and R. Solow (2001) "The Most Significant Contributions to Economics during the Twentieth Century: Lists of Nobel Laureates", *European Journal of the History of Economic Thought*, 8 (3): 289–97.

Chenery, H. and T. N. Srinivasan (1988) *Handbook of Development Economics*, vol. 1, Amsterdam: North Holland.

—— (1989) *Handbook of Development Economics*, vol. 2, North Holland.

Cohen, D. and M. Soto (2002) "Why Are Some Countries So Poor? Another Look at the Evidence and a Message of Hope", Paris: OECD Development Centre Technical Paper no. 179.

Cukierman, A. (1992) *Central Bank Strategy, Credibility and Independence: Theory and Evidence*, Cambridge, MA: The MIT Press.

de Soto, H. (2000) *The Mystery of Capital: Why Capitalism Triumphs in the West and Fails Everywhere Else*, New York: Basic Books.

Dreze, J. and A. Sen (1989) *Hunger and Public Action*, Oxford: Clarendon Press.

Editorial (2001) "Symposium on the Most Significant Contributions to Economics during the Twentieth Century: Some Nobel Laureates' Views", *European Journal of the History of Economic Thought*, 8 (3): 285.

Eichengreen, B. and J. Braga de Macedo (2001) "The European Payments Union and the Evolution of International Financial Architecture", in A. Lamfalussy, B. Snoy and J. Wilson (eds), *Fragility of the International Financial System*, Brussels: PIE Peter Lang.

Fernandez, R. and D. Rodrik (1991) "Resistance to Reform Status Quo in the Presence of Individual Specific Uncertainty", *American Economic Review*, 81: 1146–55.

Hall, R. and C. Jones (1997) "Why Do Some Countries Produce So Much More Output per Worker than Others?" *Quarterly Journal of Economics*, 114 (1): 83–116.

Harris, T. and Y. Ionnides (2000) "History vs. Expectations: an Empirical Investigation", Medford, MA: Tufts University Department of Economics Discussion Paper no. 2000–14.

Herman, B. (ed.) (1999) *Global Financial Turmoil and Reform: a United Nations Perspective*, Tokyo: United Nations University Press,

Hirschman, A. (1976) *The Passions and the Interests: Political Arguments for Capitalism before Its Triumph*, Princeton: Princeton University Press.

—— (1981) "The Rise and Decline of Development Economics" in *Essays in Trespassing: Economics to Politics and Beyond*, Cambridge: Cambridge University Press.

Kanbur, R. (2001) *The New Partnership for Africa's Development (NEPAD): An Initial Commentary*, Cornell, NY: Cornell University for the Southern African Regional Poverty Network.

Kaul, I., I. Grunberg and M. A. Stern (eds) (1999) *Global Public Goods*, New York: UNDP.

Kaul, I., P. Conceicao, K. Le Goulven and R. U. Mendoza (eds) (2002) *Providing Global Public Goods*, New York: UNDP.

Keohane, R. and J. Nye (1977) *Power and Interdependence*, Boston: Little, Brown.

—— (2001) "Power and Interdependence in the Information Age", in E. C. Kamarck and J. Nye (eds), *Democracy.com? Governance in a Networked World*, Hollis, NH: Hollis Publishing Company.

Krugman, P. (1981) "Trade, Accumulation and Uneven Development", *Journal of Development Economics*, 8: 149–61.

—— (1987) "The Narrow Moving Band, the Dutch Disease and the Competitive Consequences of Mrs. Thatcher: Notes on Trade in the Presence of Dynamic Economies of Scale", *Journal of Development Economics*, 27: 41–55.

—— (1991) "History vs. Expectations", *Quarterly Journal of Economics*, 2: 651–67.

—— (1994) *Peddlers of Prosperity*, New York: Basic Books

Lal, D. (1983) *The Poverty of Development Economics*, London: Institute of Economic Affairs.

Lin, J. Y. and J. Nugent (1995) "Institutions and Economic Development", in J. Behrman and T. N. Srinivasan (eds), *Handbook of Development Economics*, vol. 3A, Amsterdam: North Holland.

Lucas, R. (1988) "The Mechanics of Economic Development", *Journal of Monetary Economics*, 22: 3–42.

Maddison, A. (2001) *The World Economy: A Millennial Perspective*, Paris: OECD Development Centre.

Malinvaud, E. and L. Sabourin (eds) (2001) *Globalization: Ethical and Institutional Concerns*, Vatican City: Pontifical Academy of Social Sciences.

Matsuyana, K. (1991) "Increasing Returns, Industrialization and Indeterminacy of Equilibrium", *Quarterly Journal of Economics*, 106 (2): 617–50.

Musu, I. and S. Zamagni (eds) (1992) *Social and Ethical Aspects of Economics: A Colloquium in the Vatican*, Vatican City: Pontifical Council for Justice and Peace.

NEPAD (2001) *The New Partnership for Africa's Development*, NEPAD.

OECD (1996) *Shaping the 21st Century: the Contribution of Development Co-Operation*, Paris: OECD/DAC.

Oman, C. and G. Wignaraja (1991) *The Postwar Evolution of Development Thinking*, London: Macmillan, in association with the OECD Development Centre.

Pearson, L. (1968) *Partners in Development*, New York: Praeger.

Persson, T., G. Roland and G. Tabellini (1997) "Separation of Powers and Political Accountability", *Quarterly Journal of Economics*, 112 (4): 1163–202.

Ranis, G. and T. Paul Schultz (eds) (1988) *The State of Development Economics*, Oxford: Basil Blackwell.

Rosenstein-Rodan, P. (1943) "Industrialisation of Eastern and South Eastern Europe", *Economic Journal*, 53: 201–11.

Sachs, J. and A. Warner (1995a) "Economic Convergence and Economic Policies", National Bureau of Economic Research Working Paper no. 5039.

—— (1995b) "Economic Reform and the Process of Global Integration", *Brookings System on Economic Activity*, 1: 1–118.

Santiso, J. (2000) "Hirschman's View of Development, or the Art of Trespassing and Self-Subversion", Economic Commission for Latin America and the Caribbean (CEPAL/ECLAC) Review Offprint 70, Santiago: United Nations.

Seers, D. (1979) *The Birth, Life and Death of Development Economics*, Brighton, UK: Institute of Development Studies.

Sen, A. (1983) "Development: Which Way Now?" *The Economic Journal*, December, 93 (372): 742–62

—— (1990) *On Ethics and Economics*, New Delhi: Oxford University Press.

Shleifer, A. (1985) "A Theory of Yardstick Competition", *Rand Journal of Economics*, 16 (3): 319–27.

Smith, G. and M. Naím (2000) *Altered States: Globalization, Sovereignty and Governance*, Ottawa: International Development Research Centre.

Stiglitz, J. E.. (1989) "Markets, Market Failures, and Development", *American Economic Review*, 79 (2): 197–203.

Tavares, J. and R. Wacziarg (2001) "How Democracy Affects Growth", *European Economic Review*, 45: 1341–78.

Tommasi M. (2002) *Crisis, Political Institutions, and Policy Reform: It is Not the Policy, it is the Polity, Stupid*, Annual World Bank Conference on Development Economics – Europe.

Tornell, A. and P. Lane (1996) "Power, Growth and the Voracity Effect", *Journal of Economic Growth*, 1 (2): 213–41.

—— (1998) "Are Windfalls a Curse? A Non-representative Model of the Current Account", *Journal of International Economics*, 44 (1): 83–112.

—— (1999) "The Voracity Effect", *American Economic Review*, 89 (1): 22–46.

von Hagen, J. and I. Harden (1994) *National Budget Processes and Fiscal Performance*, European Economy Reports and Studies, 3: 311–418.

—— (1996) *Budget Processes and Commitment to Fiscal Discipline*, Washington, DC: IMF Working Paper no. 96/78.

Williamson, J. (1994) *The Political Economy of Policy Reform*, Washington DC: Institute of International Economics.

World Bank (1999) "Towards a Comprehensive Development Strategy", Operations Evaluation Department Precis no. 197.

—— (2001) *Partnerships and Development: a World Bank Policy Research Report*, Oxford: Oxford University Press.

—— (2002) *Globalisation, Growth and Poverty: Building an Inclusive World Economy*, Oxford: Oxford University Press.

3   Increasing returns and the division of labour in the theory of economic development[1]

Amit Bhaduri

Classical concern with economic growth and development was rekindled towards the end of the Second World War, as reconstruction and decolonization became part of an international agenda. Thinking about development and underdevelopment, some economists pursued a suggestive line of enquiry to argue that countries develop through processes that reinforce themselves over time. Thus, Rosenstein-Rodan (1943) argued in favour of a "big push", consisting of several complementary investment projects needed to set in motion such a self-reinforcing process. Myrdal found that disparities between ethnic groups (1944) and countries (1957) tend to widen due to the operation of a similar "principle of circular and cumulative causation". Kaldor explained regional and international imbalances through the self-reinforcing process of increasing returns (1989a, 1989c), and argued that standard "equilibrium economics" is incompatible with this framework of analysis (1989b, 1989d).

Self-reinforcing mechanisms appear in different fields of study, for example as auto-catalysis in bio-chemical reactions or as positive feedback in engineering systems. Examples also abound in economics. Current price rises may lead to expectations of even greater price rise to generate "bubbles"; similarly, a self-reinforcing "herd instinct" of agents may produce patterns of collective behaviour to produce "mania, panics and crashes" in the financial markets (Kindleberger 1978). Even some fundamental norms of the market culture like trust and respect for commercial contracts may be reinforced through an increasing number of market participants accepting them.

Almost since the birth of political economy, the presence of such self-reinforcing positive feedback, especially in manufacturing, has been known. Petty (1623–87) recognized not only the importance of agricultural surplus in sustaining the *social* division of labour between agriculture and manufacturing, he also pointed out the possibility of cheaper production through the *technical* division of labour and *spatial* agglomeration of manufacturing activities:

[F]or in so vast a city (like London), Manufactures will beget one another and each Manufacture will divide into as many parts as possible, whereby the work of each Artisan will be simple and easy. As for Example. In the making of a watch, if one Man shall make the Wheels, another the Spring, another shall engrave the Dial-Plate, and another shall make the Cases, then the Watch will be better and cheaper, than if the whole work be put upon any one man.

(Petty 1963: 471–2; quoted in Groenewegen 1998: 219)

Social as well as technical division of labour in a competitive economy was assigned a central role in Adam Smith's *Inquiry into the Nature and the Causes of the Wealth of Nations* (1776). In the vision he presented, greater division of labour leads to higher labour productivity that, under the classical assumption of a constant real wage rate, generates a larger surplus per worker.[2] Competition plays a critical role in the continuous reinvestment of that surplus. As the costs of production are reduced through a greater division of labour, the long-run normal prices are lowered in a competitive economy that, in turn, put pressure on the capitalists to reduce costs further by taking recourse to even greater division of labour through the reinvestment of the surplus (Kurz and Salvadori 1998). Young revived this vision by pointing out that the division of labour operates on an economy-wide scale through continuous product differentiation, the emergence of new products, industries, production methods and organization which result in a self-reinforcing process of cumulative progress. He summed it up in "the theorem that the division of labour depends in large part upon the division of labour" (1928: 233).

This grand Smithian vision of capitalistic development as a continuously self-reinforcing process, driven by the twin forces of competition and division of labour, raises many issues, some of which were more closely analysed by subsequent developments in economic theory. Ricardo (1817) brought into sharp focus the consequences of the obvious neglect of non-reproducible resources like land. It led him to the dismal view that economic development ends ultimately in a "stationary state" with zero profit. Profit tends to dwindle while the differential rent on land increases at its expense as the economy expands, bringing under cultivation less and less productive land at the margin yielding diminishing returns (Pasinetti 1959–60).

Although "capital" is a produced means of production, on the questionable assumption (Pasinetti 2000) that it can be treated in a manner analogous to land, diminishing return to capital is postulated to occur in modern neo-classical theory as the capital–labour ratio rises if capital accumulates through the reinvestment of saving at a pace faster than that of the exogenously growing labour force.[3] The Ricardian "stationary state" is then reinvented as an exogenously given "steady state" rate of growth, determined by the steady, exogenous growth rate of the labour force. The latter can be measured either in natural units without technical progress, or in efficiency units of labour if technical progress takes the specific form of augmenting only labour productivity (Solow 1956; Swan 1956).

For a return to the Smithian view that the growth process is driven endogenously by the interacting forces of competition and division of labour without any exogenously binding constraint like labour, attention has recently been focused in the neo-classical tradition on interpreting the division of labour in a manner that prevents the marginal product of capital from diminishing. Currently available endogenous models of growth explore the proposition that the growing stock of capital is generated by reinvestment of savings – itself generated by the increasing division of labour through *social* "learning by doing" (Arrow 1962) embodied in a larger stock of "human capital" (Romer 1986; Lucas 1988).

In effect, it by-passes the role of labour as an exogenous constraint by postulating that the increasing division of labour brought about by the production of further human capital can be achieved through a larger stock of physical capital (e.g. Arrow 1962; Romer 1986) or through the stock of human capital and the proportion of labour time allocated to acquiring human capital through training (Usawa 1965; Lucas 1988).

In either case, human capital is so defined as to augment the total stock of capital in efficiency units. When this efficiency effect is assumed to be sufficiently strong to neutralize the tendency of the marginal product of physical capital from falling, economic growth may be sustained endogenously, despite the exogenously given growth of the labour force.

The possibility of social learning creates a wedge between the private and the public view of economic optimality. For instance, if gross investment provides the route to social learning, private investors would fail to take this externality into account, and private optimization would result in under-investment from a social point of view. It has long been known that the so-called fundamental theorem of static welfare economics, namely that every competitive equilibrium is Pareto optimal and vice versa, runs into difficulties because of various externalities in production and consumption (Chakravarty 1973). Social learning through capital accumulation extends this argument to the dynamic context of economic growth. It also warns against the Smithian reliance on competition to do a satisfactory job of maintaining dynamic efficiency in the presence of social learning, or other forms of externalities driving the division of labour.

However, the argument goes deeper than non-optimal temporal or inter-temporal resource allocation in the presence of increasing returns, because it might render the very market form of competition *structurally* unstable. Marshall (1920) hinted at this in his famous Appendix H (see also Bharadwaj 1989). The incompatibility of his partial equilibrium analysis with the assumption of increasing returns was made explicit by Sraffa (1926). To restate the problem of structural instability of the market form with a simple example, consider two competitive firms identical in every respect, both subject to the same extent of decrease in average cost with expansion in output. A small, accidental perturbation in favour of the market share of one firm, by reducing its average cost, gives it only a slight initial competitive advantage. However, this almost negligible initial advantage might magnify cumulatively over time in a self-reinforcing manner, as lower average cost leads to higher market share to even lower average cost and so on – perhaps until one firm emerges as the monopolist, and the competitive market structure is irrevocably changed. Similar reinforcing mechanisms might also operate in the spatial competition between two industrial locations (Arthur 1994).

Or, for a more dramatic example from socio-biology, consider the social organization of insects. Ants or termites are known to practise so extensive a division of labour that the survival of the individual is practically impossible outside the group. In the construction of termites' nests, initially random deposits of building materials may occur in several places. When, by chance, one of these deposits become sufficiently large, a similar self-reinforcing process takes over, as termites begin to deposit preferentially materials on the larger heap, while the smaller deposits are abandoned altogether or joined by arches in particular cases (Nicolis and Prigogine 1977: 452–6). Thus, the emergence of structures in the formation of termites' nests, industrial districts, cities or monopolies all share the same basic mechanism of self-reinforcement.

As these examples suggest, many self-reinforcing processes over time, including dynamic increasing returns and division of labour, have consequences that are not easily dealt with in standard economic analysis. First, temporary, even small, disturbances may have large, permanent consequences, at times incorporated in a new order as our previous example of the emergence of monopoly from competition suggests. Similarly, short-term macroeconomic stabilization policies that depress output and investment temporarily may affect adversely the long-run growth prospect of the economy if, for example, they retard social "learning by doing" and human capital formation which reduces long-run productivity growth (Blackburn 1999).

Second, the cumulative processes through which initial small disturbances magnify usually take time. In a probabilistic framework, if the initial disturbances are random, fluctuations would occur initially before any cumulative process is able to gather sufficient momentum to dominate the long-run dynamics. In the previous monopoly example, the fortunes of the two competing firms would fluctuate initially, if both were subjected to random shocks. Again, in the termites' nest-building example, the prospect of the location fluctuates initially among alternative sites of deposits. Fluctuations give way to order when the self-reinforcing process becomes sufficiently strong through successive positive feedbacks in favour of one particular firm or building location. "Order through fluctuations" (Nicolis and Prigogine 1977; Haken 1978) is therefore a common phenomenon in many self-organizing systems, including economic systems which self-organize through self-reinforcing mechanisms like increasing returns and division of labour.

Third, each successive, positive feedback tends to "lock in" the system more firmly through its cumulative effect along a particular path or trajectory. In the monopoly example, as one particular firm garners the advantages of successive rounds of cost reduction through higher market share, a path-dependent outcome towards the industrial structure of monopoly becomes more probable.

One could also think of two competing technologies in the same manner. By chance, or even due to its initial superiority, as a particular technology is adopted, the firm producing that technology might enjoy initially increasing returns to scale internal to the firm due to the distribution of some fixed overhead cost over a larger volume of sales. However, over time it might also have the advantages of the distributional network becoming increasingly geared to distributing that particular technology, while training and social learning about it also become easier.

Thus, under increasing returns technological trajectories have a tendency to get trapped in a particular path. However, had the initially left-out technology been adopted, it might have become more efficient over time than the one actually adopted. Paradoxically, therefore, dynamic increasing returns and division of labour which have long been recognized as a main source of production efficiency might also turn out to be a source of inefficiency in terms of the comparative costs of foregone opportunities over time (David 1985; Arthur 1994).

Although path dependence and locking-in seem fairly generic properties of many economic, social and political processes, the formalism required to capture them is only at an early stage of development. At each stage of such a process, usually several possibilities or choices exist. Its formalization calls for a non-linear probability schema; in some cases it may be captured by a "generalized Polya process" (Arthur *et al.* 1983, 1987; reprinted in Arthur 1994).

To illustrate this process, consider the example of locating a new industry among alternative industrial districts. If the probability of it being located in a particular district is postulated to depend on the proportion of total industries located already in that district, then the self-reinforcing mechanism appears only probabilistically. The location actually chosen for the next industry may still be any one of the districts. The generalized Polya process demonstrates that, as industrial development continues, the proportion of industries located in a district ultimately reach an equilibrium (of "fixed point" of the probability function), where the (ex ante) probability of locating a new industry in a particular district equals the (ex post) proportion of total industries located already in the district. The chance element in deciding on industrial location ultimately has little influence. In general, however, several such (stable) equilibria or fixed points are possible, so that deterministic prediction of the equilibrium position may not be possible.

Contrary to Kaldor's view (1989b) that the cumulative causation of dynamic increasing returns is incompatible in general with economic equilibrium, Polya-like processes exhibit the possibility of equilibrium or multiple equilibria, because the strength of positive feedbacks tend to decrease in each successive round. Thus, if the proportion of industries in a district initially is $\frac{1}{5}$ or 20 per cent, as the next industry is located there, it becomes $[(1+1)/(5+1)] = 33\%$; with the next one $[(2+1)/(6+1)] = 43\%$, and so on. In other words, while the feedbacks remain positive and self-reinforcing, in percentage terms they decrease non-linearly in strength at each round.[4] Without this additional assumption of positive feedbacks of decreasing strength at each round, self-reinforcing processes of increasing returns may indeed rule out the existence of equilibrium.

From the macroeconomic point of view, however, a far more compelling reason limits the extent of the division of labour than the positive feedbacks of decreasing strength in a self-reinforcing process. Adam Smith (1776) had rightly observed that: The extent of the division of labour is limited by the size of the market. However, he failed to analyse clearly what determines the size of the market. The interaction between the size of the market, determined by aggregate demand as per the Keynes–Kalecki (1936, 1971) theory, and the division of labour lies at the core of the macro-dynamics of economic growth.

And yet, post-war neo-classical growth models, exogenous or endogenous, share with the Ricardian model the unfortunate common characteristic of ignoring effective demand altogether. It is simply assumed instead, in a pre-Keynesian manner, that all savings are automatically reinvested in a world ruled by Say's law. And yet, the matching between demand and supply is particularly problematic in the presence of increasing returns, as pointed out by Weitzman (1982), because suppliers inevitably become large under increasing returns, and they may fail to create adequate demand necessary to make continuous expansion of supply profitable.

Restated from a Keynesian perspective, the independence of investment from saving decisions forces us to recognize that the higher labour productivity and surplus per worker made possible by a greater division of labour need not be invested automatically by the firms. Because increasing returns exacerbate the tendency towards monopoly and market concentration, the share of profit in income may increase.

How this impacts on the incentive to invest remains an open question. While Schumpeter (1942) emphasized "creative destruction" through rapid technical progress in an oligopolistic market structure, Steindl (1952) suggested that a higher profit share under greater market concentration might push the economy towards stagnation by depressing aggregate demand. However, insofar as a higher profit share lowers consumption demand but raises the profit margin per unit of sale to stimulate investment demand, the effect on aggregate demand remains ambiguous. Depending on which effect dominates, it might result in a lower-consumption-induced stagnationist regime, or a higher-investment-led expansionist regime (Bhaduri and Marglin 1990).

Thus, the division of labour impacts in a complex way the level of aggregate demand and the size of the market. In the case of investment-led expansion with higher profit share, it can perhaps help the process of further division of labour in a self-reinforcing manner (Young 1928). But it might also hinder the same process in the consumption-induced stagnationist case. Without analysing these alternative patterns of interaction between the market size and the division of labour, we could end up telling the story of *Hamlet* without mentioning the Prince of Denmark!

Notes

1 This essay is based on an invited lecture given originally in the plenary session of the annual conference of the European Society for the History of Economic Thought, Rethymno, Crete, 14–17 March 2002, and revised subsequently during my stay at the Institute for Advanced Study in Bologna University, Italy.
2 Higher surplus per worker need not imply higher total surplus, because that depends also on the level of employment. Smith's (pre-Keynesian) discussion fails to explain how the levels of employment and output are determined.
3 Again, as in Ricardo's or Smith's discussion, the level of employment or output is not determined; instead, it is simply assumed that full-employment is maintained somehow, and that full-employment level of saving is automatically reinvested under the (pre-Keynesian) Say's law to drive the process of rising capital–labour ratio.
4 On the contrary, if in successive rounds, the next industry is not located in that district, probability decreases from 20% to $[1/(5+1)] = 17\%$ to $[1/(6+1)] = 14\%$, etc. Intuitively speaking, the intersection(s) between the increasing and the decreasing probability defines one or more Polya fixed points, at probability less than or equal to unity.

References

Arrow, K. (1962) "The Economic Implications of Learning by Doing", *Review of Economic Studies*, 29: 155–73.
Arthur, W. B. (1994) *Increasing Returns and Path Dependence in the Economy*, Ann Arbor, MI: Michigan University Press.
Bhaduri, A. and Marglin, S. (1990) "Unemployment and real wage: the economic basis for contesting political ideologies", *Cambridge Journal of Economics*, 14: 375–93.
Bharadwaj, K. (1989) "Marshall on Pigou's wealth and welfare", in *Themes in Value and Distribution*, Delhi: Oxford University Press, 159–75.
Blackburn, K. (1999) "Can stabilization policy reduce long-run growth?", *Economic Journal*, 109: 67–77.
Chakravarty, S. (1973) "Theory of development planning: an appraisal", in H. C. Bos, H. Linneman and P. de Wolff (eds), *Economic Structure and Development*, Amsterdam: North Holland.

David, P. A. (1985) "Clio and economics of QWERTY", *American Economic Review,* Papers and Proceedings, 75: 332–7.

Groenewegen, P. (1998) "Division of labour", in H. D. Kurz and N. Salvadori (eds), *The Elgar Companion to Classical Economics* (A to K), Cheltenham: Edward Elgar, 217–22.

Haken, H. (1978) *Synergetics,* New York: Springer-Verlag.

Kaldor, N. (1989a) "The case for regional policies", in F. Targetti and A. P. Thirlwall (eds), *The Essential Kaldor,* London: Duckworth, 311–26.

—— (1989b) "The irrelevance of equilibrium economics", in F. Targetti and A. P. Thirlwall (eds), *The Essential Kaldor,* London: Duckworth, 373–98.

—— (1989c) "The role of increasing returns, technical progress and cumulative causation in the theory of international trade and economic growth", in F. Targetti and A. P. Thirlwall (eds), *The Essential Kaldor,* London: Duckworth, 327–51.

—— (1989d) "What is wrong with economic theory", F. Targetti and A. P. Thirlwall (eds), *The Essential Kaldor,* London: Duckworth, 399–410.

Kalecki, M. (1971) "Determinants of profits", *Selected Essays on the Dynamics of the Capitalist Economy,* Cambridge, UK: Cambridge University Press, 78–92.

Keynes, J. M. (1936) *The General Theory of Employment, Interest and Money,* London: Macmillan.

Kindleberger, C. P. (1978) *Mania, Panics and Crashes,* New York: Basic Books.

Kurz, H. D. and Salvadori, N. (1998) "Endogenous growth models and the 'Classical' tradition", in *Understanding "Classical" Economics,* London: Routledge, 66–89.

Lucas, R. (1988) "On the mechanics of economic development", *Journal of Monetary Economics,* 22: 3–42.

Marshall, A. (1920) *Principles of Economics,* 8th edn appendix, London: Macmillan.

Myrdal, G. (1944) *An American Dilemma: The Negro Problem and Modern Democracy,* New York: Harper and Row.

—— (1957) *Economic Theory and Underdeveloped Regions,* London: Duckworth.

Nicolis, G. and Prigogine, I. (1977) *Self-Organization in Nonequilibrium Systems,* New York: John Wiley and Sons.

Pasinetti, L. L. (1959–60) "A mathematical formulation of the Ricardian system", *Review of Economic Studies,* 26: 78–98.

—— (2000) "Critique of neoclassical theory of growth and distribution", *Banca de Lavoro Quarterly Review,* 53: 383–432.

Petty, W. (1662) *A Treatise on Taxes and Contributions,* in C. H. Hull (ed.) (1899) *The Economic Writings of Sir William Petty,* Cambridge, UK: Cambridge University Press, Cambridge; reprinted New York: Augustus M. Kelly, 1963.

Ricardo, D. (1817) *Principles of Political Economy and Taxation,* in P. Sraffa (ed.) (1951) *Works and Correspondence of David Ricardo,* Vol. I, Cambridge, UK: Cambridge University Press.

Romer, P. (1986) "Increasing returns and long-run growth", *Journal of Political Economy,* 94: 1002–37.

Rosenstein-Rodan, P. N. (1943) "Problems of industrialization of Eastern and South-Eastern Europe", *Economic Journal,* 53: 202–11.

Schumpeter, J. A. (1942) *Capitalism, Socialism and Democracy,* 3rd edn, New York: Harper Brothers.

Smith, A. (1776) *An Inquiry into the Nature and Causes of the Wealth of Nations,* in R. H. Campbell, A. S. Skinner and W. B. Todd (eds) (1976) *The Glasgow Edition of the Works and Correspondence of Adam Smith*, Vol. 2, Oxford: Oxford University Press.

Solow, R. (1956) "A contribution to the theory of economic growth", *Quarterly Journal of Economics*, 70: 65–94.

Sraffa, P. (1926) "The laws of returns under competitive conditions", *Economic Journal*, 36: 535–50.

Steindl, J. (1952) *Maturity and Stagnation in American Capitalism*, 2nd edn, New York: Monthly Review Press.

Swan, T. (1956) "Economic growth and capital accumulation", *Economic Record*, 32: 343–61.

Usawa, H. (1965) "Optimum technical change in an aggregative model of economic growth", *International Economic Review*, 6: 18–31.

Weitzman, M. (1982) "Increasing returns and the foundations of unemployment theory", *Economic Journal*, 92: 787–804.

Young, A. (1928) "Increasing returns and economic progress", *Economic Journal*, 38: 527–42.

4 Endogenous growth in a stylised 'classical' model

Heinz D. Kurz and Neri Salvadori

Introduction

Interpreters from Adolph Lowe (1954) to Walter Eltis (1984) have stressed that economic growth and socio-economic development in the classical authors from Adam Smith to David Ricardo and Karl Marx were considered endogenous phenomena. In their writings, the behaviour of agents, their creativity and need for achievement and distinction, and social rules and institutions defined the confines within which the process of the production, distribution and use of social wealth unfolded. The concept of exogenous growth, as it was introduced by Gustav Cassel and then made central in Robert Solow's 1956 growth model, was totally extraneous to the way the classical economists thought. In their view the main problem the social sciences were confronted with consisted of the fact, in the words of Smith's teacher Adam Ferguson, that history is 'the result of human action, but not of human design'. What was needed was to come to grips, as best as one could, with the consequence of purposeful human actions, both intended and unintended.

In this essay we consider a very small and highly stylised aspect of the endogenous character of economic growth as envisaged by the classical authors. To keep the argument within limits, we set aside problems that cannot be dealt with in a short essay. In particular, we do not deal with the development aspect of economic growth, the technical, social, structural and institutional changes involved, the availability of an ever greater variety and quality of goods, the erosion of received patterns of consumption, of cultural styles and of social relations, and the establishment of new ones, and so forth. These themes play an important role in work of authors such as Smith and Marx. We also set aside analytical complications due to the factual intricacies of an ever more sophisticated system of the social division of labour and an ever more complex network of interdependent sectors of production.

The essay assumes essentially a one-sector economy in which 'corn' is produced by means of doses of labour-cum-capital, where capital consists only of corn and each dose of labour-cum-capital exhibits the same proportion of labour to corn. This means that labour-cum-capital can be treated as if it were a single factor of production. This bold simplification of the 'classical' approach to the problem of economic growth can only be justified if it does not misrepresent an important aspect of at least a variant of that approach. One generally engages in such simplifications only for heuristic reasons, and the heuristic perspective underlying this essay is to prepare the ground for a comparison with prominent contributions to the so-called 'new' growth literature (see Kurz and Salvadori 1996, 1998a, 1998b 1999, 2003).

Many of the models elaborated in the new growth literature are essentially one-sector models and know only a single capital good, just as our model does. By highlighting certain ideas found in the classical approach in the simplest form possible, we provide similes of some ideas found in modern contributions to growth theory. This allows us to raise the question, and provide elements of an answer to it, of continuity and change in growth theory from the classical to the modern authors. We believe that the stylised classical model elaborated in this essay following a well-known literature (see Kaldor 1955–6; Samuelson 1959; Pasinetti 1960), despite some valid criticisms that can be forwarded against it, is able to capture a number of elements of at least an important thread in classical thinking.

The following analysis will be exclusively *long period*. That is, attention will focus on positions of the economic system characterised, in competitive conditions, by a uniform rate of profit throughout the system, a uniform real wage rate, and a uniform rate of rent for each quality of land.

The composition of the chapter is as follows.

In the second section we outline the stylised 'classical' or rather Ricardesque theory of growth, and use Kaldor's well-known diagram to illustrate the endogeneity of the rate of growth. We deal both with the case in which the real wage is given and independent of the rate of growth of the workforce, and the case in which a higher rate of growth requires a higher real wage rate, reflecting a kind of Malthusian population dynamics. It is argued that the introduction of the latter does not affect the basic logic of the classical point of view, namely that in normal conditions the pace at which capital accumulates regulates the pace at which the labouring population grows. In other words, labour is considered as generated within the process of capital accumulation and economic growth.

The third section deals with neoclassical models of economic growth. It is first argued that for reasons that have partly to do with its analytical structure, which takes the initial endowments of the economy of 'factors of production' as given, the marginalist approach starts naturally from a long-term rate of growth that equals some exogenously given rate of growth of the factor(s) of production. This is exemplified in terms of the contributions of Alfred Marshall, Gustav Cassel and Robert Solow. Next, it is argued that the endogenisation of the growth rate in a class of models belonging to the so-called 'new' growth theory is carried out in a manner reminiscent of classical economics. While in the Solow growth model, for example, labour is treated as a non-producible and non-accumulable factor of production whose fixed rate of growth constrains the long-term expansion of the economic system, in some new growth models this factor is replaced by 'human capital' or 'knowledge', which are taken to be producible and even accumulable (or costlessly transferable among subsequent generations of the population). Very much like the classical assumption of a given real wage rate this is equivalent to the assumption that there is a mechanism generating 'labour'.

The final section contains some concluding remarks.

Endogenous growth in the 'classical' economists

Accumulation vis-à-vis diminishing returns in agriculture

We begin our discussion with a selection of some stylised analytical elements – and their interaction – that figure prominently in David Ricardo's work, and that are often considered to represent the building blocks of the classical position *tout court*. This invariably involves a bold reduction of the fascinating richness and diversity of classical analyses. It does not adequately represent Ricardo's much more analytically focused contribution to the problem under consideration. However, it captures some of the ideas that permeate much of his work, and this is one of the reasons why we embark on the following Ricardesque model.

The focus of our attention is on what Ricardo called the 'natural' course of the economy. By this he meant an economic system in which capital accumulates, the population grows, but there is no technical progress. Hence the argument is based on the (implicit) assumption that the set of (constant returns to scale) methods of production from which cost-minimising producers can choose is given and constant. Assuming the real wage rate of workers to be given and constant, the rate of profits is bound to fall. Due to extensive and intensive diminishing returns on land, 'with every increased portion of capital employed on it, there will be a decreased rate of production' (Ricardo [1817] 1951: 98).

Profits are viewed as a residual income based on the surplus product left after the used up means of production and the wage goods in the support of workers have been deducted from the social product (net of rents). The 'decreased rate of production' thus involves a decrease in profitability. On the premise that there are only negligible savings out of wages and rents, a falling rate of profits involves a falling rate of capital accumulation. Hence, as regards the dynamism of the economy, attention should focus on profitability. Assuming that the marginal propensity to accumulate out of profits, s, is given and constant, a 'classical' accumulation function can be formulated

$$g = \begin{cases} s(r - r_{min}) & \text{if } r \geq r_{min} \\ 0 & \text{if } r \leq r_{min} \end{cases}$$

where $r_{min} \geq 0$ is the minimum level of profitability which, if reached, will arrest accumulation (ibid.: 120). Ricardo's 'natural' course will necessarily end up in a stationary state.[1]

Clearly, in Ricardo the rate of accumulation is endogenously determined. The demand for labour is governed by the pace at which capital accumulates, whereas the long-term supply of labour is regulated by some 'Malthusian Law of Population'.[2]

Assuming for simplicity a given and constant real wage rate, Ricardo's view of the long-run relationship between profitability and accumulation and thus growth can be illustrated as in Figure 4.1 (see Kaldor 1956). The curve CEGH is the marginal productivity of labour-cum-capital; it is decreasing since land is scarce. When labour-cum-capital increases, either less fertile qualities of land must be cultivated or the same qualities of land must be cultivated with processes which require less land per unit of product, but are more costly in terms of labour-cum-capital. Let the real wage rate equal OW. Then, if the amount of labour-cum-capital applied is L_1, the area $OCEL_1$ gives the product, $OWDL_1$ gives total capital employed, and BCE total rent. Profits are determined as a residual and correspond to the rectangular WBED. As a consequence, the *rate* of profits can be determined as the ratio of the areas of two rectangles that have the same bases and, therefore, it equals the ratio WB/OW.

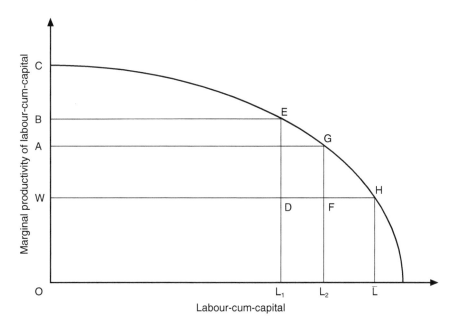

Figure 4.1 Land as an indispensable resource.

If in the course of capital accumulation and population growth the amount of labour-cum-capital rises to the level of L_2, then $OCGL_2$ gives the product, $OWFL_2$ the capital, ACG the rent and $WAGF$ profits. The rate of profit has fallen to WA/OW. Obviously, if a positive profit rate implies a positive growth rate (i.e. $r_{min} = 0$), the economy will expand until labour-cum-capital has reached the level $\bar{L}$. At that point, the profit rate is equal to zero and so is the growth rate. The system has come to a standstill; the engine of growth, profitability, has run out of steam.

In this bold simplification the required size of the workforce is considered as essentially generated by the accumulation process itself. In other words, labour power is treated as a kind of producible commodity. It differs from the other commodity, corn, in that it is not produced in a capitalistic way by a special industry on a par with the corn-growing sector, but is the result of the interplay between the generative behaviour of the working population and socio-economic conditions. In the most simple conceptualisation possible, labour power is seen to be in elastic supply at a given real (that is, corn) wage rate. Increasing the amount of corn available in the support of workers involves a proportional increase of the workforce.

In this view the rate of growth of labour supply adjusts to any given rate of growth of labour demand without necessitating a variation in the real wage rate.[3] Labour can thus place no limit on growth because it is 'generated' within the growth process itself. The only limit to growth can come from other non-accumulable factors of production. As Ricardo and others made clear, these factors are natural resources in general and land in particular. In other words, there is only endogenous growth in the classical economists. This growth is bound to lose momentum as the scarcity of natural resources makes itself felt in terms of extensive and intensive diminishing returns. (Technical change is of course seen to counteract these tendencies.)

The assumption of a given and constant real wage rate which is independent of the rate of growth of the demand for 'hands' can, of course, only be justified as a first step in terms of its simplicity. In fact, in some of his discussions with Thomas Robert Malthus, Ricardo appears to have adopted this assumption precisely for the sake of convenience. There is clear evidence that he did not consider it a stylised historical fact of long-term economic development. Reading his works, one gets the impression that the relationship between the expansion of the economic system as a whole and the wage and population dynamics is far from simple, and actually differs both between different countries in the same period and between different periods of the same country, depending on a variety of historical, cultural and institutional factors. For example, Ricardo stressed that 'population may be so little stimulated by ample wages as to increase at the slowest rate – or *it may even go in a retrograde direction*' (*Works*, VIII: 169, emphasis added). And in his *Notes on Malthus* he insisted that 'population and necessaries are not necessarily linked together so intimately'; 'better education and improved habits' may break the population mechanism (*Works*, II: 115).

However, we encounter also the following view expressed in his letter to Malthus of 18 December 1814:

> A diminution of the proportion of produce, in consequence of the accumulation of capital, does not fall wholly on the owner of stock, but is shared with him by the labourers. The whole amount of wages paid will be greater, but the portion paid to each man, will in all probability, be somewhat diminished.
>
> (*Works*, VI: 162–3)

In what follows, we formalise the idea that higher rates of capital accumulation, which presuppose higher rates of growth of the workforce, correspond to higher levels of the real wage rate.[4] We shall see that the basic logic of the argument which we have illustrated by means of the assumption of a fixed real wage rate remains essentially untouched: in normal conditions the pace at which capital accumulates regulates the pace at which labour grows.

Assume that higher growth rates of the labouring population require higher levels of the corn wage paid to workers. Higher wages, the usual argument goes, give workers and their families access to more abundant and better nutrition and medical services. This reduces infant mortality and increases the average length of life of workers. Let $(\bar{w})$ be the wage rate that must be paid in order to keep the labouring population stationary, and let $w = \bar{w}(1 + g)$ be the wage rate to be paid in order for the labouring population to grow at the rate g. Further, let the marginal productivity of labour-cum-capital (the CEGH curve of Figure 4.1) be the function $f(L)$. Then the rate of profits r turns out to be

$$r = \frac{f(L) - \bar{w}(1 + g)}{\bar{w}(1 + g)}.$$

Hence, on the simplifying assumption that $r_{\min} = 0$,

$$g = s \frac{f(L) - \bar{w}(1 + g)}{\bar{w}(1 + g)}.$$

from which we obtain a second degree equation in g:

$$\bar{w} g^2 + (1 + s) \bar{w} g - s[f(L) - \bar{w}] = 0,$$

which, for $f(L) > \bar{w}$, has a positive and a negative solution. The negative solution is insignificant from an economic point of view because it is less than -1 and would thus be associated with a negative real wage rate. The positive solution is

$$g = \frac{\sqrt{(1-s)^2\bar{w}^2 + 4sf(L)\bar{w}} - (1+s)\bar{w}}{2\bar{w}}.$$

The result of this simple exercise is that the WDFH curve (see Figure 4.2), which in Figure 4.1 was a horizontal straight line, becomes a decreasing curve:

$$\bar{w}(1+g) = \frac{\sqrt{(1-s)^2\bar{w}^2 + 4sf(L)\bar{w}} - (1-s)\bar{w}}{2}.$$

Note that if $f(L) > \bar{w}$, then $f(L) > \bar{w}(1+g) > \bar{w}$, whereas if $f(L) = \bar{w}$, then $f(L) = \bar{w}(1+g) = \bar{w}$. To conclude, the resulting modifications of Figure 4.1 do not change the substance of the 'classical' point of view expounded above.[5]

Production with land as a free good

We may now briefly turn to the hypothetical case in which the economy can grow without ever experiencing the constraint of scarce land(s). This amounts to setting land aside in Ricardo's doctrine, which might strike

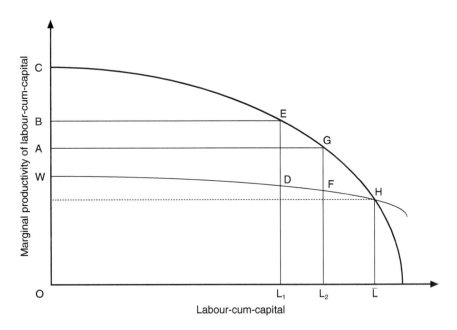

Figure 4.2 The wage rate as function of the growth rate.

the reader as something like *Hamlet* without the prince. However, Ricardo himself contemplated this case. In his letter to Malthus already referred to, he wrote:

> Accumulation of capital has a tendency to lower profits. Why? Because every accumulation is attended with increased difficulty in obtaining food, unless it is accompanied with improvements in agriculture, in which case it has no tendency to diminish profits. If there were no increased difficulty, profits would never fall, because there are no other limits to the profitable production of manufactures but the rise of wages. *If with every accumulation of capital we could tack a piece of fresh fertile land to our Island, profits would never fall.*
>
> (*Works*, VI: 162, emphasis added)

Similarly, in his letter to Malthus of 17 October 1815 he stated that

> [P]rofits do not *necessarily* fall with the increase of the quantity of capital because the demand for capital is infinite and is governed by the same law as population itself. They are both checked by the rise in the price of food, and the consequent increase in the value of labour. If there were no such rise, what could prevent population and capital from increasing without limit?
>
> (*Works*, VI: 301)

If land of the best quality were abundant (and its ownership sufficiently dispersed), it would be a free good. From an economic point of view, land can therefore be ignored like the air or the sunlight. Then the graph giving the marginal productivity of labour-cum-capital would be a horizontal line and, therefore, the rate of profits would be constant whatever the amount of labour-cum-capital. This case is illustrated in Figure 4.3. As a consequence, the growth rate would also be constant over time: the system could expand without end at a rate that equals the given rate of profits times the propensity to accumulate. As we have seen, Ricardo was perfectly aware of this implication.

In this case, if we take into account the possibility contemplated in the above that a higher rate of growth of the workforce might require a higher level of the real wage rate, then the WDF curve in Figure 4.3 would be higher, but it would still be a horizontal straight line below the CEG and above the WDF straight lines.

Production with a 'backstop technology'

However, to assume that there is no land at all, or that it is available in given quality and unlimited quantity, is unnecessarily restrictive. With the system growing without end, and setting aside land-saving technical

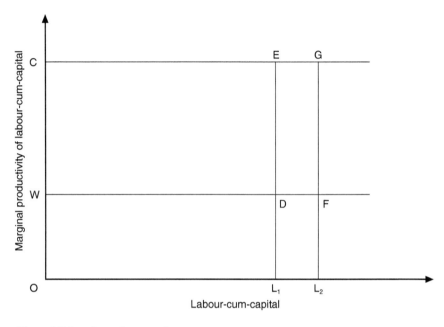

Figure 4.3 Land as a free good.

progress as contemplated by Ricardo (*Works* I, Chapter II; see also Gehrke *et al.* 2001), the point will surely come when land of the best quality will become scarce. This brings us to another constellation in which the rate of profits need not vanish as capital accumulates. The constellation under consideration bears a close resemblance to a case discussed in the economics of 'exhaustible' resources: the existence of an ultimate 'backstop technology'. For example, some exhaustible resources are used to produce energy. In addition, there is solar energy that may be considered a non-depletable resource. A technology based on the use of solar energy defines the backstop technology mentioned. Let us now translate this assumption into the context of a Ricardian model with land.

The case under consideration would correspond to a situation in which 'land', although useful in production, is not indispensable. In other words, there is a technology that allows the production of the commodity without any 'land' input; this is the backstop technology. With continuous substitutability between labour-cum-capital and land, the marginal productivity of labour-cum-capital would be continuously decreasing, but it would be bounded from below. This case is illustrated in Figure 4.4, with the dashed line giving the lower boundary. In this case, the profit rate and thus the growth rate would be falling, but they could never fall below certain – positive – levels. The system would grow indefinitely at a rate of growth which would asymptotically approach the product of the given

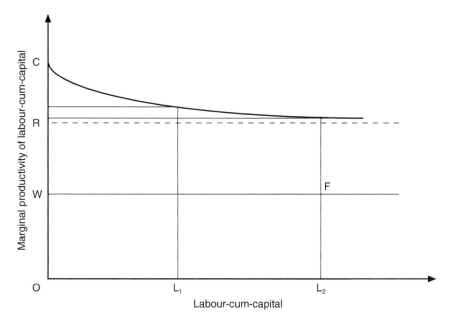

Figure 4.4 A backstop technology.

saving rate times the value of the (lower) boundary of the profit rate. In Figure 4.4 the latter is given by WR/OW.

Also in this case we may take into account the possibility contemplated in the above that a higher rate of growth of the work force might require a higher level of the real wage rate. In an expanding system the level of the real wage rate will therefore exceed the level required to keep the work force stationary. The WF curve that in Figure 4.4 is a horizontal straight line becomes a decreasing curve with the horizontal asymptote passing through the point

$$R' = \left(0, \frac{\sqrt{(1-s)^2 \bar{w}^2 + 4s\bar{w}\mathrm{OR}} + (1-s)\bar{w}}{2}\right).$$

not in the figure, where $\bar{w} < \mathrm{OR}' < \mathrm{OR}$ if and only if $\bar{w} < \mathrm{OR}$. The rate of profits would be bounded from below at a positive level.

To conclude, it must be stressed again that the Ricardesque paths of endogenous growth illustrated in Figures 4.1–4.4 depend on the fact that labour is considered as commodity that is (in some sense) 'produced' by means of corn and nothing else. In this conceptualisation the real wage rate is dealt with 'on the same footing as the fuel for the engines or the feed for the cattle', as an attentive interpreter of the classical economists remarked. Using neoclassical terminology, the straight line WF might be interpreted as the 'marginal cost function' related to the 'production' of labour. If the wage rate depends on the growth rate and thus on the amount of work employed, then the marginal cost function ceases to be a straight line.

However, this does not affect the substance of the argument. Put in a nutshell, the 'secret' of the endogeneity of growth in classical authors consists in the assumption that there is a built-in mechanism producing labour, where the rate of production is attuned to the needs of capital accumulation. In this way the *non*-accumulable factor 'labour' is deprived of the capacity to bring the growth process to a halt.

Classical and neo-classical approaches

Contributions to the classical theory of value and distribution, notwithstanding the many differences between authors, share a common feature: when investigating the relationship between the system of relative prices and income distribution, they start from the same set of data or independent variables. These are:

(C1):   the technical conditions of production of the various commodities;
(C2):   the size and composition of the social product;
(C3):   one of the distributive variables: either the wage rate or the rate of profits; and
(C4):   the available quantities of natural resources, in particular, land.

In correspondence with the underlying long-period competitive position of the economy, the capital stock is assumed to be fully adjusted to these data. Hence the 'normal' desired pattern of utilisation of plant and equipment would be realised, and a uniform rate of return on its supply price obtained.

This analytical structure is also reflected in the simple one-sector models presented in the previous section. Data (C1) and (C4) determine the curve which links the marginal productivity of labour-cum-capital to the amount of labour employed; data (C2) specifies a point on that curve; and, finally, data (C3) determines the distribution of the product. Once the latter is ascertained, growth is determined by the saving-alias-investment or accumulation function (in the case under consideration by equation $g = sr$).

By contrast, the marginalist theories of value and distribution typically start from the following data or independent variables:

(M1):   the set of technical alternatives from which cost-minimising producers can choose,
(M2):   the preferences of consumers, and

(M3): the initial endowments of the economy and the distribution of property rights among individual agents.

It is easily checked that (M1) is not very different from (C1), whereas (C2) could be thought of as reflecting (M2). What makes the two theories really different are the data (C3) and (M3). However, in the special case in which there is no labour in the economy – and therefore (C3) is automatically deleted because the rate of profits would be endogenously determined and could not be given from outside the system – (M3) would not be very different from (C4).

It will be shown that it is a characteristic feature of some of the most prominent contributions to the modern literature on endogenous growth that they eliminate labour from the picture and put in its stead 'human capital' or 'knowledge', that is something that a twentieth-century audience can accept as a producible (and accumulable) factor of production. However, the conditions of production of this *surrogate of labour* play exactly the same role played in the classical analysis by the assumption of a given real wage rate. This essay attempts first and foremost to provide a clear statement of this fact.

A theory based on the typical marginalist set of data (M1)–(M3) is hardly able to determine growth endogenously. It would presumably not be much of an exaggeration to claim that the majority of neoclassical authors have been concerned with developing theories that revolved around the concept of an *exogenously* given long-term rate of economic growth. It suffices to recall the efforts of some of the leading advocates of marginalism. Thus, in Chapter V of Book V of his *Principles of Economics*, Alfred Marshall first introduced the 'famous fiction of the stationary state' and then tried to weaken the strong assumptions required by it:

> The Stationary state has just been taken to be one in which population is stationary. But nearly all its distinctive features may be exhibited in a place where population and wealth are both growing, provided they are growing at about the same rate, and there is no scarcity of land: and provided also the methods of production and the conditions of trade change but little; and above all, where the character of man himself is a constant quantity. For in such a state by far the most important conditions of production and consumption, of exchange and distribution will remain of the same quality, and in the same general relations to one another, though they are all increasing in volume.
>
> ([1890] 1977: 306)

The resulting economic system grows at a constant rate that equals the exogenous rate of growth of population.[6] Income distribution and relative prices are the same as in the stationary economy. In modern parlance: the system expands along a steady-state growth path.

We encounter essentially the same idea in Gustav Cassel's *Theoretische Sozialökonomie* ([1918] 1932). The model of exogenous growth delineated by Cassel can be considered the proximate starting point of the development of neoclassical growth theory. In Chapter IV of Book I of the treatise, Cassel presented two models, one of a stationary economy, the other one of an economy growing along a steady-state path.

In his first model, Cassel assumed that there are z (primary) factors of production. The quantities of these resources and thus the amounts of services provided by them are taken to be in given supply. The n goods produced in the economy are pure consumption goods, that is there are no produced means of production or capital goods contemplated in the model. Goods are produced exclusively by combining primary factor services at fixed technical coefficients of production. There are as many single-product processes of production as there are goods to be produced; hence there is no choice of technique. General equilibrium is characterised by the following sets of equations: (1) equality of supply and demand for each factor service; (2) equality of the price of a good and its cost of production, that is the sum total of factor service payments incurred in its production, and thus the absence of what, in this literature, is called profit; (3) equality of supply and demand for each good produced, where the demand for each good is conceived as a function of the prices of all goods. The resulting sets of equations constitute what is known as the 'Walras–Cassel model' (Dorfman *et al.* 1958: 346). It satisfied the then going criterion of completeness: there are as many equations as there are unknowns to be ascertained.[7]

Cassel then turned to the model of a uniformly progressing economy (which he described only verbally). He introduced it as follows:

> We must now take into consideration the society which is progressing at a uniform rate. In it, the quantities of the factors of production which are available in each period ... are subject to a uniform increase. We shall represent by [g] the *fixed rate of this increase*, and of the uniform progress of the society generally.
>
> ([1918] 1932: 152, emphasis added)

In Cassel's view this generalisation to the case of an economy growing at an exogenously given and constant rate does not cause substantial problems. The previously developed set of equations can easily be adapted to it, 'so that the whole pricing problem is solved' (ibid.: 153). Cassel thus arrived at basically the same result as Marshall.

The method which marginalist economists, including those just mentioned, generally adopted up till the 1930s was the long-period method inherited from the classical authors. However, with their fundamentally different kind of analysis – demand and supply theory – they encountered formidable problems. These originated with their concept of capital. The sought determination of income distribution in terms of the demand for and the supply of the different factors of production – labour, land and capital – necessitated that they specify the capital endowment of the economy at a given point in time in terms of a 'quantity of capital' that could be ascertained independently of, and prior to, the determination of relative prices and the rate of profits.

Yet, as Erik Lindahl and others understood very well, this was possible only in the exceptionally special case of a corn model in which there was but a single capital good. In order to apply the demand and supply approach to all economic phenomena, neoclassical authors were thus compelled to abandon long-period analysis and develop in its stead intertemporal (and temporary) equilibrium analysis.

Here is not the place to enter into a detailed discussion of these developments (see, therefore, for example, Kurz and Salvadori 1995, Chapter 14). We rather jump several decades and turn immediately to the reasons for the recent resumption of (some special form of) long-period analysis in 'new' growth theory. Until a few decades ago, the number of commodities and, as a consequence, the time horizon in intertemporal general equilibrium theory was assumed to be finite and, therefore, arbitrary.

> The principal objection to the restriction to a finite number of goods is that it requires a finite horizon and there is no natural way to choose the final period. Moreover, since there will be terminal stocks in the final period there is no natural way to value them without contemplating future periods in which they will be used.
>
> (McKenzie 1987: 507)

The introduction of an *infinite* horizon turned out to be critical (see also Burgstaller 1994: 43–8). It pushed the analysis inevitably towards the long period, albeit only in the very special sense of *steady state*.[8] This was clearly spelled out, for instance, by Robert Lucas in a contribution to the theories of endogenous growth. He observed that

> [F]or *any* initial capital $K(0) > 0$, the optimal capital-consumption path $(K(t), c(t))$ will converge to the balanced path asymptotically. That is, the balanced path will be a good approximation to any actual path 'most' of the time [and that] this is exactly the reason why the balanced path is interesting to us.
>
> (1988: 11)

Lucas thus advocated a *(re-)switching* from an intertemporal analysis to a steady-state one. Since the balanced path of the intertemporal model is the only path analysed by Lucas, in the perspective under consideration the intertemporal model may be regarded simply as a step toward obtaining a rigorous steady-state setting.

Moreover, Lucas abandoned one of the characteristic features of all neoclassical theories, that is income distribution is determined by demand and supply of factors of production. If we concentrate on the balanced path, capital in the initial period *cannot* be taken as given along with other 'initial endowments'. Since distribution cannot be determined by demand and supply of capital and labour, in Lucas's model it is determined in the following way. Labour is considered the vehicle of 'human capital', that is a producible factor. Hence all factors are taken to be producible and the rate of profits is determined as in Chapter II of *Production of Commodities by Means of Commodities* (Sraffa 1960). At the beginning of that chapter (§§ 4–5), wages are regarded as entering the system 'on the same footing as the fuel for the engines or the feed for the cattle'. In this case the rate of profits and prices are determined by the socio-technical conditions of production alone – the 'methods of production and productive consumption' (Sraffa 1960: 3). The introduction of several alternative processes of production does not change the result.

The similarity between the determination of the rate of profit in Lucas' model and at the beginning of Chapter II of Sraffa's book is not surprising, since the assumption of a given real wage rate, put in a growth framework, is formally equivalent to the assumption that there is a technology producing 'labour'. The 'human capital' story could be seen as simply a rhetorical device to render the idea of a given real wage more palatable to modern scholars. As regards their basic analytical structure (as opposed to their building blocks), some of the so-called 'new' growth theories can therefore be said to exhibit a certain resemblance to 'classical' economics. In particular, in the free competition versions of the theory, the 'technology' to produce 'human capital' (or, alternatively, 'knowledge' in some approaches) plays the same role as the assumption of a given real wage rate in 'classical' economics.

From the end of Chapter II of *Production of Commodities by Means of Commodities* to the end of the book, workers may get a part of the surplus. As a consequence, the quantity of labour employed in each industry has to be represented explicitly, and the rate of profits and prices can be determined only if an extra equation determining income distribution is introduced into the analysis. The additional equation generally used by advocates of neoclassical analysis is the equality between the demand for and the supply of 'capital', which requires the homogeneity of this factor.[9] But no extra equation is required in the class of 'new' growth theories under consideration, since as in the Ricardo we dealt with here there is a mechanism attuning the size of the workforce – dubbed 'human capital' or 'knowledge' in the literature under consideration – to the requirements of an expanding economic system.

Concluding remarks

We have argued that in the classical economists economic growth and development of a nation were considered genuinely endogenous. This is exemplified with respect to a highly stylised version of one aspect encountered in the writings of the classical authors, especially Ricardo: the 'natural' course an economy would follow in the hypothetical case in which capital accumulates and the population grows but there is no technical change.

The respective argument is expounded in terms of a simple 'corn' model. In the constellation under consideration, decreasing returns will sooner or later make themselves felt due to the scarcity of land(s). With the real wage rate given and constant the rate of profits is bound to fall and the rents of land will increase. The falling tendency of the rate of profits entails a deceleration of capital accumulation and growth until the system comes to a standstill (setting aside depletable resources). Essentially the same holds true in the case in which a higher rate of growth of the workforce requires a higher real wage rate, reflecting some kind of Malthusian population mechanism. It is argued that the latter does not affect the basic logic of the classical point of view, namely that in the conditions contemplated, the pace at which capital accumulates regulates the pace at which the labouring population grows. In other words, labour is considered as generated within the process of capital accumulation and thus cannot bring growth to a halt. Growth might, however, be suffocated by the scarcity of natural resources, especially land.

Next we dealt briefly with neoclassical models of growth whose natural starting point was a system in which the long-term rate of growth equals some exogenously given rate of growth of the factor(s) of production. It is then argued that the endogenisation of the growth rate in a class of 'new' growth models is effected in a way that is reminiscent of classical economics. In the Solow model labour is treated as a non-producible and non-accumulable factor of production whose fixed rate of growth constrains the long-term expansion of the economic system. In contradistinction, in some new growth models this factor is replaced by 'human capital' or 'knowledge', which are taken to be producible, accumulable or costlessly transferable among subsequent generations of the population. Very much like the classical assumption of a given real wage rate this is equivalent to the assumption that there is a mechanism generating 'labour'.

Acknowledgements

This chapter uses some of the material contained in earlier papers by us on the so-called 'new' growth theory; see, in particular, Kurz and Salvadori (1996, 1998a, 1998b, 1999). We thank Christian Gehrke, Mark Knell and Rodolfo Signorino for useful comments.

Notes

1 This path must, of course, not be identified with the *actual* path the economy is taking because technical progress will repeatedly offset the impact of the 'niggardliness of nature' on the rate of profits.

2 Real wages may rise, that is the 'market price of labour' may rise above the 'natural' wage rate. This is the case in a situation in which capital accumulates rapidly, leading to an excess demand for labour. As Ricardo put it, 'notwithstanding the tendency of wages to conform to their natural rate, their market rate may, in an improving society, *for an indefinite period,* be constantly above it' (ibid.: 94–5, emphasis added). If such a constellation prevails for some time it is even possible that 'custom renders absolute necessaries' what in the past had been comforts or luxuries. Hence, the natural wage is driven upward by persistently high levels of the actual wage rate. Accordingly, the concept of 'natural wage' in Ricardo is a flexible one and must not be mistaken for a physiological subsistence minimum. See Stirati (1994) and Kurz and Salvadori (1995, ch. 15).

3 In the more sophisticated conceptualisations underlying the arguments of Smith and Ricardo, higher rates of growth of labour supply presuppose higher levels of the real wage rate. But as we shall see below, the basic logic remains the same: in normal conditions the pace at which capital accumulates regulates the pace at which labour grows.

4 The parallel tendency of the rate of profits and the real wage rate to fall contemplated in the cited passage has recently gained some prominence in the so-called 'New View' of the long-run trend of wages. See, in particular, Hicks and Hollander (1977). These interpreters of Ricardo (and of the classical economists at large) feel entitled to superimpose onto Ricardo's analysis the marginalist concept of a 'labour market', conceived of in the conventional way in terms of the confrontation of a demand and a supply function. It should be noted, however, that this concept is extraneous to classical thinking.

5 If $r_{\min} > 0$, then

$$\bar{w}(1+g) = \frac{\sqrt{[1 - s(1 + r_{\min})]^2 \bar{w}^2 + 4sf(L)\bar{w}} + [1 - s(1 + r_{\min})]\bar{w}}{2\bar{w}}$$

6 It should be noted that Marshal saw reason to suppose that the growth of population depended, among other things, on socio-economic factors and thus could not sensibly be treated, other than in a first step of the analysis, as exogenous ([1890] 1977, Book IV, Chapter IV).

7 The approach to the theory of general equilibrium in terms of equations was criticised by Knut Wicksell, Hans Neisser, Heinrich von Stackelberg, Frederick Zeuthen, Karl Schlesinger and Abraham Wald, and led to the development of the neoclassical theory of general equilibrium in terms of *in*equalities coupled with the introduction of the Rule of Free Goods (or free disposal assumption); see Kurz and Salvadori (1995, Chapter 13, Section 7).

8 It should be stressed that, contrary to some neoclassical interpreters, in the classical economists the long-period method was not limited to steady states. Indeed, in their analyses (as well as in early marginalist authors such as Knut Wicksell, who still shared to a considerable extent the concerns of the classical economists) the steady state played no essential role whatsoever. See on this the penetrating study of Garegnani (1976).

9 This is the famous critique of that theory put forward in the 1960s; for a review of that critique, see, for example, Kurz and Salvadori (1995, Chapter 14).

References

Burgstaller, A. (1994) *Property and Prices. Toward a Unified Theory of Value*, Cambridge: Cambridge University Press.

Cassel, G. (1932) *The Theory of Social Economy*, revised English translation of the 5th German edition of Cassel (1918), *Theoretische Sozialökonomie*, by L. Barron, New York: Harcourt Brace.

Dorfman, R., Samuelson, P. A. and Solow, R. M. (1958) *Linear Programming and Economic Analysis*, New York, Toronto and London: McGraw-Hill.

Eltis, W. (1984) *The Classical Theory of Economic Growth*, London: Macmillan.

Garegnani, P. (1976) 'On a Change in the Notion of Equilibrium in Recent Work on Value and Distribution', in M. Brown, K. Sato and P. Zarembka (eds), *Essays in Modern Capital Theory*, Amsterdam: North Holland.

Gehrke, C., Kurz, H. D. and Salvadori, N. (2003) 'Ricardo on agricultural improvements: A note', *Scottish Journal of Political Economy*, 50: 291–6.

Hicks, J. and Hollander, S. (1977) 'Mr. Ricardo and the Moderns', *Quarterly Journal of Economics*, 91: 351–69.

Kaldor, N. (1955–6) 'Alternative Theories of Distribution', *Review of Economic Studies*, 23: 83–100.

Kurz, H. D. and Salvadori, N. (1995) *Theory of Production. A Long-period Analysis*, Cambridge, Melbourne and New York: Cambridge University Press.

Kurz, H. D. and Salvadori, N. (1996) 'In the Beginning All the World Was Australia...', in M. Sawyer (ed.), *Festschrift in honour of G. C. Harcourt*, London: Routledge, vol. II: 425–43.

Kurz, H. D. and Salvadori, N. (1998a) 'The "New" Growth Theory: Old Wine in New Goatskins", in Coricelli, F., Di Matteo, M. and Hahn, F. H. (eds), *New Theories in Growth and Development*, London: Macmillan and New York: St. Martin's Press, 63–94.

Kurz, H. D. and Salvadori, N. (1998b) ' "Endogenous" Growth Models and the "Classical" Tradition', in Kurz, H. D. and Salvadori, N. (eds) *Understanding 'Classical' Economics*, London: Routledge, pp. 68–89.

Kurz, H. D. and Salvadori, N. (1999) 'Theories of "Endogenous" Growth in Historical Perspective', in Sertel, M. R. (ed.), *Contemporary Economic Issues. Proceedings of the Eleventh World Congress of the International Economic Association, Tunis. Volume 4, Economic Behaviour and Design*, London: Macmillan and New York: St. Martin's Press, 225–61

Kurz, H. D. and Salvadori, N. (2003) "Theories of Economic Growth – Old and New", in Salvadori, N. (ed.), *The Theory of Economic Growth: A 'Classical' Perspective*, Cheltenham: Edward Elgar: 1–22.

Lowe, A. (1954) 'The Classical Theory of Growth', *Social Research*, 21: 127–58.

Lucas, R. E. (1988) 'On the Mechanisms of Economic Development', *Journal of Monetary Economics*, 22: 3–42.

McKenzie, L. W. (1987) "General Equilibrium", *The New Palgrave. A Dictionary of Economics*, edited by J. Eatwell, Newman, P. and Milgate, M. London: Macmillan, vol. 2, pp. 498–512.

Marshall, A. (1977) *Principles of Economics*, reprint of the 8th edn (1920), 1st edition 1890, London and Basingstoke: Macmillan.

Pasinetti, L. L. (1960) "A Mathematical Formulation of the Ricardian System", *Review of Economic Studies*, 27, pp. 78–98.

Ricardo, D. [1817] (1951–72) *The Works and Correspondence of David Ricardo*, edited by Piero Sraffa with the collaboration of M. H. Dobb, Vols I, II, VI and VIII, Cambridge: Cambridge University Press.

Samuelson, P. A. (1959) "A Modern Treatment of the Ricardian Economy: I. The Pricing of Goods and of Labor and Land Services; II. Capital and Interest Aspects of the Pricing Process", *Quarterly Journal of Economics*, 73, pp. 1–35; 79, pp. 217–31.

Solow, R. M. (1956) 'A Contribution to the Theory of Economic Growth', *Quarterly Journal of Economics*, 70: 65–94.

Sraffa, P. (1960) *Production of Commodities by Means of Commodities*, Cambridge: Cambridge University Press.

Stirati, A. (1994) *The Theory of Wages in Classical Economics: A Study of Adam Smith, David Ricardo, and their Contemporaries*, Aldershot: E. Elgar.

5 Aspects of German monetary and development economics and their reception in Japan

Richard A. Werner

Directed credit and economic development

Following empirical work by Goldsmith (1969) and McKinnon (1973), an increasing body of evidence about a positive link between finance and growth has been accumulated in the past decade or so by, among others,[1] Gertler and Rose (1991), King and Levine (1992, 1993), and Roubini and Sala-i-Martin (1992). There has also been progress in the development of economic theories that might justify these empirical facts.[2]

Meanwhile, the role of government intervention is also the focus of a lively debate in development economics. A growing literature has pointed out that when certain assumptions (especially of perfect information) are relaxed, there may be scope for government intervention. Combined with externalities and the role of public goods, there is now a considerable body of literature that allows for a useful role of the government in economic development (Stiglitz and Uy 1996; World Bank 1997). Specifically, there is increasing evidence that government intervention in financial markets contributed to the successful performance of the Japanese and other East Asian economies.

The best-known example is the World Bank's (1993) 'East Asian Miracle' report, which concluded that 'credit policies', including directed credit by governmental institutions, were a major factor in the Asian economic miracle. Wade (1990) has argued that credit allocation was an important factor in Taiwanese post-war success. Calder (1993) has emphasized the importance of credit policies and credit allocation in post-war Japanese economic development. Directed credit has also played an important role in the development of India (Werner 2000a). Other countries that have engaged in credit-allocation policies include Indonesia, Malaysia, and Thailand.[3]

Cho and Hellmann (1993) have singled out the credit policies in Japan and Korea in terms of effectiveness. They argue that government-led credit allocation in these countries helped overcome pervasive market imperfections within a suitably designed institutional setting.[4]

Despite this evidence, the view remains widespread that government intervention in financial markets is unlikely to enhance welfare. One reason is the particular set of assumptions under which the competitive economy has been shown to be efficient in neoclassical theoretical models. They define an economy where interventions, such as by the government, cannot but reduce efficiency. As a result, economists, as well as international development organizations, have remained reluctant to endorse policies to direct credit (Vogel and Adams 1997; Noland and Pack 2001; Asian Development Bank 2002). Yet, was it really *despite* government intervention in the financial markets that Japan and other East Asian countries developed so successfully that the IMF described their 'record growth and strong trade performance' as 'unprecedented, a remarkable historical achievement' (Fischer 1998: 1)?

This essay proposes to employ an empirical methodology to contribute to the debate concerning this issue. Since agents tend to exhibit a certain degree of rationality, the revealed preference of policy makers to introduce directed credit policies in Japan at some point in the past can be seen as an indicator that those who introduced it have had specific reasons, and specific reasoning that led to their course of action. It is thus the purpose of this essay to explore the historical roots of credit-direction policies in Japan and attempt to identify their historical role and rationale.

Directed credit in postwar Japanese practice

In this essay, I am primarily interested in the strongest form of directed credit policies, namely those imposed by the central bank on much of the banking sector. These have become known under various names such as the 'credit planning scheme' in Thailand (Werner 2000b), or 'window guidance' in Korea and Japan. Such credit controls are usually employed in a dual function, namely to support the implementation of monetary policy – the quantitative aspect – and to support the allocation of resources – the qualitative aspect (Goodhart 1989). In this essay I am primarily concerned with the latter function.

What follows is a brief sketch of the key features of Japanese window guidance in the post-war era. This credit guidance consisted of regular meetings between the central bank and private-sector banks, during which the Bank of Japan essentially told the private banks on a quarterly basis by how much they were to increase their lending. The 'guidance' not only determined the total amount of loan growth in the banking system, but also intervened in its allocation among various sectors of the economy.[5] Banks always had to receive approval for the lending plans, and the central bank's Banking Department used the threat of sanctions, such as reduced loan growth quotas, to keep the banks' 'plans' identical with its own.

All loans were broken down not only into sectors (such as loans to individuals, wholesale/retail, real estate, construction) and more detailed subsectors (iron and steel, chemicals, etc.), but also by size of company (small and medium-sized businesses vs. large businesses) and by use (equipment funds, working funds).[6] All large-scale borrowers had to be listed by name.

This information on the receivers of bank loans was used to direct credit to preferred industries that had been indicated as being 'priority', or could be expected to yield a high value added. Banks were punished for over or undershooting their loan growth quotas. Compliance was assured by the monopoly power of the central bank to impose sanctions and penalties, such as cutting rediscount quotas, applying unfavourable conditions to its transactions with individual banks, or reducing window guidance quotas.[7] All these would cost banks dearly. In order not to fall behind the competition, they had no choice but to always meet their quotas. Contemporary researchers therefore concluded that window guidance was always implemented by the banks.[8]

The roots of the postwar window guidance credit policies can be traced to the early post-war era, where they were intrinsically linked to a specific person – namely Bank of Japan governor Hisato Ichimada (governor from 1946 to 1954). Governor Ichimada took a keen interest in the direction of credit. He not only engaged in directing credit to certain sectors of the economy, but also often personally decided whether a project should go ahead or not.[9] Ichimada quickly became feared and his infallible decisions over the life or death of a business project earned him a nickname – his successor as governor and close associate, Tadashi Sasaki, explained that 'he was called "pope", because under him the central bank's power was stronger than that of the government' (Nihon Keizai Shinbun, 1984, p. 3).

Where did the practice of window guidance at the Bank of Japan under governor Ichimada originate from? There is no such record of credit direction policies before the war. However, there are records of their existence in the 1920s – not in Japan, but instead in Germany. There is also evidence that governor Ichimida was personally trained in the practice of the German credit direction policies during his early years at the Bank of Japan, when he was sent to Germany. It is therefore useful next to consider the German practice and theory of credit direction and then to return to the question of their introduction into Japan.

German theory and practice

German experience with credit direction in the 1920s and 1930s

Under pressure from the victorious allies of World War I, the Reichsbank Law was changed in 1922, and the central bank was made independent from and unaccountable to any German institution including the democratically elected government and parliament.[10] At the time, the law was unprecedented.[11] The Reichsbank used its legal status to exert extra-legal control over the banking sector. Between 1924 and 1931, the Reichsbank, mainly under its President Dr. Hjalmar Schacht (1924–30), provided strict 'guidance' to the banks about their loan extension. The discount rate was still announced, but it had become more of a public relations tool, aimed at distracting from the true control tool, the credit 'guidance' (Mueller 1973).

The procedure contained both quantitative and qualitative elements. First, each bank had to apply to the central bank for its 'loan contingent', or 'credit quota' (*Kreditrahmen*) for the coming period. The banks then proceeded to allocate their contingents among lenders. Once the contingent was used up, the central bank would refuse to discount any further bills presented by that bank and would punish further credit expansions (Dalberg 1926). Since there was no legal basis for these credit controls, the Reichsbank relied on 'moral suasion', that is informal administrative pressure under the threat of sanctions that could be highly costly for the banks. One internal Reichsbank memo of 1924 notes that the central bank wields 'substantial means of exerting pressure' which 'it will not hesitate to employ'.[12]

It was only a small step further to give the banks detailed instructions about the sectoral, regional and otherwise qualitative allocation of their credits. Reichsbank President Schacht made ample use of this power.[13] The banks' sectoral allocation of loans was closely monitored and informal pressure used to direct credit into desired sectors, while suppressing it to undesirable ones.

Schacht engaged in a policy of far-reaching structural reform, favouring certain regions, sectors and institutions. The principle was to encourage credit extension for 'productive' purposes, and discourage that for others. Schacht favoured the agricultural sector, large cartels and export-oriented firms (Mueller 1973). Moreover, Schacht was an outspoken supporter of 'rationalization', a movement that gained significance during the 1920s (and today would be referred to as 'corporate restructuring' and 'structural reform'). This implied forcing many firms into bankruptcy, a process that Schacht expected to have a positive, cleansing effect on the economy. Among the sectors that were not considered priority was credit for consumption or social welfare facilities – 'loans for luxury' (Peterson 1954: 71), and margin loans that he thought fuelled stock-market speculation.

Schacht was not shy to summon top bank executives personally to give them instructions. For effect, this was combined with the threat of cutting off banks from central bank funding if they were not to comply.[14] Moreover, the Reichsbank monitored to what extent its credit was used by banks to purchase foreign currency. Reichsbank credit was not to be used to purchase foreign currency that was not 'economically justified'.[15]

Commentators noted that 'many injustices and disagreements about the details are unavoidable' (Dalberg 1926: 72). Many observers argued that, in a democracy, such vital decisions should only be made by parliament and the elected government. Based on the far-reaching influence of his credit controls, contemporaries recognized in him a 'credit dictator' or 'economic dictator'. They called the Reichsbank Germany's 'second government', since it engaged in resource-allocation decisions that reshaped the economic structure – normally something only elected governments would engage in (Mueller 1973).

The noticeable public outcry against Schacht by critics is evidence of the effectiveness of his credit controls. Even Schacht himself spoke of 'dictatorial measures' when referring to his intervention in the credit market in 1924.[16] Mueller concluded: 'His credit re-allocation policy was an active, inter-sectoral structural economic policy, agricultural policy, cartel policy, etc., for which only a government that has been legitimized by parliament is responsible, but not the Reichsbank' (1973: 59).

In 1930, the government published an evaluation of the credit supply of industry and commerce in Germany.[17] This included detailed statistics of bank credit, broken down by industrial sector of the borrower.[18] Industrial activity was divided into 39 industrial sectors. Another, similarly comprehensive study of the sectoral breakdown of bank credit was published in 1934 by the Reichsbank itself.[19]

The quantitative and qualitative controls continued in the later 1930s, as the Reichsbank obtained expanded legal powers to 'guide' bank credit. These included exchange controls that could be used to allocate credit mainly to priority and export-oriented industries. The 1935 banking law (*Reichsgesetz ueber das Kreditwesen*) required banks to regularly disclose to the newly created banking supervisory authority (*Aufsichtsamt fuer das Kreditwesen*) details of the names of the debtors receiving large-scale loans.[20] It was headed by the Reichskommissar fuer das Kreditwesen – who happened to be the President of the Reichsbank (Hjalmar Schacht).[21]

At the same time, fund-raising via the stock market or capital markets in general was severely restricted. As a result, there were few avenues by which companies could escape from the resource transfer and sectoral transformation effected by the direction of credit.[22] It is noteworthy that the banking law of 1934/35 remained in place with few changes after 1945 and, according to James, 'contributed to give shape and direction to postwar German development' (1998: 65).

Theoretical rationale of the direction of credit

Dr Schacht was a trained economist. What was his theoretical rationale for the introduction of credit 'guidance'? There may have been practical reasons: while the Reichsbank maintained the official façade of using reserve requirements and the official discount rate, in reality neither was very effective. The discount rate or short-term interest rates were not necessarily related to economic activity. And the reserve requirements were too blunt a tool to be used strictly. Therefore one rationale for the introduction of credit guidance was simply as a tool for monetary-policy implementation. This concerns the quantitative aspect of credit guidance.

The direction of credit in a qualitative sense was also of theoretical and practical importance. Although James argues that Schacht had no 'coherent concept' for the future path of Reichsbank policies (1998: 85), he also points out that the theory behind Reichsbank policies was the real bills doctrine or the banking-school view, which he believes was dominant in Germany.[23] He also sees 'variants' of the real bills doctrine, and scepticism about quantity theories, as the consistent theoretical underpinning of Schacht's policies (1998: 85). The latter seems to be the more accurate assessment.

It was a common proposition that can be traced to Mueller (1809), who recognized the problem of credit rationing. Already before the First World War, German economists demanded the establishment of a 'financial general staff' and an 'economic general staff' to work together with the military general staff towards mobilizing resources in order to maximize growth (Riesser 1906, 1913). Schumpeter's 1911 work on the link between credit and growth must also be understood as a contribution to the German mainstream.[24] During the war, credit was directed via the Reichsbank, as well as the public *Reichskassen* and *Kriegsdarlehnskassen.* National mobilization during World War I provided an impetus to the theories of directed credit.

Schacht, in line with his fellow German monetary and development economists, favoured a variant of the real bills doctrine, which argued that the extension of credit to produce new products with a higher value added could not be inflationary, since both credit and the amount of goods increased. In order to ensure that credit was not used 'unproductively', and to maximize growth, the German writers recommended the direction of credit by the authorities.[25] This was often simply referred to as *Kreditpolitik.*[26] Unproductive uses including 'speculation', that is the use of bank credit to make purely financial investments, were to be avoided. The theories that proposed directed credit all at the same time discouraged the use of the equity or capital markets and instead favoured a bank-centred economic system. One reason was that it was organizationally far more complex to direct the flows of funds in the capital markets.

Thus, an important contribution of the work of this German school of thought is the formulation of an argument to justify intervention in the credit market with the specific aim of allocating credit to high value-added sectors of the economy. Their models and theories may appear of little value from the viewpoint of classical or new classical economics. However, this is not the case when restrictive assumptions about perfect information and competition are relaxed. Thus their research and policy programme has found new support in the modern literature on imperfect information and externalities and thus remains under-appreciated in its insights.

Direction of credit as part of German monetary and development economics

At the same time, credit-direction policies must be understood as one constituent component of a broader agenda. Unlike classical British economists, German economists had mainly been concerned with the problem of economic growth and how to enhance it.

Gustav Schmoller, a leading figure of the German Historical School, was one of Schacht's teachers during his economics studies. By Schacht's own assessment, Schmoller was one of the men who had a significant influence on me then (1953: 117). Schacht wrote his PhD thesis about mercantilism and took a position similar to List's.

German economists had already recognized the importance of increasing returns to scale (Rathenau 1906), imperfect competition, incomplete markets, externalities and resulting coordination problems. They therefore argued for a greater use of large-scale industry to enhance overall economic growth as well as government intervention (Rathenau 1917a). However, government intervention was not to take the form of micromanagement as in a command economy, but the 'guidance' of credit, as discussed above, and institutional design of the provision of incentives within a market-based environment.

Walther Rathenau presented his ideas about how to efficiently organize the raw-material industry (e.g. 1915) to the authorities who recognized their potential, and was duly put in charge of raw material supplies during the First World War. Meanwhile, Rathenau became aware of the developmental advantages of a third way between private capitalism and a command economy. Already during the war he concluded that also the peace-time 'economy, which is based on the existence and cooperation of everybody, can no longer be the private matter of the individual'. He felt that the war collectivism taught the world in years what would otherwise have taken centuries to develop (Rathenau 1917b: 77, 82).

Rathenau recognized the depersonalization of ownership of large firms, its separation from control and its economic implications. He also saw that enterprises had developed already or would develop into bureaucracies that resemble the state in character (1917b). He realized that empowering managers and reducing the power of shareholders would enhance economic growth, while their actions could be coordinated top-down for national interests.[27] Rathenau's wartime associate von Moellendorff (1916) emphasized the parallels between the war economy and the medieval corporate system of trade and craft guilds, which had brought Germany prosperity in the past. He felt it could do so also in the future, if it was replaced by a modern version of large-scale businesses in cartelized and hierarchical long-term relationships. Thus the organization of each industry in business associations that operated like cartels became a key tool to guide the overall economy. Cartels had already become important before the First World War, but their role increased once their potential as a tool for economic 'guidance' from above was recognized.[28] These ideas converged with the proposals by the advocates of a 'defence economy' and the establishment of a peace-time 'economic general staff'.

Rathenau's ideas were strengthened by the success of his wartime system of cooperation between managers and government planners. After the war, he developed a proposal for the ideal economic system of the future (Rathenau 1919a, 1919b, 1919c). He calls for a just, egalitarian distribution of national income and wealth and a large-scale educational programme for the masses.[29] Rathenau's and von Moellendorff's thought was in line with earlier thinking of German development economists, and thus was quickly assimilated and advanced by others over the following two decades.

Spann (1921) and Sombart (1934), among others, also argued that private-sector trade associations, as the successors of the medieval guilds, could be used to enhance overall welfare as well for the transmission of government control. This would reduce the administrative burden, as the associations would to a great extent impose self-control according to the wishes of the bureaucrats in the various sectors. Others argued that 'Prussian state socialism' had already demonstrated that a large public sector could operate efficiently without the private profit motive.

However, few German development economists proposed the abolition of private property or nationalization, as demanded by communism or socialism. Most considered indirect state control and 'guidance' of the economy preferable to nationalization. They were aware that private incentives had to be utilized for the collective effort. Indeed, it was thought that mere economic 'guidance' by bureaucrats amounted to a more effective 'nationalization of economic life, not by expropriation but by legislation' (Spengler 1920).

Modern literature recognizes that, once assumptions such as perfect information and efficient markets are relaxed, there is no guarantee that markets left to their own devices will produce socially optimal results. By focusing on mutually beneficial cooperation and coordination, the German development economists proposed what today would be called devices for internalizing externalities, minimizing information costs and motivating individuals. Concerning the latter, it can be said in modern terminology that they recognized that 'utility functions' are inter-dependent, agents compete in hierarchical fashion and have a common desire for justice and fairness of organizational arrangements.[30]

Credit direction as core of the institutional design

Thanks to Schacht's rationalization drive, industrial concentration and the number of cartels increased steadily over the 1920s, while the top-down direction of credit strengthened the role of banks in this system.

During the 1930s, laws to restrict dividends discouraged equity finance. This, as well as increased cross-shareholdings, strengthened the position of managers vis-à-vis shareholders. As Rathenau had recognized, this was efficient from a social-welfare perspective, since the goals of managers were more in line with the overall goal of maximizing growth, and, through the industry associations, they could be used to transmit the 'guidance' of the authorities. By the late 1930s and early 1940s, industry-control associations (*Wirtschaftsgruppen, Fachgruppen*) served as the conduits for the top-down 'guidance' of the 'guided economy' (*gelenkte Wirtschaft*). The direction of credit was at the centre of an overall consistent institutional design that included the labour market, financial markets and corporate governance.

Schwenk (1937) synthesizes the theories of a growth-oriented, bank-centred economy with directed credit at its heart. Although credit coordination is arbitrary, it can ensure that money is put to productive use and to make investments that are publicly desired, while undesirable projects can be prevented. Schwenk argues that the information provided by credit data should be used by the government to assess the condition of the economy. Thus banks should be made to report regularly to the central bank about the use of credit. By contrast, internal finance and equity finance do not immediately allow the central bank or the authorities to monitor or control the use of funds, while they provide a preferable incentive structure to firms, compared with debt finance. A bank-centred economic system was thus more in line with German development economics.

How could the German economists give such advice that, in the light of the most recent theories, appears advanced? The answer must be found in its methodological outlook, which was grounded in inductivism and empiricism, instead of the theoretical and axiomatic deductivism favoured by classical literature. This had the drawback of producing theories that, to classical economists at least, did not appear rigorous or general enough to be taken seriously as 'theory'.[31] It had the advantage over classical theories, however, of delivering results that are more robust outside a restricted theoretical environment.

Influence on Japan

Japanese economists and government bureaucrats were following events in Germany closely, including the Reichsbank's policy of directed credit. Officials were regularly dispatched to Berlin, where they were based in the Japanese embassy, not far from the Reichsbank. The Japanese visitors quickly realized the potential offered by directed credit policies. In January 1923, a young Japanese central banker was assigned to the London branch of the Bank of Japan, to be posted in Berlin. The 31-year-old Hisato Ichimada was to stay until June 1926. The purpose of his stay was to study the Reichsbank's monetary policy and its implementation. The period of his stay coincided with Schacht's ascendancy to the 'credit dictatorship'.

Ichimada was in many ways deeply impressed by the experience. 'What left the strongest impression on me in Germany was central bank President Schacht', he informs us in his memoirs (1986: 38). Despite his young age, he personally became acquainted with the great credit dictator. Hints in his speeches – let alone his later policies – are suggestive that he regarded Schacht and his highly independent Reichsbank as a role model for the Bank of Japan. According to Ichimada, he visited Schacht in his office several times and each time was greeted 'with open arms' and engaged in 'a frank exchange of opinions on the state of the German economy' (1986: 38). It appears that his relationship with Schacht was more than superficial, and the two seemed to get along well; shortly after the end of the war, when Ichimada had become Bank of Japan governor, Schacht visited his Japanese acquaintance (although Schacht could not stay long, as Ichimada lamented, since he was about to be investigated by the war-crimes tribunal in Germany).[32]

After Ichimada's return to Japan, he was transferred to various posts at the central bank, including the banking department, where the central bank dealt directly with the banks. Meanwhile, the political leadership increasingly moved the Japanese economy on a war footing. With the beginning of open hostilities in China in 1937, various emergency measures and laws were passed, including a law that would allow precisely the type of credit control and allocation in which Schacht had engaged: The 1937 'Temporary Funds Adjustment Law' allowed the central bank and the Ministry of Finance to intervene in virtually all financial transactions. Funding through the stock market was reduced to a trickle and the banking system was relied upon for resource allocation, laying the foundation for the postwar bank-based financial system.

To simplify the credit guidance regime, the number of banks was drastically reduced, from about 1,400 by the end of the 1920s to merely sixty-four by the end of the Second World War. Similar to the 'control associations' in various industries, the banks were organized in so-called 'financial control associations', under the umbrella of the National Financial Control Association. As in other industries, it stayed in place in the postwar era, as the Japan Bankers' Association.

During the war, Ichimada was the secretary-general of Japan's Financial Control Association, which was created in 1942 and was operated by the Bank of Japan (BoJ). Its job was to do whatever it took to provide the priority industries with funds. This included arranging loan syndications, bank mergers, injections of BoJ funds and, most of all, the direction of credit – called *Yuushi Assen* (Loan Coordination) at the time. Just before the end of the war, Ichimada became head of the newly created and short-lived Control Department, which directed credit to large companies.[33]

The Bank of Japan acted as the control centre of the direction of credit. Its governor headed the National Financial Control Association, which was operated by the BoJ and implemented the resource-allocation plans worked out by the Planning Board. The plan was structured on a top-down basis. First, the needed output was decided upon. Then a hierarchy of manufacturers, sub-contractors and raw-material importers was determined. The banks were then required to ensure that purchasing power was made available for all the firms involved to be able to acquire the inputs into their production process. Finally, the central bank ensured that they would have sufficient resources, and direct credit appropriately. The basis for the direction of credit were detailed statistics that the banks were required to report. A detailed sectoral breakdown of bank credit has been published since 1942, when the programme of directed credit was fully implemented for the first time.

Thanks to bank credit controls, resources could be allocated to industries of strategic importance – during the war it was the munitions industry and in the postwar era the export sector. Based on plans for the overall output needs, borrowers were classified into three categories: (A) for critical war supplies, such as munitions and raw-material companies; (B) for medium-priority borrowers; and (C) for low-priority borrowers that manufactured domestic-consumption goods and items considered 'luxuries'.

The allocation of loans to the B-sectors was restricted and to sectors classified with a C almost impossible.[34] The manufacturers involved in the A category would be assigned a 'main bank', whose job it was to ensure that enough loans were given to the firm in order to meet its production targets. The firms were themselves part of a hierarchy of subcontractors and related firms, which were grouped so as to ensure fast and efficient production of allotted output targets.

This system quickly reshaped the economy. It ensured that only priority manufacturers received newly created purchasing power. Low-priority firms and industries were weakened, while the strategic firms and sectors grew rapidly. Manufacturers of luxury items, if not yet transformed to war production (such as the piano maker Yamaha, which was made to produce aircraft propellers – a war legacy that enabled the firm to diversify into motorbike production after the war), simply could not raise any external funds. Purchasing power was not used for unnecessary sectors or unproductive purposes. Loans were allocated to achieve the goals of the war economy – maximization of the desired type of output.

In 1946, with the approval of the US occupation, Ichimada became governor of the Bank of Japan. The system of directed credit worked so efficiently that it was carried over into the postwar era in its entirety. Almost all the present links between companies in the various business groups, their sub-contractors and their main banks originated in the wartime system of directed credit.[35] Thus it appears as if the desire to direct credit came first and foremost. In order to implement it efficiently, authorities decided to reorganize the financial sector and the economy at large, thereby creating a bank-based financial system.

As bank lending started to recover under his guidance, Ichimada reinstated the wartime bank-credit-guidance mechanism that determined both the quantity of new bank loans and their sectoral allocation. All that needed to be done was to switch the priority classification from war objectives to peacetime goals. Instead of munitions industries, first textile, then shipbuilding and steel, and then later automobiles and electronics became top-priority beneficiaries of allocated purchasing power. Medium priorities included most other manufacturing, as well as retail trade, agriculture, education and, on a case-by-case basis, construction. Domestic consumption-related industries fell into the lowest priority category – sectors such as real estate, department stores, hotels, restaurants, securities, entertainment, publishing and alcoholic beverages. They were without much hope of obtaining funds.[36] Ichimada judged that Japan could not afford such luxuries.

Similarly to 'credit dictator' Schacht, Ichimada earned the reputation of deciding over life and death of companies, and hence was given the perhaps more flattering nickname 'the Pope'. The system worked well in avoiding unproductive credit creation and channelling newly created money to productive activities. Japan's postwar economic development therefore has been to a large extent facilitated by directed credit.[37]

Conclusions

Directed credit, administered in the form of credit controls, has been identified as an important catalyst for high postwar economic growth in several Asian countries, including Japan, Korea, Taiwan, Thailand and Indonesia. Focusing on the country that developed earliest among these, this essay has shown that the historic origins of practice and theory of these credit controls are located in Germany. Specifically, an important impetus was derived from the practice of the Reichsbank under Hjalmar Schacht, and the thought of German growth-oriented economists of the first half of the twentieth century, whose policy advice was based on models less restricted by assumptions than those of their classical contemporaries.

The direction of credit must also be understood as a key aspect of a consistent institutional design of a 'guided' economy that transmits top-down guidance via private-sector organizations to individual firms, and that empowers private-sector managers and utilizes them for the overall goal of maximizing growth. As a result, a bank-centred, cartelized economic structure emerges that is biased towards scale-maximization, and with the direction of credit at its heart.

Both German theory and practice strongly influenced developments in Japan. To the extent that Japan's economic institutions were introduced before 1945, they were virtually equally introduced in other parts of the

Japanese empire, which at the time included today's Korea and Taiwan. The continuity of pre-1945 structures in Asia is well documented.[38] Meanwhile, in the postwar era, Dr Schacht remained active as government adviser on developmental policies in the financial sector. Specifically, he was adviser to Indonesia in the postwar era, where credit-allocation policies also continued.[39]

Acknowledgements

I am grateful for comments by participants of the Sixth Annual Conference of the European Society for the History of Economic Thought (ESHET), 14–17 March 2002, University of Crete, where this essay was first presented as a paper – especially the discussant Costas Lapavitsas and the session chair Harald Hagemann. Furthermore, Mark Metzler, Dirk Bezemer, Haim Bar-kai and Erich Streissler made valuable comments that helped me improve the manuscript of this work in progress.

Notes

1 For a survey on the literature linking financial development and economic growth, see Levine (1997).
2 Studies of ownership and control have provided some reasons: following Berle and Means (1932), Stiglitz (1985) argued that traditional control mechanisms over companies (such as shareholder meetings) do not ensure that managers of large corporations manage resources efficiently. Instead, control is exercised by banks to ensure efficient resource allocation. Studies of the 'credit channel to monetary transmission' have attempted to establish a special role for bank credit in the transmission of monetary policy, which is due to imperfect substitutability of bank loans with other forms of funding, usually for small firms.
3 On the latter, see Werner (2000b).
4 Cho and Hellmann conclude that it was

> the comprehensive involvement of the government that went well beyond the simple provision of subsidized credit programs and encompassed governance over the major participants in the development drive (both banks and firms) that seems to differentiate the Japanese and Korean experiences with credit policies from those in other countries.
>
> (1993: 26)

5 On details of Japanese window guidance, see Patrick (1962), Kure (1973, 1975), Horiuchi (1980) for the pre-1980s era, and Werner (1999a, 2002) for the 1980s and early 1990s.
6 This is why the Bank of Japan until this day maintains (and publishes) detailed loan statistics, broken down into these categories. Although the BoJ claims that '[window guidance] is employed to regulate the total amount of commercial bank credit and is not a tool for the qualitative control of lending' (Pressnell 1973: 159), empirical research such as mentioned above has disproven this claim.
7 Moreover, in the postwar era large city banks were borrowing heavily from the central bank. This rendered them even more dependent on the Bank of Japan, which used the allocation of its direct lending in support of its policy.

8 See, for instance, Patrick (1962), Kure (1973), Werner (2002).

9 As a result, the top leaders of industry, commerce and finance felt obliged to visit him frequently at the Bank of Japan to obtain his approval of their investment plans. Usually, both meeting rooms of the governor's office were occupied by captains of industry, and Ichimada dashed from room to room. For many top business leaders this was a humbling experience. The credit allocation was extra-legal and 'informal', but they had to follow every whim of Ichimada and his lieutenants. There was no committee, not much discussion and no right to appeal. It was up to the BoJ governor, who did not hesitate to refuse funding. See Werner (2001, 2003).

10 It was changed again in 1924, leaving the central bank independent from the government – but dependent and accountable to outside interests, namely the foreign-bank representatives representing the ultimate creditors of the reparations debt.

11 It remained unprecedented until the Maastricht Treaty of 1991, which established the statutes of the European Central Bank. The latter now holds the record for unaccountability and independence, since even the Reichsbank statutes did not explicitly forbid mere *attempts* by democratically elected governments to influence the decisions of the central bank.

12 Memorandum, 1924, Reichsbank (Bundesbank-Archiv).

13 James' (1998) assertion that the credit controls were primarily aimed at controlling money-supply growth is not supported by evidence, and is even contradicted later in his article.

14 Such as when he summoned the representative of the Berlin banks' association (*Stempelvereinigung*) and asked him to tell the executives of the other banks to reduce margin loans. This evidence of qualitative credit controls is mentioned by James (1998: 58). It is at variance with his earlier assertion that credit controls were primarily aimed at controlling money-supply growth.

15 An internal memorandum accompanying a freeze of the credit quotas gave these instructions: 'Bei allen Kreditgeschaeften ist ganz besonders darauf zu achten, dass die Kreditgewaehrung der Reichsbank nicht dazu benutzt wird, um Devisenkaeufe zu finanzieren, die nicht wirtschaftlich begruendet sind' 'With all credit business it must especially be taken care that the extension of credit by the Reichsbank is not used to finance the purchase of foreign exchange which are not justified economically', 'An saemtliche Reichsbankanstalten', internal memorandum, Reichsbank, 21 June 1931 (Bundesarchiv Koblenz und Berlin R28/49). This is another example quoted by James (1998: 61) that contradicts his earlier assertion that credit controls were mainly of quantitative nature.

16 Speech by Schacht on 15 May 1924, quoted in Mueller (1973).

17 Ausschuss zur Untersuchung der Erzeugungs- und Absatzbedingungen der deutschen Wirtschaft: Der Bankkredit – Verhandlungen und Berichte des Unterausschusses fuer Geld-, Kredit- und Finanzwesen (V. Unterausschuss), Berlin, 167ff.

18 The study included 32 banks, which had extended loans amounting to RM8.5bn at the end of 1928, namely the 5 Berlin *Grossbanken*, 4 regional joint-stock banks, 14 private banks, 4 government-owned banks and 5 clearing banks (*Girozentralen*).

19 Banken-Enquete of 1933; see Reichsbank (1934).

20 Reichsgesetz ueber das Kreditwesen in der Fassung vom 13. Dezember 1935, RGBl. I, 1456. According to paragraph 9 of the law, banks had to name customers receiving more than RM1m over any two-month period. Reporting had to take place in February, April, June, August, October and December. See Gaedicke (1939).

21 Finally, Schacht, again Reichsbank President from 1933 to 1939, simultan-

eously became Minister of the Economy in August 1934 and Plenipotentiary for the War Economy in May 1935.

22 Economists had by this time taken an interest in the sectoral allocation of credit. Gaedicke (1939), for instance, argued that detailed information concerning the sectoral allocation of credit provides a useful tool for the policy maker in the pursuit of governmental 'guidance' of the economy. He reasoned that the sectoral allocation of credit is of importance because it reflects the relative growth and strength of industrial sectors, and hence determines the overall state of the economy. He notices that, for example, the Bavarian Sparkassen (public savings banks) published detailed information about the sectoral division of bank credit. However, he complains that, despite the new banking law requiring banks to disclose details of their borrowers – even by name – the central bank or the bank regulatory authority has not publicly disclosed such information, thus preventing evaluation by non-privileged economists. Convinced of the importance of such information, Gaedicke proceeds to estimate the sectoral credit data from government statistics on joint-stock companies (Statistisches Reichsamt 1938).

23 James mentions as one example Adolf Weber, who argued for money endogeneity. The implication of the endogeneity of credit was reflected, he argues, in the Reichsbank argument of 1922 that it was only reacting to the strong demand for money when its policy created hyperinflation. Relevant members of the Historical School who were concerned with the role of money include Adam Mueller (1779–1829), Karl Knies (1821–91), Georg F. Knapp (1882–1926) and Adolf Wagner (1835–1917). Of course, the British Banking School differs significantly in other points from the German economists, such as its objection to government or central-bank involvement in the credit market. I thank Haim Barkai for emphasizing this fact.

24 On this, see Streissler (1994) and Hagemann (2002).

25 There were also those economists who were less convinced of the direction of credit or who maintained a more neutral stance, such as Salin (1928), who pointed out both benefits and dangers of directed credit, or Herzfelder (1930), who developed a model of credit management.

26 James (1998) argues that the German Historical School advanced the argument of endogenous money supply, which would only leave a passive role for the central bank or the authorities. However, to the contrary, their prevailing argument is one where the state should actively guide bank credit.

27 See Rathenau (1917a, 1917b, 1918, 1919a, 1919b, 1919c).

28 'This experience of the cartel system provided the foundation on which the war economy could easily be built up during World War I. The cartel system was used by the totalitarian economic system of the third Reich for its own purposes on an even higher level' (Stolper 1966: 56).

29 Rathenau proposes to bring the key question for economic development out into the open, namely the division of national income between consumption and investment. Since this ratio determines the trade-off between growth and future economic wealth on the one hand, and present standard of living on the other, he argued it should be subject to public debate.

30 Recent growth theories acknowledge the importance of the human resource aspect of 'labour'. While neglected in static models and policy advice, human resources are at the centre of the German development economics.

31 Schumpeter's case is instructive. Having been for all means and purposes a member and admirer of the Historical School until about the mid-1920s, from 1927 onwards, after his first visit to Harvard where he obtained a permanent post in 1932, he became highly critical of its research programme and its members, hinting that they were not competent theorists, but lacked

intellectual capacities. See Hodgson (2001). It is the latter view that appears to have prevailed in the English-speaking economics profession.
32 Ichimada (1986: 38–9).
33 Interview with retired former member of the *Yuushi Assenbu.*
34 Interview with retired former member of the *Yuushi Assenbu.*
35 See Okazaki and Okuno (1993), Werner (1993, 1999b).
36 See Calder (1993: 83ff.).
37 For more on the Japanese economic system and its origins, see Werner (1993, 2001, 2003).
38 For an overview on Japan, see Werner (2001, 2003).
39 Schacht was in Indonesia as adviser to the government from July to November 1951, having visited Thailand and India on the way. Schacht was later invited to advise Egypt and Iran. 'Iranian prime minister Mohammed Mossadegh had already asked the Shah for full dictatorial powers to carry out any plan of Schacht's' (Weitz, 1997: 335).

References

Asian Development Bank (2002) *Guidelines for the Financial Governance and Management of Investment Projects Financed by the Asian Development Bank,* effective January 2002, Manila: Asian Development Bank.
Berle, A. Jr. and G. Means (1932) *The Modern Corporation and Private Property,* New York: Macmillan.
Calder, K. (1993) *Strategic Capitalism,* Princeton: Princeton University Press.
Cho, Y. J. and T. Hellmann (1993) 'The Government's Role in Japanese and Korean Credit Markets: A New Institutional Economics Perspective', Policy Research Working Papers no. 1190, Financial Sector Development Department, Washington, DC: The World Bank.
Dalberg, R. (1926) *Deutsche Waehrungs- und Kreditpolitik, 1923–26,* Berlin: Reimer Hobbing.
Fischer, S. (1998) 'The Asian Crisis: A View from the IMF', Address by Stanley Fischer, First Deputy Director of the International Monetary Fund at the Mid-winter Conference of the Bankers' Association for Foreign Trade, Washington, DC, 22 January; available online at www.imf.org/external/np/speeches/1998/012298.htm.
Gertler, M. and A. Rose (1991) 'Finance, Growth and Public Policy', World Bank Working Paper, No. 814, Washington, DC: World Bank.
Goldsmith, R. W. (1969) *Financial Structure and Development,* New Haven: Yale University Press.
Goodhart, Charles A. E. (1989) *Money, Information and Uncertainty,* 2nd edn, London: Macmillan.
Hagemann, H. (2002) 'Schumpeter's Early Contributions on Crises Theory and Business-Cycle Theory', paper presented at the Sixth Annual Conference of the European Society for the History of Economic Thought (ESHET), University of Crete, 14–17 March.
Herzfelder, E. (1930) *Kreditkontrolle,* Berlin: Junker & Duennhaupt.
Hodgson, G. M. (2001) *How Economics Forgot History,* London: Routledge.
Horiuchi, A. (1980) *Nihon no kinyuu seisaku,* Tokyo: Toyo Keizai Shinposha.
Ichimada, H. (1986) *Tenki, Tsuiokuroku,* Tokuma Shoten and Yamaichi Securities, Tokyo: Economic Research Institute.

James, H. (1998) 'Die Reichsbank 1876 bis 1945', in Deutsche Bundesbank (ed.), *Fuenfzig Jahre Deutsche Mark, Notenbank und Waehrung in Deutschland seit 1948*, Munich: Verlag C. H. Beck.

King, R. G. and R. Levine (1992) 'Financial Indicators and Growth in a Cross-section of Countries', World Bank Working Paper, No. 819, Washington, DC: World Bank.

—— (1993) 'Finance and Growth: Schumpeter Might be Right', *Quarterly Journal of Economics*, 108, August: 717–37.

Kure, B. (1973) *Kinyuu seisaku – Nihon ginkou no seisaku unei*, Tokyo: Toyo Keizai Shinposha.

—— (1975) 'Nihon ginkou no madoguchi shidou', *Shikan Gendai Keizai*, 17, March.

Levine, R. (1997) 'Financial Development and Economic Growth: Views and Agenda', *Journal of Economic Literature*, 35: 688–726.

McKinnon, R. (1973) *Money and Capital in Economic Development*, Washington, DC: Brookings Institution.

Mueller, A. (1809) *Die Elemente der Staatskunst*, Berlin: Haude & Spener.

Mueller, H. (1973) *Die Zentralbank als eine Nebenregierung*, Opladen: Westdeutscher Verlag.

Nihon Keizai Shinbun (1984) 'Ko Ichimada-shi Keizai fukkou ni "ratsuwan", honou to yobarero-shushou Fukuda-shi." *Makawa-shi danwa*, 23 January 1984, p. 3.

Noland, M. and H. Pack (2001) 'Industrial Policies and Growth: Lessons from International Experience', paper prepared for the Fifth Annual Conference of the Central Bank of Chile on 'Challenges of Economic Growth', Santiago, Chile, 29–30 November.

Okazaki, T. and M. Okuno (1993) *Gendai nihonkeizai shisutemu no genryuu*, Tokyo: Nihon Keizai Shinbunsha.

Patrick, H. (1962) *Monetary Policy and Central Banking in Contemporary Japan*, Bombay: University of Bombay.

Peterson, E. (1954) *Hjalmar Schacht: For and Against Hitler*, Boston: Christopher Publishing House.

Pressnell, L. (1973) *Money and Banking in Japan*, trans. S. Nishimura, Bank of Japan, London: Macmillan Press.

Rathenau, K. (1906) *Der Einfluss der Kapitals- und Produktionsvermehrung auf die Produktionskosten in der deutschen Maschinen-Industrie*, Halle a. S., Friedrich University, Doctoral Thesis.

Rathenau, W. (1915) *Die Organisation der Rohstoffversorgung: Vortrag, gehalten in der Deutschen Gesellschaft 1914 am 20. Dezember, 1915*.

—— (1917a) *Probleme der Friedenswirtschaft*, Berlin: Fischer.

—— (1917b) *Von kommenden Dingen*, Berlin: Fischer.

—— (1918) *Die neue Wirtschaft*, Berlin: Fischer.

—— (1919a) 'Autonome Wirtschaft', *Deutsche Gemeinwirtschaft Schriftenreihe*, 16, Jena: E. Diederich.

—— (1919b) *Der neue Staat*, Berlin: Fischer.

—— (1919c) *Die neue Gesellschaft*, Berlin: Fischer.

Reichsbank (1934) *Untersuchungsausschuss fuer das Bankwesen 1933: Untersuchung des Bankwesens 1933*, 2nd part: *Teil, Statistiken. Volkswirtschaftliche und statisische Abteilung der Reich Bank*, Berlin.

Riesser, J. (1906) *Zur Entwicklungsgeschichte der deutschen Grossbanken mit besonderer Ruecksicht auf die Konzentrationsbestrebungen*, 2nd rev. edn, Jena: Gustav Fischer.

—— (1913) *Finanzielle Kriegsbereitschaft und Kriegfuehrung*, 2nd edn, Jena: Gustav Fischer.

Roubini, N. and X. Sala-i-Martin (1992) 'Financial Repression and Economic Growth', *Journal of Development Economics*, 39: 5–30.

Salin, E. (1928) *Theorie und Praxis staatlicher Kreditpolitik der Gegenwart*, Tuebingen: Mohr.

Schacht, H. (1953) *76 Jahre meines Lebens*, Bad Woerishofen: Kindler und Schier-meyer.

Schwenk, E. (1937) *Kredit-, Lohn- und Investitonskontrolle: ein Beitrag zur Konjunktur-politik*, Tuebingen: Becht.

Sombart, W. (1934) *Deutscher Sozialismus*, Berlin: Buchholz und Weisswange.

Spann, O. (1921) *Der wahre Staat*, Leipzig: Quelle u. Meyer.

Spengler, O. (1920) *Preussentum und Sozialismus*, Munich: C. H. Beck.

Statistisches Reichsamt (1938) *Abschluesse deutscher Aktiengesellschaften 1935/36 und 1936/37*, Statistik des Deutschen Reichs, vol. 525, Berlin: Statistisches Reich-samt.

Stiglitz, J. (1985) 'Credit Markets and the Control of Capital', *Journal of Money, Credit and Banking*, 17 (2): 133–52.

Stiglitz, J. and M. Uy (1996) 'Financial Markets, Public Policy, and the East Asian Miracle', *World Bank Research Observer*, 11 (2): 249–76.

Stolper, G. (1966) *Die Deutsche Wirtschaft seit 1870*, 2nd edn, Tuebingen: J. C. B. Mohr.

Streissler, E. (1994) 'The Influence of German and Austrian Economics on Joseph A. Schumpeter', in Y. Shionoya and M. Perlman (eds), *Schumpeter in the History of Ideas*, Ann Arbor: University of Michigan Press.

Vogel, R. and D. Adams (1997) 'Old and New Paradigms in Development Finance: Should Directed Credit be Resurrected?', Consulting Assistance on Economic Reform II, CAER II Discussion Paper No. 2, Boston: Harvard University Institute for International Development.

von Moellendorff, W. (1916) *Deutsche Gemeinwirtschaft*, Berlin: Verlag von Karl Siegismund.

Wade, R. (1990) *Governing the Market*, Princeton: Princeton University Press.

Weitz, J. (1997) *Hitler's Banker*, Boston: Little, Brown and Co.

Werner, R. (1993) 'Japanese-style Capitalism: The New Collectivist Challenge? An Analysis of the Nature and Origin of Japan's Political Economy and Social Order', paper presented at the Fifth Annual International Conference of the Society for the Advancement of Socio-Economics (SASE), 26–28 March, New School for Social Research, New York.

—— (1999a) Nihon ni okeru madoguchi shido to 'bubble' no keisei', *Gendai Finance*, 5 (March): 17–40, MPT Forum, Tokyo: Toyo Keizai Shinposha.

—— (1999b) 'Japans Wirtschaftsreformen der neunziger Jahre: Back to the Future' in W. Schaumann (ed.), *Japans Kultur der Reformen, Referate des 6. Japanologentages der OAG in Tokyo*, Munich: Iudicium.

—— (2000a) 'Indian Macroeconomic Management: At the Crossroads Between Government and Markets', in *Rising to the Challenge in Asia: A Study of Financial Markets, Vol. 5, India*, Manila: Asian Development Bank.

—— (2000b) 'Macroeconomic Management in Thailand: The Policy-induced Crisis', in G. Rhee (ed.), *Rising to the Challenge in Asia: A Study of Financial Markets, Vol. 11, Thailand*, Manila: Asian Development Bank.

—— (2001) *En no Shihaisha*, Tokyo: Soshisha.

—— (2002) 'Monetary Policy Implementation in Japan: What they Say vs. What they Do', *Asian Economic Journal*, 16 (2): 111–51.

—— (2003) *Princes of the Yen, Japan's Central Bankers and the Transformation of the Economy*, New York: M.E. Sharpe.

World Bank (1993) *The East Asian Economic Miracle, Economic Growth and Public Policy*, Oxford: Oxford University Press.

—— (1997) *World Development Report 1997*, Oxford: Oxford University Press.

6 The notion of the constant wage share in income-distribution theories

Hagen Krämer

> But in different stages of society, the proportions of the whole produce of the earth which will be allotted to each of these classes, under the names of rent, profit, and wages, *will be essentially different...*
>
> (Ricardo 1951–9, vol. I: 5; emphasis added)

Introduction

The long-run constancy of labour's contribution to national income, namely the constant wage share, belongs to the so-called stylized facts of economic development. This 'economic law' is known today as 'Bowley's Law'.[1] Many prominent economists belonging to a variety of theoretical schools refer to this law. For example, J. M. Keynes (1939), M. Kalecki (1938, 1954), P. Douglas (1934), P. A. Samuelson (1948), N. Kaldor (1955–6), W. Krelle (1962), O. Lange (1964), R. Goodwin (1967), J. Roemer (1978) and G. Mankiw (1997) all mention and use Bowley's Law. The alleged constancy of the wage share resulted in reactions from astonishment,[2] to the naive belief that it is a law of nature,[3] as well as annoyance about the inability refute it.[4] Bowley's Law is still one of the most important stylized facts in macroeconomic theory and is applied to growth theory as well as to the major strands of the theories of functional income distribution. All these theories, which include the neoclassical, post-Keynesian and the Kaleckian approach to distribution theory, put forward arguments as to why income distribution does not change in the long run.

The constant wage share is also an item on a longer list of so-called 'economic constants' that can be found in the economic literature and that are sometimes called 'great ratios of economics' (cf. Klein and Kosobud 1961; Darnell and Evans 1990: 44; Simon 1990). Besides its peculiarity, Bowley's Law has a special relevance because certain political conclusions can be derived from it. If it were true that the wage share does not change in the long run, every attempt by the workers and their unions to increase their share of the national product would be doomed to failure. As the first economic schools of thought developed, statements were almost immediately put forward that there is no room for manoeuvre in the determination of wages because they are strictly determined by the laws of economics. This idea can be found in the wage-fund theory of classical political economics, it can also be found in the theory of the 'iron law of wages' by Lassalles, and it reached its peak in economic debates during the dispute between Tugan-Baranowski (1913) and Böhm-Bawerk (1914) on *macht oder ökonomisches Gesetz?* (power or economic law?) in income distribution.

With the development of the marginal productivity theory of distribution, the notion that equilibrium wages determined in competitive markets are fair and any attempt to increase these wages will inevitably create unemployment found its theoretical and formal conception. However, while the old wage theories followed a static approach, the theory of the constant wage share relates to a growing economy. Therefore, the law of the constant wage share can be considered as a modern version of the theory of the wage fund (Bombach 1959: 99). Whereas in the old version an absolute measure, the wage fund, was considered to be constant, in the modern version it is a share in the increasing national product that is seen as being constant. But also in the latter case any attempt to increase that share will be either in vain or will be detrimental to labour income earners as a whole, as in the static approach. That is why Bowley's Law is frequently treated as an empirical proof of the fact that political power and class struggle cannot influence income distribution in the long run. This is why Bowley's Law is often referred to when discussing the rules and principles of an adequate wage policy.

The wage share in classical economics

The notion of a stable long-run income distribution cannot be found in classical economics. In the works of classical economists like Smith, Ricardo and Marx, income shares of the socio-economic classes are variable in the long-run according to the level of economic development.

Adam Smith treated the matter of income distribution in some depth. However, the variables he, like other classical writers, looked at most of the time were the rate of profit, the rate of rent, the wage rate and the absolute amounts of wages, profits and rent, respectively. Smith's remarks on income shares were relatively rare. He mentioned explicitly only the share of rent in national income, which he believed would increase in the long term (cf. Smith 1976, I.xi.p, 2). Later interpretations of Smith's remarks on the development of income distribution draw different conclusions, as in the case of Ricardo. Sylos-Labini (1984) refers to a passage in Smith from which he derives the notion that Smith expected wages to rise in accordance with national income in the long run. But in this case a constant wage share would only result in the absence of productivity growth. As is well known, it was Adam Smith who stressed the importance of productivity advances for the wealth of nations. If one takes technological progress into account, the assumption of a constant wage share requires that real wages rise in proportion with productivity growth. Smith, on the other hand, did not think that wages tend to rise in proportion with productivity increases:

> It is the natural effect of improvement [that] ... a much smaller quantity of labour becomes requisite for executing any particular piece of work; and though, in consequence of the flourishing circumstances of the society, the real price of labour should rise very considerably, yet the great diminution of the quantity will generally *much more than compensate* the greatest rise which can happen in the price.
>
> (1976, I.xi.o, 1; emphasis added)

But if wages do not increase in step with productivity growth, as Smith obviously assumed, this would imply a long-run tendency of the wage share to decrease instead of remaining stable.

Ricardo, in his *Principles*, not only declared the determination of the laws which regulate distribution as the principal problem in political economy, but emphasized that the income shares of the proprietors of land, of the capital owners, and of the labourers are subject to changes over time:

> But in different stages of society, the proportions of the whole produce of the earth which will be allotted to each of these classes, under the names of rent, profit, and wages, *will be essentially different*, depending mainly on the actual fertility of the soil, on the accumulation of capital and population, and on the skill, ingenuity, and instruments employed in agriculture. To determine the laws which regulate this distribution, is the principal problem in Political Economy.
>
> (1951–9, vol. I: 5; emphasis added)

It is not clear whether Ricardo's reasoning supposes the three income shares (rent, profit and wage share respectively) will rise or fall in the long run. Ricardo himself came to the conclusion that the rent share in national income would tend to increase in the long run. He derived this result from the existence of diminishing returns in agriculture. However, as Pasinetti (1960) has demonstrated, this is not a sufficient argument for assuming an increasing rent share. Diminishing returns in agriculture is also compatible with a decreasing rent share. In a similar way the development of the wage and the profit share is undetermined in Ricardo. Although Ricardo assumed that both income shares would tend to shrink in the long run, later interpretations of Ricardo's works have shown that this must not necessarily be the case (cf. Kalmbach 1972: 17; Johnson 1973: 16).

In Marx, who is considered here as another important representative of classical economics, very few passages can be found revealing Marx's thoughts about the long-run development of functional income distribution (cf. Preiser 1959: 625). Nevertheless, the development of the wage share in Marx is important for the interpretation of Marx's assumption of the increasing misery of the working class. Relative immiserization, as indicated by a decreasing wage share, can be viewed as falling behind the income progress of the other classes (cf. Mitra 1952: 11). Which direction the long-run wage share will take is a matter of controversy in post-Marxian literature. A fall of the wage share is, in principle, only possible if the rate of surplus value rises.[5] Marx is quite ambiguous concerning the development in the rate of exploitation. One can quote a remark from *Lohn, Preis und Profit* (Marx 1867) in which he considers the development of the rate of surplus value as a question of the relative strength of the classes.[6] And since the question of the development of the rate of surplus remains open, the question of the development of the wage share is also left open in Marx.[7]

These short remarks about the topic of functional income distribution in the three most important representatives of classical economics aims to make clear that classical economists, neither explicitly nor implicitly, assumed a constant wage share. However, the writings of the classical authors contain no clear statements as to which route the wage share would take in the long run.[8] One reason for this is the fact that wages were not in the centre of attention in classical analysis. This magnitude was not seen as being directly relevant for the growth process – contrary to the rate of profit and its assumed tendency to fall.[9] Therefore, in the classical framework, the development of the functional income distribution is an open question. It can be determined only via the determination of the main parameters that influence income distribution, namely productivity and wage growth. From this it follows that any reasoning about the development of income shares cannot be carried out in isolation, but has to be developed in the context of accumulation and distribution – the major themes in classical economics.

With the fundamental shift between the economic paradigms at the end of the nineteenth century from classical to neoclassical analysis, the notion of the variable wage share disappeared. It was replaced by the conception of the long-run *constancy* of income distribution. Since the beginning of the twentieth century the basic questions of functional income distribution have no longer been 'what determines income shares and what are the causes of changes?' Rather, the question 'what is responsible for the constancy of the wage share?' became the centre of interest.

The genesis of Bowley's Law

The inclusion of the wage share into the list of the so-called 'great economic magnitudes' can be traced back to the works of Arthur L. Bowley (Bowley 1900, 1920; Bowley and Stamps 1927) at the beginning of the

twentieth century in Great Britain. The term 'Bowley's Law' is an attempt
to honour the scientific work of one of the most important pioneers of
applied economics and statistics, and one of the first scholars who collected and interpreted data on wage developments.[10] In what follows I will
describe how Bowley's Law came into existence and spread in income distribution theory. Furthermore the question will be examined as to
whether the statistical methods and concepts available at Bowley's time
justify the classification of the constant wage share as one of the 'great
ratios of economics' (cf. Klein and Kosobud 1961; Darnell and Evans
1990: 44; Simon 1990).

Following the thesis that the notion of the constant wage share is one of
the cornerstones of macro-neoclassical as well as post-Keynesian theories
of income distribution that were developed in the 1950s and 1960s,
another goal is to show how the notion was taken up by the then dominant theories of functional income distribution.

Three works are viewed here as the major channels through which the
notion of the constant wage share became popular. The empirical studies
on which they relied will also be scrutinized. First, the major work for the
neoclassical macroeconomic marginal productivity theory of distribution
was the work of Paul Douglas (1934).[11] Second, the microeconomic
approach of Michael Kalecki (1938) is considered. And third, Kaldor
(1961) is identified as being responsible for the absorption of the constant
wage share idea into the post-Keynesian growth and distribution theory
and beyond.[12]

The work of Kalecki and its sources

Michal Kalecki was among the first economists who tried to develop a consistent theory about the, as he saw it, remarkably stable share of wages in
the value added by the business sector. Kalecki was also one of the first to
speak of a law in this context.[13] This phenomenon, however, received
more attention through the work of another prominent author, namely
Keynes. In the history of economic thought Keynes's 1939 article *Relative
Movements of Real Wages and Output* (*Collected Writings*, VII: 394–412) is actually better known for another reason. In this article Keynes dissociated
himself from the general validity of the so-called first classical postulate,
according to which the real wage equals the marginal product of labour.
Until then Keynes had regarded the inverse relationship between the real
wage and employment as 'one of the best established of statistical conclusion', as he wrote in 1937 in a letter to Ohlin (ibid., XIV: 190). As a result
of the empirical work of Dunlop (1938) and Tarshis (1939), Keynes
refuted his original belief. In addition to these empirical studies, Keynes
gave another piece of evidence that underpinned his original idea of an
anti-cyclical movement of the real wage had to be given up, which he
again called

...one of the most surprising, yet best-established, facts in the whole range of economic statistics ... I mean the stability of the proportion of the national dividend accruing to labour, irrespective apparently of the level of output as a whole and of the phase of the trade cycle.

(Collected Writings, VII: 408)

Keynes' view can, however, be proven to be wrong, as we will see later. Interestingly Keynes, in his 1939 *Economic Journal* article, dissociated himself from an idea that had lost empirical ground and justified his change of view with another fact that was also empirically wrong.

In order to prove the – as he called it – 'undisputed facts' (ibid.: 409) of constant wage shares in Great Britain and in the USA, Keynes, in his article, reproduces two tables from a work of Kalecki (1939). Kalecki in turn used quite different sources to build up data for the development of wage shares in Great Britain and in the USA. (cf. Tables 6.1 and 6.2). Kalecki had already published an article in 1938 in *Econometrica* (1938) about the determinants of income distribution, in which he identified the degree of monopoly as the major determining factor of influence. This article is of special interest in our context as for the first time Kalecki put together statistical figures about wage shares in Great Britain and the USA in the period from 1880 to 1935. Keynes referred to a revised version of this article that appeared one year later. It was the first chapter titled, 'The Distribution of the National Income' in Kalecki's *Essays in the Theory of Economic Fluctuations* (1939). The figures published here use more recent data and are slightly modified compared with the *Econometrica* article. The data were taken from the same authors as in Kalecki (1938).[14] The sources

Table 6.1 Relative share of manual labour* in the national income of the UK (%)

1911	40.7	1927	43.0	1931	43.7	1935	41.8
1924	43.0	1928	43.0	1932	43.0		
1925	40.8	1929	42.4	1933	42.7		
1926	42.0	1930	41.1	1934	42.0		

Source: Kalecki (1939: 199).

Note
* Shop assistants excluded.

Table 6.2 Relative share of manual labour* in the national income of the USA (%)

1919	34.9	1923	39.3	1927	37.0	1931	34.9
1920	37.4	1924	37.6	1928	35.8	1932	36.0
1921	35.0	1925	37.1	1929	36.1	1933	37.2
1922	37.0	1926	36.7	1930	35.0	1934	35.8

Source: Kalecki (1939: 200).

Note
* Shop assistants excluded.

Kalecki used were studies and calculations made by Arthur L. Bowley (1920 and 1937)[15] and Colin Clark (1937) for Great Britain. For the USA he took Wilford L. King (1930) and Simon Kuznets (1937).[16]

If one investigates the validity of the contemporary sources, many substantial differences can be found in the way wage shares are defined and calculated today. The reliability of the data is also to be questioned (cf. Krämer 1996). This is why the notion of the alleged stability of the wage share, even in the times of Keynes and Kalecki, is not free of doubts.

Data for the wage bill and for the national income

To calculate wage shares, one needs, besides data for the national wage bill, data for national income. Not surprisingly the history of calculating wage shares is closely linked to the history of national-income accounting. Great Britain was particularly prominent in the development of national income accounting methods, as this country is the place of origin not only of the first theories of income formation but also of the first empirical calculations and assessments of national income. As early as in the seventeenth century first steps were taken in this regard by William Petty and Gregory King (cf. Studenski 1958). At the end of the nineteenth century an intensive discussion developed about the correct categories of national-income accounting. These debates went on until the 1940s, when the terms and concepts of national accounting that are so well known to us today received their final shape. Until this time the definitions of national-income accounting were often changed. This partly explains why so many difficulties existed in calculating wage shares and to comparing them over time and between different countries. It became much easier to calculate wage shares when, at the end of the eighteenth century, the method of calculation for the national income changed in Great Britain. The reintroduction of income tax in 1842 provided more reliable data than those which had been taken until then from trade and production statistics. This is why in Great Britain those methods gained in importance that used the factor-earnings approach instead of the expenditure approach (cf. Studenski 1958: 111). This method was also used by Arthur L. Bowley, whose studies and publications were widely noticed and influential (cf. Darnell 1981: 151). Since Bowley, besides his interest in national income accounting, had a special interest in the income development of workers, he put much effort in the collection of wage data. In this way it was assured that sufficient data material on the wage bill in Great Britain existed.

Methods of calculating the numerator of the wage share

Today the numerator of the wage share consists of the gross income from employed persons, that is gross wages and salaries before taxes plus social contributions of the employer. The numerator of the wage share as constructed by Kalecki and his contemporaries differed from this way mainly in two respects. First, in most of the cases the social contributions of the employer is not taken into account (cf. Bowley 1937: 72). And second, and more importantly, the numerator does not include salaries.

Thanks to Bowley's works, data for the national wage bill in Great Britain is available for a much longer period, starting as early as 1860. Although the calculation of the national wage bill is not confronted with so many difficulties as the total national income, the pioneers of income accounting still faced several serious problems as Bowley had to admit: 'In brief, I do not think that the statistics are sufficient for any fine measurement of income, earnings or wages prior to 1880; there is indeed sufficient uncertainty after that date' (1937: 99).

Data revision in the 1950s concerning the wage bill in Great Britain resulted in significantly higher values in the period from 1920 to 1938 compared with the calculations made by Bowley and Clark (cf. Chapman 1953). According to the revisions in 1924 the wage bill was 11.7 per cent higher than Clark thought. In 1926 it was 1.1 per cent below Bowley's calculations, in 1935 it was 4.9 per cent higher than Clark's estimation. And finally, Bowley's data for 1938 were 9.7 per cent below the revised figures. When following the development of wage shares it is not a constant mistake that matters, but the volatility in the deviations that cause substantial errors. Here it should be noted that Chapman expected the margin of error in his own estimations to be around 5–10 per cent (ibid.: 41).

Methods of calculating the denominator of the wage share

The margin of error in determining the national income, which was calculated by estimating its single components, should be even bigger. Kuznets (1941) mentions a margin of error in the inter-war period (1919–38) of up to 20 per cent.[17] The further one goes back in history, the less reliable is the database. In addition to potentially incorrect data, a major problem is different definitions for the national product in the respective studies. This is due to the fact that no common standard in national accounting had been established at that time. It was not until the Keynesian revolution, and in face of the assembly for action in Great Britain shortly before the Second World War, that a 'statistical revolution' (Arndt 1979: 121) occurred. Only then was a precise definition of terms like 'national income' or 'gross national product' put forward. The latter term, for example, that is so common for us today, was not introduced until 1940 by Colin Clark (Cairncross 1988: 14ff.). Even in Clark's 1937 book *National Income and Outlay*, which was used by Kalecki in his 1939 article, this term did not appear.[18] It was 1952 when eventually the OECD urged its member nations to introduce a uniform and internationally comparable classification of the systems of national accounts (cf. UNO 1952).[19]

Particularly in Bowley's works, whose figures were used by Kalecki only for the years 1880 and 1913, many methods for calculating a 'national income' are doubtful from today's perspective. The three categories which Bowley used to construct his national income are 'wages', 'income assessed to income tax' and 'intermediate income'. Additionally he subdivided 'income assessed to income tax' into 'taxable income' and 'tax evasion'. It is obvious, however, that especially the latter can only be very broadly estimated. The third category, 'intermediate income', is the residual and consists mainly of non-wage income below the tax-exempted amount (cf. Bowley 1937: 79). The magnitude of the second category is based mainly on estimations made by tax authorities. These figures are subject to errors because many changes in the tax system took place in the period under consideration. The data can therefore not be considered to be very reliable and were not referred to in later studies, in contrast to the numbers Bowley created for his first category. His database on the development of wages in Great Britain became the standard of empirical income-distribution research; many later studies made reference to Bowley's work in this field. For us, the following statement of Bowley's is of high importance, since with this remark he directly pointed to his finding of a constant wage share and laid the foundations to what later became known as 'Bowley's Law':

> The general conclusion that there was no important change in the proportion of earned income to total income between 1880 and 1913 or between 1911, 1913 and 1924 remains. There is a stability of the various classes of income considered.
>
> (1937: 97)

This quotation is not Bowley's first hint as to the alleged constant long-run income distribution. Already in his important study on the development of income distribution in Great Britain that appeared in 1920, Bowley speculated about share constancy (1920: 25). But only in *Wages and Income in the United Kingdom since 1860* (1937) was he able to examine his guess in detail by using long-run data series. With this work Bowley became the first economist to explicitly formulate the thesis of a constant wage share. It is not surprising therefore that Samuelson chose Bowley as the one who gave this 'law' his name. It should not be forgotten, though, that Bowley's empirical foundations for the constant wage share are of rather doubtful value.

Similar conclusions can be made for the studies carried out by Clark (1937), King (1930) and Kuznets (1937), especially concerning the way they calculated the national product (cf. Krämer 1996: 79). Out of these four sources, with all their different definitions and conceptions, Kalecki assembled two tables about the development of the relative share of manual labour in national income in Great Britain and in the USA. Furthermore, Kalecki modified the data in some important respects (cf. ibid.). Because of the many difficulties he faced when constructing the national wage bill for both countries, he got in his own words not more than a 'hypothetical wage bill' (1939: 200). In doing this, Kalecki reached the result that the maximum value of the wage share in Great Britain was 43.7 per cent (in 1931), whereas the minimum value was 40.7 per cent (in 1911) (cf. Table 6.1).[20] For the USA, the maximum value of the wage share was 40.2 per cent (in 1925; King's measurement includes shop assistants; not in the table), whereas the minimum value was 39.3 per cent (in 1923; Kuznets's measurement excludes shop assistants; cf. Table 6.2). Kalecki concludes the empirical part of his work by stating that the share of manual labour in national income is constant in the short run as well as in the long run and could therefore be called a kind of law, which has to be explained (ibid.).

If one takes into account the many difficulties that existed in collecting reliable income data and the fact that many magnitudes were estimated with the help of some crude assumptions, Kalecki's reasoning is dubious. It was finally Keynes who, facing Kalecki's studies, demanded more accurate research and better theoretical explanations, because the constancy of the wage share seemed like a 'miracle' to him (*Collected Writings*, VII: 409).[21] As a matter of fact, many more studies on this matter were carried out later on. Twenty years later a study of similar importance to Kalecki's work was published, namely Kaldor's (1957) influential article. Before dealing with Kaldor's work we will look, for chronological reasons, at the dissemination of Bowley's Law in neoclassical analysis, since it took place at almost the same time as Kalecki's first work was published.

Neoclassical theory and the constancy of the wage share

In the textbook version of neoclassical growth theory, the use of a Cobb–Douglas production function together with the assumption of constant returns to scale, profit maximization and perfect competition implies the complete distribution of the product. From these assumptions it also follows that all income shares remain the same. The shares of profits and wages are equal to the production elasticities of capital and labour, respectively. Distribution is therefore determined 'technically'.

Paul Douglas, who gave his name to the Cobb–Douglas production function, contributed mainly to the introduction of a constant wage share into the dominant version of neoclassical growth and distribution theory.[22] Douglas's original intention was to create a production function that was capable of mirroring data series in the USA for the development of labour, capital and output. The application of the Cobb–Douglas production function on matters of income distribution was originally not a focus of Douglas's research interests. According to Bronfenbrenner, it was a subsequent idea concerning other fields of application of this type of production function (1968: 478) – it was not until his 1934 book *Theory of Wages* when Douglas mentioned functional income distribution more or less in passing. He estimated the production elasticity of labour between 60 per cent and 70 per cent and found a high correspondence with the existing wage share. It was the mathematician Charles Cobb who alerted Douglas to Euler's theorem and made clear to him that, with an elasticity of substitution of one, income shares would not be subject to changes. As a result Douglas developed *en passant* and unintentionally a theoretical 'explanation' for the constant wage share. This drew a lot of attention in the scientific community where Bowley's Law was widely accepted in the meantime.[23]

The elasticity of substitution also played a major role in a book, which was published in 1932, and had an almost identical title to Douglas's one: *The Theory of Wages* by John Hicks. Hicks developed for the first time in a systemic fashion the mutual dependence between the elasticity of substitution, income shares and the bias of technical progress. This work laid the foundation for neoclassical income share theory. Occasionally Hicks has been accused of having had the explicit intention of building his theory in a way that constant income shares would result (Scitovsky 1964: 28; King and Regan 1988: 54). And indeed Hicks later wrote about his intentions concerning the first edition of his book:

> I did have an eye on statistics, which I was trying to explain, or help to explain. These were the Bowley and Stamp calculations of the British National Income and its Distribution, which (at the time when I was writing) were available only for the two years, 1911 and 1924.
>
> (1963: 335)

However, if one looks into the first edition of Hicks's book, one finds, contrary to the quotation given above, Hicks referring to Bowley's work from 1920. In the latter the 'share of property in the National Income of Britain' in 1880 and 1913 is said to be 37.5 per cent each (ibid.: 130). Yet, Hicks modified this value in a way Bowley did himself in his later studies: Hicks subtracted the property received abroad and got as his new values 34 per cent for 1880 and 31 per cent for 1913. This means that the profit share had shown a slight decrease in that period. Having his theoretical background and knowing that the capital–labour ratio was increasing over time, Hicks concluded that the elasticity of substitution in the real economy must be smaller than one and must also fluctuate in the course of time (ibid.: 130). Therefore, when Hicks looked back later he asserted that the model developed by Douglas showed many similarities with his own but it 'was in one respect a special model. He assumed that the elasticity of substitution between capital and labour was always unity (giving constant relative shares)...' (ibid.: 312) – and it was exactly this assumption that Hicks, contrary to Douglas, *did not* use. Although with the elasticity of substitution Hicks developed a major tool for neoclassical theory, it has to be emphasized that Hicks cannot be made causally responsible for the introduction of share constancy into neoclassical distribution theory. Hicks has rather shown, in detail, the conditions that have to be fulfilled in a neoclassical framework if constant income shares are to be modelled.

A considerable influence in the dissemination of Bowley's Law can be conferred on Paul A. Samuelson's *Economics*. In this influential textbook, Samuelson coined the term 'Bowley's Law' for the constancy of the wage share.[24] Samuelson wrote in his first edition of *Economics* of 1948 about the development of income shares:

> It is rather remarkable how nearly constant are the proportions of the various categories over long periods of time, between both good years and bad. The size of the total social pie may wax and wane, but total wages seem always to add up to about two-thirds of the total.
>
> (1948: 227)[25]

Samuelson had already shown, in the first edition of his remarkable textbook, some scepticism concerning the principal validity of the law.[26] He stressed his reservations even more strongly in the fourth edition of *Economics*:

> The late Sir Arthur Bowley ... noted how remarkably constant over almost a century is wage's share of national income. No one understands why this should be so. (...in recent decades it seems to be growing more than Bowley's constancy hypothesis would indicate).
>
> (1958: 196, fn. 1)[27]

As in the middle of the 1950s neoclassical growth theory established its contours, the notion of constant income shares was present in practically all major works. In his seminal article on growth theory Solow (1956) discussed the influence of different production functions on share distribution. He stressed, several times, that it is inherent within the design of a Cobb–Douglas production function to generate a constant income distribution. Yet, Solow showed some disbelief concerning the finding of the constant wage share compared to the majority of other researchers in his field. But in his *Skeptical Note on the Constancy of Relative Shares* (1958) he challenged the alleged tendency of the aggregate wage share to fluctuate more strongly than the individual wage shares in the single industries, rather than the constancy of the wage share in the long run. Yet these signs of mistrust were very rare, as the vast amount of subsequent literature on neoclassical growth and distribution theory assumed implicitly or explicitly a constant income distribution. From the middle of the 1960s – that is ten years after Solow's (1956) and Swan's (1956) pioneering work and five years after Kaldor formulated his stylized facts – the notion of the constant wage share represented the standard premise of economic theory in this field.[28]

This was the result of the acceptance of Kaldor's stylized facts by neo-classical growth theorists. Solow explicitly referred to these stylized facts towards the end of the debate on growth theory (1970: 2). The last of the three important routes through which Bowley's Law came into distribution theory is therefore Kaldor's influential article of 1957.

The work of Kaldor and its sources

At the beginning of his article 'A Model of Economic Growth', Kaldor listed some empirical findings that he regarded as essential for any convincing model of growth: (i) constant long-run wage and profit shares, (ii) capital–labour ratio and labour productivity expanding at almost the same growth rate, which leaves the capital coefficient constant; together with (i) it follows that the rate of profit remains unchanged (1957: 260). As mentioned earlier, this collection of empirical facts appeared again in a slightly elaborated version in Kaldor (1961) where it was named *stylized facts*. The concept, the content and the methodological idea behind it found almost general acceptance in economics. This is why Kaldor's 1961 article is regarded here as one of the three major works in the history of economic thought that disseminated the notion of share constancy in economics. Kaldor had already presented this paper in 1958 at the famous Corfu conference on capital theory. Since he did not carry out any empirical studies on his own, one has to scrutinize Kaldor's sources. The main work Kaldor relied on in assembling his list of stylized facts for both of his papers was research carried out by Phelps Brown and Weber (1953). Their findings were published in 1953 in the *Economic Journal* (cf. Kaldor 1961: 2 and Kaldor 1957: 260). In what follows, this study will be briefly scrutinized as well as the one it referred to itself.

The article by Phelps Brown and Weber starts off with a statement that indicates that Kaldor referred to their work in a way that corresponded with their original intentions. Since it was the explicit purpose of Phelps Brown and Weber to build up a catalogue of empirical facts for constructing growth theories,

> It is possible to make some statistical application of the outline drawn in recent discussion of the theory of economic growth, and this paper will present estimates of capital accumulation and the components of income in the United Kingdom since 1870, in an endeavour to throw light on the relation between accumulation and productivity, the determinants of the rate of accumulation, and the effect of accumulation on the distribution of income.
>
> (1953: 263)

Phelps Brown and Weber's work was also confronted with the difficulties of accurately developing suitable definitions for statistical income categories. The authors used as a measure for income shares 'earnings' as a proportion of 'home-produced national income' (ibid.: 266). According to their findings this variable was 55 per cent between 1870 and 1914, rose to 66 per cent until 1924 and stayed at that level until 1938. The definition for national income used by Phelps Brown and Weber ('home-produced national income') was in accordance with the previously discussed historical studies. The use of earnings meant that for the first time wages and salaries were added together building a broader income category than before. Phelps Brown and Weber also referred to other studies. They used a data series collected by Phelps Brown and Hart (1952), whilst this study in turn referred to Bowley (1937) and Prest (1948). These works of Bowley and Prest are the basic studies for the 'Kaldor line', on which all other investigations in this context rest as well. As is shown in detail in Krämer (1996. 89), the Bowley and Prest studies showed similar difficulties in constructing income categories, especially for the national product.[29] The definitions vary in the course of time and a lot of guesswork was necessary to reach final results. Whereas Kalecki added depreciation to national income, Bowley and Prest did not. This means that Bowley and Prest calculated the share of wages in *net* income while Kalecki did this in *gross* income. Another important difference that influences the size of the wage share is the treatment of the income of government employees. Kalecki subtracted this income category, although with some questionable assumptions about the size of the governmental wage bill, while other studies included wages paid by the government. The third major difference consists in the addition of salaries to the national wage bill by Phelps Brown and Hart. Salaries were not included by Bowley and by Kalecki. However, sometimes the income of shop assistants was included, and sometimes even the labour income part of the self-employed, like shopkeepers, was not taken into account.

Evaluation of the empirical studies

Some of the difficulties the empirical studies faced are of a general nature with regard to income accounting, while others are of a more specific nature and have to do with the calculation of wage shares. The *general problems* were found to be threefold:[30] first, during the time considered no official authority existed that collected and evaluated economic data in a systematic manner. The pioneering work, therefore, was to put data together from different sources. Second, it was only much later that common standards were established on how to define income categories like the national product. And third, in order to come to conclusions about the development of income shares in the long run, it was necessary to make the available data compatible with each other in order to create time series data. Due to a lack of consistency this was often only possible after some far-reaching modifications. The *special problems* that existed with regard to the calculations of wage shares have not to do with the fact the contemporary definitions differ from today's. The major issue is the error that occurs when definitions of the numerator and the denominator of the wage share are *changed often and irregularly*. Additionally, definitions vary not only from author to author, but also the same researcher altered the way he constructed the respective variables from time to time.

There is one last but major point which has not been referred to, although it is one of the most important objections to all the historical studies. The share of wages in national income is subject to change simply if the number of workers (or labour income receivers) changes in relation to the number of self-employed. In this case, although the average income of a worker does not change, the wage share increases as the number of self-employed declines. This has generally been the case in most of the advanced economies, as many farmers had to give up their farms and small shopkeepers have had to close down because of the emergence of supermarkets. Under these circumstances a constant wage share implies a lower per capita income for an average worker and therefore a deterioration of the relative income position of the labourers. Amazingly enough, except for one, in none of the historical empirical studies was this influencing factor taken into account and no attempt was made to modify the wage share in this respect.[31] Tables 6.3 and 6.4 provide an overview as to how wage shares and relative wage shares (i.e. the wage share divided by the labour share at a given point in time) developed in the one-hundred year period from 1870 to 1985, as far as the data is available. It is clearly the case that income shares vary also in the long run.

Conclusions

Taking into account the important role the alleged constancy of income shares plays in the three most important strands of distribution theory, one has to assert that Bowley's Law is based on rather shaky empirical foundations. This means the validity Klein and Kosobud required for any economic measure used by economic model builders as an empirical starting point is not given: 'If ratios are in the nature of fundamental parameters, simplifications of the theory may result ... For theory construction, however, *our standards must be high...*' (1961: 173; emphasis added).

The goal of this essay has been to demonstrate that the requirements for high standards in the empirical investigations, which legitimated theorists to assume constancy of income shares in the long run, have not been met. Today we have to state that the meaningfulness of the historical studies on income distribution was not sufficient to formulate a general law of income distribution, like Bowley's Law. Since reality has proven, in

Table 6.3 The development of the absolute wage share in Western Europe, North America, Japan and Australia, 1870–1985[a]

	1870	1880	1890	1900	1910	1920	1930	1940	1950	1960	1970	1980	1985
Western Europe													
Austria	–	–	–	–	–	57.2	59.5	54.6	56.8	60.6	65.5	72.2	73.7
Belgium	–	–	–	–	–	–	–	–	53.7	56.9	63.0	77.0	72.1
Denmark	–	–	–	–	–	–	–	–	55.5	58.4	66.6	76.6	74.3
Finland	–	–	–	–	–	–	–	–	55.6	56.7	64.4	77.1	76.8
France	–	–	–	–	–	–	–	–	57.5	58.1	63.7	75.4	75.2
Germany	42.7	43.8	46.3	47.5	48.6	63.6	68.3	60.0	57.7	61.2	67.7	74.3	71.6
Greece	–	–	–	–	–	–	–	–	–	34.4	39.6	48.7	56.4
Ireland	–	–	–	–	–	–	–	–	–	–	61.3	80.8	76.0
Italy	–	–	–	–	–	–	–	–	53.1	51.4	60.2	69.2	70.4
Netherlands	–	–	–	–	–	–	–	–	47.1	57.4	69.4	74.3	66.8
Norway	–	–	–	–	–	–	48.4	46.2	55.2	65.4	73.8	76.1	70.4
Portugal	–	–	–	–	–	–	–	–	55.2	48.5	51.9	63.2	55.1
Spain	–	–	–	–	–	–	–	–	–	52.9	58.2	64.2	59.6
Sweden	–	–	–	–	–	–	59.2	52.3	55.2	62.3	77.1	86.0	80.0
Switzerland	–	–	–	–	44.6	51.6	50.8	50.5	61.2	60.8	63.3	74.5	75.1
United Kingdom[b]	–	51.3	53.0	53.3	52.8	66.8	62.6	67.5	70.9	72.5	75.3	82.7	77.3
Western Europe average[c]	48.1	–	–	–	–	–	–	–	(73.0)	74.3	74.4	82.2	84.0
Non-European countries													
Australia	–	–	–	–	–	–	–	–	65.1	65.0	66.8	68.3	66.4
Canada	–	–	–	–	–	–	–	–	62.2	69.1	73.1	72.4	71.0
Japan	–	–	–	–	–	–	–	–	45.0	50.9	54.4	68.6	69.5
New Zealand	–	–	–	–	–	–	–	–	55.2	58.1	63.9	66.7	60.9
United States	–	–	–	–	–	–	–	–	66.5	72.5	76.8	78.1	76.5

Labour-force data
Austria: 1920: 1924; 1940: 1937; 1950: 1951. Belgium: 1950: 1951. Denmark: 1950: 1951. Finland: 1950: 1951. France: 1950: 1952. Germany: 1870: 1871; 1920: 1925; 1940: 1939. Italy: 1950: 1951. Norway: 1940: 1939. Switzerland: 1920: 1924. Australia: 1950: 1951. Canada: 1950: 1951. Japan: 1950: 1952. New Zealand: 1950: 1952. United States: 1950: 1951.
Source: Kaelble and Thomas 1991: 36–7.

Notes
The absolute wage share is understood as wages in relation to the national income.
a Three-year averages.
b 1855: 55.1; 1860: 52.5.
c Weighted for each country by the number of wage earners (labour share/share of dependent labour force).

Table 6.4 The development of the relative wage share in Western Europe, North America, Japan and Australia, 1950–85[a]

	1950	1960	1970	1980	1985
Western Europe					
Austria[b]	61.2	63.1	65.4	73.9	69.0
Belgium	58.4	60.7	63.0	74.9	69.2
Denmark	60.4	62.7	66.7	73.8	69.5
Finland	63.1	62.0	64.4	75.4	75.5
France[b]	65.6	62.6	63.4	76.8	76.1
Germany	62.5	63.7	67.7	74.0	70.6
Greece	–	36.1	39.6	44.6	50.1
Ireland	57.3	58.2	61.3	78.2	68.3
Italy[c]	51.5	52.3	60.2	70.9	72.6
Netherlands	60.5	60.4	69.4	66.9	59.4
Norway	64.2	70.6	73.8	73.3	66.9
Portugal[d]	–	48.3	51.9	60.9	56.5
Spain	–	58.7	58.2	61.7	55.1
Sweden	62.7	66.1	77.1	81.5	72.2
Switzerland	68.2	63.9	63.3	70.7	–
United Kingdom[a]	71.8	73.4	75.3	84.2	79.1
Non-European countries					
Australia	67.3	66.1	66.8	68.2	67.5
Canada	70.5	71.9	73.1	70.4	69.4
Japan	58.9	57.5	54.4	66.3	66.1
New Zealand	58.8	59.0	63.9	65.4	59.5
United States	71.8	74.0	76.8	77.2	75.9

Labour-force data
Austria: 1950: 1951. Belgium: 1950: 1953. Denmark: 1950: 1951; 1980: 1981. Finland: 1950: 1951; 1980: 1981. France: 1950: 1952. Germany: 1950: 1951. Australia: 1950: 1954. Canada: 1950: 1951. New Zealand: 1950: 1951; 1980: 1981.
Source: Kaelble and Thomas 1991: 36–7.

Notes
The relative wage share is calculated as the wage share (wages in relation to the national income) divided by the labour share at a given point in time (1970 in Table 6.4). Family workers are excluded.
a Three-year averages. Base year 1970.
b Family workers could not be excluded.
c Break in data.
d The category 'unspecified' had to be included.

the last decades, that income shares fluctuate quite substantially, also in the long run, the neoclassical, post-Keynesian and, with some notable exceptions, also Kalecki's distribution theory is badly designed.[32] Since all major theories of macroeconomic income distribution still rest on the assumption of share constancy, current macro-distribution theory has to develop a modern approach that no longer rests on an invalid – or at least highly questionable – assumption like Bowley's Law.

Acknowledgements

I should like to thank Amit Bhaduri, Harald Hagemann, Peter Kalmbach, Heinz D. Kurz and Hans-Michael Trautwein for helpful discussions and their valuable comments. Any remaining misconceptions and errors are, of course, my own responsibility.

Notes

1 The term 'Bowley's Law' was coined by Paul A. Samuelson in his textbook *Economics*, honouring Arthur Lyon Bowley (1869–1957); cf. Samuelson (1964: 736).
2 Keynes (1939: 48): '...the result remains a bit of a miracle'; Schumpeter (1939: 575): '...a mystery'.
3 Weintraub (1959: 35): '...a parallel to Newton's gravitational constant g...' ibid.: 43: '...the "magic constant" of economic analysis'.
4 Robinson (1966: 81): '...the mystery of the constant relative shares remains as a reproach to theoretical economics'.
5 I am abstracting from the problem of value-price-transformation and the topic of productive and unproductive labour (cf. Moseley 1985).
6 'Die Frage löst sich auf in die Frage nach dem Kräfteverhältnis der Kämpfenden' (ibid.: 149).
7 In the post-Marxian literature on the theory of crisis some approaches exist that explain Marx's hypothesis of economic breakdown with a fall of the rate of profit, and vice versa a rise in the share of wages (Glyn and Sutcliffe 1972; Weisskopf 1979). Other approaches hold just the opposite for true (Baran and Sweezy 1966; Bleaney 1976).
8 It should be emphasized, however, that the definitions of the classical writers concerning the types of income are not completely identical with today's income categories.
9 Even though there are, of course, clear causal interrelations between the rate of profit and the wage share.
10 Bowley (1869–1957) worked as a mathematician, statistician and economist in Great Britain. Besides his empirical and methodological work on wages and national income accounts, his most important contributions to economics consist of research on mathematical economics, econometrics and statistical methods, especially sample technique (Allen 1968; Darnell 1981; Stone 1987).
11 Earlier writers on production and distribution theory following the marginalist approach were Wicksell (1893), Wicksteed (1894) and Clark (1899).
12 Kaldor is however not the first post-Keynesian writer who accepted the notion of share constancy. As is well known, there exists a variety of concepts of the neutrality of technical progress that each leaves income distribution unchanged. This feature of neutral technical progress was explicitly described and obviously held as a not unrealistic assumption by Harrod (1948: 23) and Joan Robinson (1952: 94–6; 1956: 160 and 170).
13 'As we see on the basis of statistical data the relative share of manual labour in gross income shows only small changes both in the long run and in the short period. We shall try to explain this 'law' and establish conditions under which it is valid' (Kalecki 1938: 100).
14 In total, three similar versions of Kalecki's article exist. The third version appeared in 1954 in *Theory of Economic Dynamics* as Chapter 2, entitled 'Distribution of National Income'. The sources Kalecki used there differ substantially

from the sources that were used for the first two articles. Since the articles that appeared fifteen years earlier had a greater influence for the dissemination of Bowley's Law, I focus on these works in the following.

15 In his first version from 1938 Kalecki quotes Bowley's book *The Change in the Distribution of the National Income, 1880–1913* (1920). In the second version (1939) Kalecki uses *Wages and Income in the United Kingdom since 1860* (Bowley 1937) that had appeared in the meantime and became a long-time standard in that field.

16 Kalecki (1938) uses an unpublished work of Kuznets. In Kalecki (1939) it is the meantime published work *National Income and Capital Formation, 1919–1935* (Kuznets 1937) that is quoted.

17 Similar Feinstein (1968: 127, fn. 2), who expects the potential errors of the main components of the national income to be some ±10 per cent. King (1930: 34) admits that his data could have margins of error up to 40 per cent.

18 Only in 1941 was the first official calculation of the national product of Great Britain (for the period 1938–40) published (cf. Studenski 1958: 457). In the USA the term 'GNP' replaced in 1941 the category 'national income' that had been used so far. Behind this was the necessity of creating a comprehensive economic statistic in order to lay the foundations of the 'rearmament program'. This created the basis of the US intervention in the Second World War (Gilbert and Jaszi 1944: 44ff.).

19 Even today not all nations follow the rules suggested by the OECD or the UN. In 1983 only 55 per cent of the market economies adopted the standardized concepts and definitions (Beckerman 1987: 591).

20 Keynes was concerned about the compatibility of the data series of Bowley and Clark. In a letter to Kalecki, in which Keynes commented on the galley proofs of Kalecki's *Essays in the Theory of Economic Fluctuations*, Keynes asked whether he could use Bowley's value of the wage share for 1880 (41 per cent) without modifications for a reprint of his *Economic Journal* article. In the editorial notes of Kalecki's writings his editor Osiatynski (referring to Don Patinkin's notes) assumed that either Kalecki never answered Keynes's letter or such a letter was received by Keynes too late (Kalecki CW I: 512). This assumption, however, is contradicted by the existence of the following footnote in Keynes's article: 'Dr Kalecki tells me that, if this was adjusted so as to be comparable with the figures given above, it would be about 42.7 per cent...' (1939: 409, fn. 4). This stresses the fact that Kalecki, although being aware of the problems, tried to put together data from many different sources.

21 In the third, already mentioned version of Kalecki's writing on the development of the wage share, his *Theory of Economic Dynamics* (1954), Kalecki now used a new study by Bowley (1942) for Great Britain and statistics for the US provided by the *Survey of Current Business*. Confronted with new data and the availability of longer data series, Kalecki made more careful comments concerning the wage share development in the long run: 'No *a priori* statement is therefore possible as to the long-run trend of the relative share of wages in income' (1954: 31). As a consequence Kalecki from then on focussed on the analysis of the movements of the wage share in the business cycle.

22 It should be emphasized that what later became famous as the Cobb–Douglas production function was already present in the early writings of Knut Wicksell (1893).

23 Douglas (1967) himself later described the genesis of the Cobb–Douglas production function. This interesting report makes quite clear that there are some striking similarities between neoclassical theory and Newton's physical conception of the world, which also induced Douglas to search for regularities and laws in production and distribution: 'I personally have faith that there is a fun-

damental unity in economic as in physical life . . . There is law and relative regularity everywhere else – why not in production and distribution?' (ibid.: 22).

24 The term 'Bowley's Law' appears the first time in the 6th American edition of 1964 on page 736 (cf. Samuelson 1964). In his first five editions Samuelson did not use this term, although he already referred to Bowley and his findings. About the same time as Samuelson, Robert Solow used the term 'Bowley's Law' in a talk he made at a conference on income distribution, which was organized in September 1964 by the International Economic Association in Palermo (Solow 1968: 449).

25 'Total wages' is defined by Samuelson as 'wages, salaries, and supplements earned by all employees' (ibid.: 226), that is including government employees. The labour income part of self-employed is, however, not taken into account.

26 '. . .there is nothing *sacred* about the traditional fraction of two-thirds of the national income going to wages and salaries' (ibid.: 531; emphasis added).

27 A later edition of *Economics* reads as follows: 'The share of wages and salaries in national income has edged up very slightly over the long run' (Samuelson and Nordhaus 1992: 555).

28 'Distributive shares have been remarkably constant in most western economies . . . the modern economist has almost ceased to wonder at Bowley's Law' (Drandakis and Phelps 1966: 823)

29 As Prest admitted once (1948: 31): 'It must be made clear at the outset that these figures are not by any means the most accurate that could be produced . . . Nevertheless, as there have been a number of requests for the figures, it has been decided to publish them at this stage . . .'.

30 Cf. Krämer (1996: 93) for more details.

31 It was only in Brown and Hart (1952) that this factor was mentioned. The authors presented values for the change in the relative amount of workers in the total labour force in three big countries. However, although being aware of this influencing factor, they did not calculate a modified wage share.

32 Although at the starting point Kalecki followed Bowley's Law, his theory of income distribution is open to changing income shares, since distribution is determined also by exogenous factors like the degree of monopoly or the economic power of the socio-economic classes (Sylos-Labini 1984; Krämer 1996: 251; Hein and Krämer 1997).

References

Allen, R. G. D. (1968) 'Bowley, Arthur Lyon', in *International Encyclopedia of the Social Sciences*, vol. 2, New York: Macmillan and Free Press: 134–7.

Arndt, H. W. (1979) 'Clark, Colin', in *International Encyclopedia of the Social Sciences, Biographical Supplement*, vol. 18, New York: Macmillan: 121–4.

Baran, P. A. and Sweezy, P. M. (1966) *Monopoly Capital*, New York: Monthly Review Press.

Beckerman, W. (1987) 'National Income', in J. Eatwell, M. Milgate and P. Newman (eds), *The New Palgrave: A Dictionary of Economics*, New York and London: Macmillan, vol. III: 590–2.

Bleaney, M. (1976) *Underconsumption Theories*, New York: International Publishers.

Böhm-Bawerk, E. von (1914) 'Macht oder ökonomisches Gesetz?', *Zeitschrift für Volkswirtschaft, Socialpolitik und Verwaltung*, vol. 23: 205–71.

Bombach, G. (1959) 'Die verschiedenen Ansätze der Verteilungstheorie', in E. Schneider (ed.), *Einkommensverteilung und technischer Fortschritt*, Berlin: Duncker & Humblot: 95–154.

Bowley, A. L. (1900) *Wages in the United Kingdom in the Nineteenth Century*, Cambridge: Cambridge University Press.

—— (1920) *The Change in the Distribution of the National Income, 1880–1913*, Oxford: Clarendon Press.

—— (1937) *Wages and Income in the United Kingdom since 1860*, Cambridge: Cambridge University Press.

—— (1942) *Studies in the National Income 1929–1934*, Cambridge: Cambridge University Press.

Bowley, A. L. and Stamp, J. C. (1927) *The National Income: 1924*, Oxford: Clarendon Press.

Bronfenbrenner, M. (1968) 'Neo-Classical Macro-Distribution Theory', in J. Marchal and B. Ducros (eds), *Distribution of the National Income*, London and New York: Macmillan: 476–507.

Brown, P. and Hart, P. (1952) 'The Share of Wages in the National Income', *Economic Journal*, 62, 246: 253–77.

Cairncross, A. (1988) 'The Development of Economic Statistics as an Influence on Theory and Policy', in D. Ironmonger, J. O. N. Perkins and T. van Hoa (eds), *National Income and Economic Progress: Essays in Honour of Colin Clark*, New York. Macmillan: 11–20.

Chapman, A. L. (1953) *Wages and Salaries in the United Kingdom, 1920–1938*, Cambridge and London: Cambridge University Press.

Clark, C. (1937) *National Income and Outlay*, London: Macmillan.

Clark, J. B. (1899) *The Distribution of Wealth: A Theory of Wages, Interest and Profits*, New York: The Macmillan Company.

Darnell, A. C. (1981) 'A. L. Bowley, 1869–1957', in D. P. O'Brien and J. R. Presley (eds), *Pioneers of Modern Economics in Britain*, London: Macmillan: 140–74.

Darnell, A. C. and Evans, J. L. (1990) *The Limits of Econometrics*, Aldershot: Edward Elgar.

Douglas, P. (1934) *Theory of Wages*, New York: The Macmillan Company.

—— (1967) 'Comments on the Cobb–Douglas Production Function', in M. Brown (ed.), *The Theory and Empirical Analysis of Production*, Studies in Income and Wealth, vol. 31, New York: Columbia University Press: 15–22.

Drandakis, E. M. and Phelps, E. S. (1966) 'A Model of Induced Invention, Growth and Distribution', *Economic Journal*, vol. 76: 823–40.

Dunlop, J. G. (1938) 'The Movement of Real and Money Wage Rates', *Economic Journal*, vol. 48: 413–34.

Feinstein, C. H. (1968) 'Changes in the Distribution of the National Income in the United Kingdom since 1860', in J. Marchal and B. Ducros (eds), *Distribution of the National Income*, London and New York: Macmillan: 115–39.

Gilbert, M. and Jaszi, P. (1944) 'National Product and Income Statistics as Aid to Economic Problems', *Dun's Review*, February, quoted from W. Fellner and B. F. Haley (1946) (eds for the American Economic Association) *Readings in the Theory of Income Distribution*, Philadelphia: Blakiston: 44–57.

Glyn, A. and Sutcliffe, B. (1972) *British Capitalism, Workers and the Profits Squeeze*, Harmondsworth: Penguin.

Goodwin, R. (1967) 'A Growth Cycle', in B. F. Feinstein (ed.), *Socialism, Capitalism and Economic Growth: Essays presented to Maurice Dobb*, Cambridge: Cambridge University Press: 54–8.

Harrod. R. F. (1948) *Towards a Dynamic Economics*, London: Macmillan.

Hein, E. and Krämer, H. (1997) 'Income Shares and Capital Formation: Patterns of Recent Developments', *Journal of Income Distribution*, vol. 7, no. 1: 5–28.

Hicks, J. R. (1932) *The Theory of Wages*, London; 2nd edn 1963, London: Macmillan: 1–248.

—— (1936) 'Distribution and Economic Progress: A Revised Version', *Review of Economic Studies*, vol. 4: 1–12; reprinted and quoted from, 2nd edn 1963, London: Macmillan: 286–303.

Johnson, H. G. (1973) *The Theory of Income Distribution*, London: Gray-Mills Publishing.

Kaelble, H. and Thomas, M. (1991) 'Introduction', in Brenner, Y. S., Kaelble, H. and Thomas, M. (eds) *Income Distribution in Historical Perspective*, Cambridge: Cambridge University Press: 1–56.

Kaldor, N. (1955–6) 'Alternative Theories of Distribution', *Review of Economic Studies*, vol. 23, quoted from (1980) *Essays on Value and Distribution*, 2nd edn, London: Duckworth: 209–30.

—— (1957) 'A Model of Economic Growth', *Economic Journal*, vol. 67, quoted from (1980) *Essays on Value and Distribution*, 2nd edn, London: Duckworth: 259–300.

—— (1961) 'Capital Accumulation and Economic Growth', in F. A. Lutz and D. C. Hague (eds), *The Theory of Capital*, London: Macmillan, quoted from (1978) *Further Essays on Economic Theory*, London: Duckworth: 1–53.

Kalecki, M. (1938) 'The Determinants of the Distribution of the National Income', *Econometrica*, vol. 6, no. 2: 97–112.

—— (1939) 'The Distribution of the National Income', in *Essays in the Theory of Economic Fluctuations*, London; reprinted in W. Fellner and B. F. Haley (1946) (eds for the American Economic Association) *Readings in the Theory of Income Distribution*, Philadelphia: Blakiston: 197–217.

—— (1954) *Theory of Economic Dynamics*, London: Allen & Unwin.

Kalmbach, P. (1972) *Wachstum und Verteilung in neoklassischer und postkeynesianischer Sicht*, Berlin: Duncker & Humblot.

Keynes, J. M. (1939) 'Relative Movements of Real Wages and Output', *Economic Journal*, vol. 49: 34–51, quoted from (1971) *The Collected Writings of John Maynard Keynes*, vols I–XXX, Cambridge: Macmillan, vol. VII: 349–412.

King, J. and Regan, P. (1988) 'Recent Trends in Labour's Share', in Y. S. Brenner, J. P. G. Reijnder and A. H. G. M. Spithoven (eds), *The Theory of Income and Wealth Distribution*, Brighton: Wheatsheaf: 54–86.

King, W. L. (1930) *The National Income and its Purchasing Power*, New York: National Bureau of Economic Research.

Klein, L. R. and Kosobud, R. F. (1961) 'Some Econometrics of Growth: Great Ratios of Economics', *Quarterly Journal of Economics*, vol. 75, no. 2: 173–98.

Krämer, H. (1996) *Bowley's Law, Technischer Fortschritt und Einkommensverteilung*, Marburg: Metropolis.

Krelle, W. (1962) *Verteilungstheorie*, Tübingen: Mohr.

Kuznets, S. (1937) *National Income and Capital Formation, 1919–1935*, New York: National Bureau of Economic Research.

—— (1941) *National Income and its Composition, 1919–1938*, New York: National Bureau of Economic Research.

Lange, O. (1964) *Entwicklungstendenzen der modernen Wirtschaft und Gesellschaft*, Wien: Europa-Verlag.

Mankiw, N. G. (1997) *Macroeconomics*, 3rd edn, New York: Worth Publishers.

Marx, K. (1867) *Lohn, Preis und Profit* (MEW, vol. 16: 101–52), Berlin: Dietz.

Mitra, A. (1952) 'The Share of Wages in National Income', Rotterdam (PhD thesis).

Moseley, F. (1985) 'The Rate of Surplus Value in the Postwar US Economy: A Critique of Weisskopf's Estimates', *Cambridge Journal of Economics*, vol. 9: 57–79.

Pasinetti, L. L. (1960) 'A Mathematical Formulation of the Ricardian System', *Review of Economic Studies*, vol. 27: 78–98.

Phelps Brown, P. and Hart, P. E. (1952) 'The Share of Wages in National Income', *Economic Journal*, vol. 62: 251–77.

Phelps Brown, P. and Weber, B. (1953) 'Accumulation, Productivity and Distribution in the British Economy, 1870–1938', *Economic Journal*, vol. 63: 263–88.

Preiser, E. (1959) 'Distribution (1) Theorie', in Erwin von Beckerath *et al.* (eds) *Handwözterbuch der Sozialwissenschaften*, vol. 2, Stuttgart: Fischer *et al.*: 620–35.

Prest, A. R. (1948) 'National Income of the United Kingdom, 1870–1946', *Economic Journal*, vol. 58: 31–62.

Ricardo, D. (1951–9) *The Works and Correspondence of David Ricardo*, vols I–XI, ed. by P. Sraffa with the collaboration of M. H. Dobb, Cambridge: Cambridge University Press.

Robinson, J. (1952) 'The Rate of Interest and Other Essays', quoted from 2nd edn (1979) *The Generalisation of the General Theory and Other Essays*, London and Basingstoke: Macmillan.

—— (1956) *The Accumulation of Capital*, London: Macmillan, from the 3rd edn 1969.

—— (1966) *An Essay on Marxian Economics*, 2nd edn, London: Macmillan.

Roemer, J. (1978) 'The Effect of Technological Change on the Real Wage and Marx´s Falling Rate of Profit', *Australian Economic Papers*, June: 152–66.

Samuelson, P. A. (1948) *Economics: An Introductory Analysis*, 1st edn, New York: McGraw-Hill.

—— (1958) *Economics: An Introductory Analysis*, 4th edn, New York: McGraw-Hill.

—— (1964) *Economics: An Introductory Analysis*, 6th edn, New York: McGraw-Hill.

Samuelson, P. A. and Nordhaus, W. (1992) *Economics*, 14th edn, New York: McGraw-Hill.

Schumpeter, J. A. (1939) *Business Cycles, A Theoretical, Historical and Statistical Analysis of the Capitalist Process*, vol. 1 and vol. 2, New York and London: McGraw-Hill.

Scitovsky, T. (1964) 'A Survey of Some Theories of Income Distribution', in National Bureau of Economic Research (ed.), *The Behaviour of Income Shares*, Studies in Income and Wealth, vol. 27, Princeton: Princeton University Press: 15–51.

Simon, J. L. (1990) 'Great and Almost Great Magnitudes in Economics', *Journal of Economic Perspectives*, vol. 4: 149–56.

Smith, A. (1976) *An Inquiry into the Nature and Causes of the Wealth of Nations*, vol. II of the Glasgow edition, ed. by R. H. Campbell, A. S. Skinner and W. B. Todd, Oxford: Oxford University Press.

Solow, R. M. (1956) 'A Contribution to the Theory of Economic Growth', *Quarterly Journal of Economics*, vol. 70: 65–94.

—— (1958) 'A Skeptical Note on the Constancy of Relative Shares', *American Economic Review*, vol. 48: 618–31.

—— (1968) 'Distribution in the Long and Short Run', in J. Marchal and B. Ducros (eds), *Distribution of the National Income*, London and New York: Macmillan: 449–66.

—— (1970) *Growth Theory: An Exposition*, Oxford: Oxford University Press.

Stigler, G. J. (1941) *Production and Distribution Theories: The Formative Period*, New York: The Macmillan Company.

Stone, J. R. N. (1987) 'Bowley, Arthur Lyon (1869–1957)' in J. Eatwell, M. Milgate and P. Newman (eds), *The New Palgrave: A Dictionary of Economics*, New York and London: Macmillan, vol. I: 270.

Studenski, P. (1958) *The Income of Nations*, New York: New York University Press.

Swan, T. W. (1956) 'Economic Growth and Capital Accumulation', *Economic Record*, vol. 32: 334–61.

Sylos-Labini, P. (1984) *The Forces of Economic Growth and Decline*, Cambridge, MA and London: MIT Press.

Tarshis, L. (1939) 'Changes in Real and Money Wages', *Economic Journal*, vol. 49: 150–4.

Tugan-Baranowski, M. von (1913) *Soziale Theorie der Verteilung*, Berlin: Springer.

UNO (ed.) (1952) *A System of National Accounts and Supporting Tables, Studies in Methods*, Series F, No. 2, New York: United Nations Publications.

Weintraub, S. (1959) *A General Theory of the Price Level, Output, Income Distribution, and Economic Growth*, Philadelphia: Chilton.

Weisskopf, T. E. (1979) 'Marxian Crisis Theory and the Rate of Profit in the Postwar U.S. Economy', *Cambridge Journal of Economics*, vol. 3, December: 341–78.

Wicksell, K. (1893) *Über Wert, Kapital und Rente nach den neueren nationalökonomischen Theorien*, Jena: Fischer; English translation titled *Value, Capital and Rent*, 1954 edn, London: Allen & Unwin.

Wicksteed, P. H. (1894) *Essay on the Co-Ordination of the Laws of Distribution*, rev. edn 1992, Aldershot: Edward Elgar.

Part II

Economic development and social change

Some themes from pre-classical and classical thinking

7 Nicolas Du Tot and John Law

Antoin E. Murphy

Du Tot and John Law are in some ways the economists' counterparts to that great British literary pairing, Boswell and Samuel Johnson. Boswell is Boswell and few would know his first name. Until now, Du Tot's first name has eluded generations of writers. In contemporary writings he was just referred to as Dutot. Later on the incorrect name of Charles Ferare Dutot was used by some commentators. Just as Boswell acquired the virus of excessive admiration for his subject which Macaulay in his *Essays* neologised into "lues Boswelliana", so too Du Tot appears to have acquired this virus – call it "lues Du Totiana" – in excessive praise for Law.

Certainly the early commentators of his book the *Réflexions politiques sur les finances et le commerce* (1738) appear to have thought so. Joseph Pâris-Duverney and his "ghost writer" François Deschamps severely attacked Du Tot's praise for Law in their *Examen sur les Réflexions politiques sur les finances et le commerce* published two years later in 1740. David Hume implicitly thought so too. Though quoting from the *Réflexions* in a foot-note in his essay "Of Money" (1752) to show the beneficial effects of small increases in the money supply, he certainly did not accept Du Tot's thesis on the exceptional merits of John Law.

Boswell and Johnson, Du Tot and Law. In order to understand Boswell we need to understand Johnson. In order to understand Du Tot we need to understand John Law and what he attempted to achieve in the French economy between 1716–20. This essay provides some background on John Law and on his monetary theories and policies. Against this background Du Tot's interpretation of Law and his System will be analysed.

John Law

John Law was one of the most colourful personalities in the world of early eighteenth-century money and banking. In the early part of his career he was known as a rake and philanderer. London society gave him sobriquets such as "Beau Law" and "Jessamine John". A poor gambler at this stage of his life, Law's career appeared short-lived when he was sentenced to death for killing another dandy – "Beau Wilson" – in a duel in Bloomsbury

Square in 1694. Yet, a quarter of a century later, Law was feted as a genius in France because of the success of his Mississippi Company. This success produced Europe's first major stock-market boom and had people flocking into Paris to invest in the heavily traded shares of the Company. Law's paper money had replaced specie and the shares of the Mississippi Company had replaced the bulk of the national debt.

The British – fearing that Law's system was a masterly piece of financial innovation – decided to copy it. This action produced the boom in the shares of the South Sea Company. Due to Law, the second half of 1719 and the first eight months of 1720 were periods of buoyant stock exchanges. Law's success led to his appointment as Controller General of Finances in France in early January 1720, an appointment that effectively made him Prime Minister of France. Through his shareholdings in the Mississippi Company, he was able to remark that he was the richest private individual in Europe. However, his power and wealth were not to last long. By December 1720 Law was obliged to flee France where the stock market had crashed and his paper money had become worthless.

Examination of this type of itinerary of Law's life has led many commentators to dismiss him as a charlatan, a monetary quack, and a trickster. History is harsh in the way it deals with failed innovators. Law's lifestyle, involving heavy gambling, appeared to confirm the portrait of an individual speculating with the French economy. This perception led to many economists taking a dim view of Law with Adam Smith (1776), Karl Marx (1924) and Alfred Marshall (1981) lining up to criticise him. These economists – obsessed by the view that money needed to be intrinsically valuable – dismissed Law because he believed that money is not the value for which goods are exchanged but the value by which goods are exchanged. This principle, that money did not need to be intrinsically valuable *per se*, led Law to the view that that specie money could and should be replaced with paper banknotes and deposits.

Law's vision of a specie-less economy was not fully borne out until the second half of the twentieth century when the US cut the last vestiges of the gold standard, the fixed price of the dollar in terms of gold, in 1971. Ironically, three hundred years after Law's birth, his vision of a specie-less world was fully vindicated.

There was a great deal more to Law than just an anti-metallist stance. Joseph Schumpeter, the doyen of twentieth-century historians of economic thought, attempted to rehabilitate Law, remarking: "He worked out the economics of his projects with a brilliance and, yes, profundity, which places him in the front rank of monetary theorists of all times" (1954: 295). Unfortunately, Schumpeter's analysis was incomplete and he died before providing his full assessment of Law.

Law was born into a goldsmith's family in Edinburgh in 1671. Edgar Faure, a recent biographer of Law, has interpreted Law's home background in a Freudian manner, entitling Chapter 1 of his book, "The enemy of gold was born in a goldsmith's house" (1977: 3). This appears to suggest that Law, in his rebellion against gold, was fixated to do so because of a reaction against his father. This is to misintepret banking developments in Scotland at this time. The Scottish goldsmiths of the time had no Midas fixation. They were bankers busy in the process of evolving away from deposit takers to credit creators. Credit creation necessarily meant a diminution of the role of gold. Thus Law was born into a world where gold was recognised as only part of the more exciting action of creating paper money and bank deposits.

Apparently an able youngster at school where he showed potential in both mathematics and tennis, Law left Edinburgh for the more exciting city of London in the early 1690s. There he lost considerably at the gaming tables and had to have recourse to his mother to bail him out of his debts. His duel, in 1694, with Edmund Wilson was believed to have involved a lady. However, the recent discovery of an eighteenth-century pamphlet, *Love Letters of a Noble Gentleman to Mr. Wilson,* suggests that the reason for the duel may have been a great deal more complicated – see Murphy (1997). The *Love Letters* imply that Wilson was having a homosexual relationship with a powerful English lord and politician, and that Law may have been employed as a duellist in order to rid the English lord of the embarrassments that had developed from his liaison with Wilson.

It is difficult to assess the credibility of the *Love Letters*, but documents at the Public Record Office in London show that the government of the time arranged Law's escape from prison. Was this because of the special pleading of Law's Scottish connections or was it part of the guarantee given to Law when plans were made for him to kill Wilson in the duel?

Law "escaped" from prison in 1694, and spent the next ten years travelling on the Continent through countries such as France, Holland and Italy. Touring through countries, particularly Holland and Italy, Law learnt a great deal about current banking practices. He also became an expert gambler. Indeed the description of Law as a gambler is inappropriate. He had in fact become a type of bookmaker. At the gaming tables he was always the "banker" in games such as faro. The odds were heavily tipped in favour of the "banker" in this card game, and Law used his mathematical skills to ensure that the other gamesters were gambling rather than him. Law's "bookmaking" astuteness made him a fortune of between 1.5 and two million livres by the second decade of the eighteenth century. It also brought him into contact with prominent members of the nobility in countries such as France.

During these years Law also developed his talents for monetary theorising. In 1704, he attempted – through the manuscript *Essay on a Land Bank* – to persuade Lord Godolphin as to the merits of replacing the Bank of England with a land bank. While land-bank proposals were two a penny at this time through the writings of Asgill, Barbon, Chamberlen and others,

Law's *Essay on a Land Bank* (Law 1994) did produce a major step forward in economic theory in that it contained *inter alia*:

1   a sophisticated account of value theory, most notably the first explicit use by an economic writer of supply [quantity] and demand analysis. This value theory also contains the water/diamonds paradox that Adam Smith was later to borrow without acknowledgement from Law's *Money and Trade*, where the paradox was re-stated;[1]
2   the first comprehensive assessment of the functions of money;
3   the conceptualisation of both a narrow and a broad definition of money supply;
4   the first use of the term the demand for money;
5   the first presentation of modern quantity theory in a demand for money/supply of money framework.

Money and trade

Money and Trade Considered with a Proposal for Supplying the Nation with Money (1705) incorporates many of the earlier themes raised in the *Essay on a Land Bank*. However, it goes further, much further, in its pursuit of a general macroeconomic framework along with an appropriate set of macroeconomic policy recommendations. The monetary environment that Law was addressing was an impoverished Scotland rather than the more prosperous England of the *Essay on a Land Bank*. This changed monetary environment meant that Law had to address not only the money/inflation issue, but, more importantly, the money/output issue. Law wanted to show that money was not just linked to the price level. It was also linked to output, or trade as it was then called. The name of the book *Money and Trade* said it all. Law's committed and innovative approach to macroeconomic theorising may be seen through the following discoveries:

1   the money in advance requirement;
2   the circular flow of income;
3   the emphasis on the concept of the demand for money;
4   the further analysis of international inflation in a money supply/ money demand framework; and
5   the formulation of the law of one price for a small open economy.

These are all major theoretical contributions discussed in Murphy (1997), which alongside his earlier analysis in the *Essay on a Land Bank*, entitle him to Schumpeter's praise as a great monetary theorist. What about Law the policy-maker?

The evolution of the system

The General Bank was established by Law in May 1716. It was modelled on the Bank of England in that it obtained its banking privileges from the state in return for taking up part of the national debt – part of the outstanding amount of short term *billets d'état*. The success of the General Bank enabled Law to embark on the second aspect of his macroeconomic strategy, namely the management of the national debt. To do so, he needed to create a trading company along the lines of British trading companies such as the East India Company and the South Sea Company. In August 1717, he established the Company of the West (Compagnie d'Occident), which was given monopoly trading rights over French Louisiana – an area representing half of the land mass of the United States today (excluding Alaska).

It acquired these trading rights in return for re-structuring, and accepting a lower interest rate, on part of the outstanding amount of *billets d'état*. The Company benefited in that it acquired rights to exploit the agricultural and mineral potential of this huge area. The state benefited in that part of its floating short-term debt was converted into long-term debt that bore a lower rate of interest. Shareholders, in the new company, who swapped *billets d'état* in return for the company's shares, had the prospect of large capital gains if the wealth of Louisiana was properly exploited. The nominal value of each share, which came to be known as the *mères*, issued by the Company of the West, was 500 livres. But, as they were purchased with *billets d'état*, then standing at a discount of over 70 per cent, it meant that the initial shareholders purchased their shares at a price of around 150 to 170 livres. It took nearly two years for the shares to reach their nominal issue price of 500 livres.

Initially there was little interest in the Company, and Law had difficulty in selling its shares. A year after its establishment, Law started to use the Company of the West to mount a series of spectacular takeovers and mergers. At the same time he developed the General Bank by ensuring that it was used as the government's bank for the receipt and disbursement of state funds.

In August 1718 the Company of the West acquired the lease of the tobacco farm, while in December it took over the Company of Senegal. In the same month, the General Bank's operations were re-organised and it was re-named the Royal Bank, a development showing the extent to which Law had become a key member of the Regent's inner circle.

In May 1719 Law merged the enlarged Company of the West with the Company of the East Indies and China to form the Company of the Indies. Further acquisitions in the form of the Company of Africa and the lease of the Mint were made in June and July of that year. These acquisitions and mergers required financing. Law arranged this through the issue of two tranches of shares known as the *filles* and *petites filles*.

It has already been shown that the *mères*, issued in 1717 on the establishment of the Company of the West, were subscribed for in *billets d'état*, which were standing at a very sizeable discount. Effectively they cost around 150 livres, in 1717, though issued at a nominal price of 500 livres. The second issue of shares, the *filles*, were issued in June 1719 at 550 livres – a fifty livres premium suggesting wider public interest in the shares after an interval of nearly two years. The share price jumped in July, enabling Law to issue a further batch of shares, the *petites filles*, this time at 1,000 livres each.

By the end of July 1719, Law's Company had issued 300,000 shares with a nominal value of 150 million livres, which would have cost transactors – assuming the 70 per cent discount on *billets d'état* in 1717/18 – around 108 million livres. The share price, having jumped from 500 to over 1,000 in July 1719, set the stage for a further upward gearing of Europe's first major stock-market boom. This boom was linked to Law's wish to take over completely France's national debt by swapping shares for government securities. The sheer magnitude of this operation proved to be breathtaking.

On 26 August 1719, the Regent presented Law's proposal for the Mississippi Company, as it was popularly known, to take over the tax farms and the remainder of the national debt. Law's plan was to lend the King 1.2 billion livres at an interest rate of 3 per cent so as to repay the national debt. This money would be used to repay the long-term state debts, the annuities (*rentes*), the remaining short-term floating debt (*billets d'état*), the cost of offices (*charges*) that had been or would be suppressed, and the shares of the tax farms.

Under the plan, holders of government securities were forced to give up government securities, bearing a 5 per cent rate of interest, while at the same time they were offered the possibility of acquiring shares of the Company yielding far less in terms of dividend but possessing the prospect of sizeable capital gains. With the share price jumping from 2,250 on August 1 to 2,940 on August 14, to 5,000 – and beyond this in mid-September – capital gains rather than dividends occupied the minds of most transactors. By these measures Law proposed "the radical cure" for the French economy. He aimed to transform the Company from a trading company to a trading-cum-financial conglomerate, controlling the State's finances – most notably tax collection and debt management.

Using Du Tot and Giraudeau[2] as sources, the sharp rise in the share price during August may be observed. On 1 August, the original shares – the *mères*, which, as has been shown, could have been bought for around 150 livres in 1717 – stood at 2,750. By 30 August they had risen to 4,100 and by 4 September they were at 5,000 livres, with the *filles* and *petites filles* rising *pari-passu*. Recognising the prospect of a capital gain, the debt holders were quite happy to transfer their debt into shares rather than bonds. They needed the prospect of an expected capital gain to compensate for the interest reduction on their securities from 4 per cent to 3 per cent. Their difficulty in fact became one of converting quickly enough into the shares of the Company, as the price of the shares rose very sharply during September.

Within a three-week period in September/October, the Company issued 324,000 shares, of which 300,000 were sold to the public at 5,000 livres a share – amounting in all to 1.5 billion livres. The Company had now started to operate in a different manner to that characterising its operations between August 1717 and August 1719, when it had raised around 106 million through the first three share issues.

The shares reached a 1719 high of 10,000 on 2 December. At this point, the market valuation of the Mississippi Company was 6.24 billion livres. Concomitant with these developments the banknote issue of the Royal Bank had been increased from 160 million livres in June to one billion livres by the end of 1719 as money was lent to existing shareholders to purchase further shares. France was awash with liquidity, particularly after the Company guaranteed a floor price of 9,000 livres a share in early 1720 through the establishment of a buying and selling agency known as the "Bureau d'Achat et de Vente". Effectively, the workings of this agency monetised shares.

In February 1720, the Royal Bank and the Company of the Indies were formally merged together. At this juncture, Law, who had been appointed Controller General of Finances, in January 1720, wrote: "One sees here a sequence of ideas which are interlinked and which reveal more and more the principle on which they are based" (1934: iii, 98–9).

For a while the System, in all its unifying beauty, seemed to work. Economic activity boomed, the national debt seemed to be under control, money was plentiful and the interest rate had been driven down to 2 per cent. Law had created a financial system the long-term viability of which was crucially dependent on the growth of the real economy. There had to be some equilibrium relationship between the financial system and the real economy. For a while, a temporary equilibrium existed as transactors seemed content to remain within the financial circuit trading money for shares, and shares for money. However, once money started spilling too quickly from the financial circuit into the real economy, problems arose. The real economy proved to be incapable of generating sufficient growth in commodities to match the monetary expansion, so that the excess money created inflation and balance of payments problems.

Law had always believed that the growth in the real economy, spurred on by monetary expansion, would be sufficient to mop up the newly created money. Indeed he went further and in *Money and Trade* argued that monetary expansion would lead to a balance of payments surplus. For a period Law tried to lock transactors into the financial circuit by a series of measures ranging from prohibitions on the holding of more than 500 livres of specie or bullion, to the de-monetisation of gold and a phased monthly de-monetisation of silver. These measures worked temporarily. But there was still too much liquidity in the System. On 21 May 1720, an *arrêt* was published stipulating that shares were to be reduced by four-ninths (from 9,000 to 5,000) and banknotes by half (e.g. a banknote worth 10,000 livres was to be reduced to 5,000 livres) between May and December.

This was an attempt to reduce the liquidity of the System thereby bringing the financial circuit back into line with the real economy. Despite the revocation of this 21 May *arrêt* a couple of days later – due to public pressure – the effect on confidence was so great that the System never recovered from it. The price of shares and banknotes fell continuously during the Summer (ironically, at this point the shares in the South Sea were rising rapidly) and the Autumn of 1720. Law was forced to flee the country, with the aid of the Regent, in December.

However, Law had shown that he was capable of conceptualising and establishing – albeit for a short period of time – a modern, non-metallic world at the start of the eighteenth century. It would take economists and financial leaders another couple of centuries to produce for the global economy what Law had achieved in France during 1719–20. Du Tot realised the full extent of this achievement:

> In this state, this construction was admired by everyone in France and was the envy of our neighbours who were really alarmed by it. Its beauty even surpassed all the hopes that had been placed in it since it made people despise and refuse gold and silver. It was a type of miracle which posterity will not believe. However, it is clear that there was a period, of many months, when no one wanted them [gold and silver].
>
> (1935: 106)

Nicolas Du Tot

In 1738, the *Réflexions politiques sur les finances et le commerce* was published. No author's name appeared on the title page, suggesting that the writer wished to remain anonymous. Its publication in Paris meant, however, that writers such as Voltaire would soon discover the author's surname.[3] Voltaire quickly established that it had been written by a certain M. Dutot. However, no first name was produced for the mysterious and incorrectly spelt Dutot. He appeared to be a man who wished to keep his head down. A year later, in 1739, an excessively abridged English translation of the book, *Political Reflections upon the Finances & Commerce of France*, was published in London. Again, even though we now know that Du Tot was in London at the time of its publication, no author was given for the work. We are dealing here with a man who, either out of fear or modesty, wished to maintain a very low profile.

Who was the mysterious "M. Dutot"? From the *Réflexions* it appeared that the author had worked in some capacity for John Law's System. When John Law's *Oeuvres Complètes* were published by Paul Harsin in 1934, it emerged that Law in one of his mémoires had described Du Tot as a "caissier" in the Compagnie des Indes, confirming that he had worked for him. Harsin, who located a manuscript written by Du Tot, subsequently published a further work by Du Tot to provide an "édition intégrale" of Dutot's *Réflexions politiques* in 1935.

This was not the only manuscript that Du Tot bequeathed to posterity. He also left behind a complete history of Law's System which is now located in the Bibliothèque Universitaire in Poitiers. This manuscript, *Du Tot Histoire du Système de John Law 1716–1720*, was edited by me, and published by the Institut National d'Etudes Démographiques in Paris in 2000. At the time of editing this manuscript, I had discovered a range of additional information on the author. First of all, his name was Du Tot rather than Dutot. Second, he had actually been the *sous-trésorier* of the Royal Bank rather than a cashier. Furthermore, because of the reluctance of the Royal Bank's *trésorier*, Etienne Bourgeois, to carry out his duties, Du Tot had been the *de facto trésorier* of the Bank. Third, it had been established that he had been born in Normandy, close to Cherbourg. Apart from these newly discovered facts, there were still important basic information gaps about Du Tot's life. His first name was still not known, although it had been conjectured that it was most likely to have been either Nicolas or Pierre. Furthermore his dates of birth and death were not known.

Now new information found in the Archives Nationales and the Bibliothèque Nationale fills in these gaps, and provides a more rounded account of the career of Du Tot. Let us start by working back from the day Du Tot died. Sometime between one and two in the afternoon of 12 September 1741 according to Du Tot's wife, Marie née Marchand, her husband Nicolas Du Tot had died three hours previously at his residence on the first floor of the Hotel de Lussac, rue de la Croix des Petits Champs, in the parish of St Eustache.[4] In accordance with the law of the time, seals were placed on the apartment and an inventory taken of the deceased's possessions. This inventory, along with the claims of various creditors against his estate, provide some new evidence on Du Tot's background and lifestyle.[5]

Now that his Christian name is known as Nicolas it is possible, using the Cherbourg archives, to state definitively that Nicolas Du Tot was born near Cherbourg in 1671. He was the son of Maître Nicolas Du Tot who was born in 1642 and died in February 1717. Nicolas Du Tot Sr. married Marie Robin on 19 August 1664. They had six children, three boys and three girls. Du Tot's father was a merchant described in the Cherbourg documents as a "bourgeois, marchand, conseiller du roi et lieutenant des traits foraines". Du Tot was baptised on 4 May 1671. The "scellé après le deces du Sieur Nicolas Du Tot" reveals that, at the time of his death,

Du Tot's brother Pierre (the eldest brother Jean had died in 1722) was living in Valonges close to Cherbourg.

Nothing is known about Du Tot's career prior to his commencing work for Law's Royal Bank in January 1720. Then aged forty-nine, he must have been regarded as an efficient administrator to be appointed to the position of under-treasurer of the Bank (*sous-trésorier de la banque*). Law's later confusion in describing Du Tot as a *caissier* rather than the *sous-trésorier* of the Bank suggests that Du Tot was a self-effacing administrator who worked diligently and preferred not to have a high profile.

Du Tot married Marie Marchand, the daughter of a Strasbourg "*bourgeois negociant*", on 16 August 1713. It was a marriage of a bourgeois to a bourgeois with Marie Marchand his wife bringing a dowry of 2,000 livres invested in annuities (*rentes*). There appear to have been no children born to the couple, or, if there were, they pre-deceased Nicolas Du Tot.

Du Tot lived for seventy years, but was not associated with the fashionable intellectual salons where the "*philosophes*" met. It may have been that he was a retiring type, or, alternatively, that commerce and finance were not regarded at the time as suitable subjects for the salons.

This situation would dramatically change in the 1750s when Madame de Pompadour, the King's mistress, encouraged the growth of a salon around her physician Francois Quesnay. Du Pont de Nemours, in the preface of *De l'exportation et de l'importation des grains* (1764), praised her for providing the hospitable environment in the palace at Versailles for Quesnay to first produce the *Tableau Economique*. But while Quesnay had the powerful Madame de Pompadour supporting his efforts, all Du Tot had was the memory of Law – a man whom the French regarded suspiciously.

There was, however, at least one link between Du Tot and a *philosophe* in that Baron von Holbach, the French social and political philosopher, lent Du Tot money. A representative of the Baron claimed against Du Tot's estate after his death.[6] Holbach, who was only eighteen at the time of his loan to Du Tot, may have met up with the latter because of their common interest in physics, chemistry, natural history and mineralogy. The inventory of Du Tot's house showed that he had a scientific laboratory and a wide range of mathematical and optical instruments the value of which a number of experts were commissioned to estimate.[7] From Du Tot's inventory we are able to envisage a man fascinated by scientific enquiry and passionate about building up a library of books relating to his varied interests. At his death the most valuable assets he appeared to possess were his scientific instruments and his library of books.

An assessment of Du Tot's work

When he published a further volume of Du Tot's work, Paul Harsin lauded this eighteenth-century writer for his "capital contribution to economic history" (Du Tot 1935: xxiv). At the same time, Harsin felt that, "[h]is qualities as a theorist are slighter ... in general all he does is to reproduce the views of his adversary [Melon]" (ibid.).

Now that there is a further manuscript of Du Tot's work available, can we go further than this? Was Du Tot a great economist? Overall, after reading the Poitiers manuscript, it would be incorrect to classify Du Tot as a great analytical economist. He had other strengths. He was fascinated by statistics and seems to have had the intention of providing as much statistical information as possible on the System. There is no better overall source on the daily economic history of the System than the Poitiers manuscript. This fascination with statistical material had a cost, however, for it meant that he rarely sat back to analyse in depth the material that he had presented.

Du Tot's intellectual influences combined a mixture of French and English authors. He was interested in the statistics produced by Vauban and Rademont on French income and wealth, though his interpretation of these statistics appears to have been heavily influenced by Sir William Petty's work. He showed a strong mercantilistic streak with his policy recommendations on ways to increase exports and reduce imports. These ideas evoke the policy recommendations of Sir Thomas Mun in *England's Treasure by Forraign Trade* (1664).

His dominating intellectual influence, was, however, John Law. He had worked under Law at the height of the Mississippi System, and was clearly impressed by the Scotsman's abilities. Unlike Melon and Pâris-Duverney, he had access to many of Law's unpublished *mémoires* and letters. In some parts of his writings, he paraphrased Law's views on money and the utility of banks. He became a very strong admirer of Law and his System. He described how Law arrived in France, an independently wealthy man, with a plan to improve the French economy that was based on his understanding of how the English and the Dutch had established and developed a properly functioning financial system:

> M. Law, a Scottish gentleman, was then in France where, according to some he arrived with 2 millions in sound money and according to others with sixteen to eighteen hundred thousand livres. He was a handsome, well mannered and gentle man. He traveled through all the countries of Europe with the objective of knowing their different systems of government. He reflected a great deal on the factors that had so greatly increased the revenues of the Dutch and the English relative to other nations. He had learnt that the manner of administering the finances determined the power or weakness of a state, the good or bad fortune of people and that the prodigious increase in the revenues of the Dutch and English came from their trade and that the principal reasons for this increase was in turn due to the establishment of their banks and their trading companies. He had attentively studied the regulations and method of working of these establishments. He understood that they could be established in France in less

time than elsewhere and in a more perfect manner because here all the authority is vested in the person of the King...

(2000: 55–6)[8]

Already in this extract, the reader can see Du Tot's admiration for Law. When Law was appointed Controlleur Général des Finances in January 1720, Du Tot elaborated on Law's character: "M. Law was certainly well intentioned. His principal was truth and his objective the public good. He wished to make the people happy, this glory was his only aspiration..." (ibid.: 316–17).

Du Tot added that he was under no obligation to write such praise for Law: "One must not believe that gratitude obliges me to speak in this manner. This would be to make a major mistake because I never received any favours and my situation gives adequate testimony to that fact. However, justice must be paid to the truth" (ibid.: 318).

When Law was forced to flee from France in December 1720, Du Tot reminded his readers as to how Law, who had arrived in France a rich man, left it a poor one:

I know that he had no assets abroad and that he took none with him except for 1,200 silver écus and a diamond worth two thousand écus ... It was in this way that a man, who entered the kingdom with 1,600,000 livres according to some and 1,800,0000 according to others, left it.

(ibid.: 644)

It could be argued that Du Tot lacked a sense of balance in that he always sought to justify Law's actions, and that this over-enthusiasm for both Law and his System dulled his critical faculties. From this perspective some will say that his writings lack a sense of objectivity. As against this it should be remembered that Du Tot was in a key position to witness one of the most ambitious macroeconomic experiments ever undertaken. This experiment involved (1) the attempt to remove specie from the monetary system and to replace it with paper money, and (2) the re-structuring of the national debt by the conversion of public-sector debt into equity of the Mississippi Company. The Mississippi System represented a radical attempt to overthrow the old financial system of the *Ancien Régime*. Given Law's foreign background and his unsavoury reputation it was quite remarkable that he was able to achieve what he did in less than five years.

Law was an economic theorist with great vision. Even Adam Smith referred to the "splendid but visionary ideas" of Law (1976: 317). Normally theorists are not policy-makers. Law showed, however, the dual capacity of theorist and policy-maker. Du Tot felt proud to work for Law and to be associated with his ambitious experiment, a pride which is apparent from his overall appraisal of Law's System.

From an analytical viewpoint Du Tot's writings do not rank alongside those of a Law or Cantillon (1755). Nonetheless, they are extremely useful not only in the provision of such a detailed amount of statistical material on the System, but also because they show some of the reasons as to why Law failed. Working from within the System Du Tot recognised that Law had pushed the System too far and too fast:

> His project, which was to procure abundance in France, was big and noble: but his zeal to produce results too quickly made him push credit a little too far. This excess would not have mattered if he had a year to do what he did in two months. Such a time would have made the structure more solid than it was.
>
> (2000: 486)

Later Du Tot returned to the same theme: "[W]e were too much pressed for time, we wanted to do in a month what should have taken a year, we pushed credit too far so as to produce good as quickly as possible... (ibid.: 663). In this, Du Tot may have been just paraphrasing Law's own sentiments: "I do not pretend to say that I did not make mistakes. I admit that I did and that if I was to start all over again I would act differently. I would go more slowly but surely" (in Harsin 1980: iii, 197).

This excessive enthusiasm on Law's part to implement his macroeconomic plan was not the only cause of the downfall of the System. Law's problems, from Du Tot's viewpoint, were the displacement effects that he had created in substituting a totally new system for the *Ancien Régime's* financial model. Law, in a very short space of time, had replaced the *rentiers* with shareholders, had removed most of the power base of the financiers, and – seemingly – unfettered the monarchy from the shackles of the rentier/financier classes. It was not just an economic revolution that he had produced, but also a socio-political revolution. These groups reacted to protect their financial and political base.

Du Tot continually contrasted trade ("le commerce") with finance ("la finance"). The former was good and necessary for the development of the economy whereas the latter anchored the economy and prevented it from developing:

> The new system was very useful to the state for through the introduction of trade and abundance it banished a false finance which provided many people with the means of enriching themselves at the expense of the state. It removed from the rich and the usurers the power they had for acquiring other people's goods at a very low price. It was presented by a stranger and received by a prince who had a discredited reputation. So it is not astonishing that the system encountered great opposition and many obstacles. Such is the fate of new institutions.
>
> (ibid.: 115)

This tension between trade and finance grew with the development of the System. From the beginning of the manuscript, Du Tot contrasted the different roles of the man dedicated to trade "who is 'a man dear to the state' and 'the man dedicated to finance' who, by the opposite route, works to destroy the state" (f. 12). It is a theme that Du Tot emphasised repeatedly:

> This system was useful and beneficial to the state but it was against the interests of a number of rich individuals or usurers. It removed from the latter the means of taking goods from others at an excessively low price. It diminished their wealth and their position by permitting most people to be in a situation of not needing their ruinous assistance. It decried their art in establishing that of trade, the father of abundance, before which the false finance did not dare appear without showing all its horrors. The losses of this small group of people was counterbalanced by the gains made by all the others.
>
> (ibid.: 492)

Du Tot attacked them mercilessly for their opposition, castigating the false finance, the usurers, the financiers and the rentiers (e.g. 1935: 459, 494, 658). These were the enemies from within who were attacking the System.

Who were the people in the cabal opposed to Law's policies? The cast of characters opposed to the System becomes more clearly delineated as Du Tot unveiled the step-by-step breakdown of the System in the second half of 1720. The financiers that were utterly hostile to Law constituted the "cabal" at the apex of the opposition to Law. The second layer of opposition came from the Parliament made up of members of the judiciary. The financiers and the Parliamentarians had mutual interests in the old *rentes*-driven financial system.

Law's System had, according to him, successfully replaced the old financial system. But, its success had exposed it to the self-interested attack of the financiers:

> His objective was to introduce order and simplicity into the finances, to provide a low rate of interest, to re-establish trade, to make the King independent showing to him as clearly as possible the state's business. Doubtlessly this was the secret reason that displeased those whose interest was in disorder and confusion...
>
> (ibid.: 494)

Bearing in mind Daniel Dessert's view in *Argent, pouvoir et société au Grand Siècle* (1984) that the rich nobility, fronted by the financiers, constituted the real power structure in the *Ancien Régime*, Du Tot's opinion is very much consistent with that of Dessert in that he believed it was almost impossible for Law to succeed because of the way his System was attempting to displace the financier/rentier class and their backers, the rich nobility and the judiciary.

In his account of the history of the System during 1720, Du Tot attempted to identify the key moment when the "cabal" of financiers and their followers succeeded in blocking Law's intentions and forcing the System in a direction which, according to Du Tot, Law did not want it to take. This decisive moment in the System's history arose on 5 March 1720 when the *Arrêt du conseil d'état du roy concernant les billets de banque, les actions de la Compagnie des Indes, le cours des especes, et le prix des matieres d'or & d'argent* was published. This *arrêt* contained important decisions relating to the policy of supporting share prices and increasing the attractiveness of shares and banknotes relative to specie. According to Du Tot, it was Law's enemies that forced through the 5 March arrêt.

The background to this measure was as follows. On 22 February, a decree had been made abolishing the Company's Bureau d'Achat et de Vente which up to that point had been buying its shares from the public in order to sustain their price. It looked as if tough measures to prevent the System from overheating had been introduced. Because of the removal of this prop, the share price fell by over 2,000 livres within a couple of days. This drop in the share price appears to have created intense pressure for a repeal of the 22 February measures. This repeal came quickly through the *arrêt* of 5 March. There were a number of key elements in this 5 March publication. Article ii fixed the price of shares of the Company at 9,000 livres a share; article v created a Bureau de Conversions that from 20 March would convert shares into banknotes and vice versa at the price of 9,000 livres.

Thus, the earlier policy of allowing the price to be determined by market forces was reversed. The Bureau de Conversions was just another name for the Bureaux d'Achat et de Vente. More significantly, Law, by providing a guaranteed price of 9,000 livres per share, had monetised the shares of the Mississippi Company.

The 5 March measures deepened the disproportionate gap that emerged between the value of paper money and specie. First of all, they created a situation in which the banknote issue would go out of control when the public sold shares for banknotes. Second, article ix declared that: "[T]he banknote was a money which was not subject to any variation." Combining this with the 11 March *arrêt* stipulating the progressive reduction in value and the eventual demonetisation of specie, it effectively meant that value of specie would decline progressively relative to the banknotes. Law's later comments in a memoir written in 1723 suggested that he was aware of this problem from March onwards.

According to both his own accounts and those of Du Tot, the Scotsman wished to dampen down the System in March 1720 by introducing the measures that he later attempted to introduce on 21 May. Du Tot's account stressed that the situation would never have arisen if "the state had been less charged with indebtedness when the Regency was established". Law had been forced to attack not only the monetary crisis, but also the financial crisis created by the overhang of the Crown's debt. It was necessary to expand credit "so as to open the doors to abundance" (1935: 418). But in March, Law realised that credit had been over-expanded and that he had to sacrifice the banknote in favour of shares:

> Mr. Law had been considering this operation since the previous March when he saw that it was impossible to maintain the creditworthiness of the banknote and that it was necessary to sacrifice it in favor of shares so as to enable all the debtors to be in a position to free themselves. This operation was contained in the outline of a decree that he sent to the Regent. The latter appeared happy with it. It reduced the banknote by half and shares by four ninths for the first of December next   that is to say that the share was reduced by successive monthly reductions from 9,000 to 5,000. He also sent this project to certain members of the council who greatly approved it. However, at the bottom of their hearts they looked upon it as a favorable occasion for getting rid of its author. From that moment they prepared their guns for firing on the publication of the decree.
>
> (ibid.: 418–19)

So, instead of granting Law permission to dampen the System in March 1720, he had been forced (1) to guarantee shares at 9,000 livres, thereby creating the possibility of a sizeable expansion in the banknote issue, and (2) to make the banknote invariable to domestic exchange-rate changes. This latter measure meant that with each reduction in the value of specie, as specified by the 11 March *déclaration*, the value of banknotes would increase relative to specie.

There were therefore two problems for the paper-money supply. In the first place, it would be increased when the public sold shares in exchange for banknotes. Second, the value of the paper banknote issue would increase relative to specie when the latter was reduced each month. Du Tot was strongly against these developments. He believed that there was a fixed relationship between the paper-money supply and the specie money supply (ibid.: 398–9).

Du Tot displayed considerable admiration for Law's theories and policies. However, when the System ran into difficulties in 1720, Du Tot invoked a principle that he felt had been forsaken. This principle involved restricting the amount of banknotes in circulation to the estimated amount of specie in circulation. He calculated that the specie money supply at the start of 1720 amounted to 1.3 billion livres. At that stage the banknote issue was below this at one billion livres. But once the Company started purchasing its own shares, and, after this, when the price of shares

were guaranteed at 9,000 livres each, the banknote issue shot up between
February and May 1720 to over 2.7 billion livres.

This broke the "égalité" or "parité" that Du Tot believed should have
been maintained between banknotes and specie. He devoted eleven folio
pages (ibid.: 30–40) in the *article second contenant l'origine et les principes du
credit public, et son utilité* to an attempt to provide a rationale for this parity
approach. He argued that in a state without mines, if there was a shortage
of specie, the monarch could supplement this deficiency by creating
credit. What did he mean by credit? For him "the first use of credit was to
represent money by paper: (ibid.: 30). Here Du Tot showed that he
believed that there was a strong link between specie and credit. Banknotes, because of their high velocity of circulation, were the ideal form of
credit to create. He did recognise that the basis of credit was confidence,
and this in turn meant that it was undesirable to create an excessive
amount of banknotes. He came up with a simple rule that the amount of
banknotes should equal the amount of specie:

> To re-assure people on this point it appeared that in a state like this
> one where the public was not used to credit it was first of all necessary
> to double the money and trade by a credit which did not exceed the
> sum of the specie in circulation in the state so that it could always be
> convertible into specie on demand...
>
> (1935: 34)

This parity rule was specific to the circumstances of France, which was
unaccustomed to this type of banking.

Du Tot contended that the parity principle that he advocated was
broken by the *arrêt* of 5 March which: (1) monetised shares by guaranteeing their price at 9,000 livres and (2) made banknotes invariant to
domestic exchange rate changes in specie. The first element of the 5
March *arrêt* led to a very rapid expansion of the banknote issue when the
public sold shares for banknotes. The second element meant that banknotes kept increasing in value relative to specie after the 11 March *déclaration* stipulating continuous monthly reductions in the value of gold and
silver. This resulted in the following:

> Public credit was forced and overdone by increasing the banknote
> issue up to 2,736,540,000 livres without at the same time increasing
> the specie that the banknotes represented. There was therefore no
> longer any parity between the banknotes and specie, the proportional-
> ity between supply and demand was broken...
>
> (1935: 513)

I doubt very much that Law would have agreed with Du Tot's view on
the need to have the currency issue limited to the size of the gold and

silver in circulation. Law wanted to go a great deal further than this, and to create a true paper money system that was de-coupled from gold and silver. Du Tot, as shown earlier, expressed awe, admiration and incredulity at Law's achievements in the early part of 1720. However, despite his enthusiasm for Law and his System, he does not appear to have understood the extent to which Law intended the System to be revolutionary. Law wanted to have a specie-less France. Du Tot did not agree with this and his proposal for a type of 100 per cent metallic money for banknotes was very much at odds with Law's approach.

It is noticeable that Du Tot's manuscript finished in December 1720, the period in which Law made what proved to be a permanent departure from France. The great macroeconomic experiment was over. Du Tot was left to become a type of curator of Law's ideas and policies – a work to which he seems to have applied himself with considerable diligence for the rest of his life. Johnson once remarked to Boswell: "You have two topics, yourself and me, and I'm sick of both." I do not believe Law would have said this of Du Tot, for the latter helped put in perspective many of the issues and problems that Law sought to solve during the period 1716–20. He would, however, have insisted on heavily editing Du Tot's interpretation of the System's replacement of metallic money by paper credit.

Notes

1 Smith (1976: 45).
2 Du Tot, (2000); Giraudeau, "Variations exactes de tous les effets en papier, qui ont eu cours sur la place de Paris, a commancer au mois d'Aout 1719 jusques au dernier mars 1721", in the Bibliothèque de l'Arsenal, Ms. 4061.
3 Voltaire, "Lettre sur l'ouvrage de M. Du Tot et sur celui de M. Melon", *Pour et contre* (1738: 296–312); "Lettre à M. Thiriot sur le livre de M. Dutot", Bibliothèque Française, XXIX (1739: 108–21).
4 Archives Nationales Y 13092, Scellé après le deces du Sieur Nicolas Dutot Bourgeois de Paris, du 11 Septembre, 1741. (My thanks to Dr Loic Charles for his assistance in helping to locate this document.)
5 Archives Nationales, Minutier Central, LIII/299, "Inventaire 25 Septembre 1741 après le décès du Sieur Nicolas Du Tot".
6 Archives Nationales 13092, Scellé après le décès ... folio 19. The Baron's interests were represented by Nicolas Daine.
7 Ibid.: 32–3.
8 The folio references are to the original manuscript which is now reproduced in *Du Tot: Histoire du Système de John Law 1716–20.*

References

Anonymous (1723) *Love-letters between a certain late nobleman and the famous Mr. Wilson: discovering the true history of the rise and surprising grandeur of that celebrated beau,* London: A. Moore.
Cantillon, R. (1755). *Essai sur la nature du en general,* London: Fletcher Gyles (Paris: Guillyn).

Dessert, D. (1984) *Argent, pouvoir et société au Grand Siècle*, Paris: Fayard.

Du Pont de Nemours, P. S. (1764) "De l'exploration et de l'importation des grains," in Geuthner, P. (ed.), *Collection des Economistes*, Paris, 1911.

Du Tot, N. (1738) *Réflexions politiques sur les finances et le commerce*, The Hague: Les Frères Vaillant & Nicolas Prevost.

—— (1935) *Réflexions politiques sur les finances et le commerce*, ed. P. Harsin, Paris: Sirey.

—— (2000) *Histoire du Systême de John Law 1716–20*, ed. A. Murphy, Paris: Institut National d'Études Démographiques.

Faure, E. (1977) *La Banqueroute de Law*, Paris: Gallimard.

Harsin, P. (1935) "L'argent est-il le nerf de la guerre?" *Revue des Sciences Politiques*, 18.

Hume, D. (1752) *Political Discourses*. Edinburgh: R. Fleming for A. Kincaid and A. Donaldson.

Law, J. (1705) *Money and Trade Considered with a Proposal for Supplying the Nation with Money*, Edinburgh: A. Anderson.

—— (1934: 1980) *John Law: Oeuvres Complètes*, cd. P. Harsin, Paris: Vaduz.

—— (1994) *John Law's Essay on a Land Bank*, ed. A. E. Murphy, Dublin: Aeon Publishing.

Marshall, A. (1924) *Money, Credit and Commerce*, London: Macmillan.

Marx, K. (1981) *Capital, vol. 3*, New York: Penguin.

Mun, T. (1664) *England's Treasure by Forraign Trade*, London: Thomas Clark, reprinted, New York: August M. Kelley, 1968.

Murphy, A. (1986) *Richard Cantillon: Entrepreneur and Economist*, Oxford: Oxford University Press.

—— (1997) *John Law: Economic Theorist and Policy-Maker*, Oxford: Oxford University Press.

Pâris-Duverney, J. (1740) *Examen du livre intitulé Réflexions Politiques*, The Hague: V & N Prevôt.

Schumpeter, J. (1954) *A History of Economic Analysis*, Oxford: Oxford University Press.

Smith, A. [1776] (1976) *An Inquiry into the Nature and Causes of the Wealth of Nations*, ed. R. H. Campbell, A. S. Skinner and W. B. Todd, Oxford: Clarendon Press.

8 Genesis of Hume's political economy of "manners"

Tatsuya Sakamoto

Introduction

In this essay, I clarify what was original about the particular way in which Hume discussed economic subjects – ranging from apparently theoretical issues such as the origin of commerce, money and economic development to more practical and political questions including the moral quality of luxury and the use and abuse of paper money and public credit. It is impossible within this limited space to provide a systematic analysis of these subjects. Rather, I seek here to shed analytical light upon a specific idea with a view to providing a more systematic answer to the question of the precise place of David Hume against the background of the Scottish Enlightenment.

In Book III, Chapter IV of the *Wealth of Nations*, Smith gives an interesting account of three reasons why "the increase and riches of commercial and manufacturing towns, contributed to the improvement and cultivation of the countries to which they belonged". The first of these reasons is that commercial and manufacturing towns provide "a great and ready market" for the agricultural products of the country. Second, the city merchants are "commonly ambitious of becoming country gentlemen" and are "generally the best of all improvers" of the otherwise uncultivated country estates. Third, and most remarkably, Smith contends that "commerce and manufacturing gradually introduced order and good government, and with them, the liberty and security of individuals, among the inhabitants of the country" (1776/1976: I, 412).

Of particular importance in this connection is Smith's following comment: "This, though it has been the least observed, is by far the most important of all their effects. Mr. Hume is the only writer who, so far as I know, has hitherto taken notice of it" (1776/1976: I, 412). Editors of the Glasgow edition say that Smith's comment is "a little odd", considering the fact that there had been predecessors in the discovery of the civilizing effect of commerce such as Adam Ferguson, John Millar and William Robertson. They even suggest that Smith possibly wrote that particular part at a very early stage of his composition when Hume was still the only writer who had made the "discovery". However, apart from the simple fact that Smith was too meticulous an author not to have amended the earlier-written part immediately before its final publication, there seems to be an important sense in which his exclusive mention of Hume's name is to be taken as a deliberate act.

Smith singled out Hume as the "only writer" who grasped the true sense in which "the silent and insensible operation of foreign commerce and manufactures" (1776/1976: I, 418) of the towns was the decisive historical cause of the individual liberty of the country. Smith was possibly critical of those authors who discussed the same subject in a similar fashion after Hume, but who did not make due acknowledgement as they should have. Even if this were the case, Smith probably believed that this was not due to any lack of their respect for the common friend, but was a result of their failure to understand the true nature of the question.

Polity and commerce in civilized monarchy

Hume's inquiry into this subject started as early as 1741 and 1742 when he published *Essays Moral and Political*. In closely linked two chapters, "Of Liberty and Despotism" and "Of the Rise and Progress of the Arts and Sciences", Hume proposed a fundamental criticism of the prevailing Whiggish distinction between republican liberty and monarchical despotism. According to this traditional distinction, commerce on the one hand and the arts and sciences on the other never flourish except in free governments (i.e. republics and limited monarchies).

Hume refutes this classical republican view by employing ancient and modern historical sources to conclude that modern civilized monarchies represented by French and English "absolute" monarchies were far from despotic. On the contrary, Hume praises the security of individual property that the civilized monarchy ensures and the resulting economic prosperity. Even if far removed from the level of the security of property guaranteed by parliamentary legislation, as was the case in the post-Revolution England, nonetheless the security of property under civilized monarchies was effective enough in Hume's view for generating individual economic activities at the early stage of market economy in Europe.

Hume's insight into the "modern" nature of European monarchies was founded upon his idea of market economy as an essentially modern historical phenomenon. Market economy as propelled by individual self-interest and expanding by the international division of labour was necessarily transforming the nature of the post-feudal, early-modern and so-called "absolutist" government.

The English republican prejudice against the European monarchies as despotic misunderstood their changing nature. Hume says that Machiavelli, the founder of modern politics, made the same mistake: "[H]is reasonings especially upon monarchical government, have been found extremely defective…" (1741–2/1987: 88). The vital significance of trade and commerce for modern states in general, be it republican or monarchical, has escaped the attention of political writers until recently. "Trade was never esteemed an affair of state till the last century; and there scarcely is any ancient writer on politics, who has made mention of it" (ibid.).

It was quite easy to know the reason why ancient Greek and Roman writers on politics were completely silent on the commercial nature of government. These societies themselves were essentially non-commercial as illustrated by the universal prevalence of "agrarian laws". Hume's theory of civilized monarchy provided a vital starting point for his further inquiry into the mutual relationship between commerce, liberty and political constitution. But it must be remembered that at this stage of his argument Hume was discussing under the dominant preoccupation of the republic–monarchy dichotomy. His belief in the peculiarly modern and commercial character of civilized monarchies nonetheless ultimately derives from the Whig stereotypical distinction between liberty and despotism, as stated so clearly in his following comments:

> However perfect, therefore, the monarchical form may appear to some politicians, it owes all its perfection to the republican; …It must borrow its laws, and methods, and institutions, and consequently its stability and order, from free governments. These advantages are the sole growth of republics.
>
> (ibid.: 125)

In this remark, Hume makes an explicit distinction between two types of monarchies, the "civilized" and the "barbarous". Indeed, Hume was convinced that only the former type was able to generate the rule of law by borrowing it from republican government. But I notice here a circularity in his argument. In Hume's view only the "great wisdom and reflexion" of that particular prince or monarch could have achieved the rule of law under the civilized monarchies. The fundamental question here is: what produced this "wisdom and reflexion" in the first place? Hume's answer was as follows:

> But such a degree of wisdom can never be expected, before the greater refinements and improvements of human reason. These refinements require curiosity, security, and law. The first growth, therefore, of the arts and sciences can never be expected in despotic governments.
>
> (ibid.: 118)

On the one hand, the "great wisdom and reflexion" of a particular monarch must be logically preceded by the more universal diffusion and refinement of the "human reason" in general. But, on the other hand, this enhanced intellectual level of the people in general must be further pre-supposed by the introduction by the monarch of the rule of law from republican or free governments.

Hume's view confirmed and enlarged by his trip to Europe

From early 1748 for almost a year Hume made an extensive tour over the Continent as a member of the diplomatic expedition of Lieutenant-General James St Clair. On their way to the final destination, Turin, he called at major cities of Germany, Austria and Italy. Among many interest-ing events and episodes which Hume encountered on route, I would like to draw special attention to his discovery of the primacy of the moral over physical causes as the determining factor of national characters. This was to develop into a systematic study in a new essay entitled "Of National Characters" added in the 1748 edition of the *Essays Moral and Political.*

Regarding the date of composition of this essay, there is a well-known case presented by Paul Chamley (1975: 274–305). In this brilliant work, Chamley seeks to establish that the basic ideas of Hume's essay on national characters were originally inspired by his knowledge of Mon-tesquieu's *L'Esprit des lois*, which was still in the printing process in Geneva, to be published in November 1748. On the basis of admirable historical research, Chamley concludes that "Since the *Essay* fits in exactly with the part of *L'Esprit des lois* dealing with the influence of climate on national characters, Hume's information must have gone at least as far as that" (ibid.: 296).

I suggest, on the contrary, that Hume's essay as fundamental criticism of the climatic theory of national character was an inevitable by-product of his extensive tour of European countries. In particular, on the basis of his first-hand observation of the differences and varieties in the moral, polit-ical and economic conditions of those countries, Hume came to realize that these differences could not be attributed to purely climatic or phys-ical causes. This should not be surprising when we are reminded of the long-standing European debate with respect to the relative importance between the moral and physical causes.

Furthermore, in Hume's case, the theory of civilized monarchy served as an effective tool for understanding the striking social realities of Euro-pean countries that were totally different from what the British nation was made to believe. Notably, Germany, as Hume observed with his own eyes, had a tremendous impact to lead him to doubt the truth of the commonly held prejudiced against the country. He foresaw that, should Germany be unified in the future, it would surely achieve a formidable national wealth and political power in Europe.

This observation stood in sharp contrast with what Hume was to experience during the course of his travels in Austria. It was an infinite variety of the conditions in which people lived under the same rule of Austria. Hume was shocked to see extreme poverty at Knittelfeld in Stiria, just 120 miles distant from Vienna (see Greig 1932: I, 130). However, as Hume travelled further into Tirol, he was surprised to find the opposite social condition as represented by "An Air of Humanity, & Spirit & Health & Plenty is seen in every Face" (ibid.: I, 131).

This brief survey is informative enough to reveal the extent to which Hume had already grasped what were to become more systematic arguments against the climatic theory. Regardless of the question of Paul Chamley's interesting point concerning when and how Hume encountered *L'Esprit des lois*, he had independently developed his thoughts about the relative superiority of the moral and physical causes in the making of national characters, and his answer was unequivocally clear. The main thrust of his criticism of climatic theory was that not only physical, climatic and geographical causes, but also political or constitutional conditions of a given society are equally unable to explain the variety of its social and economic conditions. This discovery must also have derived from Hume's theory of civilized monarchy. In other words, this extensive tour led him to the conviction that the fundamental causes which determine the type of social and economic development of a nation are neither physical, nor political.

In the published essay, Hume resolves the vulgar notion of "national character" into "a peculiar set of manners" in an empiricist fashion and attempts to give a variety of senses in which the moral causes determine manners. Hume defines the moral causes as "all circumstances, which are fitted to work on the mind as motives or reasons, and which render a peculiar set of manners habitual to us" (1741–2/1987: 198). In this definition, Hume understands manners to be something which are worked on (an object) and the moral causes as something which works on (a subject); the moral causes include political, economic and geopolitical circumstances.

However, I must hasten to add that Hume's position in this essay is still transitional. Indeed the essay is a clear statement about the primacy of the moral causes as against climatic and physical influences to determine the variety of national characters. But it does not provide any systematic reasoning that reveals the mutual relationship between moral causes and the "peculiar set of manners" on the one hand, and the relationship between political and non-political kinds of moral causes on the other.

Economic development as the knowledge-productive pattern of social development

Political Discourses, published in 1752, was the chief means by which Hume developed his version of modern commercial society. Notwithstanding its apparent want of systematic character in the formal sense, the theoretical core of Hume's economic thought as a whole is his view of economic development. It is further divided into two argumentative components. The first is a systematic analysis of the mutual relationship between commerce and luxury, and the second is an attempt to provide the theory of money as both logical and historical extension of the first argument. Here I would like to indicate my conclusion in advance by noting that the central organizing principle of these two components is the idea of the "manners".

Hume's idea of luxury means a mutually developing relationship between production and consumption within the market economy and the social division of labour. Not only that, it involves a definitely political dimension. This is made clear by the fact that Hume's argument was directed against three traditional views of luxury. First, the classical republican or Agrarian; second, the Medieval and Calvinist; and third, the Mandevillian. All these traditions or positions were not only profoundly hostile to the moral efficacy of luxurious consumption in different senses of the term, but also were seriously suspicious about the politically corruptive influences of luxury.

Against all these, Hume attempts to present a consistent justification of luxury by way of its radical reformulation as "the refinement in the arts" (the new title after the 1760 edition). As Hume believes, commerce generates popular wealth; popular wealth further generates a popular demand for the rule of law and a regular constitutional government. This was indeed a classic reformulation of the "commerce-liberty" theme in the eighteenth century.

I say this was a re-formulation because the commerce-liberty theme itself was not any invention by Hume, but had long been the focus of moral and political debates ever since the civil war in the seventeenth century. It was "vulgarized" in eighteenth-century debates as the theoretical ground of the ideological defence of the Revolution settlement. In the nineteenth century and after, the commerce-liberty theme grew into the liberal-capitalist or the Marxist versions to bring about different historical consequences.

Not only in general historiography, but also in the development of Hume's own thought, this subject had already formed the substance of his theory of "civilized monarchy". It demonstrated his insight into the commercial nature of the modern civilized government regardless of its formal constitution. But, as it still implicitly remained within the conceptual framework of the liberty–despotism dichotomy, another theoretical step was to be made in the essay on national characters in which Hume substituted the concept of "manners" by way of reducing the analytical importance of constitutional factors.

So what was truly original in Hume's reformulation of the "Commerce-Liberty" theme in *Political Discourses*? I hold that it was a further reformulation of the concept of "manners" as the central principle in such a way as to upgrade the concept from something passive and objective as an historical product of the moral causes to something active and subject-ive as the motivating force of civilization. This transformation was achieved by the introduction of "knowledge" as the primary engine of growth in a civilized society.

Hume identifies two principal roles for knowledge in the civilizing process. One is knowledge as the source of technological and industrial progress. In Hume's view, industry promotes knowledge, and knowledge promotes industry. But here the relationship between the two is neither mutual nor reciprocal. Hume believes that industry originally produces knowledge, and not vice versa. Hume also contends that once the know-ledge-productive or producing pattern of industrial growth is set in motion, then the knowledge-produced pattern of economic growth imme-diately begins to develop with an almost equal force.

By contrast, the second role of knowledge is more of a political and legal nature. It is not only that a nation whose wealth is large enough as a result of the knowledge-productive pattern of economic growth affords "a kind of storehouse of labour, which, in the exigencies of state, may be turned to the public service". More significantly, it necessarily prepares an intellectual and, for that matter, a social and institutional foundation of the rule of law. Notably enough Hume introduces this argument in a rhetoric that makes readers feel that this was exactly what he was driving at in his overall defence of luxury:

> Laws, order, police, discipline; these can never be carried to any degree of perfection, before human reason has refined itself by exer-cise, and by an application to the more vulgar arts, at least, of com-merce and manufacture. Can we expect, that a government will be well modelled by a people, who know not how to make a spinning-wheel, or to employ a loom to advantage?
>
> (1752/1987: 273)

Hume's particular emphasis upon the vital role of knowledge as the intellectual foundation of the rule of law deserves special attention in the context of the genesis of Hume's thought in at least two following senses.

First, it dissolves the circular argument of 1742 as quoted earlier. Here in 1752, it turns out that that "greater refinements and improvements of human reason" are able to take place "by an application to the more vulgar arts, at least, of commerce and manufacture". The knowledge-productive type of economic development in the age of the Tudor absolute monarchy explains why it could have transformed itself into a civilized monarchy without the Tudor monarchs apparently borrowing the laws from any republic.

Second, this argument provides an almost final solution of the problem posed in the essay on national characters of 1748 by clarifying the causal relationship, first between the moral causes in general and manners, and second that between political and non-political causes within the moral causes themselves. In the earlier essay Hume could not give an adequate account of the causes of the seemingly irregular distribution of wealth and poverty in those countries that he visited either by physical or political causes. Now Hume is able to offer an alternative account of the same question by appealing to the varying degrees of realization of the industrious and knowledge-productive pattern of economic development.

Money versus manners in Hume's monetary theory

Hume's monetary theory has long been the most influential and the most widely known part of his economic thought. In particular, the relative importance or centrality in Hume between the quantity theory and the inflationist theory has remained the focal point of interpretation to this day. I do not intend to contribute something to this controversy itself, but rather attempt to shed new light on it by way of theoretical and historical application of Hume's concept of manners in such a way as to attach a somewhat revised significance to the so-called inflationist elements of his theory. Put in a different way, I hold that Hume's idea of manners played a vital role of substantially coordinating the two formally inconsistent or even contradictory theories of money.

Largely overlapping with the three targets of Hume's defence of luxury, his monetary theory is presented as a fundamental criticism of two dominant contemporary views. One was the mercantilist, and the other was the classical republican or agrarian. Furthermore, in line with his strategic deployment of the idea of manners in refuting their views of luxury, Hume went on to make a full use of the same concept when he presents his own monetary theory in a consistent fashion. Viewed in this way, two different monetary theories in Hume reappear in a refreshing light as commonly rooted in and ultimately deriving from the theory of manners.

After explaining the essence of the quantity-theory as if it was a commonly held view, Hume goes on to say: "I shall finish this essay on money, by proposing and explaining two observations, which may, perhaps, serve to employ the thoughts of our speculative politicians" (1741–2/1987: 285). In so saying, he develops the substance of the chapter. The two observations are Hume's account of economic and political consequences of manners as apparently resulting from the large or small quantity of money.

The first observation is an unquestionable rise of commercial activities in Europe as a consequence of the steady increase of money after the discovery of the West Indies. The second is the poverty of many European countries that was generally understood to have proceeded "as is commonly supposed, from the scarcity of money". These two phenomena had something fundamental in common in the sense that both of them were generally believed to have derived from monetary causes. However, as Hume observed them, they are inevitable consequences of different "manners and customs" of European peoples.

Regarding the first question, Hume shrewdly contrasts in the essay "Of Money" those countries represented by England where the increase of money supply resulted in the real rise in commercial and industrial activities with the other group of countries where this did not happen. Hume deliberately excludes Spain and Portugal from the former category by saying that "since the discovery of the mines in AMERICA, industry has encreased in all the nations of EUROPE, except in the possessors of those mines" (1752/1987: 286). With respect to his second observation concerning political strength and the quantity of money, Hume notes in the same essay that "a greater disproportion between the force of GERMANY, at present, and what it was three centuries ago" should be attributed to "manners and customs of the people" rather than to monetary causes as generally imagined (ibid.: 289).

The popular opinion was not entirely wrong in each case because Hume himself believes that the increase or scarcity of money undeniably had a causal connection with each phenomenon. Hume's point was that the monetary causes were only secondary or mediating causes, and they themselves were historical effects of the ultimate and more profound cause, that is people's manners. If this were the case, then it follows that Hume was in a uniquely ambiguous theoretical situation in terms of the grasp of the neutrality of money. In Hume's view, monetary causes were merely external and neutral to economic development in the fundamental sense, but they were not necessarily so in the secondary or historical sense.

At this point of my argument, it may safely be claimed that Adam Smith's commentary on the priority of the "Commerce-Liberty" theme, mentioning Hume's name to the exclusion of all the possible names, was written after deliberate and intentional consideration. It was a reflection upon the unprecedented depth of Hume's theory of economic development as the system of manners.

References

Chamley, P. E. (1975) "The Conflict between Montesquieu and Hume: A Study of the Origins of Adam Smith's Universalism", in A. S. Skinner and T. Wilson (eds), *Essays on Adam Smith*, Oxford: Oxford University Press.

Greig, J. Y. T. (ed.) (1932) *The Letters of David Hume*, 2 vols, Oxford: Oxford University Press.

Hume, D. (1741–2/1987) *Essays, Moral, Political and Literary,* ed. E. F. Miller, rev. edn, Indianapolis: Liberty Classics.

—— (1752/1987) *Political Discourses,* ed. E. F. Miller, rev. edn, Indianapolis: Liberty Classics.

Smith, A. (1776/1976) *An Inquiry into the Nature and Causes of the Wealth of Nations,* ed. R. H. Campbell and A. S. Skinner, Oxford: Oxford University Press.

9 The French debate on the morality and the political economy of luxury

From Boisguilbert to Quesnay

Walter and Shelagh M. Eltis

Introduction

There were great inequalities in income and wealth in the seventeenth and eighteenth centuries. All who wrote on economies and societies therefore confronted the question of whether the extraordinary and often ostentatious consumption of the wealthiest undermined or boosted the economies within which they spent so extravagantly.

This was a more acute issue in France than in Great Britain. It was entirely clear that the British economy was outperforming the French, and British writers were therefore more inclined to take a favourable view of the central elements in the evolution of their economies, including the extraordinary inequalities in personal expenditure which accompanied the undiluted right of the wealthy to dispose of their property in whatever way they wished.

France in contrast had suffered periods of famine and a succession of crises in the state's finances. These produced three seventeenth-century defaults, the desperation of John Law's financial experiments and the subsequent failure of attempts at reform by a succession of Controllers-General. Every aspect of France's economy and society therefore became a subject of critical debate.

Economic publication increased enormously in France in the 1750s. The number of books published on the economy doubled from 1745–9 to 1750–4, and it doubled again between 1750–4 and 1755–9. French political economy was also notable for the social and political distinction of the authors of some of its leading contributions. As in Britain, leading philosophers together with bankers and merchants published on political economy; but the early French writers also included thirty-seven ministers and intendants who published on economics between 1750 and 1789 (Théré 1998, p. 37). The leading economic writers who contributed substantially to the luxury debate included Argenson, Boisguilbert, Cantillon, Forbonnais, Melon, Mirabeau and Quesnay.

Fénelon, Montesquieu, Rousseau and Voltaire also wrote extensively and influentially on luxury. They were deeply concerned with every aspect of French society, and philosophers and theologians no less than ministers and intendants were interested in the impact of luxury on the economy and society.

The various authors attached very different meanings to luxury. It normally denoted inequality, but in addition, did it divert money from essential expenditure elsewhere, or lock it up unproductively? The debate pitted town against countryside and the old nobility against *nouveau riche* financiers and tax farmers. Sumptuary laws which laid down the clothing each social rank was permitted to wear had been designed to contain the consumption of social inferiors within their station but few actually survived into the eighteenth century. It is interesting how late in the century dress codes were still being advocated by social conservatives.

A few economic writers understood that a successful economy needed industry, agriculture and commerce, and therefore hesitated to categorise swathes of their fellow citizens as members of a potentially redundant luxurious class.

This essay will present a broad outline of the luxury debate until François Quesnay's brilliant development of the new macroeconomics in Richard Cantillon's *Essai sur la nature de commerce en général* of 1755. With extraordinary additions and refinements, he created what Philippe Steiner (1998, p. 5) has described as "the new science of political economy", but at the same time he abandoned the social and political issues which had preoccupied his predecessors and presented the influence of luxury within the constraints of the economic model he had invented – his celebrated *Tableau économique.*

The luxury debate before the physiocrats

Pierre de Boisguilbert is sometimes regarded as the founder of French political economy and he opened the economic dimension of the luxury debate in the final decades of the reign of Louis XIV. Heavy war taxation had brought concern that France's taxable base was being eroded, as impossible burdens on the peasantry caused crops to be abandoned and land to be withdrawn from cultivation. Boisguilbert expressed this in his published works and in impassioned communications to successive Controllers-General of Finance. He had the profound insight that, despite their individual lowly status, the spending of peasants, given their preponderance in the population, had a huge impact on the economy, bringing a downward spiral to wealth and population if it was damaged (1966, pp. 619–21). Boisguilbert's attacks on the unjust nature of the main land tax, the *taille,* and its inefficiencies as a revenue producer together with his views on how indirect taxes prevented goods coming to market – his striking example was of Norman peasants being obliged to drink water rather than cider (p. 279) – were not matters for dispute. Concern that France's population had fallen lay behind much subsequent debate on luxury.

Boisguilbert cited Henri IV's minister, Maximilien de Bethune, duc de Sully, as setting a precedent in support of his belief in the need to restore the consumption of the peasant class. Sully, he said, supported the grain market through free trade at a price which allowed the exploitation of land of every condition, and left the roads free for the transport of grain which he called the greatest source of revenue for the King and the people. He claimed that Sully saw that taxes were fairly spread on people as well as goods; that customs and the *gabelle* (the tax on salt) were not too high and that fixed capital was sacred (ibid., p. 432). Boisguilbert was hostile to the usual government response to distress, namely to hold down the price of grain either from concern for the poor or for considerations of public order. He believed that such action had reduced rents to unsustainable levels where land was taken out of cultivation, which resulted in even higher prices in years of poor harvests (ibid., pp. 886–7).

In the eighteenth century other writers who thought that the agricultural sector was starved of manpower or investment also praised Sully, but it was often to attack Jean Baptiste Colbert, minister under Louis XIV, who was seen as having diverted government support to industry to the detriment of agriculture. Since luxury goods were largely imported, or the product of protected new industries such as the manufacture of silks and porcelain to substitute for such imports, it was a temptation to declare them unnecessary and harmful.

The Court of Louis XIV used ostentation in dress, jewels, theatrical displays, fountains, statues, and so on, as a deliberate statement of the splendour of royalty. This luxury and Louis XIV' s wars were financed through the sale of offices and recourse to tax-farmers who bought the right to raise taxes on behalf of the king. Revenues were anticipated for several years.

An aristocratic view of what was needed to place society on its proper path is seen in the Plan de Gouvernement proposed in 1711 to the due de Bourgogne, then heir to the throne. Known from its place of drafting as the *Tables de Chaulnes*, it blamed luxury for corrupting the behaviour of the whole nation and declared that it made merchants wealthy at the expense of the nobility. At court the reformers required moderation in furniture, clothing, horses and food, while they insisted on sumptuary laws on the Roman model. They also had measures to restrict positions to nobles alone, attacked marriages where social standing was unequal and sought to deny noble titles to commoners who bought noble lands. The programme was not wholly backward-looking since it proposed that nobles should be permitted to engage in the wholesale trade and be able to join the magistrature without loss of noble status (Galliani 1989, p. 144).

The prospective heir to the throne on whom these plans depended actually died before Louis XIV and the proposals died with him. But one of their authors, his former tutor, the aristocratic archbishop of Cambrai, François de Salignac de la Mothe Fénelon, had written a book in the 1690s, *Les aventures de Telemaque,* to impart lessons in kingship in a palatable form and this contained the same ideas. The book proved immensely popular and Fénelon's attacks on luxury were influential, not least on Rousseau. He set his story in Greek mythology. Subsequent debate cites classical models – praising Sparta if hostile to commerce and luxury; and Athens, if generally favourable to the arts, commerce and technical progress. The study of History was expected to teach practical lessons and most argument began with an historical survey. Though Fénelon chose a pagan setting, his ethos is Christian and looks to an after-life. Fénelon regarded wars as the greatest evil inflicted on mankind and said that good kings, far from attacking their neighbours, should act as mediators to prevent wars. Settled peace is needed before population can expand. His ideal monarch encourages agriculture, and to supply manpower for it, transports idle artisans from the towns to the countryside (ibid., p. 222). Fénelon links excessive taxation with the peasant's unwillingness to marry and raise a family. Though not wholly hostile to trade (ibid., p. 72) he wants to reduce the "prodigious number of merchants" who are blamed for importing luxuries from abroad. Undesirable luxury is also seen as home-grown and as bringing *la mollesse* (soft-living), and corrupt behaviour in its wake. Since Fénelon's recognition of human imperfections did not allow him to suppose that war could be eliminated, the effect of *mollesse* on a nation's fighting capacity worried him and he expressly linked a simple agricultural life with the toughness needed to campaign (ibid., p. 109). He praised the Spartan model which his state Salente adopted and there is a dress code to distinguish ranks.

In the final years of Louis XIV's reign war debt mounted and focused attention on paper credit and the money market. The collapse of John Law's Mississippi Company was a searing experience for French investors whereas the Bank of England fought off rival banks and became invaluable to successive British governments. Since France seemed self-evidently a richer country in natural endowment and her rival's wealth appeared to depend much on trade and colonial expansion, pro-industrial policies which favoured luxury were increasingly defended in France as potentially productive of wealth and employment. It is probably no coincidence that French writers such as Melon, Montesquieu and Voltaire who defended luxury had spent long periods in England. They were familiar with the provocative arguments of Mandeville's *Fable of the Bees*.

Jean-François Melon, former secretary to John Law, produced arguments in favour of luxury in his *Essai politique sur le commerce* (1734). This went through some twenty editions, and it was substantially enlarged in 1736. His views on war, population and agriculture are similar to Fénelon's. He defined luxury as

> an extraordinary sumptuousness which is bestowed by the wealth and security of a government; it is the necessary consequence of every well-administered society. The man who finds himself with plenty

wishes to enjoy it; he has there refinements which the less well-off cannot afford, and this refinement is always relative to the age and to the individual. What was luxury for our fathers is now taken for granted; and what is luxury for us will not be for our nephews.

(1736, p. 106)

This echoed the British mercantilist writers who argued that the acquisition by the mass of the population of what one generation regarded as luxuries would act as a spur to ambition and effort (Perrotta (1997) and Eltis (1999)).

Melon also noted that at a particular time people would view luxury according to their own circumstances; to the village-dweller it would be evident in the town, and to the town-dweller the Capital would be its glaring example (1736, p. 107). Since luxury was relative to the individual in a hierarchical society which had great disparities of wealth, Melon's luxury is sometimes no more than economic activity which raises the living standard of the poorest.

Melon saw limitless technical progress as creating new employment and he mocked those who wished to preserve outmoded jobs (ibid., pp. 89–90). In his eyes it was always desirable that what had been made by two men should be made by one. He was, however, concerned that domestic rather than foreign workmen should produce the added value in turning flax into fabric, or, more profitably, lace. So he concluded that, "What must be allowed as luxury must often be forbidden as importation" (ibid., pp. 144–5).

The theatre, largely court-based, had often been attacked as a prime example of luxury and extravagance: this had been Boisguilbert's opinion (1966, p. 988). Melon dealt with it in a sentence, "Displays cannot be too grand, too splendid, nor can there be too many of them; it is a commerce where France always receives without giving" (1736, p. 125). For him the highest and even the most absurd form of luxury was costly foodstuffs. Yet he defends these as providing an income for the market-gardener, bringing happiness and hope into his family's life (ibid., pp. 123–4). He claimed that the farmer or winegrower was his prime concern and he praised Henri IV who wanted the peasant to afford a chicken in his pot. But he believed that if the peasant were over-taxed, a downward spiral of the kind Boisguilbert had discussed (1966, pp. 298–9) would result, affecting the whole society.

Melon knew that the main critics of luxury were Churchmen. In Catholic France the Church was opposed to much that was readily accepted in Protestant England as normal for the functioning of commerce. Catholic theology on the evil of usury had hardly changed since mediaeval times though financial instruments and networks had greatly developed. Indeed it was not until the Revolution that it became legal to take interest on loans; although the casuists had softened outright prohibition to the faithful and in practice interest was paid: an individual would be dependent for absolution upon his confessor's attitude. The Crown had exemption from these laws (McManners 1998, II, pp. 264–5).

While making some emollient remarks about charitable institutions, Melon attacked the Church on many fronts. He believed that clerical and monastic celibacy reduced the population; excessive religious holidays cut production, while attacks on usury and new forms of dealing in paper financial instruments upset the necessary circulation of wealth. Melon strongly defended *agiotage* (stock-jobbing) against religious objections (1736, pp. 260–4). He pointed out that certain market activities had become acceptable, such as dealing in contracts on the City of Paris and in the main land tax, the *taille*. As for other forms of *agiotage*, he accused the Church of hypocrisy since a famous *agioteur* had named bishops, great lords and magistrates among those with whom he dealt.

He provocatively praised Lucullus, a by-word for luxury in the ancient world, attacked Lycurgus's Spartan sumptuary laws and insisted that austere Sparta was not more conquering or better governed than "voluptuous" Athens (ibid., p. 114). He said that the reformer who through the harshness of his personality wants to make life harder may sometimes be admired by the populace; but that he is always scorned by the sage whose yardstick is the sweetness of society (ibid., pp. 114–15).

For him, idleness was the greatest vice and he was ready to blame it for sedition, civil war and the fall of the Roman Republic (ibid., pp. 99–100). He referred to the occupation of begging being passed on from father to son, and this will have been seen as an attack on preachers encouraging alms-giving (ibid., p. 33). Luxury, on the contrary, he called the destroyer of laziness and idleness. He maintained that the rich man would soon see his wealth disappear if he did not work to keep it and to acquire new riches (ibid., p. 109).

Melon met the fear that luxury created *mollesse* by claiming that it was far removed from the ordinary soldier or junior officer, while no army had been beaten because of the grand style of the General Corps. Indeed he claimed that ambition to emulate senior officers was a spur to action (ibid., pp. 108–9).

In his poem *Le Mondain*, published in the same year as Melon's first edition, Voltaire celebrates luxury in the most provocative fashion. He had read and admired Melon's book (Morize 1909, p. 113) and he was in London in 1728 when the fifth edition of Mandeville's *Fable of the Bees* was much discussed. Voltaire is confrontational in tone:

> I thank wise Nature who, for my good, caused me to be born in this age that is so decried by our poor Doctors: this profane time is just right for my conduct. I love luxury, and even soft living [*la mollesse*], all the pleasures, each branch of the Arts, cleanliness, good taste, adornments.
>
> (lines 4–11)

He calls excess a very necessary thing and praises foreign trade which brings new goods. He insults Adam, the first man, describing him as having filthy, black, hooked long nails. In a state of Nature, neither the food nor hard ground as a bed appeals to him. Rather he delights in paintings, silverware, tapestries and mirrors reflecting fountains. In case anyone should doubt his targets he makes a dig at Fénelon, addressing him as Monsieur du *Telemaque*. Voltaire challenged: "Praise away your little Ithaca, your Salente and its wretched walls where your Cretans, sadly virtuous, poor in belongings and rich in abstinence, lack everything to have plenty" (lines 113–17).

In the *Defense du Mondain* of 1739 Voltaire claimed that luxury made a large state wealthy even if it ruined a small one. The rich man was born to spend generously. Melon supported this in a letter to the countess de Verne in which he alluded to the number of families supported by her expenditures on the arts. He maintained that if people ceased to love paintings, engravings and every type of curiosity, at least twenty thousand men would be ruined in Paris and forced to look for work abroad (Morize 1909, p. 152).

Montesquieu's *De l'esprit des lois*, published in 1748, became the starting point of much discussion. He had already touched on luxury in 1721 in his *Lettres persanes* where he confronted the argument that luxury led to *mollesse*. As a leading member of the nobility and a wealthy landowner he was imbued with a sense of the importance and the duties of noble rank. He saw the nobility as the natural military defenders of France. *Mollesse* would be serious if it were the natural consequence of luxury. His fictional Persian calls Paris the most sensual city in the world. Disparities in wealth are vividly suggested, yet Montesquieu observes:

> In Paris you can see a man with enough to live off till the day of judgement, who works incessantly and runs the risk of shortening his life in order to accumulate, as he says, enough to subsist.
>
> The same spirit seizes the nation: one only sees work and industry. Where then is this effeminate people of whom you speak?
>
> ([1721]1951, letter 107)

The argument that whereas equality and a modest style of living was right for a small republic it was out of the question for a large state such as France and incompatible with monarchical government was widely used. Though contemporary Britain was manifestly not a republic it was a trading and maritime nation and as such it was treated as apart from other monarchies. It is interesting that Montesquieu appended an optimistic view of Britain's future to his summary of the causes of the fall of the Athenian republic, and what he saw as the corruption of the Italian republics of his time. The argument that luxury led to the collapse of states was implicitly met when he wrote in the *Grandeur et decadence des*

Romains that a free government could reform itself through its own laws ([1734] 1951, ch. 8, p. 396).

Montesquieu held certain opinions which were socially conservative. He showed his dislike of parvenu tax-collectors in *Lettres persanes* ([1721]1951, letter 48), and he voiced it even more strongly in *De l'esprit des lois* where he said that they had destroyed the Roman Republic. He held that it would be destructive of a monarchy if theirs became an honoured profession ([1748] 1961, Bk XIII, ch. 20). He maintained that the nobility should not be involved in commerce (ibid., Bk XX, ch. 21). Though hostile to financiers, Montesquieu supported the taking of interest on loans and wished it to be made legal (ibid., Bk XXII, ch. 19, and 1991, p. 767).

It is in *De l'esprit des lois* that Montesquieu has most to say about luxury. He gives an important definition:

> Luxury is always in proportion to the inequality of incomes. If wealth is equally spread out in a state there will be no luxury; because it is only based on the commodities which one awards oneself from the work of others.
>
> ([1748] 1961, Bk VII, ch. 1)

Montesquieu had great faith that the hard work which is associated with commerce would prevent luxury from corrupting behaviour. Though he saw the character of republics as depending on equality of wealth and frugality, he made an exception for republics such as ancient Athens, which were based on commerce.

> It is true that, when the democratic state is based on trade, it may very well happen that some individuals in it have great wealth, and that behaviour there is not corrupted. This is because the spirit of commerce brings with it that of frugality, of economy, of moderation, work, wisdom, tranquillity, order and law. Thus, so long as this spirit endures, the wealth it produces has no bad effect.
>
> (ibid. Bk V, ch. 6)

He stated that banks did not have a place in monarchies because any considerable accumulation of their wealth is liable to become the Prince's treasure. His opinions on mercantile companies are interesting as, after arguing that they do not normally suit a monarchy, he continued:

> I say further: they are not always appropriate in States where people carry out trade in essentials; and, if enterprises are not so large that they are beyond the scope of individuals, one would do even better not to hinder freedom of trade in any way through exclusive privileges.
>
> (ibid., Bk XX, ch. 10)

Montesquieu saw a place for sumptuary laws, especially in republics, which might need to preserve the spirit of frugality. However he cautioned against their use in monarchies (ibid., Bk VII, ch. 5). A limit on the ability of governments to regulate their citizens was noticed by Montesquieu (Bk XIX, ch. 27) and by Melon (1736, p. 112) who each referred to tax exiles.

While Melon, Voltaire and Montesquieu were in their different ways sympathetic to the growth of luxury, and comfortable that France should follow Great Britain in its principal manifestations, a powerful adversary, Jean-Jacques Rousseau, entered the debate in the 1750s. The talent he displayed in his *Discours sur les sciences et les arts* brought him patronage from wealthy aristocrats and the protection of Chretien-Guillaume de Lamoignon de Malesherbes, who was running the censorship. Renato Galliani argues convincingly that the views Rousseau expressed in his early writings, before *La nouvelle Héloïse* (1761), reflected traditional aristocratic attacks on luxury (1989, p. 272). His censors perceptively noted Rousseau's "fatal eloquence", which made him so influential despite the contradictions in his own life and the defects he saw in his own early work. Rousseau argued from a supposed state of nature in which man was blessedly ignorant and happy, to the evils of present society:

> There you see how luxury, dissoluteness, and enslavement have been in every age the punishment for the presumptious efforts we have made to leave the happy ignorance in which eternal wisdom had placed us.
>
> ([1750] 1992, p. 40)

Rousseau saw luxury as making a nation less able to fight (ibid. p. 47). Not surprisingly Sparta was his classical model (ibid., p. 111). He attacked paintings which did not glorify martial heroes but put forward, "with great care all ancient mythology's aberrations of heart and mind" (ibid., pp. 49–50). This is close to Fénelon. Soon he moved on to attack the evils printing had brought and to approve the burning of books 1 (ibid., p. 52n.). Louis XV's father-in-law, the former King of Poland, replied to this first treatise, and Rousseau in his response said, "luxury corrupts everything; both the rich man who enjoys it, and the wretch who covets it" (ibid., p. 88). In his *Dernière réponse* Rousseau stated:

> Luxury sustains a hundred poor in our towns, and causes the death of a hundred thousand in our countryside: the money which circulates through the hands of the rich and artists to supply their excesses is lost from the farm-worker's subsistence; and it is precisely because the others must have braid that he has no cloak ... We must have powder for our wigs; there you have the reason why so many poor folk have no bread.
>
> (ibid., p. 107n.)

D'Alembert had come to the defence of the arts and sciences in the *Discours préliminaire de l'Encyclopédie* of 1751, arguing that they made society more agreeable even if they did not improve it. Rousseau riposted in the preface to his play *Narcisse* in 1752 that, "The appetite for literature, philosophy and the fine arts destroys love for our prime duties and for true glory." He returned to the subject in the *Discours sur l'Origine et les fondements de l'inegalité parmi les hommes*:

> At the same time as industry and the arts spread out and flourish, the cultivator, disregarded, weighed down by taxes needed to support luxury and condemned to spend his life between work and hunger, abandons his fields to seek in the towns the bread he should be carrying there.

> ([1755] 1992, p. 187)

In his *Discours sur l'économie politique* of 1755 Rousseau proposed that heavy taxes should be placed on luxury goods such as carriages, mirrors, furniture, materials, gilding, the courts and gardens of private residences, on every kind of entertainment. In contrast to Melon he believed that once entrapped by luxury men would not give it up, and they would rather starve than die of shame.

In his *Contrat social* of 1762 Rousseau made several references of a laudatory nature to the marquis d'Argenson whose *Considérations sur le Gouvernement ancien et present de la France* he knew in manuscript. They shared an admiration for the republics of the ancient world (Larrere 1992, pp. 61–5) and d'Argenson was eager to increase the popular element in France's government under its monarchy.

D'Argenson's professed aim was to show in his *Considérations* that popular government under the sovereign would increase the state's power and promote the happiness of the people. He wanted to replace royal officers with municipal ones chosen by the people. He also criticised the government for interfering in commerce, echoing Melon's words when he said, "Commerce only needs protection and freedom and perhaps the one should be abandoned in order to enjoy the other more fully" (1764, pp. 66–7). He was not hostile to the arts but he argued that, whereas a country like Russia needed laws to encourage the arts (the word then included what we would call crafts), France needed to return to agriculture which it had neglected (p. 15).

Argenson said that it was just that those who consumed most for their own luxury should pay the most to the State whose capital they diminished (p. 228). He considered that Spain had been ruined by luxury and inequality (p. 78). He blamed financiers and finance ministers since Colbert for policies such as alterations of the coinage, the trickery of false letters of credit and double assignations of revenue (p. 185). He attacked the sale of offices as impeding democracy (p. 156) as well as for the tax exemptions they entailed, resulting in the tax burden falling on the weakest shoulders. He wanted wealthy men to be ennobled (p. 190) but not through the purchase of offices (p. 311).

He expressed the wish that nobles and wealthy men should reside on their country properties. He wanted lands to be free of feudal dues and he scorned these personally: "I prefer a good walnut tree which bears fruit to a fief which is just idiocy" (quoted in Larrere 1992, p. 192). He scorned rank which only relied on birth as leading to laziness and he wished people to be equal among themselves so that they could work in accordance with their talents (pp. 308–9).

In many of his Journal entries from 1747 to his final entry in January 1757, d'Argenson refers to spectacular examples of luxury expenditure on the royal favourite, Madame de Pompadour. In November 1748 he wrote, "Yesterday eight country houses and private residences were counted where work was in progress for the Marquise de Pompadour." In July 1750 he wrote of the King having ordered more than 800,000 livres worth of Vincennes china for his country houses and especially for her chateau de Bellevue. In May 1751 he notes that she appeared at Marly in a gown embellished with English lace costing more than 22,500 livres and he adds that the public notices these expenditures. This was doubly objectionable since in 1752 he reports the fear that the King will have to declare bankruptcy. In February 1753 he notes that the English are building forty new ships and that they have paid off 200 million livres worth of public debt since the war. He prophesies that with these numerous fleets the English will wipe France out in the three areas of the world where it has colonies. Indeed this largely occurred in 1763 at the end of the Seven Years War when France lost Canada and various West Indian islands, while it was marginalised in India.

In December 1754, after describing the taking of royal troops by smugglers, d'Argenson stated that the people favour the smugglers because they are at war with the tax-farmers who are considered too rich and the people want goods more cheaply.

In his journal entry for 5 October 1749 d'Argenson reported his neighbours as saying that the rural population had declined by more than a third in ten years. He blamed the corvee for driving labourers to the towns. The towns had their problems too: on 12 July 1750 he noted that Lyon was full of the poor, not because bread was dear, but because a fall in the supply of silk from Piedmont had led to lay-offs. The Farmers-general, he reports in June 1754, had complained to the Controller-General of Finances, Machault, that trade and manufactures were decaying and that foreigners were working up French raw materials. Machault's response was, "So much the better! That is all the more workers to return to the land."

This was not everyone's solution but by the 1750s the luxury debate was increasingly becoming one between agriculture and industry. In 1755 an anonymous work was published entitled significantly *L'Abeille* [the bee], *ou recueuil de philosophie de litérature et d'histoire*. It had every sign from its contents of seeking to appeal to the circle of Mme de Pompadour and the duc de Choiseul. The author devoted pages to famous women in history and defended tax-farmers – her family was involved in tax-farming – while he was eager to build up the navy, Choiseul's particular concern.

The eleventh chapter of the book begins, "Happy is the State which possesses the Merchant & Manufactures!" After enumerating stages in the preparation of hemp, flax, wool, and so on, he continued:

> Let us assume that all these activities are suppressed; and cast our eyes on the consequences of so many people being out of work. It is easy to see that we shall soon cease being happy and peaceful: we shall fall bit by bit into the condition of Savages: & the State will suffer from it in many ways. Thus China in her wisdom does not allow anybody to avoid work in the length and breadth of that vast Empire, much more populous than France or Holland.
>
> (Anon 1755, p. 106)

The author of *L'Abeille* suggested that only a third of the population was needed for agriculture. He argued that manufactures bring demand for more animals, fields are brought under cultivation, the soil is improved, income rises and trade expands (ibid., p. 112).

François Veron de Forbonnais argued similarly that luxury assists the whole economy in his *Elements de commerce* of 1755:

> It is luxury alone, or the abundance whose fruit it is which gives the spirit this activity which is so prodigious in its effects. If abundance is widespread an equal and lifegiving warmth will spread through all the parts of the body politic.
>
> (ch. 13, "Du luxe")

He added, "The greatest of all abuses would be that the rich spent nothing; all would be poverty-stricken around them, the state would be almost without warmth and lifeless" (ibid.).

There is an interesting contrast between the pro-industrial analyses of Melon and Forbonnais, and d'Argenson's argument where agriculture is of central importance. A further penetrating and highly influential analysis of the central role of agriculture emerged when Richard Cantillon's *Essai sur la nature du commerce en general* was published in 1755. He had been a brilliant millionaire banker who had understood and exploited the inconsistencies in Law's scheme (Murphy 1986, pp. 172–5) and he set out the first complete account of the financial circulation of an economy.

The influence of Cantillon's penetrating analysis

Cantillon died in 1734, or shortly afterwards, apparently in a fire in his London home. Several copies of his influential and penetrating book circulated in manuscript, and it was published in 1755 through the sponsorship of Vincent Gournay. Its influence can be judged by the extent to which the greatest French economists of the 1750s, the 1760s and the 1770s quoted extensively from it, but they also went on to develop and refine his path-breaking analysis, which was especially relevant to the luxury debate.

Cantillon estimated that twenty-five workers could provide the necessities of life, the food, clothing and housing required by 100 "according to the European standard" ([1755] 1931, p. 87).

Half the population would make no kind of direct contribution "with their hands ... to the different needs of men", which left twenty-five persons out of 100 who would be capable of working but were not required to create subsistence goods. Some of these might be employed to work up the subsistence goods produced by the twenty-five to a higher standard "like making fine linen, fine cloth, etc." while knives and forks, nicely wrought, "are more esteemed than those roughly and hastily made". Cantillon added that it would make little difference to a state if people wore coarse or fine clothing, but "the States where fine Cloths, fine linen, etc. are worn, and where the Feeding is dainty and delicate, are richer and more esteemed than those where these things are ruder" (ibid., pp. 87–9).

The twenty-five spare workers out of 100 could alternatively be employed as servants or soldiers, and Cantillon added:

> If enough employment cannot be found to occupy the 25 persons in a hundred upon work useful and profitable to the State, I see no objection to encouraging employment which serves only for ornament or amusement. The State is not considered less rich for a thousand toys which serve to trick out the ladies or even men, or are used in games and diversions, than it is for useful and serviceable objects.
>
> (ibid., pp. 91–3)

The production and consumption of luxury goods and services would therefore only be damaging if the resources devoted to them exceeded the surplus created by the twenty-five workers out of 100 who produced the nation's subsistence goods.

The twenty-five spare workers would ideally be employed to produce reserve stocks above the yearly consumption "like Magazines of Cloth, Linen, Corn, etc., to answer in bad years, or war. And as Gold and Silver can always buy these things, even from the Enemies of the State" these were crucial elements in the relative size of the reserve stocks of the European nations which determined "the comparative greatness of Kingdoms and States" (ibid., pp. 89–91).

Cantillon thus regarded an economy's potential to create an economic surplus and the importance of the purposes to which this was directed as of central importance. In his analysis, surpluses were generated especially in agriculture which produced the incomes of the landlord class, and he explained some of the necessary interconnections in a manner which those who followed him in the 1750s, the 1760s and the 1770s went on to develop in a variety of ways.

He assumed that a country's available land which generated the agricultural surplus was fully farmed, and that the size of the agricultural labour force would depend on the customary standard of living of labouring families. If peasants lived frugally, the product of $1\frac{1}{2}$ acres would support an agricultural labourer, but he would need twice this to persuade him to marry and bring up a family. These three acres were required for each labouring family in the southern Provinces of France where the labourer would "rarely eat meat, will drink little wine or beer, and will have only old and shabby cloaths which he will wear as long as he can". If the customary standard of living was higher, as in the English county of Middlesex where farm workers could expect wine, meat woollen cloaths, and so on, a labourer might "without drunkenness or gluttony or excess of any kind consume the produce of four to ten acres of Land of ordinary goodness" (ibid., p. 37) and he would require twice this to bring up a family. Hence the rural population would depend on the extent of a country's cultivated territory and the standard of living at which labourers were prepared to marry and raise a family. The more frugal their standard of living, the greater the population.

These considerations determined the extent of a nation's agricultural population, but there would also be an urban population and its size would depend on the expenditure of the agricultural surplus. This was paid to the landlords and to those who organised agriculture. The processes through which an agricultural surplus consisting of foodstuffs would be transformed by merchants and entrepreneurs into monetary rents in the hands of landlords who would spend these to create effective demand in the cities is brilliantly explained. Cantillon assumed that one-third of total agricultural output would go to the landlords, and that the remaining two-thirds would go to those who actually farmed. Half of this or one-third of each harvest would go to agricultural entrepreneurs and the agents of the landlords who organised farming, while the remaining third would consist of the costs they incurred, mainly payments to the unskilled farm labourers who would each require the product of between three and twenty acres to subsist and bring up their families. It is these farm labourers who would provide the labour which enabled twenty-five to provide subsistence for 100, while two-thirds to three-quarters of what they produced would go to those who owned the land, and the entrepreneurs

and agents of the landlords who organised its cultivation. Cantillon
assumed that landlords would use the whole of their third of the nation's
agricultural output to maintain artisans and performers of personal services in the cities, while agricultural entrepreneurs with their returns over
costs of one-third of agricultural output would exchange half their net
incomes for urban manufactures and services. In Cantillon's words:

> on this supposition the Farmer who has two thirds or four sixths of
> the Produce of the Land, pays either directly or indirectly one sixth to
> the Citizens [of the Cities] in exchange for the merchandise which he
> takes from them. This sixth with the one third or two sixths which the
> Proprietor spends in the City makes three sixths or one Half of the
> Produce of the Land.
>
> (ibid., p. 45)

This calculation that half of total agricultural output is consumed in the
countryside and half in the towns and cities supports his statement that "It
is generally calculated that one half of the Inhabitants of a kingdom
subsist and make their Abode in Cities, and the other half live in the
Country" (ibid., p. 45).

The particular manufactures a nation consumed would depend substantially on the lead set by the greatest landlords who held the most
powerful and prestigious positions in the state:

> The example of the Prince, followed by his Court, is generally capable
> of determining the inspiration and tastes of the other Proprietors of
> Land, and the example of these last naturally influences all the lower
> ranks.
>
> (ibid., p. 93)

When a nation's master craftsmen and entrepreneurs in easy circumstances vary their expenses, "they always take as their model the Lords and
Owners of the Land" (ibid., p. 63). Hence if the Court and the richest
landlords consume recherché luxury manufactures, so will the lesser aris-
tocracy and the richer farmers who would follow their lead. This has
important implications for a nation's welfare. Cantillon suggested that in
Poland half the income of the landlords and therefore of the wealthier
farmers also was apparently spent on imported manufactures:

> If a Proprietor or Nobleman in Poland, to whom his Farmers pay
> yearly a rent equal to about one third of the Produce of his Land,
> pleases to use the Cloths, Linens, etc. of Holland, he will pay for these
> Merchandises one half of the rent he receives and perhaps use the
> other half for the subsistence of his Family on other Products and
> rough Manufactures of Poland: but half his rent on our supposition

corresponds to the sixth part of the Produce of his Land, and this sixth part will be carried away by the Dutch to whom the farmers of Poland will deliver it in Corn, Wool, Hemp and other produce. Here is then a sixth part of the Land of Poland withdrawn from its People.

(ibid., p. 75)

Moreover, if the Farmers who received the other two thirds "imitating their Masters consume foreign Manufactures" still more of "the produce of the Land in Poland would be "abstracted from the Food of the People, and, what is worse, mostly sent to the Foreigner and often serving to support the Enemies of the State" (ibid., pp. 75–7).

Hence to the extent that manufactures are imported, a country would actually contribute to the subsistence of potential enemies. In contrast, if the recipients of the agricultural surplus spend this on domestically manu-factured goods and services, it would sustain domestic employment over and above that provided by agriculture itself. Cantillon therefore offered a clear answer to a question which George Berkeley set out in *The Querist* in 1735 (query 150): "Whether an Irish Lady, set out with French Silks, and Flanders Lace, may not be said to consume more Beef and Butter than fifty of our labouring peasants?" Cantillon calculated, from detailed data which should have formed a Supplement to his book, but was probably destroyed in the fire in his London home:

If the Ladies of Paris are pleased to wear Brussels Lace, and if France pays for this Lace with Champagne wine, the product of a single Acre of Flax must be paid for with the product of 16,000 acres of land under vines ... Suffice to say here that in this transaction a great amount of the produce of the Land is withdrawn from the subsistence of the French, and that all the produce sent abroad, unless an equally considerable amount of produce be brought back in exchange, tends to diminish the number of People in the State.

(ibid., p. 77)

If, in contrast, a nation achieves an export surplus of manufactures, its employment and population would benefit. If its goods were superior to those manufactured overseas and produced net inflows of gold and silver, its prices would rise, the terms of trade would move in its favour and it would become increasingly powerful. But these favourable conditions would prove unsustainable. Beneficiaries of the favourable export trade and of the higher prices and incomes it generated (first merchants in the export industries, and after that lawyers, followed by the whole popu-lation: Cantillon had unfortunate experiences in the law courts of both England and France) would adopt habits of luxury which undermined the balance of trade because the goods they bought would mainly be imported:

abundance will not arise without many wealthy individuals springing up who will plunge into luxury. They will buy Pictures and Gems from the Foreigner, will procure their Silks and rare objects, and set such an example of luxury in the State that in spite of the advantage of its ordinary trade its money will flow abroad annually to pay for this luxury. This will gradually impoverish the State and cause it to pass from great power into great weakness.

(ibid., p. 185)

The leading economists of the 1750s, the 1760s and the 1770s absorbed and developed elements of Cantillon's analysis.

François Quesnay was Cantillon's most notable successor. He was physician to Madame de Pompadour, to Louis XV and indeed to Adam Smith when his pupil, the Duke of Buccleuch, fell ill in Paris. By the 1760s, the new excitement about the economy which was inducing so many to publish had begun to centre on his powerful and original contributions. He quoted Cantillon directly (on p. 483 of the encyclopedia article "Grains" of 1757) in his account of how agricultural rents found their way to the cities where the expenditure of the landlords would be a crucial element in the determination of the demand for both food and manufactures. Victor Riqueti, Marquis de Mirabeau, who became Quesnay's principal collaborator after 1759, had possessed a manuscript copy of Cantillon's book since the 1740s and this had a far-reaching impact on the original 1756 edition of *L'Ami des hommes* which caused Mirabeau himself to be widely described as "the Friend of Mankind". In 1776 Cantillon's book was one of the few which the abbe de Condillac actually quoted from in *Le Commerce et le Gouvernement: consideres relativement l'un a l'autre*, and he followed Cantillon precisely in his demonstration that a country would support a smaller population, the greater the refinement of tastes of labouring families, because more acres would be required to support each worker (1776, Part I, ch. 25); and in his statements that only landlords are free to spend as they wish while everyone else is dependent for his employment on the expenditure of others (ibid., Part I, ch. 28).

Quesnay's analysis in collaboration with Mirabeau was the most influential, and the many points at which they adopted elements of Cantillon's analysis will become evident. But they arrived at a different conclusion from Cantillon's in their analysis of the influence of the consumption of luxury manufactures. According to Cantillon the consumption of such goods would only prove damaging to output and population in so far as they were imported. Quesnay's and Mirabeau's analysis insisted that an increased demand for manufactures could undermine the economy, even if the extra industrial goods were produced by France herself.

Quesnay's analysis of the influence of luxury consumption

Quesnay and Mirabeau developed an entirely technical approach to the luxury question, which removed it from debate about incentives and social inequality. For Quesnay, all non-agricultural economic activity was "sterile" because it generated no economic surplus or *produit net*, and it was the luxury element in a nation's sterile expenditure which was most liable to undermine the long-term viability of economies. At the margin, increased sterile expenditure was always attributed to excessive *"luxe de décoration"* which was the element in the expenditure on the products of industry and commerce which might be so high as to destabilise the economy.

In the *Tableau economique* which Quesnay first created in 1758–9 in the Palace of Versailles where King Louis XV is said to have played a part in the correction of the proofs, he followed Cantillon in his assumption that the expenditure of rents is the crucial element in the determination of the comparative size of industry and agriculture. Quesnay's calculations of the necessary interconnections between the level of agricultural rents and employment in industry and agriculture are far more detailed and sophisticated, but their overriding structure based on the relative expenditure of each class on their products is similar. Quesnay concluded that the economy would be in stationary state equilibrium when the proportion of expenditure on the products of industry and commerce, including *luxe*, was 50 per cent, while there would be disastrous consequences if *luxe* rose above this:

> It can be seen from the distribution delineated in the tableau that if the nation's expenditure went more to the sterile expenditure side than the productive expenditure side, the revenue would fall proportionately, and this fall would increase in the same progression from year to year successively. It follows that a high level of expenditure on *luxe de décoration* and on conspicuous consumption is ruinous. If on the other hand the nation's expenditure goes on the productive expenditure side the revenue will rise, and this rise will in the same way increase successively from year to year. Thus it is not true that the type of expenditure is a matter of indifference.
>
> ([1758–9] 1972, p. 12)

In 1760 he created a detailed series of Tableaux which set out precisely how this would occur in "Tableau economique avec ses explications", which he appended to the 1760 edition of *L'Ami des hommes*. In 1763, further collaboration between Quesnay and Mirabeau led to the publication of *Philosophie rurale*, a comprehensive account of the economics of the growing physiocratic school, over which Quesnay presided intellectually, and Mirabeau socially. It included sequences of tableaux which sought to provide a complete account of the circumstances in which the French economy would grow or decline. One of these describes how it would decline if the propensity to consume manufactures including those describable as *"luxe de décoration"* came to exceed the critical 50 per cent. They followed Cantillon in assuming that extra luxury consumption would not be confined to the wealthiest. It was led from Versailles: "The Prince's taste for magnificence" turned "an emporium of baubles, of metallic objects and of changing fashions into the principle of feeding a nation on which nature had lavished the dew of heaven and the fat of the land" ([1764] 1972, Part III, p. 22) and it spread for: "When *luxe de décoration* is dominant in a nation, it extends to all classes of men" (ibid., Part III, p. 33).

Quesnay and Mirabeau also followed Cantillon in his calculation that a limited proportion of output could safely be spent on luxury goods without damaging the economy. In their analysis, the principal question concerning the impact of luxury consumption was the amount the economy could safely spend on the sterile side of the Tableau. What could be safely spent in this way would conform to the needs of men and be:

> in a proportion compatible with the expenditures which are distributed in the economic order of an agricultural Nation, establishing themselves regularly, as a result of the revenues of its territory, when their natural progress is not disturbed or forced by its political Government.
>
> Luxury which animates and which follows the stations in life and the ordered fortunes of Citizens is not a luxury which damages. It is not even, strictly speaking, luxury. This requires a just understanding founded on principles: and its demonstration necessarily obliges us to briefly summarise our leading economic maxims.
>
> (ibid., Part III, pp. 26–7)

Quesnay and Mirabeau then proceeded to deploy extremely sophisticated elaborations of the *Tableau economique* to set out the precise circumstances in which luxury was not "strictly speaking" luxury, because it conformed to the natural order, and when it would be excessive and therefore damaging.

They demonstrate through the Tableaux set out below that the expenditure of 50 per cent of total revenues on sterile industry and commerce is compatible with the continual reproduction of the economy's capital stock, and especially its agricultural advances, so that up to this limit, additional industrial expenditures were not luxurious. As soon as expenditures on the sterile side of the Tableau exceeded the critical 50 per cent, agricultural advances would be encroached upon and the economy would decline, so that spending more than half of rents on manufactures (and because of social emulation, similar excess expenditures by merchants, artisans and entrepreneurial farmers) would become luxury which under-mined the economy.

Cantillon also had a formula. He had calculated that the economy would not be undermined if the workers producing non-necessities of life did not exceed the twenty-five out of 100 who produced necessities for the whole population. The derivation of Quesnay's and Mirabeau's formula to arrive at their apparently comparable result was far more complex.

In the series of Tableaux from *Philosophie rurale* presented in Figures 9.1–9.3, Quesnay and Mirabeau set out the full impact on the whole economy of an increase of one-tenth in the propensity to consume the products of industry and commerce. These marginal changes are always referred to as increases in the propensity to consume *luxe*.

Figure 9.1 shows the Tableau of *Philosophie rurale* in its equilibrium sta-tionary state. The economy makes advances (i.e. capital investments) of 2000 in the productive sector (shown at the head of the Tableau on the left), which it invests in agriculture, and advances of 1000 in the sterile sector (at the head of the Tableau on the right), which it invests in indus-try and commerce. These investments produce reproducible agricultural wealth of 5000 which is the total shown at the foot of Figure 9.1. This 5000 is just sufficient to enable farmers to pay rents of 2000 (the Revenue shown in the centre at the head of the Tableau) and to retain 3000 for the following year's investments. Rents are 2000 because annual agricultural advances of 2000 create a *produit* net of 100 per cent which is the yield *la grande culture* generates. Farmers will be able to use the 3000 of the 5000 which they retain to invest 2000 in agricultural advances for the next harvest, while their further 1000 will cover what Quesnay calls interest to make good the one-tenth rate of depreciation which he assumes on their total farm capital (*avances primitives & annuelles*) of 10,000. The details are explained in the Appendix of this chapter. Because the initial agricultural investment of 2000 creates reproducible agricultural wealth of 5000, this will continue to be just sufficient to pay rents of 2000, to furnish the following year's farm investments of 2000 and to provide 1000 to cover the depreciation of farm capital. The economy can continue to produce these returns and sustain a stationary state in which agricultural investment is always 2000 and agricultural output is always 5000.

Figure 9.2 shows what will occur if, in the subsequent year, the propen-sity to consume *luxe* increases by one-fifth. There will be the same invest-ments at the start of the year as in Figure 9.1, of 2000 in agriculture and 1000 in industry and commerce, but because there is an increased propensity to consume *luxe* by all classes, less of the economy's effective demand will return to agriculture. As a consequence of the reduced finan-cial flows to agriculture (the details are set out in the Appendix), farmers' reproducible wealth at the foot of Figure 9.2 is 4680 in place of the 5000 at the foot of Figure 9.1. If out of this reduced reproduction of agricultural wealth, farmers retain the 3000 they would need to maintain

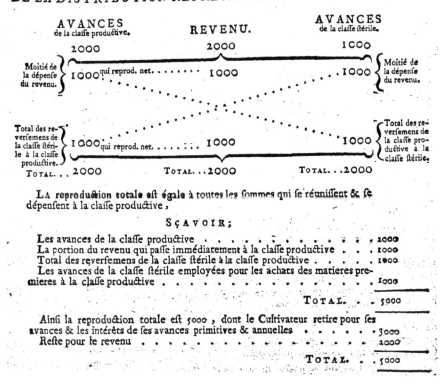

Figure 9.1 The Tableau in equilibrium (source: Mirabeau and Quesnay, Philosophie rurale, I: 123).

agricultural investment at its previous level, they would only have 1680 with which to pay rents, 320 less than the 2000 they were contractually obliged to pay. Quesnay assumes that this shortfall of 320 in the resources available to pay rents will be divided equally between farmers and landlords who will each lose 160. Hence in the following year, illustrated in Figure 9.3, agricultural investment (*Avances*) is 1840 in place of the former 2000, and rents (*Revenu*) are 1840 in place of 2000. Both are therefore reduced by 8 per cent.

Hence at the head of Figure 9.3, which shows what will occur in the second year of an increased propensity to consume *luxe*, because agricultural advances are merely 1840, and Revenue at the head of the Tableau is also only 1840, there is an 8 per cent reduction in food output (because investment is 8 per cent lower) and expenditure on food is also 8 per cent lower because purchases of food from the revenue and by

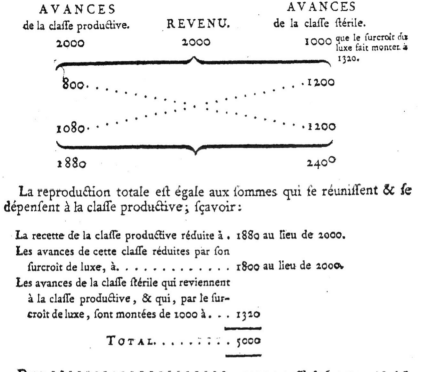

AVANCES
de la claffe productive.

REVENU.

AVANCES
de la claffe ftérile.

2000

2000

1000 que le furcroît du luxe fait monter à 1320.

800 1200

1080 1200

1880

2400

La reproduction totale eft égale aux fommes qui fe réuniffent & fe dépenfent à la claffe productive ; fçavoir :

La recette de la claffe productive réduite à . 1880 au lieu de 2000.

Les avances de cette claffe réduites par fon
furcroît de luxe, à. . . . . 1800 au lieu de 2000.

Les avances de la claffe ftérile qui reviennent
à la claffe productive, & qui, par le furcroît de luxe, font montées de 1000 à. . . 1320

TOTAL. 5000

Dont. . . . . 320 ont repaffé, & font retenus à la claffe ftérile, où ils ont augmenté de 320 les avances de cette claffe, qui fe- roient reftées à 1000, fi le luxe n'a- voit pas augmenté.

Refte 4680

Dont le Cultivateur retire pour fes reprifes 3000

Refte pour le revenu . . . . 1680 au lieu de 2000.

TOTAL. 4680

La perte de 320 livres, que le calcul fait tomber en totalité fur le revenu, étant repartie également fur les avances de la claffe producti-ve & fur le revenu, eft pour chacun 160 livres ; ce qui réduit la re-production des avances de la claffe productive à 1840, & celle du revenu également à 1840.

Figure 9.2 Initial impact of a 20 per cent increase in luxury consumption (source: Mirabeau and Quesnay, Philosophie rurale, III: 36–7).

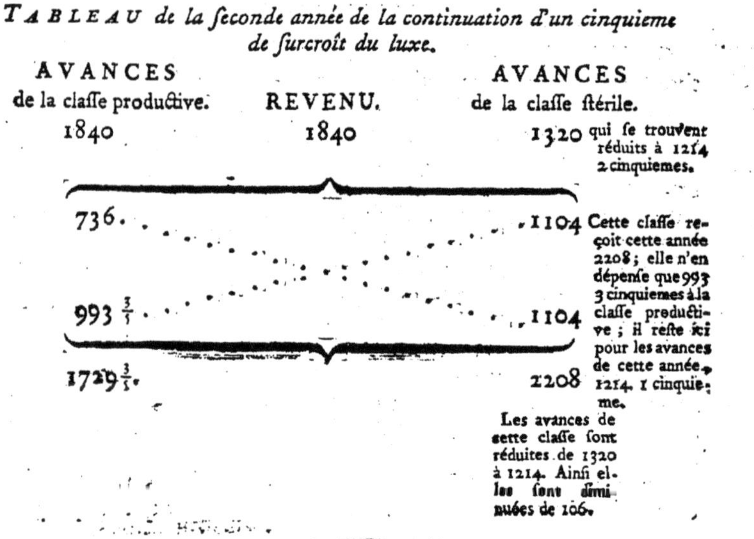

AVANCES
de la claffe productive.
1840

REVENU.
1840

AVANCES
de la claffe ftérile.
1320 qui fe trouvent
réduits à 1214
2 cinquiemes.

736 . . .

. . . 1104 Cette claffe re-
çoit cette année
2208; elle n'en
dépenfe que 993
3 cinquiemes à la
claffe producti-
ve ; il refte ici
pour les avances
de cette année,
1214. 1 cinquie-
me.

993 $\frac{3}{5}$ . . .

. . . 1104

1729 $\frac{3}{5}$.

2208

Les avances de
cette claffe font
réduites de 1320
à 1214. Ainfi el-
les font dimi-
nuées de 106.

La reproduction totale eft égale aux fommes qui fe réuniffent &
fe dépenfent à la claffe productive; fçavoir :

La recette de la claffe productive. . . . . . 1729 $\frac{3}{5}$.
Les avances de cette claffe, réduites par
l'excès de fon luxe, de 1840 à 1656
Les avances de la claffe ftérile de 1320,
defquelles il n'eft dépenfé cetteannée que
1214, dont 106 font pris fur les 1320
de ces mêmes avances, & conformé-
ment à cette reprife, elles fe trouvent
réduites à . . . . 1214 $\frac{1}{5}$.

TOTAL. 4600

Dont 294
Refte 4306

ont repaffé, & font retenus à la claffe
ftérile, & y foutiennent les avances de cette claffe à 1214, lef-
quelles, fans l'excès de luxe, n'au-
roient été que de 920, c'eft-à-
dire, égales au quart des fommes
des avances productives, & du
revenu, prifes enfemble.

Le Cultivateur retire pour { Avances. . . . . . 1840 l.
fes reprifes   { Intérèts. 920

TOTAL 2760

Refte pour le produit net. . . . . 1546 au lieu de 1840.

TOTAL 4306

Ce déchet de 294 étant reparti entre les avances de la claffe productive & le revenu, les réduifent de part & d'autre, à 1703.

Figure 9.3 Impact in second year of a 20 per cent increase in luxury consumption
(source: Mirabeau and Quesnay, Philosophie rurale, III: 39–40).

farmers themselves are 8 per cent less. Total reproducible agricultural wealth (at the foot of Figure 9.3) is 4306 in place of the 4680 of the previous year (presented at the foot of Figure 9.2) which was 8 per cent lower than the reproduction of 5000 in the stationary state which was illustrated in Figure 9.1. Hence in the second year of increased *luxe* that is illustrated in Figure 9.3, output and the resources available to pay rent and to invest are each reduced by 8 per cent from the already reduced levels illustrated in Figure 9.2. The economy will continue to decline at a rate of 8 per cent per annum for so long as the 60 per cent propensity to consume the products of the sterile sector, including especially, *luxe* persists.

The rates of decline predicted in Figures 9.2 and 9.3 (and by the equations which explain Quesnay's results in the Appendix) are very large. Quesnay's Tableaux demonstrate that an economy's propensity to consume *luxe* will have a significant impact on its rate of growth, and that a propensity which exceeds the equilibrium ratio of 50 per cent has the potential to produce a sharp sequence of decline.

It has been widely argued that Quesnay's assumption that the direction of internal consumption influences the rate of growth is flawed. The essence of Quesnay's argument is that because only agriculture generates a *produit* net, a diversion of demand away from agriculture and towards luxury manufactures will reduce the economy's investable surplus and therefore its rate of growth. But Negishi (1989) in particular has suggested that if demand within an agricultural kingdom shifts in favour of manufactures as in Figures 9.2 and 9.3, the economy could continue to produce the same quantity of food as before and therefore create an unchanged *produit* net, by selling the food that is no longer marketable within France in world markets. The additional manufactures which the French population desired in place of food could be imported in exchange for these higher exports of food. The use of international markets to export any food which had become surplus to French requirements in order to import the extra manufactures French consumers now desired would allow the economy to adopt the pattern of production which realised the highest economic surplus it could achieve. Negishi's solution requires an unlimited potential to exchange food for manufactures in world markets at unchanging terms of trade. His assumption is, in effect, that France is a "small country" which faces world prices for food and manufactures which are independent of the quantities it exports and imports.

But eighteenth-century France was not a "small country" which faced export prices for food and import prices of manufactures which were independent of the quantities it sought to export and import. In *Philosophie rurale*, Quesnay and Mirabeau actually considered the possibility that a shift in consumer preferences from food to manufactures could be met by exporting the food which was no longer in demand in France, and importing additional manufactures:

> Could it not be said that an excessive taste for manufactures [*luxe de décoration*] would be damaging only to nations which lacked the opportunity of freedom of external trade in their own agricultural produce; because these would be unable to compensate by the sale of their foodstuffs abroad for a loss on domestic sales caused by an excessive demand for manufactures? But would the opportunity for foreign trade and all round freedom to conduct it be enough to put right this derangement? Such external trade might perhaps greatly slow the progress of the destructive impact of an excessive demand for manufactures. But even this trade does not extend to the export of every kind of agricultural product; for most of these can only be consumed in the region which produces them. Besides, this external trade itself can only be sustained in so far as it is reciprocal. The merchant himself wishes to transport and bring back goods to cover his costs and gain a profit. Now, through what purchases will a nation, intent on manufactures, carry on with foreigners trade in the sale of its natural products?
>
> ([1764] 1972, pp. III.32–3)

Here Quesnay and Mirabeau demonstrate that they have the same awareness as Negishi that an unlimited potential to trade would allow an economy with a large agricultural *produit* net to remain predominantly agricultural. But they also summarise the difficulties in financing greatly increased imports of manufactures through additional agricultural exports.

When they wrote in the eighteenth century there was not free trade in agricultural produce in France, or anywhere else in Europe. Much agricultural produce was untradable: it had to be consumed close to where it was harvested, and this was especially the case with the eighteenth century's primitive transport facilities. There were also deep-rooted reasons why many countries would not allow unlimited food imports to undermine their own agriculture. That was as true in the eighteenth century as it still is in the twenty-first. Quesnay's and Mirabeau's argument that the propensity to consume agricultural products influences the rate of growth is therefore not flawed in the manner that Negishi supposes.

Quesnay and Mirabeau were convinced that the invention of the Tableau provided a basis for the calculation of the impact of particular policies. They told their critics: "Will you again say that you do not understand what there is to gain in having more income or more revenue, and paying more for what one buys? ... If you are able to calculate, you will easily penetrate this mystery" (ibid., p. I.233). They believed that the Tableau provided a basis for the calculation of the growth which France could achieve through the adoption of appropriate policies. At the same time inappropriate policies could all too easily continue the economic decline from which they believed France was suffering.

Quesnay's and Mirabeau's brilliant and sophisticated Tableaux show how *luxe* can be even more damaging to the long-term viability of economies than their many predecessors had supposed. But by analysing the impact of *luxe* within the Tableau in this technical manner, they and other physiocratic writers like Nicholas Baudeau, the editor of *Les ephemerides du citoyen* in 1765–72 and 1774–6, reiterated that an economy in stationary state equilibrium was free to spend 50 per cent of all incomes on the sterile side of the Tableau which included luxury manufactures. Previous opponents of *luxe* had regarded all expenditures of this kind as economically and socially harmful.

Quesnay, Mirabeau and Baudeau therefore replaced the large and important questions which France's political philosophers had regarded as central to the luxury debate with an economists' formula for the level of *luxe* which was compatible with the stationary-state equilibrium of the economy. Therefore, according to the greatest physiocrats, the acceptable level of luxury would not depend on the nature of society, or upon inequalities and incentives to advancement, or on the kinds of goods produced, although these were condemned in many eloquent passages in *Philosophie rurale*.

It will be evident that the physiocrats abstracted virtually all that was socially and politically significant from the luxury debate, and grafted an economic model of immense originality and sophistication onto their supposition that the manufacture of luxuries generated no kind of economic surplus. This assumption was rapidly shown to be false, not least by Adam Smith in Great Britain in 1776 in the *Wealth of Nations* and in France in the same year by Condillac, who, in the opinion of the French Nobel Prizewinner in Economics, Maurice Allais, had developed "a general theory of the generation of surpluses, of general economic equilibrium, and of maximal efficiency" in *Le Commerce et le Gouvernement*, which was superior to Adam Smith (Allais 1992, pp. 37 and 192). Both showed that manufactures can be hugely surplus-generating. Their development of economics beyond the physiocratic model suggests that the contribution of the earlier writers, whom Quesnay and his disciples briefly superseded, should not be overlooked.

Appendix: the explanation of the impact of a one-fifth increase in expenditure on *luxe de décoration* in Quesnay's Tableaux in *Philosophie rurale*

In what is said below, for expositional simplicity, what Quesnay and Mirabeau describe as the productive sector will be referred to as "agriculture", which produces "food", while the sterile sector will be referred to as "industry", which produces "manufactures".

In Figure 9.1, a and b represent the expenditure on food from the non-agricultural classes, while c and d represent the expenditure on manufactures from outside the industrial sector. Half of landowners' total revenue or rents of 2000 are spent on food and half on manufactures, so a and c are each 1000. The farmers spend half their advances of 2000 on manufactures, so d is 1000. The principal complication in the explanation of Figure 9.1 concerns b, manufacturers' expenditures on food. Quesnay states that "The total of the payments of the manufacturing class to the agricultural class equals one-half of the receipts of the manufacturing class" ([1764] 1972, p. I.328). As these receipts are represented by c and d which are each 1000, b which is $\frac{1}{2}(c+d)$ also equals 1000. Quesnay adds that "the manufacturing class receives 2000 of which 1000 remain to replace its advances, and 1000 are employed for the subsistence of those who work in it" (ibid., pp. I.328–9). It is simplest to suppose that b represents the purchases of food by manufacturers for their subsistence, which absorbs 1000 of the 2000 they have received (via c and d) while the remaining 1000 they receive is used after the completion of the transactions set out in Figure 9.1, to purchase the advances they will require for the following year.

When the Tableau becomes more complex in Figures 9.2 and 9.3, the key to whether output will expand or decline is whether total agricultural wealth which is reproduced rises or falls. It is therefore necessary to understand how this total is arrived at. At the foot of Figure 9.1, Quesnay writes, "The total reproduction is equal to all the sums which in combination are spent within agriculture." Viz:

1	Farmers' advances	2000
2	That part of the revenues of the landlords which is immediately spent on food (a)	1000
3	Purchases of food by the manufacturers (b)	1000
4	Advances of the manufacturers which are used to buy raw materials from the farmers	<u>1000</u>
		5000

Thus the reproduction totals 5000, of which farmers retain for their advances and the "interest" they require to maintain their total capital	3000
There remains for revenue to pay to the landlords	2000

As Figure 9.1's total revenue in the initial year is 2000, farmers retain enough to pay a similar rent in the following year. The 3000 they retain for themselves is sufficient to sustain their annual advances at 2000 and to provide the 1000 which Quesnay assumes they will require to cover the depreciation of one-tenth of their total capital of 10,000 which is made up of the annual advances of 2000 which the Tableau shows, and primary advances (of long-term fixed capital) of 8000 which are four times as great. Hence the conditions required to sustain a stationary state will be continually reproduced.

Figure 9.2 shows the impact on this basic Tableau of an increase of one-fifth in the propensity of all classes to purchase manufactures where these additional manufactures represent *luxe*. In Quesnay's words the Tableau shows "the deterioration caused by an excess of luxury of one-fifth" (ibid., p.

III.36). In Figure 9.1, landowners, farmers and manufacturers each spent half their incomes on food and half on manufactures. Now these each spend four-tenths on food and six-tenths on manufactures, that is an additional two-tenths or one-fifth is now spent by each class on manufactures. The expenditure of landowners on food (a) and manufactures (c) is readily calculable as 800 and 1200 (that is 40 and 60 per cent of their total rents of 2000). Farmers' expenditures on manufactures at 1200 (d) are also a straightforward 60 per cent of their advances of 2000 in place of the previous 50 per cent. The figure which is less straightforward to interpret is b, manufacturers' expenditure on food, which Quesnay writes down as 1080. In the stationary state of Figure 9.1 they spent one-half of their total receipts of (c + d) on food. If they are now to spend one-fifth less on food because, like the rest of the population, they now have a greater propensity to consume manufactures, they would spend four-tenths of their enhanced receipts of 2400 on food, that is 960 in place of the former five-tenths which would produce 1200. But Quesnay actually says that they spend 1080. The explanation of this discrepancy is that only half of manufacturers' total receipts of 2400 are allocated to the financing of subsistence and it is merely to this half that the one-fifth reduction in the propensity to buy food applies. The overall reduction in manufacturers' propensity to buy food will therefore be one-tenth and not one-fifth, and a one-tenth reduction in the 1200 that half of (c + d) produces is the 1080 which Quesnay shows for b in Figure 9.2. The economy's total reproduction which was 5000 in the stationary state presented in Figure 9.2 is now describable as follows:

1   Farmers' expenditures on food from their own advances
    in place of the former 2000. Their "interest" (depreciation
    of capital) of 1000 is spent entirely in agriculture, and four-
    tenths of their advances of 2000 are spent in agriculture,
    so they spend 1800 in all on agricultural produce   1800
2   Farmers' receipts from landowners (a) which are
    four-tenths of their rents of 2000   800
3   Purchases of food by manufacturers (b)   1080
4   Purchases of raw materials by manufacturers
    (manufacturers' advances of 1000 at the head of the
    tableau)   1000
                                                                         4680

The economy's total reproduction is therefore 4680 in place of the 5000 of the previous year when the Tableau was in stationary-state equilibrium. Quesnay assumes that the 320 by which farmers' receipts fall short of the 5000 they would require in a stationary state will be divided equally between a 160 reduction in revenues paid to landowners and a reduction of 160 in the incomes of farmers.

Manufacturers are in the apparently happy situation that they have received 2400 and spent 1080 of this on food, and 1000 on materials and they therefore have a financial surplus of 320 which they retain for the future. In Quesnay's words under Figure 9.2, "320 have passed to and are retained by the manufacturers."

Because agriculture is in financial deficit by 320 in Figure 9.2, and half of this is taken from the incomes of farmers, their annual advances in the following year, which is represented in Figure 9.3, will fall by 160 from the 2000 of Figure 9.2 to 1840, that is by 8 per cent. Because landlords forgo the remaining half of agriculture's financial deficit, rents are also reduced by 8 per cent from 2000 in Figure 9.2 to 1840 in Figure 9.3. Indeed in Figure 9.3, all the totals are reduced by precisely the 8 per cent by which agricultural advances fall, since all the quantities in a Quesnaysian economy are multiples of annual agricultural advances, and in Quesnay's calculations these have fallen by 8 per cent.

Thus the totals in Figure 9.3, the Tableau of the second year, of an increase in the propensity to consume *luxe* from 50 to 60 per cent, correspond precisely to the Tableau of the previous year, with a, b, c and d each 8 per cent lower than in Figure 9.2. A general formula for the economy's rate of decline in the conditions Quesnay assumes, which confirms his calculations in Figures 9.2 and 9.3, can readily be derived.

Farmers' annual advances in the initial year when the Tableau is in stationary-state equilibrium can be written as A: it is 2000 in Figure 9.1. Total rents or revenues are thus also A with Quesnay's assumption of a rate of return of 100 per cent on annual agricultural advances. The propensity to consume food of all classes can be written as q: this is 0.5 in Figure 9.1. Then the reproduction of the economy is as follows:

1 Farmers' expenditures on food from their own advances will be HA from the expenditure of interest plus qA from their expenditures on their own subsistence, i.e.: $(\frac{1}{2}+q)A$
2 A fraction q of total rents of A will be spent in agriculture, i.e.: qA
3 Farmers and landlords each spend $(1-q)A$ on manufactures, so industry receives $2(1-q)A$. Half of this is retained to finance advances. Of the remaining $(1-q)A$, half is sensitive to variation in q, and therefore becomes $q(1-q)A$ while the remaining half is independent of q and continues as $\frac{1}{2}(1-q)A$. Hence manufacturers' expenditures on food total: $\frac{1}{2}+q(1-q)A$
4 Manufacturers' advances are one-quarter of the sum of agricultural advances and rents, i.e. $\frac{1}{4}$ of 2A or: $\frac{1}{2}A$
The economy's total reproduction, for which X can be written, is the sum of 1., 2., 3. and 4. or $(1\frac{1}{2}+2\frac{1}{2}q-q^2)A$. Hence:

$$X = (1\frac{1}{2}+2\frac{1}{2}q-q^2)A \tag{1}$$

When the economy is in stationary-state equilibrium, q is 0.5 and X is 2MA, as in Figure 9.1 where A is 2000.

When q is 0.4 instead of 0.5, X, the total reproduction, is 2.34A or 4680 as in Figure 9.2 where A is initially 2000. If the extent to which the total reproduction falls is divided equally between reduced agricultural advances and lower rents as Quesnay assumes, these will each be reduced by half the fall in X, i.e. by half of 0.16A or by 0.08A. In Figure 9.2, A is 2000, and agricultural advances fall by 0.08A to 1840 in Figure 9.3.

The formula for the rate of decline (or conversely growth) of annual agricultural advances, and therefore of every total in the Tableau, is the change in annual agricultural advances as a fraction of agricultural advances at the start of the year. The change in advances is half the change in the economy's total reproduction:

The reproduction changes from $2\frac{1}{2}q$ to $(1\frac{1}{2}+2\frac{1}{2}q-q^2)A$, i.e. it changes by $(2\frac{1}{2}q-q^2-1)A$

The change in annual agricultural advances is half the change in the reproduction or $(1\frac{1}{4}q-\frac{1}{2}q^2-\frac{1}{2})A$ and the economy's rate of growth of annual agricultural advances, g_A is this as a fraction of A. Hence:

$$g_A = (1\tfrac{1}{4}q - \tfrac{1}{2}q^2 - \tfrac{1}{2}) \tag{2}$$

When q = 0.5 as in Figure 9.1, g_A is zero, while it is −0.08 when q = 0.4 as in Figures 9.2 and 9.3.

References

Alembert, Jean le Rond (1751) *Discours preliminaire de l'Encyclopedie*, ed. F. Picavet, Paris: Armand Colin, 1929.

Allais, Maurice (1992) "The general theory of surpluses as a formalization of the underlying theoretical thought of Adam Smith, his predecessors and his contemporaries", in Michael Fry (ed.), *Adam Smith's Legacy*, London: Routledge, pp. 29–62, 166–97.

Anon. (1755) *L'Abeille, ou recueuil de philosophie de litterature et d'histoire*, Hague.

d'Argenson, Marquis (1764) *Considerations sur le Gouvernement ancien et present de la France*, Amsterdam.

d'Argenson, Marquis (1859–67) *Journal et Memoires*, ed. E. J. B. Rathery, 9 vols, Paris.

Baudeau, Nicholas (1765–7) "Principes de la science morale et politique sur le luxe et les lois sumptuaires", *Les Ephemerides du citoyen*.

Berkeley, George (1735–7) *The Querist*, 3 vols, Dublin.

Boisguilbert, Pierre de (1966) *Oeuvres manuscrites et imprimees de Boisguilbert*, vol. II of *Pierre de Boisguilbert ou la naissance de l'Economie Politique*, Paris: L'Institut National d'Etudes Demographiques.

Cantillon, Richard (1755) *Essai sur la nature du commerce en general*, Paris; reprinted and translated by Henry Higgs for the Royal Economic Society in 1931, London.

Condillac, E. Bonnot, abbe de (1776) *Le Commerce et le Gouvernement*, Paris; trans. and ed. 1997 by Shelagh M. and Walter Eltis, *Commerce and Government*, Aldershot: Edward Elgar.

230 *Walter and Shelagh M. Eltis*

Eltis, Walter (1999) "Does luxury consumption promote growth?" in Roger E. Backhouse and John Greedy (eds), *From Classical Economics to the Theory of the Firm: Essays in Honour of P.P. O'Brien*, Cheltenham: Edward Elgar, pp. 87–103.

Fénelon, François de Salignac de La Mothe (1699) *Les aventures de Telemaque*, Paris; reprinted in 1995 in Paris: Gallimard.

Forbonnais, François Veron de (1755) *Elements de commerce*, Amsterdam.

Galliani, Renato (1989) *Rousseau, le luxe et l'ideologie nobiliaire*, Oxford: Voltaire Foundation of the Taylor Institute.

Kuczynski, Marguerite and Meek, Ronald L. (eds) (1972) *Quesnay's Tableau Economique*, London: Macmillan.

Larrere, Catherine (1992) *L'invention de l'economie au XVIIIe siecle*, Paris: PUF Leviathan.

McManners, John (1998) *Church and Society in Eighteenth Century France*, 2 vols, Oxford: Clarendon Press.

Mandeville, Bernard de (1714) *The Fable of the Bees: or Private Vices, Public Benefits*, London; after 1729 editions also included the Second Part.

Melon, Jean-François (1734) *Essai politique sur le commerce*, Paris; edition augmentée 1736.

Mirabeau, Victor Riqueti, Marquis de and François Quesnay (1756–60) *L'Ami des hommes*, 8 Parts, Avignon (including "Le Tableau economique avec ses explications").

Mirabeau, Victor Riqueti, Marquis de and François Quesnay (1763) *Philosophie rurale*, Paris; 2nd edn in 3 vols 1764; reprinted in 1972 by Scientia Verlag Aalen.

Montesquieu, Charles-Louis de Secondat, baron de la Brede (1721) *Lettres persanes*; reprinted in 1951, ed. Emile Faguet, Paris: Nelson.

Montesquieu, Charles-Louis de Secondat (1734) *Considerations sur les causes de la grandeur des Remains et de leur decadence*, reprinted in 1951 in Lettres persanes, Paris: Nelson, pp. 331–523.

Montesquieu, Charles Louis de Secondat (1748) *De l'esprit des lois*, 2 vols; reprinted in 1961, Paris: Garnier frères.

Montesquieu, Charles Louis de Secondat *Pensées et Spicilege*, ed. Louis Desgraves 1991, Paris: Robert Laffont.

Morize, Andre (1909) *L'Apologie du luxe au XVIII65 siècle et Le Mondain de Voltaire*, Paris: H. Didier.

Murphy, Antoin (1986) *Richard Cantillon: Entrepreneur and Economist*, Oxford: Clarendon Press.

Negishi, T. (1989) "Expenditure patterns and international trade in Quesnay's *Tableau Economique*", in *Developments in Japanese Economics*, Tokyo: Academic Press/Harcourt Brace Jovanovich, pp. 85–97.

Perrotta, Cosimo (1997) "The pre-classical theory of development: increased consumption raises productivity", *History of Political Economy*, vol. 29: 2, pp. 295–326.

Quesnay, François (1757) "Grains", reprinted in 1958 in *François Quesnay et la Physiocratie*, 2 vols, Paris: Institut National d'Etudes Demographiques, pp. 459–510.

Rousseau, Jean-Jacques (1750) *Discours sur les sciences et les arts*; reprinted in 1992, ed. Jacques Roger, Paris: Flammarion, pp. 23–55.

Rousseau, Jean-Jacques (1752) *Dernière réponse de J. J. Rousseau*; reprinted with *Discours sur les sciences et les arts*, pp. 97–126.

Rousseau, Jean-Jacques (1755) *Discours sur l'economie politique*; reprinted in *Oeuvres completes*, ed. B. Gagnebin and M. Raymond, Paris: Gallimard, 5 vols, 1959–95, vol. Ill, pp. 241–78.

Rousseau, Jean-Jacques (1755) *Discours sur l'origine et les fondements de l'inegalite, parmi les hommes*; reprinted with *Discours sur les sciences et les arts* in 1992, pp. 145–257.

Rousseau, Jean-Jacques (1762) *Du contrat social*; reprinted in *Oeuvres completes*, vol. Ill, pp. 279–470.

Rousseau, Jean-Jacques (1764) *Preface to "Narcisse"*; reprinted in *Oeuvres completes*, Vol. 11, pp. 959–74.

Smith, Adam (1776) *The Nature and Causes of the Wealth of Nations*, London.

Steiner, Philippe (1998) *La "Science Nouvelle" de l'economie politique*, Paris: PUF.

Théré, Christine (1988) "Economic publishing and authors, 1566–1789", in Gilbert Faccarello (ed.), *Studies in the History of French Political Economy: from Bodin to Walras*, London: Routledge, pp. 1–56.

Voltaire, François Marie Arouet de (1734) *Le Mondain*; reprinted in Morize (1909), pp. 133–9.

Voltaire, Francois Marie Arouet de (1739) *La Défense du Mondain*; reprinted in Morize (1909), pp. 153–8.

10 French political economy, industrialism and social change (1815–30)

Philippe Steiner

Any examination of the French political economy of the first half of the nineteenth century must take into consideration the extraordinary social and political context of the time: the aftermath of a French Revolution and the Napoleonic endeavour which, having overthrown the royal family in France, had brought conflict to the whole of Europe. How was it possible to understand the workings of society after the collapse of a dynasty that had reigned for many centuries over one of the most powerful nations of Europe? How should social progress, so clearly set out in Turgot's early texts and in Condorcet's final work, be considered in this new context?

These were the sorts of questions that taxed the minds of social scientists and, more generally, of all those who comprised the French intellectual milieu from the end of the eighteenth century onwards. The economists, or rather the small group who did not refute this appellation, were no exception. Jean-Baptiste Say, Charles Dunoyer and Charles Comte, Henri Saint-Simon and Auguste Comte – not to mention Adolphe Blanqui, Jean-Antoine Chaptal and Charles Dupin who, although they may be less well known now, had a widespread influence at the time – all presented their contemporaries with their ideas on what society could expect from industry.

This essay first examines the import and value that Say attached to industry, since it is he who by general consent is the founding father of reflection on this topic. Next, I explore how this doctrine poses the key question of elite adapted to the nascent social system: should this elite be drawn, and if yes in what way, from the new social classes, that is to say the industrial classes? Such questions go beyond the boundaries of economic thought in the narrow sense of the term and require that economic questions also be considered in the light of the desired development of a society, as demonstrated by the opinions carried in a variety of journals, *Le Censeur européen*, *L'organisateur*, *La Revue encyclopédique* and *Le Producteur*, and by the debates between the different factions of industrialist thought, dealt with in the third section of this chapter.

Say's conception of production as the foundation of industrialism

In the first chapter of the *Traité*, Say provides a clear formulation of the goal of the entire first book of the *Traité*: 'There is therefore only real production of wealth when there is creation or increase of utility. *Let us discover how this utility is produced*' (1817: I, 7; my italics). Later, Say finishes his Chapter 3 with a strong statement of the goal envisaged for the *work as a whole*:

> Let us therefore conclude that wealth, which lies in the value that human industry with the aid of natural agents gives to things, that wealth, I say, is susceptible to be created, destroyed, increased or reduced according to the means one applies. This is a significant truth because it puts within man's reach the goods which, with good reason, he desires to possess, provided he knows and wishes to use the means necessary to obtain them. The development of these means is *the aim of this work.*
>
> (1817: 21–2; my italics)

In other words, the entirety of the work aims at elucidating the means by which men can produce the goods they require in increasing quantities. In order to follow the development of the author's thought and to appreciate the significance of his conception of political economy for his contemporaries, it is therefore to the question of the means of wealth production that one must turn.

Human industry, natural agents and knowledge

The duty of political economy is to study the wealth that we would not possess were it not for the way 'human industry triggers, complements, completes the operations of nature' (ibid.). Thus, in his definition of industry, Say puts the emphasis on the relationship that exists between industry and nature. First, production signifies a use that humans make of the nature that is at their disposition. Production is a combination of the materials provided by nature in order to give them a utility that they would not naturally have. This utility can be direct or indirect. Say introduces the term capital as an intermediary between industry and nature, signifying the stock of products already existing at industry's disposal prior to the contribution of nature. This is the triptych that defines the conditions of modern production: industry (or human work), capital and nature; or put another way, the productive action of labour, capital and natural agents.

Second, the benefits that men can anticipate from nature will lead them to attempt to appropriate it; with the exception of those cases where nature is a free good (the wind, the sea, the laws of nature – ibid.: 34) nature can be appropriated thanks to a positive legislation which assures its possessor its exclusive usage, as is the case, for example, with land. The relationship between production and nature is therefore dependent on social organisation; and this domain is one where a particular effort is required, as the author of the *Traité* makes very clear. From Chapter XIV onwards he introduces an examination of property rights, of administrative rules and regulations relating to production, and so on, citing them specifically as social causes for the improvement or impediment of production.

Third, nature is a 'powerful tool' to the extent that it constitutes a resource that permits the materials it harbours to be put into action. The production of utility therefore relies on the implementation of knowledge of the laws of nature, laws that in effect are so many means of putting nature to the service of society. Knowledge is thus an integral element in human industry; it enables a *collective appropriation* of nature. Say attaches great importance to this dimension of human industry. Human beings' relationship to nature can either be that of the *use* of materials present on or in the terrestrial globe, the *appropriation* of certain amongst them and the *knowledge of the laws* that drive natural phenomena.

These three dimensions of industry are founded on the three classes that participate in the production process. The scientist makes possible the collective appropriation of nature by providing the knowledge needed to master the 'powerful tool' that is nature. The workman carries out the immediate work destined to transform nature. The entrepreneur plays an intermediary role by hiring the productive services of the two preceding categories, to which are added the services of the capital hired from capitalists and those of the land hired from landowners.

In this way Say gathers together the elements that enable him to define this new, previously unknown, form of society. He is thus able to mark his position off as quite distinct from that defended by Smith when it comes to the question of modern society and the causes of wealth.

The division of labour and machines

An attentive comparison of the 'Preliminary Discourse' of the first two editions of the *Traité* shows that, from 1814 onwards, Say vigorously critiques the *Wealth of Nations*. Smith's theory of production is no exception since the division of labour, which is one of its central elements, is submitted to a rigorous critique.

It is nonetheless true that Say, in his turn, reworks Smith's famous description of the pin factory, but in doing so he limits its importance. First, Say puts the emphasis on the importance of the division of labour at the heart of the world of the scientists – that is to say those who study nature in order that society can collectively appropriate the resources offered by natural agents. The division of intellectual labour is an important element that Say introduces through the concept of the productive service of the scientist, which he sees as one of the constitutive elements of industry. Second, Say reproaches Smith for not having accorded machines greater importance than the division of labour when it came to giving an account of the accumulation of wealth (ibid.: xlix–l).

By machine, Say understands all the means that industry can employ to harness the non-appropriated forces of nature through a mastering of the laws of nature by science. This therefore constitutes a considerable departure from Smith's thought, as is underlined by two important consequences that Say draws from this change of perspective. It is not exchange that is at the heart of society, but production. Or, to put it another way, the exchanges between men and nature facilitated by the use of machines.

In place of the Smithian approach of trying to uncover the rules which people naturally follow in exchange (1776: I, 44), Say's major concern is the rules which people follow socially in the exchange with nature in order to produce utility. The synthetic definition of the concept of production costs provided in the *Epitôme* is explicit on this point:

> [P]*roduction* being an exchange where one gives production costs in order to receive the *utility* produced, it results that the more the utility produced is considerable in relation to the production costs, the more the exchange is advantageous. A more efficient use of *natural agents* procures greater *utility* produced in relation to production costs and as a consequence makes the exchange through which man receives created *values* against production costs more advantageous.[1] Natural hazards, such as hail, frost, or human hazards such as war, damage or taxes, by removing a part of the values produced, make the exchange less advantageous.
>
> (1817: II, 452–3)

These rules depend on the state of a society because they depend on the level of command that people have over the laws of nature, but they also depend on the rules according to which people organise themselves socially. In fact, Say never omits to mention 'human hazards' or the lack of development of 'moral and political sciences' amongst the phenomena that thwart production. Furthermore, the entrepreneur is at the centre of his approach precisely because he is the essential mediator through whom this Society–Nature relationship can take place:

> It is in this way that nature is nearly always in a community of work with mankind; and in this community we gain all the more when we are more successful in economising on our work and that of our capital, which is necessarily costly, and when we succeed in causing

nature to produce a greater output. Smith went to great lengths to
explain the abundance of products to be found amongst civilised
peoples in comparison with the penury of less developed nations,
notwithstanding the multitude of unemployed and unproductive
labourers that abound in our societies. He sought the source of this
abundance in the division of labour; and there is indeed no doubt
that the separation of occupations, as we follow him in understanding
it, adds greatly to the productive power of labour. It is nonetheless an
insufficient explanation for this phenomenon as a whole, whereas if
the power of the natural agents that civilisation and industry harness
for our profit are taken into account this phenomenon no longer
seems at all surprising.

(ibid.: I, 30–1)

Modern society is not therefore Smith's *commercial society*, but the *industrial
society* that Say, Saint-Simon and the editors of the *Censeur Européen*,
Dunoyer and C. Comte, Dupin,[2] Blanqui and Michel Chevalier,[3] take as
their principal object of study in the first half of the nineteenth century.

It is important to take full stock of the importance that Restoration
publicists accorded to industry. For this, there is no more indicative event
than the 1819 exposition of the products of French industry. Launched by
François de Chateauneuf, with assistance from Chaptal, this exposition
was conceived of as a way of demonstrating French industrial progress
after the terrible upheavals of the Revolution,[4] and the Napoleonic wars. A
journal like the *Revue encyclopédique*, whose overall intellectual project
required that it should treat such a subject, did not fail in its obligations as
can be seen from its first volumes which contain a review of Chaptal's
work by Dupin (1819), a review of the exposition itself (Le Normand
1819) – not to mention the reviews dealing with the subject of applied
mechanics,[5] a term which designates what might in other words be called
the science of the engineer.[6]

Dupin's review of Chaptal is of interest above all for the idea it gives of
the divide between those who champion industry and free trade and those
who, with Chaptal and Dupin at their head, having serious reservations
with regard to free trade, see the future in an association between industry
and the state through what today would be called industrial policy.

The review of the exposition written by Le Normand, a regular contrib-
utor to the *Revue encyclopédique* on the subject of practical mechanics, is of
a very different nature. From the outset, industry is linked to the peaceful
competition that ranks different nations in relation to one another. The
article, which is written in a descriptive tone, depicts the general satisfaction of visitors to the exposition as well as their desire to capture the
marvels of industry on display with their gaze. In conclusion, the author
finishes on a note very close to Say's tone when the latter vaunts the merits
of the 'production of sameness (*mêmeté*)' (1803: I, 136–40) over the pro-

duction of exceptional products which would be expensive and therefore
out of the reach of the majority of the population:

> Manufacturers should be fully aware of the goal at which they must
> aim. They should not be especially preoccupied with producing
> objects of outstanding beauty and consequently of great expense.
> Rather, they should strive to manufacture objects of widespread
> utility, of solid construction, of excellent quality and of a price that
> makes them available to widest section of the population.
>
> (Le Normand 1819: 154)

Alongside this general public journal are a series of others in which the
political dimension is more prominent. Here, publicists progressively
define industrialism, by which they mean a social and political order
organised for and by industry. The most significant periodicals in this
respect are that of Charles Comte and Dunoyer, *Le Censeur européen*, and
the more ephemeral publications launched by Saint-Simon with the help
of some gifted secretaries (Augustin Thierry and Auguste Comte) such as
L'industrie, Le politique, L'organisateur, Du système industriel and *Le catéchisme
des industriels*. At the beginning of this period the two groups were tightly
linked,[7] as can be observed by examining first the publications of Saint-
Simon and Thierry in 1817 and then following their echo in *Le Censeur
européen* (III: 193–208).

As indicated by its title, the journal *L'industrie* puts useful activity at the
heart of social life.[8] What does this useful activity, whether theoretical or
practical, intellectual or manual, require in order to develop? First, it
needs to be conscious of itself, of its strength and its importance, and of
the real unity constituted by all the industrialists of the nation, and more
generally of Europe. Then it needs freedom without which it is unable to
bring forth its true fruit; government must therefore be of non-interventionist in order to allow society, or rather industry, to decide what is best
for industry. The required social system must therefore be one where:

> [W]orkers, whose agglomeration forms the essence of a true society,
> can exchange the products of their various labours between one
> another with an absolute freedom; a form of administration such that
> society alone might know what it requires, what it wishes and what it
> prefers, and thus might be the sole arbitrator of the merit and the
> utility of work.
>
> (Saint-Simon and Thierry 1817: 166)

Nevertheless, even at this early stage, Say is reproached for not having felt
the true political implications of his political economy and for not having
taken his thought to its natural conclusion: that of clearly stating the need
for modern society to reconstitute itself as an industrial society (ibid.:

185–6). Once this transformation has been effected, the authors have no qualms about affirming that politics will simply become a question of political economy, since at this stage Saint-Simon still conceives of self-interest as the only social bond that links people:

> There is an order of interests felt by all people, the interests that pertain to everyday life and to well-being. This order of interests is the only one on which all people can agree and on which they have to agree, the only one where they have to think and act in common, the only order therefore about which politics should preoccupy itself and which should be taken as the sole measure in the critique of all social institutions and organisation. To resume, therefore, politics is *the science of production*, that is to say the branch of learning that has for its object the order of things that is the most favourable for all types of production.
>
> (ibid.: 188)

Politics reduced to 'the science of production'; political economy transformed into 'the science of industry' (1817: II, 158)! In terms of social and political outlook, no one could ever offer anything closer to Say's thought. It is therefore no coincidence that Comte and Dunoyer publish large extracts of *L'Industrie* in volume 2 of *Le Censeur européen*, approving its general direction and in particular applauding ideas that specifically relate to the place of industry, to liberty and to non-interventionist government.

It is therefore no surprise to find Saint-Simon making a number of references to Say's work in this period (Saint-Simon and Thierry 1817: I, 182–91 and II: 151–8). The admiration does not go unreciprocated, as Say had read and admired certain of Thierry's works, Say provided finance for certain of Saint-Simon's publications and, in the middle of the twenties, he was still in relation with A. Comte. For its part, *Le Censeur européen* published a long review of the *Traité*, another of the *Petit volume contenant quelques aperçus sur les hommes et la société* and a third of *Des canaux de navigation dans l'état actuel de la France*, a booklet that Say wrote on this most industrialist subject.

As Saint-Simon is clearly not one of those who shirks programmatic declarations, it is no surprise to find him taking his reflection to the level of demanding the organisation of a new social system which he closely associates with industry. The prospectus for *L'organisateur* from August 1814 is a prime example:

> *L'organisateur* will have as its object: 1. to posit the principles which should serve as the basis for a new political system; 2. to present the project of the organisation of a scientific workshop capable of creating a social doctrine that befits the current level of man's know-

ledge; 3. to prove that it is in the interest of all social classes that this work be carried out as speedily as possible; 4. to indicate the means of maintaining public tranquillity during the organisation of this new system.

(Saint-Simon and Comte 1819–20: 8)

The two journalists would develop these principles from a study of history structured by the law of progress, according to which the French Revolution was a moment of critical illness (the primary meaning of the French word 'crise' at this time was above all a medical one). That is to say that 'the passage from the feudal and theological system to an industrial and scientific one [constitutes a crisis] that will inevitably last until the process of forming a new social system is in full swing' (Saint-Simon and Comte 1821: 3).

From political economy to social theory

The roots of the link between political economy and social theory are to be found in the physiocrats, in Turgot and Condorcet, and then in the turbulence of the Revolution, and especially in the political positions expressed in social science in the years, or even months, that immediately precede the Terror.[9] The *Cours d'organisation sociale* given at the Lycée by Pierre-Louis Roederer (1793) provides one excellent example of this, and the economic teaching of Alexandre Vandermonde (1795) at the Ecole normale another. Both make a case for the defence of self-interest and efficiency against the proponents of virtue.

However, the way in which these questions take on renewed urgency at the moment when the question of putting the Revolution to an end emerges requires direct consideration. The social elite of the Ancien Régime is directly called into question on the basis of criteria brought to light by political economy. The question is no longer that of how to regenerate the old elite by reorienting the land-owning nobility towards agriculture and commerce, but of replacing them with a new elite tied to the objectives and values of industrial civil society: that is to say to efficiency and modern virtue.

Liberation through the market

The choice that Say (1803) and Jean-Charles-Léonard Simonde de Sismondi (1803) both make simultaneously and independently in favour of Adam Smith over physiocracy means that both are able to make clear the major rupture that has occurred during the Revolution when it comes to the social status of industrial men. As early as the second chapter of his great work, Smith (1776: I, 26) suggests that market relations liberate people from the constraints associated with personal relations.

This line of argument aims at demonstrating the profound difference between the social exchanges that take place through political relations, that is to say the relations in which domination is at work, and the market relations in which individuals are freed from any constraint, whether political, familial or affective. Smith returns to this question in book IV of the *Wealth of Nations*, but it is clear that Say and Sismondi had already not only understood this message perfectly, but also retained and developed it. A clear expression of this is to be found in the manuscript that Sismondi (1801: 273) seeks to publish; the same theme is also developed in a brief chapter of the *Traité d'économie politique*, in which Say treats the question of social independence in modern society. This chapter is in book IV, which deals with the distribution of wealth – and more precisely comes between the chapters on industrial revenues (those of the scientist, the worker and the entrepreneur) and those on revenues to be gained from land and capital.

For Say, this chapter is above all a chance to affirm 'the independence that industrial revenues have procured in modern societies for a class whose members are spread as wide as society itself: that is to say those who possess neither land nor capital' (1803: II, 262). Here Say mounts a strong defence of the thesis which states that the possessor of industrial capacity is socially free from the wealthy in the measure that, through the market, he can serve the public without being dependent on a handful of powerful figures:

> In a social system of this type, the majority of a nation finds that there is little profit to be gained in serving the great and much to be gained from serving the public, that is to say by making use of their industry. From this point on, there is no more patron–client relation: the most meagre citizen can do without a patron, putting himself rather for his survival under the tutelage of his talent.
>
> (1803: II, 264)

There is no clearer affirmation of the idea that the development of the market frees the average citizen from the personal subordination of the hierarchical chain to be found under the Ancien Régime, as set out in its ideal form by Alexis de Tocqueville in the second volume of his *Démocratie en Amérique*. As soon as individuals are endowed with some industrial capacity, a capacity on which their economic independence is based, they also obtain a social independence, that is to say the essential basis on which social equality can be developed between individuals, all equally economically independent and equally able to make use of their reason.

Constant's manuscripts from the beginning of the nineteenth century are marked by Say's influence and, more particularly, by the influence of the brief chapter discussed above which sees social independence as the property of industrious individuals freed from personal submission to the powerful thanks to the market (Steiner 1998b: 141–56). According to the genealogy established by Dunoyer (1827a: 370–3), Constant's political writings, including his famous lecture, *De la liberté des modernes* (given at the Athénée Royal, the institution where Say gave his first public lectures on political economy) are to be counted amongst the founding texts of industrialism alongside those of Say and count Montlosier.

Social independence, industry and peace have become the central values around which the political life of the moderns revolves. In this sense, liberation through the market implies more than the social independence of industrialists freed from any personal dimension; as a theory of the market, political economy becomes a political theory. It is therefore in no way surprising to discover that the theory of economic growth developed by Say amongst others should be associated with a theory of social and political development, and more particularly with an in-depth reflection on the nature of the social elite that would be fit to lead an industrial society.

Industrial society and the rise of the middle class

In *Olbie*, Say – taking the opposite point of view from that of Rousseau – considers that the education of adults is an essential element for the regeneration of a corrupt society (1800: 4–5). In the wake of the physiocrats and the Ideologues, he makes education a key criterion for those wishing to accede to the government elite:

> [T]he first book of morality for the Olbiens was a sound treaty of political economy. They instituted a type of academy that they charged with the function of depository for this book. Any citizen who wished to be nominated to the position of first magistrate, was required to be publicly interrogated on the principles of this science, principles which he was free to choose to defend or attack. All that mattered for the academy to award him with the education diploma was that he had a good grasp of these principles, without which any passage to higher office would not be possible for him.
>
> (ibid.: 25–6)

Three years later, in the preliminary notes for the first edition of the *Traité d'économie politique*, examining the social conditions thanks to which his work could contribute to social change, Say explains that government – that is to say political elite and those in the higher positions of political administration – were not the main audience of his work. Those that it was vital to reach were to be found in the nation itself, and more precisely in the middle class (1803: I, xxviii). Say is thus here making a strong affirmation that social structure and education are linked. This he reinforces with an argument that one might be tempted to term a sociology of public action:

> Even if a monarch and his leading ministers were fully familiar with the principles on which the prosperity of nations were founded, what use would their knowledge be if they were not seconded every step of the way at all levels of their administration by men able to understand them, to collaborate with their views and to transform their conceptions into reality? The prosperity of a town, of a province can sometimes depend on a minor task carried out in an office, and often the head of a small administrative section, by provoking an important decision, exerts a much greater influence than that of the legislator himself.
>
> (ibid., I: xxviii–xxix)

But even this is not enough, says Say, because the main body of society itself also has to have educated enough to be ready to receive the measures proposed:

> Finally, if one supposes that all those who participate in the management of public affairs, at all levels, are well-versed in political economy without the nation being so, admittedly an altogether improbable scenario, imagine what resistance they would encounter in the prejudices of those very people whom their operations would favour the most? For a nation to get best advantage from a good economic system, it is not enough that its chiefs be in a position to adopt the best plans in all domains, it is also vital that the nation should be in a fit state to receive them.
>
> (1803: xxix)

Traces of this line of thought are also to be found in the critiques addressed to the land-owning class: they are seen as the owners of a property of dubious legitimacy (ibid.: II, 140–1) and they are less remarkable citizens since the nature of their wealth tends to make them timid vis-à-vis the powers. This is in contrast to those who possess mobile property, whose strength lies in the fact that they can escape bad government by leaving the country along with their wealth (Say *Mss* K44.334).

Furthermore, Say is suspicious of the predominance of the administration and the phenomenon of the 'quest for positions' which drains the nation of a part of its strength/blood – whilst it is not the action of government that he considers most important for the health of the nation (1819: 146–8, 163; 1828–9: II, 528–37) – without taking into consideration the actual capabilities of those to whom a position is conferred. It is economically inefficient and it endangers the principle of social independence that Say sees as the basis for the new social order.

Say pins his hopes on public opinion, as long as this is well informed as to the real needs and potential of a nation (*Mss* K454, K455), even if, in a text that probably dates from the first years of the Restoration, he states that he does not consider the enlightened part of the nation to be greater than 50,000 out of the thirty million people that then constituted the population of France (*Mss* K.454.858). This will take time. Such a point of view does not make of Say a thinker satisfied with the prevailing social order, far from it. Simply he is aware that social change takes time and that any attempts that do not respect this prerequisite are destined for failure as he would have experienced first hand during the Revolution. Time must be used for the diffusion of the social sciences (*Sciences morales et politiques*) learning which would enable a new elite to emerge from the industrial classes.

In effect, in contradistinction to the 'legislators, the administrators of public affairs to whom the principles of social economy remain alien' (Say 1828–9: I, 29) – that is to say in contradistinction to the political elite sprung from the Ancien Régime who do not know the basic principles of the functioning of society – Say calls for the formation of an elite, political or not, enlightened by the knowledge of political economy:

> I am of the opinion that this branch of study will soon be the neces-
> sary element to any liberal education; people will seek to avoid a dis-
> advantage equivalent to that which hinders those who do not know
> how to read when they are surrounded by people who benefit from
> this medium of information.
>
> (ibid.: 36)

What political class for industrial society?

By making political economy the mainstay of politics seen as empirical science, Saint-Simon and his secretaries emphasise a dimension of Say's thought that the latter does not manage to address in a satisfactory way, even in his own eyes, as is demonstrated by his inability to complete and publish his *Essais de politique pratique*. Saint-Simon's insistence on this point stems from the fact that he considers that political science, whether in France or in Europe, has failed to keep pace with contemporary developments in industry.

In *Le politique*, Saint-Simon formulates the problem by opposing a national or industrial party with an anti-national party. The former comprises industrialists (direct producers, entrepreneurs, those who lend capital to those who produce goods useful). The second is composed of pure consumers, those who do not contribute to the creation of utility and those whose political doctrines are opposed to the interests of industrialists (Saint-Simon and Comte 1819: 195–6). In *L'organisateur*, a distinction is drawn between power (of man over man) and capacity (of men over things) (ibid.: 85–7). This enables the development of a simple definition of the political capacity of industrialists from which emerges the idea that at the basis of positive political science lies political economy:

What today amounts to the highest degree of political capacity? My response is simple and easy. Since men have become equal in the eyes of the law, political rights are now only founded on the possession of money or of things that one can procure with money. The greatest, the most significant of the powers confided in government is that of taxing its citizens: it is from this right that stem all the others that it possesses. Political science therefore today consists essentially in making a good budget. And the capacity necessary to make a good budget is an administrative capacity, from which it emerges that administrative capacity is the prime political capacity. Let us now deduce who, between industrialists and individuals whose capital is not engaged in industrial enterprises, for the good governance of their affairs has the greatest need of administrative capacity. It is evident that administrative capacity is a capacity without which industrialists would be quite unable either to get rich or even to maintain their wealth; whereas property owners merely need not to spend more than their income in order to conserve their wealth and to economise on their revenues in order to get richer.

(ibid.: 200–1)

This thesis, which is also taken up by A. Comte in his writings of this period (1822, 1825, 1826), foregrounds the striking argument that industrial policy carried out to industry's advantage should be made by the industrialists themselves, since political capacity is directly based on the administrative capacity which is their forte. This position remains linked to that of Say to the extent that the latter had also emphasised the importance of knowledge, particularly of practical knowledge, under which heading he specifically included knowledge aimed at social organisation. A. Comte and Saint-Simon's position is therefore the development of one of the major axes of Say's thought; this proximity explains the fact that the latter had given Saint-Simon's secretary warm encouragement, as A. Comte mentions to Mill in 1844.

Nonetheless, a discrepancy between the lines of thought becomes visible when the two publicists foreground the cultural and normative dimension of social life. This dimension is nothing new, since it is already a visible feature of the last four books of *L'industrie*, those on which the young A. Comte collaborated after the departure of Thierry (Gouhier 1941: 172–94). However, it was to grow ever stronger to become one of the two major aspects of the industrialist thought of Saint-Simon and A. Comte as it emerges in *Du système industriel.* For they now start to insist on the moral dimension of social change in the move to industrial society – a dimension which eludes both political revolution as it does purely economic transformation. A stable social order demands a common moral doctrine:

A society cannot continue to exist without common moral ideas; this community is as necessary on a spiritual level as a community of interests is on a temporal level. These ideas cannot be common if they do not have as their base a philosophical doctrine universally adopted in the social edifice. This doctrine is fundamental: it is the link that unites and consolidates all the parties.

(Saint-Simon and Comte 1821: 51)

From this period onwards, the idea that egoism – which they view as rampant – should be balanced by a moral link founded in altruism emerges as a strong principle in their writing on industrialism (ibid.: 51–2, 85–95). This change of perspective, which reduces the role accorded to liberty and to economic liberty,[10] has an important consequence for the political organisation of the industrial class. In fact, from 1821 onwards, but more stridently in the *Catéchisme des industriels*, the two men exhort industrialism to mark itself as distinct from liberalism.

What are the arguments called upon to justify this separation? First, they affirm that liberalism is essentially a critical doctrine developed during the period when industrialists were submitted to theological and military government. Liberalism therefore has a dimension that is essentially a defence against the threats which then hung over the industrialists. This is at the root of the reproach henceforth addressed to this doctrine of being ambiguous and imprecise in failing to designate the principles of the new social system that would be the industrial system (Saint-Simon and Comte 1823–4: IV, 52–3, 180–9).

Second, even though liberalism as a political party is constituted by a membership of industrialists, its leaders are nonetheless always imbued with ideas of domination (of man over man). As a consequence, the liberal political elite perverts industrial policy by sticking to outdated maxims, and by seeking to profit from a period of crisis (in the sense of the passage from one social system to another): 'The real slogan of the heads of the [liberal] party is: get out of there, so I can get there myself. Their stated aim is to rid us of corruption, but their actual aim is to exploit corruption to their advantage' (ibid.: 53). Once rid of its out-of-date political elite, industrialism becomes a party composed uniquely of industrialists, workers included, based around its own fundamental ideas – those of Saint-Simon and A. Comte of course. The industrial monarch is bound to appeal to the new administrative elite marked by its competence in industrial administration. This is all the more certain since, in their opinion, politics no longer has anything very much to do with constitutional subtleties, but is reduced to making a good budget, that is to governing with as little intervention as possible (1821: 171–80; 1823–4: IV, 7–8).[11] Industrialists should occupy themselves with industrial policy and leave behind all those 'windbags' and 'scribblers' of the liberal party who hinder industrialists from seizing their destiny in their own hands (1821: 171–80; 1823–4: IV, 131–2).

This is where divisions within the industrialist camp of Say, Constant, Dunoyer and A. Comte start to emerge. Say was clearly annoyed by the way in which Dunoyer criticised him in the pages of the *Revue ency-clopédique* (Dunoyer 1827b) over his theory of immaterial services and on account of the absence of political vision in his *Traité* (Steiner 1997: 38–44).

Certain of the nuances that the *Cours complet* contains are no doubt a consequence of this dispute, notably when Say enlarges the scope of political economy or when he draws political conclusions from economic developments. However, he does not succeed in providing a clear response to the questions asked of him concerning political organisation. This is demonstrated. for example, by his hesitation over the way to select and remunerate public servants (Say 1828–9: II, 61–4, 354–8), since an economic solution would rely on the existence of a mechanism of competition which in this instance does not exist.

Dunoyer, for his part, extends Say's theory of productive services in order to propose a new classification of industries. This classification is founded on the idea that all socially useful professions fall under the aegis of industrial science and that because of this there is a tight relation between industrial science (political economy) and social science – that is to say the science of 'the laws according to which society will progress towards perfection' (Dunoyer 1827a: 368).

Dunoyer considers the classic tripartite division between agricultural, commercial and manufacturing industry as trivial. He above all reproaches Say for having restricted himself to those industries that produce things. Rather, he claims, industries that act on individuals, either physically or morally, are just as important.[12] With this extension of industry to include all personal services (1845: I, x), even government comes to have a place within the field of political economy, which thus comes to have a significantly wider scope:[13]

> Government in essence belongs within the number of arts that act directly on men, in opposition to those which direct their activity directly on material nature [. . .]. Its particular task, in this common labour, is to teach men to live well with one another, to instil justice and reasonableness in their most essential relations. We would say, if we can be forgiven the use of such language, that government is the producer of sociability, of good civil habits.
>
> (1852a: 837)

It goes without saying that in Dunoyer's very liberal approach, the state must limit itself to facilitating free transactions between the providers of personal services and those who purchase them in order to increase their human capital, whether in the sphere of action on matter (knowledge) or in the moral dimension (civil habits). The true task of government is the

'production of men submitted to public order and obedient to the functioning of justice' (1852b: 443).

These differences between Say and Dunoyer's liberal industrialism
demonstrate as well strong differences with Saint-Simon and A. Comte.[14] In
direct opposition to Saint-Simon and his school whose theories appear in
Le producteur, Dunoyer (1827a: 379–80) explains that the state is unable to
provide personal services itself. Rather it should content itself with assuring
social order and enabling 'free and unlimited competition in all professions' (ibid.: 376). Dunoyer even goes further, suggesting a commodifica-
tion of services related to social relations and the production of morality.

This approach clashes sharply with the religious endeavours of Saint-
Simon, the Saint-Simonians and A. Comte. It is true that Dunoyer is sensitive to the fact that this extension of the market might seem morally
unacceptable to a number of people and therefore seeks a rhetoric that,
thanks to an opposition between things (stock) and the service which
allows the production of a service (the flux), can make the whole argument acceptable:

> We are well aware that such a way of presenting these truths [on
> moral, political, etc. production] might give them a somewhat shock-
> ing appearance. Are you about to, people will say, transform feeling,
> taste and education into an item for sale and make morality into an
> object of commerce? Such reactions must be avoided. For it is not so
> difficult to express these ideas in a language that is scientifically
> precise and which seems offensive to no one. In reality, it is not taste,
> or knowledge, or morality that become an object of social commerce:
> what, however, is subject to market forces is the services which
> produce these precious products. These services are subject to remu-
> neration and who could possibly find it shocking that this should be
> the case.
>
> (1852a: 637–8)

The second difference emerges over the question of whether there is a
need for a specific political class devoted to a particular task that no industrialist (in Saint-Simon's sense of the word) could accomplish:

> Political capacity is a specific capacity, perfectly distinct from that
> which is demanded by other professions. It consists in the knowledge
> of the general laws according to which all good professions develop
> and in the knowledge of the social regime which best suits their
> progress.
>
> (1827a: 389)

In summary, Dunoyer considers that politics is a specific profession, even
when it is limited to the industrial politics of an industrial society.

A third noticeable difference appears when Dunoyer rejects the idea that knowledge, including knowledge in the moral sphere, can be provided by an institution that has the rational organisation and organic unity of industrial society as its goal. In opposition to those who see competition as leading to anarchy, Dunoyer maintains that competition, which he assimilates with intellectual liberty (1827a: 390), is an essential prerequisite for the discovery of truth.[15]

The reaction of Constant (1826) to this question on the publication of Dunoyer's work is indicative of the deep division that the former perceives between his own thought and Dunoyer's radical development of Say's economistic and utilitarian conception of society. Constant concurs with Dunoyer in rejecting the approach of Saint-Simon's followers (gathered in the journal *Le producteur*) to the extent that, like him, Constant defends the beneficial nature of a diversity of opinions and rejects the Saint-Simonian idea of an industrial scientocracy as the ideal form of government for an industrial society.[16]

This agreement, however, does not prevent a profound discord vis-à-vis the utilitarian nature of Dunoyer's approach. Other important disagreements, such as notably on the role of race, which do not concern the main object of our analysis will not be considered here. Constant does not accept the idea that liberty is no longer to be considered an unalienable right of the human race, to be thought of rather as the result of a utilitarian calculation. Rather, Constant is concerned about the political consequences of utilitarianism in a period in which, according to is own view of the industrial society (1814), individuals are ready to abandon their liberty in the name of order, or to give up on politics in order to have fuller enjoyment of their material comforts:

> This state of civilisation tends towards stability, and, if you will, towards good order more than towards moral virtue. But, good order, a useful thing, a thing indispensable for progress is more of a means than an end. If, in order to maintain it, one is forced to sacrifice all generous emotion, man is thereby reduced to a condition little different from that of certain other industrious animals, whose well-ordered hives and artistically constructed cells, could nonetheless never be the beautiful ideal of the human race. It is therefore important to counterbalance this effect of civilisation by awakening, by developing as much as possible, noble and disinterested feelings. This is important in order to preserve civilisation from the dangers that result for society from its own internal tendencies.
>
> (1826: 421)

This idea, that should on the one hand be related to the influence of German philosophy on the Coppet group (Jaume 1997), and to the importance of religion in Constant's thought on the other, is in concordance with an essential dimension of the thought of A. Comte. In his *Système de politique positive*, the latter explains that the sociocracy of the new religion of humanity that he proposes has as its principal task that of countering 'the great human problem, that of the ascendance of altruism over egoism' (1851–4: II, 173).

Curiously, it is at this juncture that A. Comte finds merit in Dunoyer's work (1845). In effect, what he appreciates in Dunoyer's work is the 'constructivist' idea – of which Constant to say the least is not particularly fond – according to which society results from the government, through the production of morality and of fundamental axioms which permit progress in political organisation. It is thus that, despite his out-of-hand rejection of classical economic theory and the competition principle, he considers an anarchistic principle unfitting to industrial society. A. Comte appreciates Dunoyer's work to the point of recommending it to Mill.

Conclusion

The discussion between the French economists and publicists has its roots in the way Say's political economy emphasises the basic importance of production as organised by the entrepreneur who – with the help of nature – combines industry, science and capital to extract from nature the utility of benefit to men in their social life. However, this discussion quickly leads to propositions that transform political economy into an overall science of society. These are not necessarily positions that Say would have refused, but he certainly did not come anywhere near developing them with the same boldness.

Political economy therefore constitutes a new political discourse: new on account of the motivations that it foregrounds (self-interest), new on account of the behaviour that it highlights (industry, that is to say the production of utility), new on account of the type of politics that it proposes (the administration of things), new finally on account of the classes that it calls to take power. This novelty also finds expression in the elements whose importance political economy reduces or considers as nil: honour, war, the power of men over men and, more generally, to put it in Saint-Simon's terms, the idle drones that parasite the industrial hive.

Within this new discourse, a significant rift between the proponents of industrialism would rapidly occur. According to Saint-Simon and A. Comte, political economy must first be reformed such that its social dimension be given its full worth. But this quickly no longer seems fully satisfactory to them. They soon come to suggest that it is necessary to go beyond political economy – or rather to critique it in order to give birth to a genuine science of the social, in both its static and dynamic dimensions. This is what A. Comte baptises sociology. By doing this, they put the emphasis on the normative dimension of social life (altruism) and on the development of the moral capacities (philanthropy) that must accompany the progress of civilisation because, without denying the importance of material self-interest, they see it as in itself insufficient to guarantee a stable political order.

This moral and normative dimension in the one (Saint-Simon author of *Nouveau christianisme*) as in the other (A. Comte author of *Système de politique positive*) leads to the formulation of a religion adapted to the new industrial order. It also leads them to reinforce the central idea of an economic order under the control of experts, of the extension of the industrial order to the whole of society, and to the call to create a new social elite characterised by being drawn from the world of the industrialists.

These proposals draw vigorous ripostes on the part of the liberals. Dunoyer and Constant reject these calls for social organisation, underlining rather the virtues of spontaneous order and the socially beneficial character of the disorder engendered by economic activity. This does not prevent these liberals from opposing one another over the role of a utilitarian morality, a form of morality that Constant rejects.

This investigation of the debate on industrialism in France between 1817 and 1830 demonstrates that economic theory does not progress in a simple linear fashion, and that one should always bear in mind that conflicts between alternative depictions of new realities are an essential ingredient in understanding the evolution of political economy (Steiner 1998b). In this respect, it is surprising to note that Friedrich Hayek (1952) omits – without making the slightest reference to it – Dunoyer's liberal position, even though he studies in detail that of the protagonists of the constructivist position defended by Saint-Simon, Comte and the subsequent followers of Saint-Simon.

This is a curious oversight indeed! Dunoyer is certainly the figure who does the most to advance the formal rationalisation of economic theory by proposing that personal services are exchanged on the basis of decentralised decisions regulated by competition. By extending Say's arguments on the production of utility and productive services to personal services, to those that touch the development of the individual's moral and cultural dimensions most closely, Dunoyer takes a great stride in the direction of spontaneous order. Hayek's strange omission means that he does not see the conflict which from the outset opposes those who reduce economics to rational instrumental action (Max Weber's *Zweckrationalität*) and those who, without denying the force of this type of action, nevertheless maintain the importance of values, emotions and traditions (Weber's concept of *Wertrationalität* and non-rational forms of action). By masking this dimension of the history of economic ideas, Hayek can find no other explanation than a scientific error symbolised by the Ecole Polytechnique, for what was in fact nineteenth-century society's rejection of the extreme free-market ideal proposed by Dunoyer.

From this point of view, the debate has not fallen into disrepair. Certainly, we no longer have to choose between A. Comte and Dunoyer, but contemporary societies are confronted by similar dilemmas. Do we accept, in relation to personal services, to knowledge and morality, to health and the body, options that push – in the name of efficiency and the justice of the free market – towards the extension of market forces in the social sphere? Or do we rather take the axiological dimensions of social life seriously and strive to limit the scope of the market?

Notes

1 In a footnote, Say is careful to introduce machines in order to explain the phenomenon that he has in mind (1803: 168, 452).

2 Dupin makes himself the apostle of the machine and the human knowledge that makes its use possible. This is the major lesson that emerges from the lectures that Dupin gave at the Conservatoire des Arts et Métiers (1825) where he was Say's colleague, but also from his major work, *Les forces productives de la France* (1827).

3 A former student of the Ecole Polytechnique, Chevalier made the link between liberal political economy and the Saint-Simonian school of thought in his teaching in the Collège de France. In the first years of his teaching, he accorded a significant place to technical and technological considerations, and above all to the predominance of production over any question of distribution (Steiner 1998a).

4 Chaptal's work (1819) had, amongst others, the goal of demonstrating the losses and gains of French industry during 1815–19 in comparison to the 1789 situation.

5 The works in question are those of J.-A. de Borgnis, *Traité complet de mécanique appliqué aux arts* (three articles by Le Normand between 1819 and 1821) and of Gérard-Joseph Christian, the director of the Conservatoire des arts et métiers where Say taught from 1819 onwards, with his *Vues sur le système des opérations industrielles ou Plan de technonomie*.

6 See Antoine Picon's work (1992) on the engineers of the Ponts et Chaussée or John Hubbel Weiss (1982) on the Ecole Centrale. It is worth remembering that Comte, a former student of the Ecole Polytechnique, distinguishes between the scientist, the engineer and the industrialist. The former is distinct from the second by being devoted to theory, which creates a role for the engineer as a 'permanent and regular intermediary between scientists and industrialists for all specific works' (1825: 173).

7 On the occasion of a stay with Say in Paris, John Stuart Mill mentions that Saint-Simon and his secretaries formed part of the salon that Say held in conjunction with C. Comte, Say's son-in-law, and Dunoyer. As Henri Gouhier (1941) and Ephraïm Harpaz (1959, 1964) have noted, during the period 1817–24 the two sets of journalists have a common vision of industry and social change, even if, as will be demonstrated below, they later come to differ on an essential point.

8 Society is entirely reliant on industry. Industry is the only guarantee of its existence, the unique source of all its wealth and prosperity. The state of things that is the most favourable for industry is therefore in itself the most beneficial for society as a whole. This is both the starting point and the goal of all our efforts: to show the importance of industry in its true light, to show the political influence which it can and should exert, to make its interests known to itself, to make it increasingly aware of the

nature of its forces and its means, to show it the obstacles that it has to van-
quish, to support and second it in its enterprises, and to watch over it
unceasingly on the one hand to contain despotism and on the other to
prevent revolutions. By fortifying industry, to build a constitution that is
industrial in essence: this is our task.

(*Prospectus* cited in *Le Censeur européen*, 1817: I, 372)

9 The major directions in which the 'new science' of political economy
developed in its initial stages have been considered in a previous article
(Charles and Steiner 1999).

10 From this period onwards, the two publicists progressively distance themselves
from the notion of liberty: Liberty, they argue, was essential as long as industrialists were submitted to a government that was essentially theological and military, but now that they were freed from this government – and this they see as
the principal achievement of the French Revolution – it no longer had such a
central role in the industrialist agenda (Saint-Simon and Comte 1821: 15–17).
All the more so, since liberals tended to distort the meaning of liberty by transforming it into a doctrine of 'laissez-faire' which A. Comte sees as a doctrine of
'rien-faire' (Comte 1828a, 1828c).

11 This line of thought is largely due to the influence of A. Comte to the extent
that Saint-Simon charged him with the task of 'reforming political economy'
when he became his secretary in 1817 (Gouhier 1941: 189–98). This aspect of
A. Comte's work emerges very clearly in the articles he publishes in his own
name during that period (1819).

12   I will consider this social state [the industrial one] according to the different classes of labour and functions of which it is comprised, starting with
the industries that act on things, such as: the extractive industry, the trans-
portation industry, the manufacturing industry, the agricultural industry. I
will then go on to examine the arts which have men as their object, such as
those that are preoccupied with our physical improvement, those which
have as their object the cultivation of our imagination or our feelings,
those which aim at developing our intelligence, and those finally which
aim at improving our moral habits.

(Dunoyer 1845, I: 15–16)

It does not appear that in the period under consideration Dunoyer's theories
received an especially positive reaction (Coquelin 1852b); but given the development of the service industry and the political economy linked to it, it cannot
be said that these ideas were fruitless.

13 Here again Dunoyer does not seemed to have been crowned with great success,
and the debate between him, Chevalier and Victor Cousin within the pages of
the *Journal des économistes* in 1851–2 shows the serious reservations that his position provoked (Allix 1911; Augello 1979: 25–38; Pénin 1991).

14 It is worth remembering that there is something quite specific about the relations between A. Comte and Dunoyer in that Comte makes a remarkable
exception when it comes to Dunoyer's contribution to social science. In effect,
in the *Catéchisme positiviste*, it is Dunoyer who is seen as the principal inheritor
of Smith in the field of political economy. Moreover, Comte makes an exception to his rule of cerebral hygiene of no longer reading the intellectual production of his contemporaries, by reading Dunoyer's 1845 work which he
recommends to Mill (Mill 1899: 409–11 – letter from Comte to Mill, 28 February 1845).

15   By working to overcome the obstacles in the way of the free and legitimate
exercise of the human faculties, [the critical philosophy which Saint-

Simon and his disciples reject] on the contrary aims towards an extremely positive goal: that of putting humanity in a position where its faculties can develop more easily. The progress of the human faculties: this is the real, and assuredly very positive goal that it has set itself.

(Dunoyer 1827a: 390–1)

16   You do not want, you [the Saint-Simonians] say, the beneficial domination that is inevitably exerted by enlightened men on all classes of society. This influence will always be felt and has no need of your spiritual power to maintain its authority. No matter how you organise it, this spiritual power will always simply be an inquisition lacking of the religious prestige of the type with which the priests of Egypt or the Spanish inquisition adorned themselves. This beneficial influence has nothing to fear from what you call moral anarchy; quite on the contrary it is in reality the natural, desirable, happy state of a society in which everyone, according to the level of his knowledge, can believe or examine, conserve or improve, can in one word make a free and independent use of his faculties. Anarchy of this nature is as necessary for intellectual life as air is for physical life. The truth is above all precious on account of the activity that inspires in man the need to discover it.

(Constant 1826: 434)

References

Allix, E. (1910) 'Say et les origines de l'industrialisme', *Revue d'économie politique*, 24(2–3): 303–13, 341–63.

—— (1911) 'La déformation de l'économie politique libérale après J.-B. Say: Charles Dunoyer', *Revue d'histoire des doctrines économiques et sociales*, 4(1): 115–47.

Augello, M. (1979) *Charles Dunoyer. L'assolutizzazione dell'economia politica liberale*, Roma: Edizioni dell'Ateneo & Bizzarri.

—— (1981) 'Il dibattito in Francia su economia e società e la soluzione "industrialista" (1814–1830)', *Rassegna economica*, 1: 7–38.

Blanqui, A. (1828) 'Essai sur les progrès de la civilisation industrielle des principales nations européennes', *Revue encyclopédique*, 38: 598–612.

Censeur Européen, Le 1817–19, Paris (12 volumes).

Chaptal, J.-A. (1819) *De l'industrie française*, Paris: Imprimerie nationale (reprinted 1993).

Charles, L. and Steiner, P. (1999) 'Entre Montesquieu et Rousseau. La physiocratie parmi les origines intellectuelles de la Révolution française', *Etudes Jean-Jacques Rousseau*, 11: 83–159.

Comte, A. (1818) 'Deux lettres à Saint-Simon', in *Auguste Comte: Ecrits de jeunesse 1816–1828*, Paris and The Hague: Mouton (1970).

—— (1819) ' Du budget', in *Auguste Comte: Ecrits de jeunesse 1816–1828*, Paris and The Hague: Mouton (1970).

—— (1822) 'Plan des travaux scientifiques nécessaires pour réorganiser la société', in *Système de politique positive ou traité de sociologie instituant la religion de l'humanité*, 3rd edn (1851–4, vol. 4), Paris: chez l'auteur (reprinted 1890).

—— (1825) 'Considérations philosophiques sur les sciences et les savants', in *Système de politique positive ou traité de sociologie instituant la religion de l'humanité*, 3rd edn (1851–4, vol. 4), Paris: chez l'auteur (reprinted 1890).

—— (1826) 'Considérations sur le pouvoir spirituel', in *Système de politique positive ou traité de sociologie instituant la religion de l'humanité*, 3rd edn (1851–4, vol. 4), Paris: chez l'auteur (reprinted 1890).

—— (1828a) 'Compte rendu de J-B. Bidaut "Du monopole qui s'établit dans les arts industriels et dans le commerce"', in *Ecrits de jeunesse 1816–1828*, Paris and La Hague: Mouton (1970).

—— (1828b) 'Compte rendu de col. Swan "Courtes observations sur l'état actuel du commerce et des finances de l'Europe"', *Ecrits de jeunesse 1816–1828*, Paris and La Hague: Mouton (1970).

—— (1828c) 'Economie politique: revue industrielle', in *Ecrits de jeunesse 1816–1828*, Paris and La Hague: Mouton (1970).

—— (1830–42) *Cours de philosophie positive*, Paris: Hermann (reprinted 1975).

—— (1851–4) *Système de politique positive ou traité de sociologie instituant la religion de l'humanité*, 3rd edn, Paris: chez l'auteur (reprinted 1890).

—— (1852) *Catéchisme positiviste ou sommaire exposition de la religion universelle*, Paris: Garnier (reprinted 1922).

—— (1970) *Ecrits de jeunesse 1816–1828*, Paris and La Hague: Mouton.

Constant, B. (1814) 'De l'esprit de conquête et de l'usurpation dans leurs rapports avec la civilisation européenn', in *Œuvres de Benjamin Constant*, Paris: Gallimard (reprinted 1957).

—— (1826) 'compte rendu de L'industrie et la morale considérées dans leur rapport avec la liberté', *Revue encyclopédique*, 29: 416–35.

—— (1852) 'Industrie', in C. Coquelin and G.-U. Guillaumin (eds), *Dictionnaire de l'économie politique*, vol. 1, Paris: Guillaumin.

Dunoyer, C. (1827a) 'Esquisse historique des doctrines auxquelles on a donné le nom d'industrialisme, c'est-à-dire des doctrines qui fondent la société sur l'industrie', *Revue encyclopédique*, 33: 268–94.

—— (1827b) 'Compte rendu du *Traité d'économie politique*', *Revue encyclopédique*, 34: 63–90.

—— (1845) *De la liberté du travail ou simple exposé des conditions dans lesquelles les forces humaines s'exercent avec le plus de puissance*, Paris: Guillaumin.

—— (1852a) 'Gouvernement', in C. Coquelin and G.-U. Guillaumin (eds), *Dictionnaire de l'économie politique*, vol. 1, Paris: Guillaumin.

—— (1852b) 'Production', in C. Coquelin and G.-U. Guillaumin (eds), *Dictionnaire de l'économie politique*, vol. 2, Paris: Guillaumin.

Dupin, C. (1819) 'Compte rendu de *De l'industrie française*', *Revue encyclopédique*, 3: 30–45.

—— (1825) *Discours et leçons sur l'industrie, le commerce, la marine, et sur les sciences appliquées aux arts*, Paris: Bachelier.

—— (1827) *Forces productives et commerciales de la France*, Paris: Bachelier.

Gouhier, H. (1941) *La jeunesse d'Auguste Comte et la formation du positivisme*, Paris: Vrin (reprinted 1970).

Harpaz, E. (1959) '*Le Censeur européen*. Histoire d'un journal industrialiste', *Revue d'histoire économique et sociale*, 2: 185–218 and 3: 328–57.

—— (1964) '*Le Censeur européen*. Histoire d'un journal quotidien', *Revue des sciences humaines*, 114: 139–259.

Hayek, F. (1952) *The Counter Revolution of Science: Studies on the Abuse of Reason*, Indianapolis: Liberty Press (reprinted 1979).

Jaume, L. (1997) *L'individu effacé ou le paradoxe du libéralisme français*, Paris: Fayard.

Le Normand, L. (1819) 'Notice sur l'exposition des produits de l'industrie française au Louvre, année 1819', *Revue encyclopédique*, 4: 131–55.

Mill, J. S. (1899) *Lettres inédites de John Stuart Mill à Auguste Comte*, Paris: Alcan.

Pénin, M. (1991) 'Charles Dunoyer 1786–1862: l'échec d'un libéralisme', in Y. Breton and M. Lutfalla (eds), *L'économie politique en France au XIXe siècle*, Paris: Economica.

Picon, A. (1992) *L'invention de l'ingénieur moderne L'Ecole des Ponts et Chaussées 1747–1851*, Paris: Presses de l'Ecole Nationale des Ponts et Chaussées.

Roederer, P. L. (1793) *Cours d'organisation sociale*, in P. L. Rœderer *Œuvres du comte Pierre-Louis Rœderer*, vol. 8, Paris: Firmin-Didot (reprinted 1857).

Saint-Simon, H. (1966) *Œuvres de Saint-Simon*, Paris: Anthropos.

Saint-Simon, H. and A. Comte (1819) 'Le politique', in H. Saint-Simon, *Œuvres de Saint-Simon*, vol. 2, Paris: Anthropos (1966).

—— (1819–20) 'L'organisateur', in H. Saint-Simon, *Œuvres de Saint-Simon*, vol. 2, Paris: Anthropos (1966).

—— (1821) 'Du système industriel', in H. Saint-Simon, *Œuvres de Saint-Simon*, vol. 3, Paris: Anthropos (1966).

—— (1823–4) 'Catéchisme des industriels', in H. Saint-Simon, *Œuvres de Saint-Simon*, vols 4 and 5, Paris: Anthropos (1966).

Saint-Simon, H. and A. Thierry (1814) 'De la réorganisation de la société européenne', in H. Saint-Simon, *Œuvres de Saint-Simon*, vol. 1, Paris: Anthropos (1966).

—— (1817) 'De l'industrie, ou discussions politiques, morales et philosophiques, dans l'intérêt de tous les hommes livrés à des travaux utiles et independents', in H. Saint-Simon, *Œuvres de Saint-Simon*, vols 2 and 3, Paris: Anthropos (1966).

Say, J.-B. (1800) *Olbie, ou essai sur les moyens de réformer les mœurs d'une nation*, Paris: Déterville.

—— (1803) *Traité d'économie politique*, 1st edn, Paris: Déterville.

—— (1815) 'De l'Angleterre et des Anglais', in J.-B. Say, *Cours d'économie politique et autres essais*, Paris: Flammarion (1996).

—— (1817) *Traité d'économie politique*, 3rd edn, Paris: Déterville.

—— (1819) 'Cours à l'Athénée royal', in J-B. Say, *Cours d'économie politique et autres essais*, Paris: Flammarion (1996).

—— (1827) 'Réclamation – Lettre à M. A. Jullien, directeur de la *Revue encyclopédique*', *Revue encyclopédique*, 36: 559–60.

—— (1828–9) *Cours complet d'économie politique pratique*, Paris: Guillaumin (1852).

—— Mss, *Manuscrits in the Bibliothèque Nationale de France*, Paris: BNF.

Sismondi, J.-C.-L. Simonde de (1801) *Recherches sur les constitutions des peuples libres*, Genève: Droz (reprinted 1965).

—— (1803) *De la richesse commerciale ou Principes d'économie politique appliqués à la législation*, Genève: Pashoud.

Smith, A. (1776) *An Inquiry into the Nature and the Cause of the Wealth of Nations*, Indianapolis: Liberty Press.

Steiner, P. (1997) 'Politique et économie politique chez Jean-Baptiste Say', *Revue Française d'Histoire des Idées Politiques*, 5: 23–58.

—— (1998a) 'Production, répartition et passion de l'égalité: l'économie politique de Michel Chevalier', *Revue européenne des sciences sociales*, 110: 97–119.

—— (1998b) *Sociologie de la connaissance économique: Essai sur les rationalisations de la connaissance économique (1750–1850)*, Paris: Presses universitaires de France.

Vandermonde, A. (1795) 'Leçons d'économie politique', in D. Nordman (ed.), *L'Ecole normale en l'an III: leçons d'histoire, de géographie, d'économie politique*, Paris: Dunod (1994).

Weiss, J. H. (1982) *The Making of the Technological Man: The Social Origins of French Engineering Education*, Cambridge MA: MIT Press.

11 Sloth and greed

Mercantilist and classical views on human nature and economic development

Alain Clement

Most mercantilists and classical economists with an interest in the causes of the wealth of their nations and in strategies for their development sought explanations in political, social, institutional, environmental and moral factors rather than in purely economic terms. Mercantilists, for instance, indicated that self-sufficiency should be favoured for political reasons. The quest for wealth could not be conceived of outside its national context. In explaining development, the early economists took account of environmental factors as well as the location of activities and populations, while taking care to distinguish between renewable (agricultural) and non-renewable (mining) natural resources.

They attributed greater importance to the conditions of economic activity than to the nation's potential wealth in manpower and primary resources. Thus analysing labour was more a matter of observing attitudes towards work and examining the conditions that promoted employment rather than merely computing the level of employment, because it was believed that people's natural inclination to idleness was the major obstacle to development.

Contrasting with this approach where human behaviour lay at the centre of development were interpretations of the causes of economic development and also suggestions for more appropriate strategies. Although a harsh natural environment or intense demographic pressure might prove instrumental in the development of some countries, for others, alternative strategies could be devised to attain the same standard of economic development whether through authoritarian policies (compulsory labour and low wages) or through more active and incentive policies (participation of a country in international trade). In both cases, the means proposed might be an answer to the poverty of nations and to one of the fundamental handicaps of economic development in the form of those basic characteristics of human nature – idleness and sloth.

The political factors of development

The early seventeenth century knew no real theory of economic development but just a typology and a classification of the activities in which a country had to engage in order to figure among the wealthiest and the most developed of nations. These three activities were, by order of preference, trade, industry and agriculture. Nevertheless, a highly materialistic conception of wealth, power and development prevailed.

This was true of Bodin who in the late sixteenth century described his homeland as a privileged, naturally rich place: 'Depuis que Dieu posa la France entre l'Espagne et l'Italie, l'Angleterre et l'Allemagne, il pourveut aussi qu'elle fût la mère nourrice portant au sein le cornet d'abondance qui ne fut onques et ne sera jamais vuide' ([1576] 1986, p. 418).

Sully wrote enthusiastically in *Mémoires des sages et royales économies* that:

> La France est mieux fournie qu'aucun autre royaume dans le monde, (à l'exception de l'Égypte) et ces produits qui consistent en grains, végétaux, vins, teintures, huiles, cidre, sel, chanvre, laine, lin,... sont la cause de tout l'or et l'argent qui entrent en France et en conséquence ces produits sont bien meilleurs que toute la soierie que produisent la Sicile, l'Espagne et l'Italie.
>
> ([1638] 1942), p. 16)

Montchrétien also vaunted the wealth of France which: 'dispose des cinq sources inépuisables de richesse naturelle [...] le bled, le vin, le sel, les laines, les toiles' ([1615] 1889, p. 239). This potential could feed 'le nombre infini de ses habitants'.

Richelieu described those same characteristics of France: 'si fertile en blés et si abondante en vin et si remplie de lin et de chanvre pour faire les toiles et les cordages nécessaires à la navigation' ([1632/1638] 1947), p. 448). Similar analyses were to be found in English pamphlets. Mun wrote that England was provided with natural wealth

> both in the sea for fish and on the land for wool, cattle, corne, lead, lin, iron, and many other things for food, raiment and munition; in so much, that upon strickt tearmes of need, this land may live without the help of any other nation.
>
> ([1621] 1971, p. 50)

All these commentaries emphasised two essential points: first of all the pre-eminence of natural resources in producing wealth and satisfying needs; second the political dimension of development. Without necessarily referring to the concept of self-sufficiency, economists concerned themselves with a style of development effected within a national context. The drive for national self-sufficiency, which these authors claimed was the source of a state's political independence, was indisputable proof of this.

Montchrétien was the first to speak of autarky:

> Toute société ne doit point emprunter d'ailleurs ce qui lui tient de nécessaire, car ne le pouvant avoir qu'à la merci d'autrui, elle se rend faible d'autant [...] il n'y a que la seule nécessité qui doive contraindre de prendre d'ailleurs ce que l'on n'a point.
>
> ([1615] 1889, p. 66)

He thought it better to forgo foreign trade: 'Que le pays fournisse le pays' (ibid., p. 112). Likewise, Montchrétien conceded, 'si les Espagnols pouvaient faire assez de bleds pour se nourrir, aurions nous juste occasion de nous plaindre d'eux de ce qu'ils ne voudraient plus acheter les nostres' (ibid., p. 155).

This point of view was shared by Mun although more guardedly. It seemed especially important not to be dependent on foreign powers for the provision of essential supplies; in particular, it was useful that

> we may peradventure employ our selves with better safety, plenty, and profit in using more tillage and fishing, than to trust so wholly to the making of cloth; for in times of war or by other occasions, if some forraign Princes should prohibit the use thereof in their dominations, it might suddenly cause much poverety and dangerous uproars, especially by our poor people, when they should be deprived of their ordinary maintenance.
>
> ([1664] 1965, p. 73)

Ensuring the country's self-subsistence was seen as a way of wielding power and of consolidating the nation's domination over others: 'Le royaume qui peut soy même fournir à ses propres necessitez est toujours plus riche, plus fort, plus redoutable' (Montchrétien [1615] 1889, pp. 131–2). In short, mercantilists advocated national economic independence not simply as a matter of making savings on imports; a political risk was perceived, which might induce a decline of the national economy.

Awareness of this danger was more clearly expressed in nineteenth-century writings and in particular in the works of Malthus and his followers. In the debate against Ricardo and Ricardian economists, Malthus returned to the subject of economic dependence/independence. Although economic interdependence was not greatly developed, each country was subjected to economic risks from other nations. A crisis in one country had repercussions for others, especially if the country was largely dependent on the wider world for its activity, and particularly for foodstuffs and the raw materials used in industry. The country would be entirely dependent '[u]pon the demands of its customers, as they may be variously affected by indolence, industry or caprice, [also] it is subjected to a necessary and unavoidable diminution of demand in the natural progress of these countries' ([1803/1826] 1986, vol. 2, p. 397). A country which exported manufactured goods and imported agricultural produce might consider that a symmetrical relationship could be established with other states. However, this would depend on its capacity to supply manufactured goods on a permanent basis. This could not be guaranteed because '[i]t is generally an accidental and temporary, not a natural and permanent division of labour, which constitutes one state the manufacturer and the carrier of others' (ibid., p. 397). Nor was the problem a narrowly economic one. The political aspect was fundamental.

Public opinion was capable of forcing a government to prohibit trade:

> It has, perhaps, not been sufficiently attented to in general, when the advantages of a free trade in corn have been discussed, that jealousies and fears of nations, respecting their means of subsistence, will very rarely allow of a free egress of corn, when it is in any degree scarce.
>
> (Malthus [1815] 1970, p. 145)

W. Jacob depicted this danger most forcefully. Imagining the case of a war with a country's supplier, Jacob put the problem in these terms:

> Must we relinquish that tone of dignity which we have so long, and so ably supported, from the apprehension, that the countries on which we have rendered ourselves dependant for bread should inflict the punishment of famine, if we claim our rights?
>
> (1814, p. 167)

The same arguments were developed in France by Sismondi. Fearing the dependence of a nation on foreign traders' plans, he specifically addressed this question in its political context, much as Jacob did:

> Sur quelle sécurité pourra compter la nation, si sa subsistance dépend tout entière des étrangers, et en particulier de ceux qui peuvent le plus facilement devenir ses ennemis, des gouvernements les plus barbares et les plus despotiques de l'Europe, de ceux qui seront le moins arrêtés quand ils voudront lui causer du dommage, par le dommage qu'ils causeront en même temps à leurs propres sujets? Que deviendra l'honneur de l'Angleterre, si l'empereur russe, toutes les fois qu'il voudra obtenir d'elle une concession quelconque, peut l'affamer, en fermant les portes de la Baltique?
>
> ([1819] 1971, p. 212)

For all these mercantilist or liberal allies of Malthus, economic independence was held to be a country's best protection against impoverishment, even though not a sufficient condition. This historical debate recurs today in very similar terms and with similar arguments (Clément 1999) in controversies about food security for Third World countries (national food independence or opening up to the world market). And even today the political dimension of the problem has not been superseded by purely economic arguments.

Physical and human factors of development

Mercantilists initially underscored the role of natural resources in creating national wealth. Yet they soon came to realise that a harsh natural environment could, paradoxically, foster development. Such an environment was viewed as a stimulus to economic activity that would otherwise remain low due to innate slothfulness.

In the seventeenth century, Holland was developing faster than other countries with significantly greater natural resource endowments. At the time, Thomas Mun, Director of East India Company, wrote:

> [I]t seams a wonder to the world, that such a small countrey, not fully so big as two of our best Shirses, having little natural wealth, victuals, timber, or other necessary munitions, either for war or peace, should notwithstanding posses them all in such extraordinary plenty, that besides their own wants they can and do likewise serve and sell to other Princes, ships, ordnance, cordage, corn, powder, shot, and what not, which by their industrious trading they gather from all the quarters of the world.
>
> ([1664] 1965: 74)

Counter to the trends of the time in which natural endowments were considered the sine quo non for development, the mercantilists focused on explaining this conundrum in terms of the industriousness of the Dutch as vs. the sloth of the likes of the Irish or the French. They argued that generous natural endowments might encourage a people to give in to their natural sloth, whereas a harsh natural environment would press them to overcome it.

The example of Ireland was often used in contrast: it was rich in natural resources but had failed to move beyond the economic subsistence level. In his *Observations*, William Temple argued that, given this plenty, the lack of development in Ireland could be attributed to laziness of the Irish people ([1673] 1972: 109). We find a similar analysis in the majority of English writings until around 1750. Charles Davenant, intellectual heir to Petty, argued that: '[A] rich soil is apt to make a people lazy' ([1695–9] 1771: I, 391) while 'when great numbers are confined to a narrow compass of ground, necessity puts them upon invention, frugality and industry; which, in a nation, are always recompensed with power and riches'.

In France, Colbert, too, viewed natural wealth as an obstacle to a country's development, engendering idleness and lack of dynamism:

> L'abondance et la fertilité de la France retient et empesche l'industrie et mesme la parcimonie car les choses faciles ne produisent point ou peu de gloire et d'avantages; les difficiles au contraire, si à la puissance naturelle de la France, le Roy y peut joindre celle que l'art et l'industrie du commerce peut produire [...] l'on jugera facilement que la grandeur et la puissance du Roy augmenteront prodigieusement.
>
> (1861–2: vol. 2, annex CCLXVI)

It was thus common throughout the eighteenth and nineteenth centuries for a low standard of development to be explained by the favourable natural environment compounded by humankind's inclination to idleness. Supporting this argument about human nature, in the second edition of his *Essay*, Malthus argued that '[A] state of sloth, and not of restlessness and activity, seems evidently to be the natural state of man' ([1803/26] 1986: vol. 2, 61). In *Principles* he, also using the example of Ireland, argued that natural wealth diminished human effort and engendered economic stagnation; while in countries facing greater difficulties of production, effort was necessary from the beginning and was what stimulated economic activity. He concluded: '[T]he fertility of the soil alone is not an adequate stimulus to the permanent increase of wealth' ([1820] 1986: vol. 6, 281).

Was this propensity to laziness an innate trait of human nature, in which case it would be difficult to act? Or was it the result of particular circumstances, and, in that case, could strategies to combat idleness be created? Observations by economists from Petty to Malthus were ambiguous on this count. In effect, they could not distinguish cause from effect – laziness as the effect of a favourable environment as opposed to a trait of human nature exacerbated by a favourable environment. What these commentators actually seem to be describing is rural underemployment as discussed in more recent analyses of the Third World (Rosenstein-Rodan 1943; Nurkse 1953; Lewis 1954). The big difference is that in contemporary analyses, this phenomenon is attributed to a demographic surplus with regard to what the farming sector can absorb in the way of labour, while the pre-industrial economists reported a correlation between a low standard of development and a low density of population.

In sum, these early economic writers were making the general claim that natural resources are not an essential factor in development. In fact, a pleasant climate, a large geographic area and propitious natural conditions exert a somewhat negative impact on development because they incline the inhabitants towards inactivity and laziness. Difficult living and working conditions on the other hand have a stimulating effect on economic activity and on development. Wealth is obtained by human labour.[1]

Without making too rash an interpretation of these writings, it seems that demographic characteristics were considered of greater importance than environmental ones in explaining development levels. Population sizes, densities, location as well as attitudes towards work were seen as the key factors fuelling development.

For Petty, population and land in England accounted for five-sixths of its wealth; population was a source of wealth in itself just like money or property. In addition to the quantitative effect, a potential advantage was achieved through a better division of labour and the possibility of saving. However, a plentiful population was viewed as a source of wealth provided that economic activity was made a priority.

Temple, Petty, Colbert and Davenant all observed that a high concentration of people in small areas (as in Holland), or in poor lands, produced a creative tension – an incentive for everyone to work and a reduction in people's natural propensity to laziness. Natural conditions that induced hard and difficult work fostered the capacity for hard work because, without such effort, people would die.[2] Holland was the perfect illustration of this: the difficult conditions of production because of over-population[3] rather than the shortage of fertile ground were a plausible hypothesis for the beginnings of its successful agriculture.

Malthus again resorted to the demographic argument to express several differences. While he showed that demographic pressure could play favourably on food resources so that in order to satisfy population growth, more should always have to be produced (this is the principle of self-sustaining demand for agricultural produce), he also pointed out that beyond maximum limits imposed by diminishing returns,[4] this situation would have little chance of arising. Malthus observed that a certain laziness of the inhabitants precluded any rapid increase in wealth and maintained them in a state of poverty. He thus downplayed the effect of demographic pressure on economic development and emphasised instead the failings of human nature.

These arguments of these economists are close to those made by E. Boserup (1965), S. Kuznets (1967) and Julian Simon (1981, 1986), who maintain that pressures exerted on the productive system by a growing population induce technological, institutional and economic change. A contrary situation was illustrated by the slow development of Irish agriculture,[5] which implicitly was based on the low density of the population. This failed to provide a strong enough stimulus to modernise the sector and to make it more productive.

Elements for development strategies: from urban agglomeration to compulsory labour

Having analysed the causes of national wealth, mercantilist and classical economics authors naturally felt inclined to propose strategies for development. What solutions were on offer in countries where favourable conditions did not prevail (low population density, good natural environment)? Could an environment similar to that observed in Holland be re-created? This became Petty's project. Institutional reforms, in particular labour policies, also came up for consideration, as did the countering of sloth by fostering of greed/desire to emulate others using luxury goods.

Promoting urban agglomeration

In order to reconstitute an economic environment similar to that of Holland, Petty suggested for England a sort of artificial urban agglomeration. Indeed, the Greater London project (Petty 1662) was a step in that direction. Petty analysed the economic advantages of such a project with regard to the reduction of production costs (of transport in particular), and to the likely transformation of agriculture. On both counts it was found that the success of Holland was due not only to efficient agriculture, but also to the development of an efficient and dense network of communications that greatly reduced the costs of transport.[6]

Ideally for Petty, comments Dockès (1990), there would be a short economic circuit where all activities would be concentrated within a single city. This was one of the reasons Petty imagined London (1683) with 4,690,000 inhabitants, while the rest of England would have only 2,710,000 inhabitants. The production of necessities for the supply of London would cover an area thirty-five miles in diameter! A second advantage in this concentration of population in urban zones was that it would make the surrounding area more productive, because a high density of population would prompt improvement in production technology In turn, a more successful agriculture would help to cut manufactured goods production costs and would ensure cheaper food for the urban population. It would bring about a shift away from subsistence agriculture towards commercial farming (Roncaglia 1985).[7]

The introduction of compulsory labour policies and of low wages

Whether laziness and lack of discipline were the true nature of the poor or, as mercantilists claimed, the effect of the absence of a stimulating environment, they were a major cause of poverty and of economic backwardness in England. So mercantilists suggested introducing rudimentary

Sloth and greed   265

social policy by drawing a distinction between the good and bad poor, and by suggesting that alms be reserved for the disabled and voluntary poor (clerics for the greater part). As for the working poor who until then enjoyed the benefit of public charity, they would have to take care of themselves. If they could not work of their own initiative, they would then be forced to do so in the workhouses, thus contributing to the enrichment of the nation. In this way social policies and economic voluntarism were combined to some degree. The poor had to be gainfully employed, and not a drain on the nation's economy.

The fight against idleness was conducted in the name of the defence of moral virtues: '[L]e travail ôte à l'âme l'occasion de mal faire..., donne le repos, et faict trouver les choses bonnes et agréables . . . La justice, les loix, ny la paix ne peuvent subsister sans le travail' (Laffemas 1604: 4). As Richelieu suggested, it was also conducted for more obviously economic reasons:

> Et pour ce qu'il y a en ce Royaume un grand nombre de mandians et vagabons, lesquels bien que propres au travail passent néantmoings leur vie à la gueuserie et à l'oyseveté, qui les portent pour la pluspart à des vices et à des desbauches pernicieuses, de telle sort qu'ils sont non seullement inutiles mais à charge du Royaume, au lieu qu'estant employez ilz pourroient servir à eulx et au public.
>
> (1624–6: 332)

National laws were gradually brought into agreement with this conception of work. Montchrétien proposed confinement and compulsory manufacturing work for adults. In England, the employees' statute of 1563[8] was the most important law in the fight against idleness. Bridewell were founded in the late sixteenth century. At the end of the seventeenth century, the first municipal workhouses were opened. By favouring cheap, disciplined labour and by creating competition against the putting out system, these workhouses became highly advantageous for entrepreneurs.

Petty also suggested, in addition to confinement, intensifying work to increase productivity.[9] He notably proposed measures such as the reduction of the midday break to one half hour or the abolition of certain meals (such as the Friday evening meal) ([1691] 1963: 110).

Unlike the other mercantilists, Petty also claimed that productivity would be higher if wages were low ([1691] 1963). He advanced two arguments in defence of low wages. The first relied on the idea that hunger pangs made people work;[10] the second argument was based on the savings on production costs brought about by low wages. Petty ([1690] 1963) suggested maintaining workers at a strictly minimum standard of living to induce them to work harder and for longer. De Mandeville captured the spirit of the time:

> [W]hen we see an artificer that cannot be driven to his work before Tuesday, because the Monday morning he has two shillings left of his last week's pays; why should we imagine he would go to it at all, if he had fifteen or twenty pounds in his pocket?
>
> ([1714] 1997: 98)

The policy of assistance to the poor was geared to advancing the economic system and creating the biggest possible economic surplus regardless of any principle of social justice. The objective of the maximum enrichment of the nation supposed that the poor had to remain poor. This approach was followed in the late eighteenth century by the precursors of Malthus, and by J. Townsend in particular. Townsend remained favourable not only to the progressive disappearance of public charity, but also to a practice of low wages because:

> In general it is only hunger which can spur and goad them on to labour. . . . Hunger is not only a peaceable, silent, unremitting pressure, but, the most natural motive to industry and labour, it calls forth the most powerful exertions.
>
> ([1786] 1971: 23, 24)

Hunger not only produced the most economical and the most effective means to incite people to work, but it had, Townsend claimed, an educational value: 'hunger will tame the fiercest animals, it will teach decency and civility, obedience and subjection, to the most perverse' (ibid.: 27). This conception naturally led its author to reject the Poor Laws.

Such hostility towards social policies is more easily understood in the light of analyses developed by most mercantilists and classical economists. The arguments put forward foreshadowed contemporary neo-liberal positions on the negative effects of social policies (Murray 1984; Katz 1989) and on ties between distribution, poverty and economic growth (Kuznets 1955).

Like most of the economists of his generation, Malthus thought that the poor laws discouraged work and encouraged laziness. They vehemently condemned these laws that had become a mechanism for manufacturing poverty and remained a prime cause of population growth. They argued that this system could not achieve the objective of correcting disparities because the transfer of resources from one individual to another could not increase the total quantity of food a country might need. These laws promoted growth of the numbers of the poor. They also resulted in greater impoverishment of the immediately superior social classes, because any increase in the price of necessities brought about by the demographic effects of the poor laws would reduce the purchasing power of these people.

Ricardo argued that these laws intensified the lack of foresight of poor people in their carefree state: '[T]he operation of the system of poor laws has been directly contrary to this. They have rendered restraint superfluous, and have invited imprudence, by offering it a portion of the wages of prudence and industry' ([1817] 1951: 107). The poor were sure to take advantage of the common wealth, which normally would fall to those who showed care and application in their work. Such measures, rather than reducing poverty, generalised it and encouraged irresponsible behaviour. Only farmers, claimed Malthus, were still loath to seek such assistance.[11]

The other side of the coin: fostering greed through foreign trade

As of the end of the seventeenth century, there was an alternative strategy being discussed on how to combat laziness in lifting nations out of a state of underdevelopment: It involved stimulating demand so as to induce people to engage in economic activity. By relying on other traits of human nature such as envy and a taste for novelty – on greed, in short – solutions equally effective to the punitive ones proposed by the early mercantilists and the Malthusians were available. It was the proponents of high wages who argued along these lines, but they were not the only ones to defend the positive impact of consumption on economic development. While the absence of genuine needs made people reluctant to work and perpetuated the low standard of development, wants could be created through demand for luxury goods – the stimulation and satisfaction of which required foreign trade.

As we have seen, mercantilist thinking emphasised – as in the Dutch case – the need for a country to grow richer rapidly by producing and selling abroad more than one consumed domestically, and for the populace to be hard-working, sober and efficient (Temple [1673] 1972: 109). Late seventeenth-century analysis was different. Some mercantilists took a particular interest in the concept of demand that they had just discovered (Appleby 1978). The economic challenge of providing more than just subsistence goods had also gained in importance. Henceforth, economists were convinced that it was demand which stimulated production (Coke 1671).

England, for example, was seen as a large market where domestic demand could be stimulated by envy, competition and love of luxury:

> The main spur to trade, or rather to industry and ingenuity, is the exorbitant appetites of men, which they will take pains to gratifie, and so be disposed to work, when nothing else will incline them to it, for did men content themselves with bare necessaires, we should have a poor world.
>
> (North [1691] 1907: 528)

Consumption was considered the root cause of business and prosperity. Not to spend, Barbon claimed, would be just as dangerous for the state as a foreign war. Luxury was no longer condemned, but was seen as a stimulus for industry as a whole. Food consumption, although essential, provided work for only a few people. Conversely, consumption of housing and clothing seemed boundless. North and Barbon showed that this potentially unlimited demand was the cause of enrichment both at home and abroad: 'It is from fashing in cloaths, and living in cities, that the king of France's revenues is so great, by which he is become troublesome to his neighbours' (Barbon [1690] 1905: 34).

The author of *Fable of Bees* emphasised the role of consumption as a mechanism for economic development, even though it involved consumption by a minority of the population. Potentially infinite demand for luxury goods provided work for the poor. In *Fable*, de Mandeville noted that: '[L]uxury employ'd a million of the poor, and odious pride a million more' ([1714] 1924: 33). On the other hand, sobriety and contentment destroyed industry, for '[B]are virtue can't make nations live in splendor' ([1714] 1924: 40).

Most classical economists agreed with this view. It was obvious that lack of wants other than for subsistence requirements was a cause of stagnant development. Few workers remained idle when wages rose. For Smith, people were driven by their unlimited wants, over and above the needs of subsistence, and would always try to work more, even to excess especially when paid in return: 'Mutual emulation and the desire of greater gain, frequently prompted them to over-work themselves, and to hurt their health by excessive labour' ([1776] 1976: 100).

This analysis implies that without unlimited wants, economic agents have no interest in producing more than what was necessary to satisfy their primary needs. Development requires creating a demand for manufactured products, not just by producing agricultural goods. Development 'can only be effected by the introduction of manufactures, and by inspiring the cultivator with a taste for them' said Malthus ([1803/26] 1986: vol. 2, 106). By creating new wants other than the need to feed the population, farmers were saved from '[t]heir injurious sloth' (ibid.: 108), thereby hiring and providing a living for more people.

Mercantilist and liberal positions on foreign trade were radically different in many areas. But in some mercantilist and classical works, the two strands had a common line of reasoning linked to the idea of arousal of desire and the creation of wants – which would stimulate domestic economic activity and development – via foreign trade. A way of stimulating wants was to imitate consumption patterns imported from abroad by means of business connections.

The thesis of favourable balance of trade – exporting more than was imported – predominated throughout the sixteenth and seventeenth centuries. It implied more or less wholesale condemnation of imported luxury items (Perrotta 1991). This view continued to be defended into the eighteenth century, inter alia by Steuart ([1767] 1966)[12] and Cantillon ([1755] 2001).[13] However, by the late seventeenth century, some authors saw not only the necessity for overseas trade, but saw in such trade the stimulus for domestic economic activity. For some mercantilists, 'foreigners imports were justifiable because they dazzled people with their novelty and promoted industry by way of the acquisitive instinct' (Appleby 1978: 171).

This was Barbon's position, arguing that the consumption of luxury goods, including their import, was beneficial to consumption and to the production of new products and therefore a positive factor for domestic economic development:

> There is the same wants of the mind in Foreigners, as in the English, they desire novelties; they value English-cloths, hats and gloves and foreign goods more than their native make: So that, tho' the wearing or consumming of forreign things, might lessen the consuming of the same sort in England; yet there may not be a lesser quantity made; and if the same quantity be made; it will be a greater advantage to the Nation, if they are consumed in foreign countries than at home.
>
> ([1690] 1905: 35–6)

In his *Essays on Economics*, Hume very clearly expressed a position probably shared by most classical economists as well:

> It [commerce with strangers] rouses men from their indolence; and presenting the gayer and more opulent part of the nation with objects of luxury, which they never before dreamed of, raises in them a desire of a more splendid way of life than what their ancestors enjoyed. And at the same time, the few merchants, who possess the secret of this importation and exportation, make great profits; and becoming rivals in wealth to the ancient nobility, tempt other adventurers to become theirs rivals in commerce. Imitation soon diffuses all those arts; while domestic manufacturers emulate the foreign in their improvements, and work up every home commodity to the utmost perfection of which it is susceptible.
>
> ([1752] 1955: 14)

These analyses can be regarded as particularly relevant to countries which had no industry, and which lived in a 'primitive state' in which no one wished to become rich and individuals never suffered from the attempts of other individuals to get rich. In this vein, authors such as J. S. Mill ([1848] 1965) could assert that foreign trade could modify this state of affairs. People would be able to enjoy a higher standard of living if they effectively wished to enjoy a better mode of existence. People in poor countries needed to experience the most direct possible contact with the situation and achievement of rich countries – this greater exposure to the possibilities of consumption and production revealed by international relations would be the main incentive to their development. Hence, every effort had to be made to open up underdeveloped countries to international trade. Local business was seen an extremely powerful generator of new wants, a means of disseminating new ideas and new aspirations.

This was, before its time as it were, the theory of the international effect of demonstration (Nurkse 1953) derived from an extension of Duesenberry's theory. The opening up of poor countries to trade with rich countries tends to stimulate their demand for imported goods, but it also incites them to produce and to export primary products for which they enjoy a decisive comparative advantage.

Summary

Early mercantilist works on wealth and economic development adopted a multifaceted approach. First, their analyses highlighted the importance of natural resources to show that they were a necessary but not a sufficient condition of development and enrichment. Even more important than land area or fertility, the location of the land was decisive in creating wealth, since areas located at the crossroads of numerous and varied channels of communications contributed more to the wealth of a country than its natural resources per se.

The human factor was a second – and ultimately more important – factor affecting development not just for mercantilists, but also for the early liberals and then for many classical economists. More than the volume of labour, it was the population's fitness and propensity to work that were decisive. As the majority of authors from the mercantilists until Malthus in the nineteenth century believed that people were indolent by nature and little inclined to engage in economic activity, they were interested in the role of natural resources and other institutions which encouraged economic activity. For some economists, a hostile natural environment, generally compounded by demographic pressure, was decisive in stimulating economic progress. At the same time, institutional means were not overlooked: compulsory labour, especially in the seventeenth century; low-wages policies suggested by some mercantilists; opposition to the poor laws was made by the classical writers at the end of the eighteenth and at the beginning of the nineteenth century. In contrast, later mercantilist and classical authors contended that the fostering of greed – through the opening up of economies to the world market to create new needs through emulation – could prove an even more effective solution than hunger pangs used to prod persons to work.

On all of these issues, mercantilists and early liberals foreshadowed contemporary development economic writings. The debate initiated by Boserup in the 1960s on the effect of demographic pressure, the debate on the opening up of the world market, are examples of concerns that were widely debated from the seventeenth century through to the nineteenth century.

Notes

1 I adopt the definition of economic activity by W. A. Lewis (1955), which is remarkably similar in substance to that given by the mercantilists:

> By economic activity, we understand effort to increase the return on a work or on a given resource, or to reduce the cost of the given return. To say that the economic activity is a necessary condition of the growth means simply saying that the people have chances to obtain more possessions than if they try hard there. The economic growth is the result of a human effort.

2 In *The Theory of Economic Growth* published in 1955, W. A. Lewis addressed the question of work, considering attitudes towards work as an explanatory factor of economic development. He confirmed this mercantilist point of view with the only difference being that in the countries where it was excessively difficult to earn one's living, any effort could be discouraged, while an intermediate situation was the most conducive where reasonable effort guaranteed a decent standard of living (1955: 44).

3 Petty noted that in Holland there was about one acre of good land per capita as compared to four acres in France and England, and ten in Ireland.

4 Even fertile soil cannot infinitely produce grains for an ever-growing population, even though '[a] fertile soil gives at once the greatest natural capability of wealth that a country can possibly possess' (Malthus [1820] 1986: vol. 6, 266). When the population used all the available land, the only way to increase agricultural output was to improve land, and unfortunately: '[T]his is a fund, which, from the nature of all soils, instead of increasing, must be gradually diminishing' ([1803/26] 1986: vol. 2, 10). While the European nations had not yet reached this natural limit, others like China and Japan were less fortunate. Malthus doubted that '[T]he best directed efforts of human industry could double the produce of these countries even once in any number of years' (ibid.).

5 The mercantilists analysed Irish agriculture rather finely, because they described a relatively extensive type of agriculture that required little in the way of labour. In this farming system, natural grasslands, moors, woodland and closed fields all remained. Although cereals were still important, they were no longer the primary output but were overtaken by secondary crops, timber and livestock.

6 See also Boserup's (1991) analysis of the advantages of a high density of a rural population on reductions in the costs of transport.

7 Boserup's (1965) analyses which develop the thesis of the positive effect of demographic pressure in changing agriculture clearly confirm these observations and the role played by the concentration of population in the appearance of a highly productive agriculture as seemed to be the case of Dutch agriculture.

8 Statute of Artificiers, Labourers, Servants of Husbandry and Apprentices.

9 Workhouses cost the parishes a lot, and came to be viewed as a complete failure: output was very low.

10 Cf. Coats (1958). Mathias (1979) reminds us of the argument citing low wages as an incentive to work while high salaries were argued to instigate idleness and debauchery. This point of view was developed with Calvinist ideas. More recently Wiles (1968) reports opposition between mercantilist proponents of low wages and those favourable to high wages. He compares the contemporary opposition between classical economists and Keynesians, between those who analyse wages as an element of production costs and those who consider them as a potential stimulant for demand. See also Brewer (1992).

11　Such opinions were not universal. J. R. McCulloch, an economist of the Ricardian school, thought on the contrary that to grant aid to capable but nevertheless unemployed working people could not be considered incitement to laziness. Although of a more conservative tradition, W. Lloyd was among the fervent defenders of the poor laws. He embraced the conception of distributive justice in the mediaeval Christian tradition and in his conferences on poverty he upheld the right of the poor to assistance ([1826] 1967: 38).
12　See Diatkine in Béraud and Faccarello (1992).

References

Appleby, J. O. (1978) *Economic Thought and Ideology in Seventeenth Century England,* Princeton: Princeton University Press.
Barbon, N. ([1690] 1905) *A Discourse on Trade,* Baltimore: Lord Baltimore Press.
Béraud, A. and G. Faccarello (eds) (1992) *Nouvelle histoire de la pensée économique,* vol. 1, Paris: La découverte.
Bodin, J. ([1576] 1986) *Les six livres de la République,* Paris: Fayard.
Boserup, E. (1965) *The Conditions of Agricultural Growth,* London: G. Allen & Unwin.
—— (1991) 'Causes and effects of disequilibria in food production', in F. Gendreau (ed.), *Les spectres de Malthus,* Paris: ORSTOM.
Brewer, A. (1992) 'Petty and Cantillon', *History of Political Economy,* 24 (3): 711–28.
Cantillon, R. ([1755] 2001) *Essay on the Nature of Commerce in General,* Somerset: Transaction Publishers.
Clément, A. (1999) *Nourrir le peuple: entre état et marché (XVIe–XIXe siècle),* Paris: l'Harmattan.
Coats A. W. (1958) 'Changing attitudes to labour in the mid-eighteenth century', *The Economic History Review,* 11 (1): 35–51.
Coke, R. (1671) *Treatise where in is Demonstrated that the Church and State of England are in Equal Danger with the Trade of it, Treatise I,* London: Henry Brome.
Colbert, J.-B. (1861–2) *Lettres, Instructions et Mémoires,* Paris: Pierre Clément.
Davenant, C. ([1695–9] 1771) *The political and Commercial Works, Collected and Revised by Sir Charles Whitworth,* London: R. Horsfield.
Dockès, P. (1990) 'Birth of the trading space (17th–18th centuries)', *Journal of the History of Economic Thought,* 12 (2): 124–45.
Hume, D. ([1752] 1955) *Writings on Economics,* ed. E. Rotwein, Madison: University of Wisconsin Press.
Jacob, W. (1814) *Considerations on the Protection Required by British Agriculture and on the Influence of the Price of Corn on Exportable Productions,* London: J. Johnson & Co.
Katz, M. B. (1989) *The Undeserving Poor: From the War on Poverty to the War on Welfare,* New-York: Pantheon.
Kuznets, S. (1955) 'Economic growth and income inequality', *American Economic Review,* 14 (1): 1–28.
Kuznets, S. (1967) *Modern Economic Growth,* New Haven: Yale University Press.
Laffemas, B. de ([1604] 2003) *Mémoires sur le commerce,* Paris: Paléo Editions.
Lewis, W. A. (1954) 'Economic development with unlimited supplies of labour', *Manchester School,* 22 May, pp. 139–91.
Lewis, W. A. (1955) *The Theory of Economic Growth,* London: G. Allen & Unwin.
Mahieu, F.-R. (1997) *Petty, Fondateur de l'économie politique,* Paris: Economica.

Malthus, T. (1803/1826) *An Essay on the Principle of Population*, London: J. Johnson; reprinted in Edward Anthony and William Pickering (eds) (1986) *The Works of Thomas Robert Malthus*, vols 2 and 3, London: Wrigley.

—— (1814) *Observations on the Effects of the Corn Laws, and of a Rise or Fall in the Price of Corn on the Agriculture and General Wealth of the Country*, London: J. Johnson; reprinted in A. McKelley (ed.) (1970) *T.R. Malthus, The Pamphlets* (95–131), New York: Augustus McKelley.

—— (1815) *The Grounds of an Opinion on the Policy of Restricting the Importation of Foreign Corn*, London: J. Murray & J. Johnson and Co; reprinted in A. McKelley (ed.) (1970) *T.R. Malthus, The Pamphlets* (137–73), New York: Augustus McKelley.

—— ([1820] 1836) *Principles of Political Economy Considered with a View of their Practical Application*, London: J. Murray, 2nd edn; reprinted in E. A. Wrigley and David Souden (eds) (1986) *The Works of Thomas Robert Malthus*, volumes 5 and 6, London: Pickering & Chatto.

Mandeville, B. ([1714] 1997) *The Fable of the Bees and Other Writings*, Indianapolis: Hackett Publishing Company.

Mathias, P. (1979) *The Transformation of England: Essays in the Economic and Social History of England in the XVIIIth Century*, London: Methuen.

McCulloch, J. R. (1826) *A Treatise on the Circumstances which Determine the Rate of Wages, and the Condition of the Labouring Classes Including an Inquiry into the Influence of Combinations*, Edinburgh: Black & Tait; reprinted in 1967, New York: Augustus McKelley.

Mead L. W. (1986) *Beyond Entitlement: The Obligations of Citizenship*, New York: Free Press.

—— (1992) *The New Politics of Poverty: The Nonworking Poor in America*, New York: Basic Books.

Mill, J. S. ([1848] 1871) *Principles of Political Economy with Some of Their Applications to Social Philosophy*, London: John Parker, 2nd vol., 7th edn; reprinted in J. M. Robson (ed.) (1965) *Collected Works of John Stuart Mill*, Vols 2 and 3, Toronto: University of Toronto Press, Routledge & Kegan Paul.

Mun, T. ([1664] 1965) *England's Treasure by Foreign Trade*, London; reprinted New York: McKelley.

—— ([1621] 1971) *A Discourse of Trade*, London; reprinted New York: McKelley.

Murray C. (1984) *Losing Ground: American Social Policy 1950–1980*, New York: Basic Books.

North, D. ([1691] 1907) *Discourses upon Trades; Principally Directed to the Cases of the Interest Coynage Clipping Increase of Money*, Baltimore: Lord Baltimore Press.

Nurkse, R. (1953) *Problems of Capital Formation in Underdeveloped Countries*, Oxford: Oxford University Press.

Perrotta, C. (1991) 'Is the mercantilist theory of the favourable balance of trade really erroneous?' *History of Political Economy*, 23 (2): 301–35.

Petty, W. (1662–91) *The Economics Writings*, ed. Charles Hull, Cambridge, UK: Cambridge University Press; reprinted in 1963, New York: Augustus McKelley.

Ricardo, D. (1817) *On the Principles of Political Economy, and Taxation*, London: J. Murray; reprinted in 1951/5, ed. Sraffa, P., Cambridge: Cambridge University Press.

Richelieu, J. A. ([1622–1624] 2002) *Mémoires: An conseil du roy*, tome 4, Paris: Paléo Editions.

—— (1632–8) *Testament Politique,* reprinted in 1947, ed. L. André, Paris: Robert Laffont.

—— (1975) *Les papiers de Richelieu,* Paris: éditions Pedone.

Roncaglia, A. (1985) *Petty, the Origins of Political Economy and Taxation,* London: Everyman Classics.

Rosenstein-Rodan, P. N. (1943) 'Problems of industrialization in Eastern and South Eastern Europe', *Economic Journal,* 53: 202–11.

Simon, J.-L. (1981) *Ultimate Resource,* Princeton: Princeton University Press.

—— (1986) *Theory of Population and Economic Growth,* New York: Basil Blackwell.

Smith, A. (1776) *An Inquiry into the Nature and Causes of the Wealth of Nations,* London: W. Straham & T. Cadell; reprinted in R. H. Campbell and A. S. Skinner (eds) (1976) *The Glasgow Edition of the Works and Correspondence of Adam Smith,* Oxford: Oxford University Press.

Steuart, J. (1767) *An Inquiry into the Principle of Political,* London: A. Millar & T. Cadell; reprinted in 1966, ed. A. S. Skinner, Chicago and Edinburgh: University of Chicago Press and Oliver.

Sully, Maximillien de Béthune, Duc de ([1638] 2001) *Mémoires des sages et royales oeconomies d'Etats de Henry le Grand* (tome 1), Paris: Paléo Editions.

Temple, W. (1673) *Observations upon the United Provinces of the Netherlands;* reprinted in 1972, ed. G. Clark, Oxford: Clarendon Press.

Wiles, R. C. (1968) 'The theory of wages in later English mercantilism', *Economic History Review,* 21: 113–26.

12 The two paths of economic development in Adam Smith's thought

Sandrine Leloup

Introduction

It was commentators in the tradition described by Brown (1997) as revisionists who were the first to claim that Smith's economic theory was not as optimistic as we might have been inclined to believe. Indeed, these critics go as far as challenging the idea that Smith was a liberal, and emphasise the fact that natural constraints were not the only brakes on capital accumulation. According to the author of *Wealth of Nations*, projectors' investments imply wastage of capital and therefore hinder capital accumulation. On the contrary, virtuous, prudent men, concerned about the approval of the impartial spectator, unfailingly contribute to the growth of wealth (Reisman 1976; Pesciarelli 1989; Prasch 1991; Sen 1993; Hollander 1999). This point of view is also shared by philosophers like Dwyer (1998) and Griswold (1998), according to whom Smith was of the opinion that the increase in national wealth is hindered if individuals are not virtuous.

In line with the revisionists, I think there is a strong connection between morals and economics in Smith's thought. I claim that, for Smith, if there is a link between economics and virtue, it apparently only runs from virtue to economics, not vice-versa. In this light, the *Theory of Moral Sentiments*, an essential part of Smith's work, is necessary for an understanding of the economic concepts developed in *Wealth of Nations*.

Nevertheless, there are several obstacles to the revisionist interpretation. First of all, the revisionist tradition usually neglects the analytical dimension of Smith's economics. It suggests that economic development proceeds through four consecutive stages of development, each based on a particular mode of subsistence: hunting, pastoral, agricultural and commercial. The latter – commercial society – is the one in which wealth is maximal, but as men are immoral, the nation nonetheless tends towards decline. Development would be more rapid if economic actors were virtuous.

But what these commentators fail to take into account are the technical factors involved in economic development.[1] Moreover, if we follow the revisionist interpretation, we are forced to conclude that investments presided over by projectors always turn out to be negative in terms of economic wealth. However, a close analysis of Smith's argument leads to a rather different conclusion.

In *Wealth of Nations*, Smith makes a distinction between the *natural course of things* and "the order contrary to the natural course of events" or the *retrograde order* (1776: 380). In the first case, agriculture is the main sector and the development of manufactures depends upon that of agriculture, whereas, in the second case, the expansion of manufactures takes priority over agriculture. The first path of development is followed when the economic actors are prudent, whereas the second is provoked by projectors' investments.

According to the revisionist interpretation, the second type of development would necessarily lead to the impoverishment of nations. However, European nations developed in line with the order contrary to the natural course of events, and, astonishingly, this neither prevented them from increasing their wealth, nor from reaching an advanced state of development. In the *Theory of Moral Sentiments*, Smith himself recognised the merit of ambitious men in having "changed the face of the world" (1759: 256). That is to say, in other words, that their investments may have positive consequences for economic wealth.

How can this contradiction be explained? Are the *natural course of things* and the *retrograde order* in fact one and the same? Do the two processes lead to the same endpoint? In the first section, I will show that the *natural course of things* that excludes projectors is associated with an optimal and ideal path of development (Rosier 1987). Great Britain's development, however, diverged from this natural course, because of the role of projectors in the expansion of manufactures. We will see in the second section that their investments affected the speed of economic development, so that this was less rapid than it might have been, but that access to opulence was not compromised.

The *natural course of things*: when the path to virtue crosses the path to fortune

The Enlightenment was a time of enthusiasm and fear, but also a time of important inventions. In this turbulent world, we find men whose aim was not the avid pursuit of profit but "the provision of a modest competency" (Moore 1998: 24). Characters of this type are present in Smith's world: these are the prudent men.[2] In *Wealth of Nations*, Smith wrote that their businesses were not "marvellous" (1776: 362) when compared to the great manufacturing enterprises which were developing during this period, but that they had the advantage of being more "solid" and "lucrative" than the gigantic concerns run by ambitious entrepreneurs.

The relationship between agriculture and manufactures

In the first era of development or the primitive state, all nations are identical. Men start to invest their funds in agriculture in order to provide the population with the means to live. At the second stage, the population increases and human needs become more subtle; it is then that manufacturing activities and commerce both develop.

These stages have often been highlighted in the history of economic development: the originality of Smith's analysis of the *natural course of things* lies in the balance between the different sectors, a balance due to the presence of virtuous, prudent men. Smith's prudent men always avoid putting themselves in situations that are too difficult and from which they would have difficulty extricating themselves. Moreover, as frugal men, their needs are simple and not sophisticated. They prefer improving agriculture not only because investments are less risky, but also because their primary concern is basic needs. So, in the first instance small-scale factories were intended to lead to the perfection of agriculture. It is only at a third stage that a nation would develop bigger factories that would require more capital and more sophisticated production techniques.

The singularity of this ideal development process, designated by the term the *natural course of things*, is the manner in which manufactures are introduced into the economic sphere. The expansion of manufactures depends on agricultural surplus (π_a),[3] and the surplus earned in manufacture (π_m) has as its objective an increase in agricultural surplus.[4] Small-scale industries can be developed to provide for the growing population and to employ labour under-utilised in agriculture. If we note P_a, the agricultural product and P_m, the manufacturing product, we can summarise this process as shown in Figure 12.1.

Regarding agriculture as an important economic sector was in no way original, for, in the eighteenth-century economy, agriculture was of considerably greater importance than industry. Several decades later, Bentham, for example, reached the same conclusion: in the PostScript to *Defence of Usury*, he explained that without agriculture, industry could not have developed.[5] Nevertheless, since he considered projectors to be the real heroes of economic development, he also claimed that manufacture had become the dominant sector, taking predominance over agriculture.

In opposition to this, Smith argued that agriculture must remain the leading sector in order that a nation accede rapidly to opulence. His point

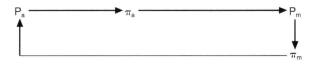

Figure 12.1 Relations between agriculture and manufacturers in the "natural course of things".

of view is close to that of the physiocrats: even though agriculture's maximum rate of profit can never exceed that of industry, it is nonetheless the sector which offers the most "durable" increase in annual product:

> That which arises from the more solid improvements of agriculture is much more durable and cannot be destroyed but by those more violent convulsions occasioned by the depredations of hostile and barbarous nations continued for a century or two together, such as those that happened for some time before and after the fall of the Roman empire in the western provinces of Europe.
>
> (1776: 427)

It is significant that the vocabulary used with reference to agriculture is similar to that used in relation to prudent men: the adjectives "durable" and "solid" recur constantly. However, Smith does not mean that prudent men must necessarily be cultivators and, in contradistinction to the physiocrats, he never claimed that agriculture is the only sector of productive activity. Agriculture must develop earlier than industry, but the expansion of industry and commerce must not imply the sacrifice of agriculture.

Productive labour and labour productivity in the "natural course of things"

This balance between agriculture and manufacture has consequences for the way the different production factors should be used. According to Smith, entrepreneurs have the choice of increasing either productive labour or labour productivity. Productive labour is opposed to unproductive labour: whereas the first "adds to the value of the subject upon which it is bestowed", the second "has no such effect" (1776: 330). Labour productivity, on the other hand, relies on an augmentation of the division of labour. The introduction of manufactures implies an acceleration of the second factor, the benefits of which, underlined by most commentators, can be summarised as follows: When the specialisation of work increases, both labour productivity and the skill of each worker will increase. "The division of labour, however, so far as it can be introduced, occasions, in every art, a proportionable increase of the productive powers of labour" (ibid.: 15).

> [T]he improvement of the dexterity of the workman necessarily increases the quantity of the work he can perform; and the division of labour, by reducing every man's business to some one simple operation, and by making this operation the sole employment of his life, necessarily increased very much dexterity of the workman.
>
> (ibid.: 16)

Being more skilled, the worker is then able to create new machines:

> I shall only observe, therefore, that the invention of all those machines by which labour is so much facilitated and abridged seems to have been originally owing to the division of labour. Men are much more likely to discover easier and readier methods of attaining any object when the whole attention of their minds is directed towards that single object than when it is dissipated among a great variety of things. [...] A great part of the machines made use of in those manufactures in which labour is most subdivided, were originally the inventions of common workmen, who, being each of them employed in some very simple operation, naturally turned their thoughts towards finding out easier and readier methods of performing it.
>
> (ibid.: 19–20)

The Smithian's argument suggests a functional relationship between the division of labour and worker productivity.[6] This means that, like labour and capital, the productivity of workers could be described as an endogenous variable, dependent upon the extent of the division of labour (Reid 1989). But, contrary to the claims of other commentators, according to Smith labour productivity is not the sole production factor. Indeed, as we know, prudent men are not ambitious entrepreneurs. They invested in little factories – small units involving about ten men (1776: 14)[7] – and not in gigantic factories swarming with numerous workers. So, in the *natural course of things*, the division of labour is introduced gradually.

However, a further problem remains. Smith was writing in a period when agriculture was still the main sector of activity, but both manufacturing activities and international trade were becoming more and more important. This is the reason why the question as to whether agriculture is always able to function as the main driving force in all societies, whatever the period, is a legitimate one.

Is it not inherent in the division of labour to have a spontaneous tendency to expand, thus leading to the alienation of workers? Smith did not give a specific answer to this question. It can be supposed that, thanks to the influence of prudent men, the expansion of the manufacturing sector would permanently remain subordinate to that of agriculture. In this case, the development of the division of labour would be gradual, less rapid than the development of inventive capacities, and thus the negative effects of the division of labour would be avoided.

According to Smith, the natural course of things is possible in a particular society, with particular characters. These are not the monomaniacs who produce simply for the sake of production, but virtuous economic actors – the prudent men – who engage themselves in investments with a profit rate never much higher than the average rate of profit. The examples Smith gives of nations that follow the natural course of things are the North American colonies. The men who lived in these colonies were Quakers, people whose behaviour resembles that of the prudent man. They privilege the development of agriculture and consider that manufactures for distant sale are not their main priority: when a producer "has acquired a little more stock than is necessary for carrying on his own business [. . .], he does not, in North America, attempt to establish with it a manufacture for more distant sale, but employs it in the purchase and improvement of uncultivated land" (1776: 379). By following this order of development, these colonies enjoyed a "rapid advance" with regard to European nations.

Scotland at the end of the eighteenth century: the *retrograde order*

The hypothesis of the natural course of things was considered by Smith as having restrictive conditions, since in order to achieve it, the economic actors had to be prudent. This was not the case for the nations of Europe, where all the actors involved in the economy did not moderate their passions following the example of prudent men. On the one hand, amongst bankers we encounter fearful and cowardly men who wanted to get rich rapidly. On the other, projectors are primarily interested in high profit; under the impetus of strong passions, they often push to invest in large and dangerous investments.

The opposite order: from manufactures to agriculture

Thanks to the usury laws, the investments of prudent men benefited from being able to utilise a large proportion of the funds available. Indeed, the interest rate required by the entrepreneur's high-risk investments was higher than the legal limit, fixed by usury laws. Bankers refused to finance the projectors, because the law stopped them from obtaining an interest rate that corresponded to this kind of business, that is to say a rate of 8 per cent to 9 per cent.[8]

However, the credit-market situation was far from optimal: finding themselves unable to increase the rate of interest, bankers increased their discounting activities. This behaviour would not have had dire consequences if the beneficiaries of all the bills of change had been prudent entrepreneurs. But the problem was that some projectors broke the law and used the stratagems described in Chapter II, Book II of *Wealth of Nations*.[9]

Consequently, not all projectors were excluded from the credit market. High-risk investments slipped through the net, and were started despite the presence of the usury laws.[10] Their integration into the economic arena has been all the more facilitated by the numerous laws encouraged manufactures. According to Bowles (1985), "the manufacturing centres had received special encouragement" and "manufacturing development had preceded agricultural advance in Europe". Smith wrote:

> From the beginning of the reign of Elizabeth too, the English legislature has been peculiarly attentive to the interests of commerce and manufactures, and in reality there is no country in Europe, Holland itself not excepted, of which the law is, upon the whole, more favourable to this sort of industry. Commerce and manufactures have accordingly been continually advancing during all this period. The cultivation and improvement of the country has, no doubt, been gradually advancing too; but it seems to have followed slowly, and at a distance, the more rapid progress of commerce and manufactures.
>
> (1776: 424)

These manufactures contributed to such rapid development of industry and foreign commerce that these sectors became the cause of the improvement in agriculture. This expansion succeeded in leading the course of events in a direction opposed to the natural course of things. Speaking about "all the modern states of Europe", Smith wrote:

> The foreign commerce of some of their cities has introduced all their finer manufactures, or such as were fit for distant sale; and manufactures and foreign commerce together have given birth to the principal improvements of agriculture. The manners and customs which the nature of their original government introduced, and which remained after that government was greatly altered, necessarily forced them into this unnatural and retrograde order.
>
> (ibid.: 422)

This order can be summarised in the following way. Rather than being dedicated to the perfection of the agriculture, the manufacture's surplus (π_m) is above all destined for big manufactures. According to this developmental order, manufactures and foreign trade developed first, thereby, becoming the leading sectors and themselves driving progress in agriculture (see Figure 12.2).

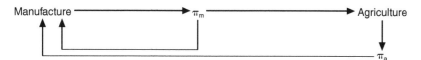

Figure 12.2 Relations between agriculture and manufacturers in the retrograde order.

A fine machine but fragile machine

The *retrograde order* is founded in the power of large manufacturing concerns created by projectors. Many scholars have shown that Smith criticises the behaviour of the projectors, accusing them of wasting the productive capital of the nation. So it is easy to deduce that he would be hostile to the process of development these men imply. It is, therefore, astonishing to see that he considers that the development of big manufactures provides numerous advantages for the nation. First of all, he showed how these innovations lead the nation from the primary stage of development to an advanced level. In part IV of the *Theory of Moral Sentiments*, he wrote that ambitious men had "changed the face of the world". Second, in *Wealth of Nations:* "I [Smith] shall endeavour to show hereafter; and at the same time to demonstrate that, though some countries have by this course attained to a *considerable degree of opulence*" (1776: 380). Are we thus to conclude that, in the final analysis, from an economic standpoint the retrograde course is equally as successful as the natural course of events?

Just after writing in the *Theory of Moral Sentiments* that ambitious men "changed the face of the world", Smith adds another point relating to the nature of the wealth, resulting from their labour. The wealth earned by these men contributed to important improvements, but it remained synonymous to great instability:

> Power and riches appear then to be, *what they are*, enormous and operose machines contrived to produce a few trifling conveniencies to the body, consisting of springs the most nice and delicate, which must be kept in order with the most anxious attention, and which in spite of all our care are ready every moment to burst into pieces, and to crush in their ruins their unfortunate possessor. They are immense fabrics, which it requires the labour of a life to raise, which threaten every moment to overwhelm the person that dwells in them, and which while they stand, though they may save him from some smaller inconveniencies, can protect him from none of the severer inclemencies of the season. They keep off the summer shower, not the winter storm, but leave him always as much, and sometimes more exposed than before, to anxiety, to fear, and to sorrow; to diseases, to danger, and to death.
>
> (1759: 182)

This passage from the *Theory of Moral Sentiments* has often been interpreted as expressing a single idea. Scholars generally argued that Smith, ironic about the stoic idea of riches, was simply mocking the feelings of a man worn out by a life spent chasing after fortune (Diatkine 1991, 1996). However, the phrase "what they are", concerning power and riches at the beginning of the quotation, proves that not only was the author giving a personal opinion, but, above all – and it is this that constitutes the originality of his exposition – he was making a scientific analysis. Dramatic innovations suddenly introduced into the economic sphere enable the opening up of an admirable and refined system, but this is based on a fragile structure that may collapse at any moment.[11]

Judging from the example of continental Europe, we learn in *Wealth of Nations*, the process of development associated with this fragile system is according to Smith "necessarily both slow and uncertain" (1776: 422–3) and, as the author wrote several chapters earlier in *Wealth of Nations*, likely to be "perturbed and interrupted by numerous accidents". Smith gives no specific information about why the investments of projectors slow down the process of economic development. What "threats" do they represent for the economic system? What are the hindrances mentioned by Smith in *Wealth of Nations*? To answer this double question, it is necessary to study the impact of the projectors' innovations.

According to Smith, the entrepreneur is an ambitious man and not an inventor, as Bentham was to claim in the "Defense of Usury" (1787). He engaged in enterprises in order to rapidly improve his condition. Contrary to the Smithian prudent men, he was interested in developing large-scale manufactures in order to obtain a higher rate of profit than the ordinary rate. Certainly, Smith was able to admit that these investments might imply a great increase in the national product. Nonetheless, he also focused on two very important drawbacks.

First of all, projectors' investments are risky projects. Like a lottery, their probability of failure is high; it is possible to make huge gains in one go, but one can equally lose a lot too. Therefore, a spectacular increase in national product in the case of success is quite hazardous, and it may easily be followed by an abrupt decrease the next year. This is the reason why Smith wrote that the *retrograde order* is "uncertain, perturbed and interrupted by numerous accidents". These "numerous accidents" are the projectors' failures, which entail a waste of capital.

Second, we know that Smithian projectors preferred investing in large-scale manufactures to investing in little factories as the prudent men did. In these large-scale manufactures, the projectors extended the division of labour to an extreme rather than increasing productive labour. In European commercial society, that is to say a society developed according to the *retrograde order*, the intricate division of labour implies numerous disadvantages which Smith discusses in *Lectures on Jurisprudence* and in book V of *Wealth of Nations*: "Where the division of labour is brought to perfection, every man has only a simple operation to perform. [...] It is remarkable that in every commercial nation the low people are exceedingly stupid" (1776: 539). Smith goes on to say:

> In the progress of the division of labour, the employment of the far greater part of those who live by labour, that is, of the great body of

the people, comes to be confined to a few very simple operations, frequently to one or two. [...] The man whose whole life is spent in performing a few simple operations, of which the effects are perhaps
always the same, or very nearly the same, has no occasion to exert his
understanding or to exercise his invention in finding out expedients
for removing difficulties which never occur. He naturally loses, therefore, the habit of such exertion, and generally becomes as stupid and
ignorant as it is possible for a human creature to become. The torpor
of his mind renders him not only incapable of relishing or bearing a
part in any rational conversation, but of conceiving any generous,
noble, or tender sentiment, and consequently of forming any just
judgment concerning many even of the ordinary duties of private
life [...]. His dexterity at his own particular trade seems, in this
manner, to be acquired at the expense of his intellectual, social, and
martial virtues.

(1776: 781–2)

For many commentators (Marglin 1976; Herrera and Vercellone 2000),
Smith's criticisms are limited to this negative comment about the division
of labour. For, in any case, it has to be admitted the stupidity of the opera-
tives did not inhibit the wealth-creating process of the nation. A closer
reading of book V of *Wealth of Nations*, however, proves the contrary.
Smith's argument can be summarised as follows. The main problem as he
saw it was not simply the reduction in labour productivity. Smith feared
that alienation destroys all the most noble qualities and virtues. For this
process would lead to workmen being unable to judge what is good or
bad, so they may therefore come to neglect the approbation of the impartial spectator. They do not consider the virtuous prudent man a hero, but
praise the projectors, who, as they see it, possess the means to greater happiness. So, like them, they rush into hazardous projects and rather than
building up their own capital, borrow directly from bankers to invest in
hazardous stratagems.

Smith worries about the destruction of frugality, the origin of capital
accumulation. We can better understand what Smith meant in *Wealth of
Nations* when he wrote that, in European commercial society, a high rate
of profit:[12]

seems everywhere to destroy that parsimony which in other circumstances is natural to the character of the merchant. When profits are
high that sober virtue seems to be superfluous and expensive luxury
to suit better the affluence of his situation. But the owners of the great
mercantile capitals are necessarily the leaders and conductors of the
whole industry of every nation, and their example has a much greater
influence upon the manners of the whole industrious part of it than
that of any other order of men.

If his employer is attentive and parsimonious, the workman is very likely to be so too; but if the master is dissolute and disorderly, the servant who shapes his work according to the pattern which his master prescribes to him will shape his life too according to the example which he sets him. Accumulation is thus prevented in the hands of all those who are naturally the most disposed to accumulate, and the funds destined for the maintenance of productive labour receive no augmentation from the revenue of those who ought naturally to augment them the most. The capital of the country, instead of increasing, gradually dwindles away, and the quantity of productive labour maintained in it grows every day less and less. Have the exorbitant profits of the merchants of Cadiz and Lisbon augmented the capital of Spain and Portugal? Have they alleviated the poverty, have they promoted the industry of those two beggarly countries?

(1776: 612)

So, it should be noted that whether they are a success or a setback, projectors' innovations hamper economic development. In the case of an unfavourable outcome, the negative consequences appear especially rapidly in a decrease of the national product (Duboeuf 1994; Diatkine 1995: 38). Success, on the other hand, implies a faster increase in economic growth, but the economic system is not stable: the following year, growth may decrease because of a failure. Besides, in the *retrograde order*, the division of labour, when pushed to the limit, destroys the inventive capacity of individuals and excludes in addition the formation of human capital, which would be added to physical capital. But, according to Smith, the most worrying aspect of all is that, by destroying the moral qualities of individuals, the division of labour also destroyed parsimony, the main source of wealth.

For the time being, Smith certainly did not see the economic situation as catastrophic, because the projectors were few in number and, the usury laws, even if they were inefficient, allowed the prudent men to be the dominant influence in the nation. But what would happen if these laws were abolished? This problem is worth considering because in Smith's time there were violent polemics between those who wanted to keep the usury laws and those who wanted to do away with them, claiming they were a hindrance to the development of trade. It is well known that Smith belonged to the former intellectual current. Maybe he was afraid that if the usury laws were relaxed, bankers would choose to finance the investments of the projectors, which would in turn have the effect of raising the general level of interest. For the prudent men who did not want to borrow at above a rate of 5–6 per cent interest, the situation would probably become disadvantageous. Smith wrote:

> If the legal rate of interest in Great Britain, for example, was fixed so high as eight or ten per cent, the greater part of the money which was to be lent would be lent to prodigals and projectors, who alone would be willing to give this high interest. Sober people, who will give for the use of money no more than a part of what they are likely to make by the use of it, would not venture into the competition. A great part of the capital of the country would thus be kept out of the hands which were most likely to make a profitable and advantageous use of it, and thrown into those which were most likely to waste and destroy it.
>
> (1776: 357)

If the credit market was liberalised, Smith feared that most of the funds would go to the projectors at the expense of the prudent men. The business of the latter would therefore be hindered at the cost of giving advantage to the projectors. Small manufacturing businesses would gradually disappear and would leave the way open for more large-scale manufacturing enterprises. In such a situation, the "retrograde" order would work against the creation of wealth in the nation. The associated growth regime would be degenerate and economic development would be impeded.

Conclusion

According to Smith, the natural course of things does not stand in opposition to the *retrograde order* in terms of economic development. The second is only slower than the first. The interventions of institutions play an important role in avoiding disaster. What Smith means by this is that institutions are able to prevent the *retrograde order* from descending into a deteriorating one, but their interventions are not enough to restore the natural course of things.

We can assume that the projectors' activities are costly in the long run as they reduce the incentives for capital accumulation. Nevertheless, after 1833 – the date of the suppression of the laws – chaos did not occur. Perhaps the increase of the number of projectors was not as spectacular as Smith feared. The number of projectors always remained small in proportion to the overall economic sphere. So, if the capitalism system is condemned to follow a path of non-optimal development, chaos is not the long-term outcome.

Acknowledgements

I wish to thank Daniel Diatkine, André Lapidus, Arnaud Orain, Michel Rosier and Nathalie Sigot for their helpful comments and suggestions.

Notes

1 On the contrary, by neglecting the relations between ethics and economics in Smith's thought, other commentators only emphasise Smith's determinants of economic growth: the division of labour, productive labour and labour productivity are therefore considered the main factors in the creation of wealth.

2 On the concept of prudence in Smith's thought, see Sen (1987), Pack (1991), Charlier (1996) and MacCloskey (1998).

3 See Dwyer (1998).

4 In the natural course of things, "the progressive wealth and increase of the towns would, in every political society, be consequential, and in proportion to the improvement and cultivation of the territory or country" (Smith 1776: 378).

5 "Agriculture without manufactures makes men more numerous, and less wealthy: agriculture with manufactures makes men more wealthy, and consequently less numerous" (Bentham 1787: 206).

6 On positive effects of the division of labour, see Young (1928), Rosenberg (1976) and Arrow (1979).

7 Like Kindleberger (1976), I think that Smith ignored the Industrial Revolution.

8   Where the legal rate of interest, on the contrary, is fixed but a very little above the lowest market rate, sober people are universally preferred, as borrowers, to prodigals and entrepreneurs. The person who lends money gets nearly as much interest from the former as he dares to take from the latter, and his money is much safer in the hands of the one set of people than in those of the other. A great part of the capital of the country is thus thrown into the hands in which it is most likely to be employed with advantage.

                                  (Smith 1776: 357)

9   When two people, who are continually drawing and redrawing upon one another, discount their bills always with the same banker, he must immediately discover what they are about, and see clearly that they are trading, not with any capital of their own, but with the capital which he advances to them. But this discovery is not altogether so easy when they discount their bills sometimes with one banker, and sometimes with another, and when the same two persons do not constantly draw and redraw upon one another, but occasionally run the round of a great circle of entrepreneurs, who find it for their interest to assist one another in this method of raising money, and to render it, upon that account, as difficult as possible to distinguish between a real and fictitious bill of exchange; between a bill drawn by a real creditor upon a real debtor, and a bill for which there was properly no real creditor but the bank which discounted it, nor any real debtor but the entrepreneur who made use of the money.

                                  (Smith 1776: 311–12)

10   The paper which was issued upon those circulating bills of exchange, amounted, upon many occasions, to the whole fund destined for carrying on some vast and extensive project of agriculture, commerce, or manufactures; and not merely to that part of it which, had there been no paper money, the entrepreneur would have been obliged to keep by him, unemployed and in ready money for answering occasional demands.

                                        (Smith 1776: 311)

11 See Hoselitz (1970: 142).

12 See Anspach (1976).

References

Anspach, R. (1976) "Smith's Growth Paradigm", *History of Political Economy*, 8(4): 494–514.

Arrow, K. (1979) "The Division of Labour in the Economy, the Polity, and the Society", in G. P. O'Driscoll (ed.), Adam *Smith and the Modern Political Economy*, Ames, Iowa: Iowa State University Press.

Bentham, J. (1787) "Defence of Usury", in W. Stark (ed.) (2004) *Jeremy Bentham's Economic Writings*, London: Routledge, vol. 1.

Bowles, P. (1985) "Adam Smith and the 'Natural' Progress of Opulence", *Economica*, 53: 109–18.

Brown, V. (1997) " 'Mere Inventions of the Imagination': a Survey of Recent Literature on Adam Smith", *Economics and Philosophy*, 13(2): 281–312.

Charlier, C. (1996) "The Notion of Prudence in Smith's *Theory of Moral Sentiments*", in *History Economic Ideas*, 4(1–2): 271–97.

Diatkine, D. (1991) "Introduction", *La richesse des nations*, Paris: Flammarion.

—— (1996) "Adam Smith et le projet colonial ou l'avenir d'une illusion", *Cahiers d'Economie Politique*, 27–8.

Diatkine, S. (1995) *Théorie et Politique monétaire*, Paris: Armand Colin.

Duboeuff, F. (1994) "Monnaie et banques dans la *Richesse des Nations*", *Revue Economique*, 45: 5, pp. 1199–212.

Dwyer, J. (1998) *Age of Passions: an Interpretation of Adam Smith and Scottish Enlightenment Culture*, East Linton: Tuckwell Press.

Griswold, C. L. (1998) *Adam Smith and the Virtues of Enlightenment*, Cambridge, UK: Cambridge University Press.

Herrera, R. and Vercellone, C. (2000) "Transformation de la division du travail et théories de la croissance endogène une revue critique", *Cahiers de la Maison des Sciences Economiques*, 33, Paris: CNRS.

Hollander, S. (1999) "Jeremy Bentham and Adam Smith on the Usury Laws: a 'Smithian' Reply to Bentham and a New Problem", *European Journal of the History of Economic Thought*, 6(4): 523–51.

Hoselitz, B. F. (1970): *Les théories de la croissance*, Paris: Dunod.

Kindleberger, C. P. (1976) "The Historical Background: Adam Smith and the Industrial Revolution", in Skinner, A. and Wilson, T. (eds), *Essays in Honour of Adam Smith*, Oxford: Oxford Clarendon Press.

MacCloskey, D. (1998) "Bourgeois, Virtue and the History of P. and S.", *Journal of Economic History*, 58(2): 297–317.

Marglin, A. (1976) "Origines et fonctions de la parcellisation des tâches", in *Critique de la division du travail*, Paris: Le Seuil.

Moore, B. (1998) *Moral Aspects of Economic Growth*, Ithaca, NY: Cornwell University Press.

Pack, S. J. (1991) *Capitalism as a Moral System: Adam Smith's Critique of the Free Market Economy*, New York: E. Elgar.

Pesciarelli, E. (1989) "Smith, Bentham, and the Development of Contrasting Ideas on Entrepreneurship", *History of Political Economy*, 21(3): 521–36.

Prasch, R. E. (1991) "The Ethics of Growth in Adam Smith's *Wealth of Nations*", *History of Political Economy*, 23(2): 337–51.

Reid, G. (1989) *Classical Economic Growth: an Analysis in the Tradition of Adam Smith*, Oxford: Blackwell.

Reisman, D. A. (1976) *Adam Smith's Sociological Economics*, London: Croom Helm.

Rosenberg, N. (1976) "Another Advantage of the Division of Labor", *Journal of Political Economy*, part I, 84(4): 861–8.

Rosier, M. (1987) 'Le und è le de reproduction et d'accumulation d'Adam Smith', *Recherches Economiques de Louvain*, 53(2).

Sen, A. (1987) *On Ethics and Economics*, Oxford: Basil Blackwell.

—— (1993) "Money and Value: on the Ethics and Economic of Finance", *Economics and Philosophy*, 9(2): 203–27.

Smith, A. (1759) *Theory of Moral Sentiments*; trans. M. Biziou, C. Gautier and J.-F. Pradeau (1999) *Theorie des sentiments moraux*, Paris: Léviathan.

—— (1776) *An Inquiry into the Natures and Causes of the Wealth of Nations*; reprinted in 1976, ed. A. S. Skinner, Oxford: Oxford Liberty Classics.

Young, A. A. (1928) "Increasing Returns and Economic Progress", *Economic Journal* 38, 152: 527–42.

13 Ricardo, machinery and comparative advantage

Andrea Maneschi

Introduction

The machinery question was a pivotal economic and social issue as the industrial revolution gathered strength in Britain. The public's attitude toward machinery was an ambiguous one. While the benefits – indeed the wonders – of machinery were a visible manifestation of sweeping economic change, broad segments of the working class regarded it as a threat to their livelihood. The destruction of machinery by the Luddites, and the riots of workers who lost their jobs due to mechanization, became frequent occurrences. The implications of machinery inevitably became a lively item of debate among the growing number of adherents of the English classical school of political economy. In a period that Thomas Carlyle called the "Age of Machinery", it is not surprising that the opinion held on such a burning issue of the day by an economist of the calibre of David Ricardo, the presumptive leader of the classical school, would be highly regarded.

Chapter 31 "On Machinery", that Ricardo added to the third edition of the *Principles of Political Economy and Taxation* of 1821, gave rise to much controversy, even among Ricardo's followers, in part because it contradicted Ricardo's own previous assertion that the introduction of machinery would not cause the demand for labour to fall. Ricardo had even convinced John McCulloch to abandon the argument he made in the *Edinburgh Review* in 1820 that investment in fixed capital must displace a greater quantity of circulating capital, thus lowering rather than increasing the wage rate. McCulloch recanted this view in the *Edinburgh Review* in 1821, claiming instead that machinery could only improve a labourer's condition. But in the same year, Ricardo adamantly argued, in the third edition of his *Principles*, "that the opinion entertained by the labouring class, that the employment of machinery is frequently detrimental to their interests, is not founded on prejudice and error, but is conformable to the correct principles of political economy" *(Works: vol. I, 392).*

In the words of John Hicks (1969: 151), Ricardo showed "candour and courage" in pointing out an important eventuality that most classical economists had failed to note, or the validity of which they doubted: the sudden introduction of machinery can spell ruin for workers in the short run.[1] Ricardo centred his argument on a numerical example which assumes that the introduction of machinery requires more fixed capital and less circulating capital. The resulting increase in the fraction of a given amount of capital devoted to fixed capital necessarily causes some labour (whose maintenance depends on the wage fund or circulating capital available) to become redundant in the short run.

This example and Ricardo's revised views on machinery gave rise to many critiques, both in his lifetime and after it. Some of these critiques are well taken. Several observers pointed out that Ricardo never integrated chapter 31 with the previous chapters of his book, nor did he describe fully the economic equilibrium after machinery is introduced.[2] These critiques, however, do not affect the validity of Ricardo's qualified conclusion that:

> All I wish to prove, is, that the discovery and use of machinery may be attended with a diminution of gross produce; and whenever that is the case, it will be injurious to the labouring class, as some of their number will be thrown out of employment.
>
> (*Works*: vol. I, 390)

Granting this conclusion, this chapter will focus on the implications of Ricardo's views on machinery for his theory of comparative advantage, and why the dire consequences that he predicted for workers offered no licence for discouraging the use of machinery. The second section investigates Ricardo's views of the effects of machinery on the welfare of workers, and on a country's comparative advantage and the associated pattern of trade. The third section examines the policy implications that Ricardo drew for the introduction of machinery, and shows that the national gains that he expected from it, despite the adverse consequences for workers, are similar in nature to the gains from trade highlighted in chapter 7 of the *Principles*. The final section compares the lessons to be drawn from chapter 31 to those yielded by other chapters of the *Principles*.

Implications of machinery for income distribution and foreign trade

The prospect of a continuous increase in money wages in England due to diminishing returns to labour on a fixed amount of land, in the face of unchanged commercial policies and in the absence of adventitious improvements in technology, is a leitmotif of Ricardo's *Principles*. Because of the inverse relation between wages and profits, this would lower the profit rate and the rate of accumulation that depended on it. The immediate policy implication on which Ricardo insisted was the repeal of the Corn Laws that kept the price of corn and the money wage artificially high. The failure to do this would imply a steady loss of dynamism and Britain's gradual descent toward the stationary state.

The alleged pessimism underlying this model of growth followed by stagnation has been contested by some authors. Mark Blaug interprets the stationary state in Ricardo's *Principles* as a "methodological fiction". He argues that in Ricardo's view: "For all practical purposes, the limits to economic progress were political and not economic in character" (1958: 32). Samuel Hollander (1979) contends that Ricardo was optimistic about Britain's economic future even in the absence of Corn Law repeal. Taking her cue from Blaug, Hollander and M. Dobb, Berg seeks "to refute the standard view of Ricardo's pessimism by a close textual analysis of his writing on technical change, interpreted in the context of his works as a whole" (1980: 44). According to her, the model that Ricardo presented in the *Principles*, based on diminishing returns to land, a declining profit rate and a tendency to the stationary state, "was a counterfactual, set up precisely in order to emphasize the significance of the factors from which Ricardo abstracted – free trade and technological improvement. Trade and technical progress both produced social and economic changes which considerably modified the 'natural state' of limited land" (ibid.: 47). In chapter 31, Ricardo contrasts the trends of wages in England and in America:

> Machinery and labour are in constant competition, and the former can frequently not be employed until labour rises. In America and many other countries, where the food of man is easily provided, there is not nearly such great temptation to employ machinery a in England, where food is high, and costs much labour for its production.
>
> (*Works*: vol. I, 395)

Aside from the loss of dynamism entailed by the failure to reform Britain's trade policies that he stressed in earlier chapters, Ricardo now identified another consequence of the Corn Laws: the incentive for firms to substitute machinery for labour, with an immediate detrimental effect on the welfare of workers. This incentive exists because improved machinery, given the rising cost of labour, allows a reduction in the cost of production of commodities, so that firms can compete more effectively both at home and abroad.

Ricardo's attention to the distributional consequences of machinery in chapter 31 is not surprising in light of his focus in the *Principles* on the shares of national income accruing to the various social classes. As he observed in the Preface:

> In different stages of society, the proportions of the whole produce of the earth which will be allotted to each of these classes, under the

names of rent, profit, and wages, will be essentially different ... To determine the laws which regulate this distribution, is the principal problem in Political Economy.

(ibid.: 5)

With regard to the share accruing to labour, in chapter 5 of the *Principles*, "On Wages", Ricardo asserted that:

Notwithstanding the tendency of wages to conform to their natural rate, their market rate may, in an improving society, for an indefinite period, be constantly above it; for no sooner may the impulse, which an increased capital gives to a new demand for labour be obeyed, than another increase of capital may produce the same effect; and thus, if the increase of capital be gradual and constant, the demand for labour may give a continued stimulus to an increase of people.

(ibid.: 95)

This optimistic scenario prevails "if the increase of capital be gradual and constant". But chapter 31 depicts a different scenario, with adverse consequences for the share of national income accruing to labour. The condition for this to occur is "that improved machinery is *suddenly* discovered, and extensively used" (ibid.: 395). "But", Ricardo added, "the truth is, that these discoveries are gradual, and rather operate in determining the employment of the capital which is saved and accumulated, than in diverting capital from its actual employment" (ibid.).

Ricardo thus wished to impress upon his readers that machinery is not necessarily something to be feared as the harbinger of economic disaster for workers. In the usual course of events, an increase in fixed capital is accompanied by an increase in circulating capital, which comprises the wage fund that allows more workers to be employed. In a country like Britain: "The demand for labour will continue to increase with an increase of capital, but not in proportion to its increase; the ratio will necessarily be a diminishing ratio" (ibid.). In light of the statements in chapter 31 that stress the unlikely possibility, rather than the likelihood, of dire consequences for workers from the adoption of machinery, it is difficult to interpret that chapter as an expression of pessimism regarding Britain's economic prospects.

In addition to the effects of machinery on employment and income distribution, Ricardo's observations provide new insights into his theory of comparative advantage. In chapter 7 of the *Principles*, "On Foreign Trade", Ricardo set up his well-known numerical example of trade between England and Portugal. Despite international differences in wages and profit rates, he noted that capital and workers tend to be immobile between countries, in contrast to their mobility between regions of the same country. After expounding the principle of comparative advantage, he concluded that "the produce of the labour of 100 Englishmen may be given for the produce of the labour of eighty Portuguese, sixty Russians, or 120 East Indians" (ibid.: 135).

But in chapter 31, Ricardo allowed for the international mobility of capital, and noted the consequences this would entail for his theory of comparative advantage. It is argued by many economists, especially in text-books on the theory of international trade, that this theory is Ricardo's major contribution to economic theory. It certainly marks the beginning of the theory of international trade as the oldest applied field of eco-nomics. Statesmen and economists in developing countries have some-times claimed that Ricardo's theory of comparative advantage is static, and that countries that try to implement it become locked into a pattern of trade that may be disadvantageous to them.

In contrast to this view, I believe that the classical economists, and Ricardo in particular, held a dynamic view of comparative advantage, which is continually modified by factors such as diminishing returns to labour on land, or the introduction of machinery (Maneschi 1992, 1998). Chapter 31 offers a prime example of the fluidity of comparative advant-age in the face of government policies such as the discouragement of the adoption of machinery.

A notable feature of Ricardo's theory of comparative advantage is that it depends on technological differences between countries. It contrasts sharply with the Heckscher–Ohlin theory of trade, which postulates that technology is everywhere the same and that factors of production are always fully employed. Comparative advantage depends on factor endow-ment differences between countries, and on the fact that commodities employ factors of production in different proportions at the same factor prices. A country that is relatively well endowed with a certain factor exports commodities whose production employs that factor intensively. The Stolper–Samuelson theorem, a logical implication of the Heckscher–Ohlin theory, states that trade increases the real reward of a country's abundant factor of production and reduces that of the scarce factor (Stolper and Samuelson 1941).

In chapter 31 of Ricardo's *Principles*, the Heckscher–Ohlin theory can explain neither the changes in comparative advantage resulting from the introduction of machinery, nor their implications for income distribution or for employment. The change in income distribution highlighted by Ricardo, where the innovating capitalist's profits are enhanced in the short run while workers become unemployed, is unrelated to any change in factor abundance or factor scarcity. The sudden introduction of machinery in a country's industry improves its technology and alters com-parative advantage in its favour, leading both to an increase in trade and an adverse impact on workers in that sector.

Gains from trade and gains from machinery

After he used a numerical example in chapter 31 to argue that machinery can be harmful to the welfare of workers, at least in the short run, one might have expected Ricardo to show some ambiguity about the wisdom of public policy that fosters improvements in machinery. Instead he argued vigorously that if the government prevented these improvements in order to alleviate their impact on labour, England's economic position would suffer:

> The employment of machinery could never be safely discouraged in a State, for if a capital is not allowed to get the greatest net revenue that the use of machinery will afford here, it will be carried abroad, and this must be a much more serious discouragement to the demand for labour, than the most extensive employment of machinery; for, while a capital is employed in this country, it must create a demand for some labour; machinery cannot be worked without the assistance of men, it cannot be made but with the contribution of their labour. By investing part of a capital in improved machinery, there will be a diminution in the progressive demand for labour; by exporting it to another country, the demand will be wholly annihilated.
>
> (*Works:* vol. I, 396–7)

The countries that adopt the improved technology will be enabled to export the very commodities that England would have produced and exported instead.

In the final paragraph of chapter 31, Ricardo provided a quantitative measure of the gains accruing to a country that, by adopting machinery, can conquer the world market for a commodity instead of importing it from another country that had welcomed rather than discouraged this technology. This paragraph, in which Ricardo addresses his readers directly using the pronoun "you" and the adjective "your" for greater rhetorical effect, is worth quoting in its entirety:

> The prices of commodities, too, are regulated by their cost of production. By employing improved machinery, the cost of production of commodities is reduced, and, consequently, you can afford to sell them in foreign markets at a cheaper price. If, however, you were to reject the use of machinery, while all other countries encouraged it, you would be obliged to export your money, in exchange for foreign goods, till you sunk the natural prices of your goods to the prices of other countries. In making your exchanges with those countries, you might give a commodity which cost two days labour, here, for a commodity which cost one, abroad, and this disadvantageous exchange would be the consequence of your own act, for the commodity which

you export, and which cost you two days labour, would have cost you only one if you had not rejected the use of machinery, the services of which your neighbours had more wisely appropriated to themselves.

(ibid.: 397)

The gains realized by a country that adopts improved machinery are quantified in an analogous way to that in which Ricardo measured the gains from trade in chapter 7 of the *Principles*. Those accruing to England are described as follows in that chapter:

> The quantity of wine which she [Portugal] shall give in exchange for the cloth of England, is not determined by the respective quantities of labour devoted to the production of each, as it would be, if both commodities were manufactured in England, or both in Portugal.
>
> England may be so circumstanced, that to produce the cloth may require the labour of 100 men for one year; and if she attempted to make the wine, it might require the labour of 120 men for the same time. England would therefore find it her interest to import wine, and to purchase it by the exportation of cloth.

(ibid.: 134–5)

Hence England "produces" wine indirectly by manufacturing cloth with the labour of 100 men, and exchanging it for wine that would have cost 120 men if she produced it directly. The gains from trade are the amount of labour saved, consisting of $120 - 100 = 20$ men. This measure is consistent with what Jacob Viner referred to as the "eighteenth-century rule" for the gains from trade, which states that "it pays to import commodities from abroad whenever they can be obtained in exchange for exports at a smaller real cost than their production at home would entail" (1937: 440).[3]

The gains from trade are illustrated in Figure 13.1, where the horizontal and vertical axes represent the quantities of labour L_w and L_c required to produce the amounts of wine and cloth traded. In England these are given by $L_w = OC$ (120 men) and $L_c = OA$ (100 men). If AB is a 45-degree line through A intersecting the L_w axis at B, the distance BC measures England's gains from trade. Its length, given by twenty men, represents the saving of labour that England realizes by exchanging cloth for wine with Portugal instead of producing the wine directly.

Figure 13.2 illustrates the gains that the country described in the final paragraph of chapter 31 quoted above (presumably England) realizes if she adopts machinery to produce a commodity, instead of importing it from the country to which its production migrates if England were to discourage the use of machinery. Ricardo argued that: "In making your exchanges with those countries, you might give a commodity which cost two days labour, here, for a commodity which cost one, abroad" (*Works:*

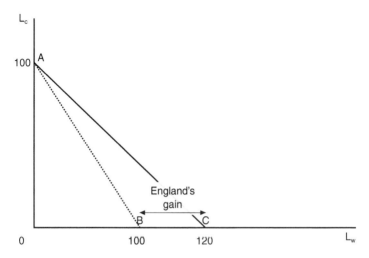

Figure 13.1 England's gain from trade.

vol. 1, 397). Let the vertical and horizontal axes in Figure 13.2 represent the amounts of labour L_1 and L_2 used to produce commodities 1 and 2. If she fails to adopt the improved machinery for commodity 1, England would have to assign $L_2 = 200$ units of labour to the production of commodity 2, shown by the distance OC on the L_2 axis, in order to import 100 units of commodity 1. If England adopts this machinery, she would need to devote only 100 units of labour, measured by OA on the L_1 axis, to produce the same 100 units of commodity 1. The "gain from machinery", analogous to the "gain from trade" depicted in Figure 13.1, is given by BC in Figure 13.2, and amounts to $200 - 100 = 100$ men, where B is the point of intersection on the L_2 axis of a 45-degree line through A.

The adoption of machinery leads to a reversal of comparative advantage, as indicated by Ricardo's observation that: "By employing improved machinery, the cost of production of commodities is reduced, and, consequently, you can afford to sell them in foreign markets at a cheaper price" (ibid.). Comparative advantage can thus be altered by a prejudicial government policy that "rejected the use of machinery, the services of which your neighbours had more wisely appropriated to themselves" (ibid.). Chapter 31 of the *Principles* thus identifies the "gain from machinery" by measuring the "loss from trade" when England imports a commodity that she could have produced more cheaply than the foreign country. It thus points to the advantages that may accrue to a country that practices what was later named "import substitution".

Although the policy to adopt machinery results in the elimination of imports, this is not an autarkic policy directed at self-sufficiency, as was mostly true when it was carried out by developing countries after World

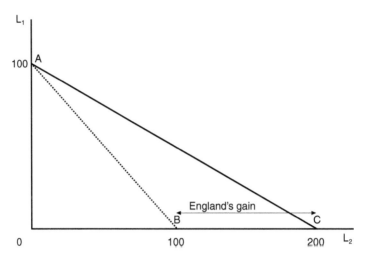

Figure 13.2 England's gain from machinery.

War Two. The policy, instead, leads to an increase in global trade, since England is able to establish herself as the lowest-cost worldwide producer of commodity 1.

Conclusions

Ricardo's remarkable chapter 31 contains important lessons for an economy that, like the British one, was in the throes of the industrial revolution. Contrary to the conventional wisdom that prevailed among his fellow classical economists, Ricardo asserted that the sudden introduction of machinery can indeed harm the working class by causing some workers to become redundant. It is symptomatic of Ricardo's intellectual honesty and independence that he did not hesitate to proclaim a conclusion that he knew would upset some of his friends, and was even diametrically opposed to one that he himself had held a short time before. The form in which he announced his new insight was by writing a brand new chapter for the third edition of the *Principles*, which Piero Sraffa (1951: 1, vii) refers to as "the most revolutionary change" in that edition.

Despite the adverse consequences that machinery can inflict on workers, Ricardo was unequivocal in asserting that its introduction should not be discouraged by the government. In earlier chapters of the *Principles*, Ricardo also frequently elaborated on the positive effects of machinery. In chapter 1 he argued that: "Thus then is the public benefited by machinery: these mute agents are always the produce of much less labour than that which they displace, even when they are of the same money value" *(Works*. vol. I, 42). In chapter 7, he stressed the importance of reducing the prices of wage goods, thus lowering the money wage and increasing the profit rate, and showed that this can be achieved in one of two ways: by the introduction of machinery or of cheap foreign goods that enter workers' consumption baskets:

> It has been my endeavour to shew throughout this work, that the rate of profits can never be increased but by a fall in wages, and that there can be no permanent fall of wages but in consequence of a fall of the necessaries on which wages are expended. If, therefore, by the extension of foreign trade, or by improvements in machinery, the food and necessaries of the labourer can be brought to market at a reduced price, profits will rise.
>
> (ibid.: 132)

Hence technical change ("improvements in machinery") and foreign trade are equivalent ways of pursuing the national goal of raising the rate of profit.

In chapter 31 Ricardo attracted attention to the fact that machinery, while beneficial to the country, can have a harmful side effect on a social group such as workers. This is one of several instances in the *Principles* where Ricardo noted that enlightened policies can have significant transitional costs, but should still be fostered because of the long-run gains that they can bring. Another example occurs in chapter 19, "On Sudden Changes in the Channels of Trade", where Ricardo argued that the inability to withdraw capital from the land was no reason to stop cheap corn from being imported. He chided as follows those who thought otherwise:

> They do not see that the end of all commerce is to increase production, and that by increasing production, though you may occasion partial loss, you increase the general happiness. To be consistent, they should endeavour to arrest all improvements in agriculture and manufactures, and all inventions of machinery; for though these contribute to general abundance, and therefore to the general happiness, they never fail, at the moment of their introduction, to deteriorate or annihilate the value of a part of the existing capital of farmers and manufacturers.
>
> (ibid.: 271)

In this case, it is farmers and manufacturers that suffer rather than workers, and once again Ricardo is willing to sacrifice their short-run interests to a greater social good.

By altering comparative advantage, improvements in machinery can change the direction of trade. The parallelism between the effects of technology and trade that is apparent in the *Principles* is such that Ricardo even measured their benefits in the same way. The saving of labour that they both occasion, as illustrated above in Figures 13.1 and 13.2, results from a superior allocation of economic resources. If improved technology or freer trade affects the commodities consumed by workers, an additional gain is a rise in the rate of profits. Against these gains must be set the associated short-run adjustment costs, such as the dislocation of existing production lines or a sudden deterioration in the economic welfare of the workers. While Ricardo took pains to draw attention to these costs, they were clearly subordinate in his view to the long-run gains that technology and trade can convey.

Notes

1 One of the economists who persuaded Ricardo to change his mind on the machinery issue was John Barton, whose book (1817) he cited at some length in chapter 31. Barton presented a numerical example that must have inspired Ricardo to come up with his own. As Eltis (1985: 261) points out, Ricardo devised "a far sharper example than Barton's". In realizing that machinery can be labour-saving and hence can cause unemployment and social conflict, Barton was preceded by Lord Lauderdale, who observed that: "The profit of stock employed in machinery is paid out of a fund that would otherwise be destined to pay the wages of the labour it supplants" (1804: 167, cited in Berg 1980: 34).

2 See, for example, St Clair (1957), Blaug (1958, 1997), O'Brien (1975) and Rashid (1987). St Clair, noting the hurry with which the third edition of the *Principles* was prepared for publication, observes that: "[I]t was too late to bring the old chapters into harmony with the new one [chapter 31]. It might be possible here and there to insert a footnote, but many statements in the old text inconsistent with the new theory had to be left standing, to the perpetual bewilderment of the reader" (1957: 237). Blaug (1997: 130) comments that: "[T]his chapter [31] seems glued on to the rest of the book as an afterthought."

3 The numbers 120 and 100 are two of what Paul Samuelson (1969) refers to as the "four magic numbers" in Ricardo's numerical example of comparative advantage. The other two numbers are those relating to the production of Portugal's exports of wine (eighty men) and the labour she would have required to produce her imports of cloth (ninety men). Most economists have assumed that these four numbers represent unit labour input coefficients, denoting the amounts of labour needed to produce one unit of wine and cloth in each country. Ruffin (2002) has argued instead that the four numbers indicate the amounts of labour needed in each country to produce the total amounts of the commodities exported and imported. Maneschi (2004) expands on Ruffin's article by showing that Ricardo's four numbers yield each country's gains from trade by simply subtracting two of the numbers from the other two. The same four numbers do double duty by also revealing the pattern of comparative advantage in England and Portugal.

References

Barton, J. (1817) *Observations on the Circumstances which Influence the Condition of the Labouring Classes of Society*, London: Arch.

Berg, M. (1980) *The Machinery Question and the Making of Political Economy 1815–1848*, Cambridge, UK: Cambridge University Press.

Blaug, M. (1958) *Ricardian Economics: A Historical Study*, New Haven: Yale University Press.

—— (1997) *Economic Theory in Retrospect*, 5th edn, Cambridge, UK: Cambridge University Press.

Eltis, W. (1985) "Ricardo on machinery and technological unemployment", in G. A. Caravale (ed.), *The Legacy of Ricardo*, Oxford: Basil Blackwell.

Hicks, J. (1969) *A Theory of Economic History*, Oxford: Oxford University Press.

Hollander, S. (1979) *The Economics of Ricardo*, Toronto: University of Toronto Press.

Lauderdale, J. M. (1804) *An Inquiry into the Nature and Origin of Public Wealth*, Edinburgh: Constable.

McCulloch, J. R. (1820) "Taxation and the corn laws", *Edinburgh Review*, 33: 155–87.

—— (1821) "Effects of machinery and accumulation", *Edinburgh Review*, 35: 102–23.

Maneschi, A. (1992) "Ricardo's international trade theory: beyond the comparative cost example", *Cambridge Journal of Economics*, 16: 421–37.

—— (1998) "The dynamic nature of comparative advantage and of the gains from trade in classical economics", *Journal of the History of Economic Thought*, 20: 133–44.

—— (2004) "The true meaning of David Ricardo's four magic numbers", *Journal of International Economics*, 62 (2): 433–43.

Mill, J. S. (1848) *Principles of Political Economy*, London: Parker & Co.

O'Brien, D. P. (1975) *The Classical Economists*, Oxford: Clarendon Press.

Rashid, S. (1987) "Machinery question", in J. Eatwell, M. Milgate and P. Newman (eds), *The New Palgrave: A Dictionary of Economics*, Vol. 3, London: Macmillan.

Ricardo, D. (1951–73) *The Works and Correspondence of David Ricardo* (11 vols), ed. P. Sraffa, Cambridge, UK: Cambridge University Press.

Ruffin, R. J. (2002) "David Ricardo's discovery of comparative advantage", *History of Political Economy*, 34: 727–48.

Samuelson, P. A. (1969) "The way of an economist", in P. A. Samuelson (ed.), *International Economic Relations: Proceedings of the Third Congress of the International Economic Association*, London: Macmillan.

Sraffa, P. (1951) "Introduction to" *The Works and Correspondence of David Ricardo*, vol. I, Cambridge, UK: Cambridge University Press.

St. Clair, O. (1957) *A Key to Ricardo*, London: Routledge & Kegan Paul.

Stolper, W. F. and Samuelson, P. A. (1941) "Protection and real wages", *Review of Economic Studies*, 9: 58–73.

Viner, J. (1937) *Studies in the Theory of International Trade*, New York: Harper.

Index

Italic page numbers indicate figures not included in the text page range.

eBooks – at www.eBookstore.tandf.co.uk

A library at your fingertips!

eBooks are electronic versions of printed books. You can store them on your PC/laptop or browse them online.

They have advantages for anyone needing rapid access to a wide variety of published, copyright information.

eBooks can help your research by enabling you to bookmark chapters, annotate text and use instant searches to find specific words or phrases. Several eBook files would fit on even a small laptop or PDA.

NEW: Save money by eSubscribing: cheap, online access to any eBook for as long as you need it.

Annual subscription packages

We now offer special low-cost bulk subscriptions to packages of eBooks in certain subject areas. These are available to libraries or to individuals.

For more information please contact webmaster.ebooks@tandf.co.uk

We're continually developing the eBook concept, so keep up to date by visiting the website.

www.eBookstore.tandf.co.uk

For Product Safety Concerns and Information please contact our EU
representative GPSR@taylorandfrancis.com
Taylor & Francis Verlag GmbH, Kaufingerstraße 24, 80331 München, Germany

www.ingramcontent.com/pod-product-compliance
Ingram Content Group UK Ltd.
Pitfield, Milton Keynes, MK11 3LW, UK
UKHW021444080625
459435UK00011B/360